San Fransicko

Also by Michael Shellenberger

Apocalypse Never: Why Environmental Alarmism Hurts Us All

San Fran- sicko

Why Progressives Ruin Cities

Michael Shellenberger

HARPER

An Imprint of HarperCollins*Publishers*

HarperCollins books may be purchased for educational, business, or sales promotional use. For information, please email the Special Markets Department at SPsales@harpercollins.com.

FIRST EDITION

Library of Congress Cataloging-in-Publication Data has been applied for.

ISBN 978-0-06-309362-1

21 22 23 24 25   LSC   10 9 8 7 6 5 4 3 2 1

For Helen

Go, Francis, and repair my house, which as you see is falling into ruin.[1]

—instruction to Saint Francis

Contents

Contents

Introduction

When I first heard last June that a group of people had taken over a neighborhood in downtown Seattle, ostensibly in response to the killing of an unarmed black man, George Floyd, by a police officer in Minneapolis, I couldn't understand what had happened. *It wasn't like a bunch of heavily armed anarchists had erected traffic barricades and kicked the police out of their precinct building*, I thought, and went back to whatever it was I was doing. It was only after I had learned of the killing of two black teenagers in the occupied area that I came to understand that the anarchists had, in fact, done exactly that. *But why? And why did the Seattle police and mayor let them?*

I am not unfamiliar with radical politics. As a socialist youth in the late 1980s I had read books by America's most famous anarchist, Noam Chomsky, excoriating US imperialism in Latin America. From 1996 to 1999, I worked with eco-anarchists seeking to save old-growth forests in California and the Pacific Northwest. And in 1999, I protested alongside so-called black bloc anarchists against economic globalization in the streets of Seattle. While I knew anarchists wanted to abolish government, it never dawned on me that a major city government would actually participate in its own abolition. *What was going on?*

Though my curiosity was piqued, I wasn't in much of a position to find out. In the 1990s I had worked on a broader set of progressive causes, including advocating for the decriminalization of drugs and alternatives to prison. But for most of the last two decades my research and writing has focused on the environment. And, in the early summer of 2020, I was busy running my nonprofit research organization and preparing for the release of my book on the topic.

It was anarchy of a different sort that motivated me to write *San Fransicko*. During the pandemic, a growing number of people in floridly psychotic states were screaming obscenities at invisible enemies, or at my colleagues and me, on the sidewalks or in the street, as we went to and from our retail office in downtown Berkeley, near the University of California. Others were angrier than ever, often inexplicably. One morning a young man came up to me as I was unlocking our front door and coughed in my unmasked face. Another man threatened to assault a colleague. In both cases our mistake appears to have been that, rather than averting our eyes, we had looked at the men.

Many of the problems stemmed from COVID-19. California's prisons, jails, and homeless shelters were under orders to reduce their occupancy. Fewer people were being arrested for public intoxication and aggressive behavior. More people started sleeping in front of our office, the boarded-up secondhand clothing store next door, or the former S&M shop next to it, frequently leaving their trash and waste for us to clean up in the morning. And we started finding people passed out on the sidewalk, sometimes with their pants around their knees.

But none of these problems started with the pandemic. Between 2008 and 2019, eighteen thousand companies, including Toyota, Charles Schwab, and Hewlett-Packard, fled California due to a constellation of problems sometimes summarized as "poor business climate."[1] California has the highest income tax, highest gasoline tax, and highest sales tax in the United States, spends significantly more than other states on homelessness, and yet has worse outcomes.[2] "I came out here in 1983," said HBO's Bill Maher to Representative Adam Schiff in the fall of 2020. "I found paradise. I love California. I do. I don't want to leave. But I feel like I'm living in Italy in the '70s or something. . . . I don't know what I'm getting for my super high taxes."[3]

I was as confused as Maher. Though I have been a progressive and Democrat all of my adult life, I found myself asking a question that sounded rather conservative. What *were* we getting for our high taxes? And why, after twenty years of voting for ballot initiatives promising to address drug addiction, mental illness, and homelessness, had all three gotten worse? And why had progressive Democratic elected officials stopped enforcing many laws against certain groups of people, from unhoused people suffering mental illness and drug addiction in San Francisco, Los Angeles, and Seattle, to heavily armed and mostly white anarchists in Seattle, Portland, and Minneapolis?

I wrote *San Fransicko* because I didn't have the answers to those questions and felt I needed them. What I discovered in the process was that much of what I and other progressives had believed about cities, crime, and homelessness was all wrong, and that we needed to get it right.

Just as no police officer believes it's good for neighborhood safety to abandon a precinct building, no sane psychiatrist believes that enabling and subsidizing people with schizophrenia, depression, and anxiety disorders to use fentanyl and meth is good medicine. Yet that is what San Francisco, Seattle, and Los Angeles are, in effect, doing. What California does with its 100,000 unsheltered residents, most suffering mental illness or drug addiction while living in violent, dangerous, and degrading encampments, is mistreatment of the foulest sort and in many instances far worse than the mistreatment of mentally ill people in the first three quarters of the twentieth century. How did we go from the nightmare of mental institutions to the nightmare of homeless encampments?

In *San Fransicko* I explore how the conversation around how to use law and order to advance civil rights gave way to a debate over whether law and order is an obstacle to social justice. The question used to be carrots versus sticks. Do you reward people for not committing crimes, or do you punish them when they do? But that's been superseded by a question from progressives: what if it's a form of victimization to try to influence people's behavior at all? The governing majority in some of America's cities seems to believe that the only real public policy problem is how to pay for letting people do whatever they want, from turning public parks into open-air drug encampments, to using sidewalks as toilets, to handing over whole neighborhoods to people who are heavily armed and purposefully unaccountable.

Some will take offense at this book's subtitle, but I am not suggesting that progressives *only* ruin cities, nor that they never save them. Nor am I suggesting that conservatives never ruin them. But I am saying that when progressives do ruin cities, they do so in similar ways, and for similar reasons. And while the crisis of disorder I am describing is strongest in progressive West Coast cities, it is spreading east, like many trends in America do.

Progressives have been in charge of San Francisco, Los Angeles, and Seattle, as well as California and Washington, during most of the decades in which the problems I describe here have grown worse. And on the fundamental policies relating to mental illness, addiction, and housing for the homeless, moderate Democrats, conservatives, and Republicans have either gone along with the liberal and progressive agenda or been powerless to prevent it since the 1960s. And it was Democrats, not Republicans, who played the primary role in creating the dominant neoliberal model of government contracting to fragmented and often unaccountable nonprofit service providers that have proven financially, structurally, and legally incapable of addressing the crisis.

Not long after I began my research, I read what I felt then, and still feel now, were the three best books on homelessness, all published in the early 1990s, and all authored by liberals or progressives.[4] At first the books inspired me. I felt as though three wise elders had reached forward through time to pass along essential truths. But then it dawned on me that, despite those three books having been widely reviewed and well received, including by America's most influential newspapers, the crisis of untreated mental illness and addiction, as well as what we call homelessness, had grown worse, not better. What would prevent *San Fransicko* from suffering a similar fate?

That night, I confessed to my wife, Helen, that all I might be able to do was write a book that warned other places what *not* to do. She grew quiet and looked away. After I asked her what was the matter, she said, "We *live* here." I needed to be as constructive as I was critical, she felt. And so at the heart of *San Fransicko* is a positive proposal for how to restore human dignity, not just law and order, to progressive West Coast cities. At both philosophical and policy levels it will, I hope and believe, resonate with the heads, hearts, and guts of reasonable conservatives and reasonable progressives.

Having shared my motivations as well as I understand them myself, it is to the breakdown of civilization on America's West Coast that we can now turn.

San Fransicko

1

"I Just Want to Clean Up the Mess"

In 1977, a candidate for the San Francisco Board of Supervisors invited reporters to a press conference at a local park. He said he was going to announce legislation essential to improving the quality of life in the city. With a pack of cameras waiting for him, the man walked across the grass toward them before stopping, making a face, and lifting up his foot to look at the bottom of his shoe only to discover, in feigned horror, that he had stepped in dog poop. After pretending to be surprised, and flashing a big smile, the man turned toward the cameras and announced legislation he would introduce, once elected, that required San Franciscans to pick up their dogs' poop.[1]

It was a savvy and ultimately successful move for the handsome forty-something-year-old candidate. The number one quality-of-life issue for San Franciscans had become the large amount of uncollected dog feces on sidewalks and in parks. The man had run for supervisor twice before, coming in tenth the first time and seventh the second time. But he never connected with a majority of voters. This time, having identified an issue that people cared about, he was elected to the Board of Supervisors.[2] His name was Harvey Milk.

Today we remember Milk as perhaps the most significant gay rights leader of all time. He is the person who unlocked the secret to reducing prejudice against same-sex relationships, by people disclosing to friends and family that they were gay. Sean Penn won an Oscar after immortalizing Milk's life in a 2008 film. But Milk owed his political career to dog poop.

Shortly after taking office in 1978, Milk introduced the "Scoop the Poop" Act,[3] which by the end of the summer the Board of Supervisors had passed.[4] Afterward, a journalist said to Milk, "The police department says it may be hard to enforce this," to which Milk replied, beaming, "I think it will be easy based on peer pressure. It's going to be hard to write citations. But when a San Franciscan is walking down the street and sees someone breaking the law you say 'Hey!'—with a smile—'You broke the law.' And after a while, when enough people do that, the message will be clear. It will be an education process. I really hope not one single citation is ever issued. . . . I don't want to put anybody in jail. I don't want to fine anyone. I just want to clean up the mess."[5]

People overwhelmingly complied. It's true that dog owners still sometimes fail to pick up after their dogs. But dog owner behavior has changed drastically, and for exactly the reason Milk predicted it would: peer pressure. Dog owners felt, and feel, a moral obligation to take responsibility for their pets. As such, Milk's campaign to remove poop from San Francisco's parks and sidewalks was a resounding success. At least, that is, when it came from dogs.

In 2018, San Francisco's mayor, London Breed, held a walking tour with television cameras and newspaper reporters in tow. "I will say that there's more feces on the sidewalks than I've ever seen," said Breed. "Growing up here, that was something that wasn't the norm."

"Than you've ever seen?" asked the reporter.

"Than I've ever seen, for sure," she said. "And we're not just talking about from dogs. We're talking about from humans."[6]

Complaints about human waste on San Francisco's sidewalks and streets were rising. Calls about human feces increased from 10,692 to

20,933 between 2014 and 2018.[7] In 2019, the city spent nearly $100 million on street cleaning—four times more than Chicago, which has 3.5 times as many people and an area that is 4.5 times larger. Between 2015 and 2018, San Francisco replaced more than three hundred lampposts corroded by urine after one had collapsed and crushed a car.[8]

The underlying problem was homelessness. Between 2013 and 2016, complaints of homeless encampments to the city's 311 line rose from 2 per day to 63 per day.[9] In 2018, a major medical association decided to host its annual convention, worth about $40 million for the local economy, elsewhere, after decades of holding events in San Francisco.[10] The condition of the homeless in San Francisco is internationally recognized as inhumane. In 2018, the United Nations' special rapporteur visited San Francisco and said, "There's a cruelty here that I don't think I've seen, and I've done outreach on every continent."[11]

Many of San Francisco's homeless live in densely populated, centrally located areas. The most infamous of these is the Tenderloin, a downtown neighborhood that borders government buildings including City Hall, a major shopping district with several large tourist hotels, and many of the city's concert venues and museums.

Some argue that the homelessness situation in San Francisco isn't worse than other cities. "New York City has a worse per-capita homelessness problem than San Francisco," wrote a *New Yorker* reporter in 2020. "California's proportion of homeless residents trails that of New York; Washington, D.C.; and Hawaii."[12] The difference is that San Francisco has a far higher number who are unsheltered, sleeping on the streets or in tents rather than in homeless shelters.

Many studies show that warmer climates and more expensive housing are major factors behind higher rates of homelessness, both sheltered and unsheltered, in San Francisco, Seattle, and Los Angeles.[13] In much of California, one can sleep outside for most of the year without freezing. Half of the unsheltered homeless population in the United States is in

California and Florida alone, even though the two states are home to just 19 percent of the population.[14] High-tech companies like Salesforce, Twitter, and Stripe, progressives noted, had attracted thousands of employees who had driven up rents, resulting in tenant evictions.[15]

In 2016, representatives from San Francisco's business, philanthropic, and media communities committed to halve the city's chronic homeless population in five years. They created a media initiative called the SF Homeless Project, and raised over $130 million in the first year, with $100 million raised by an organization called Tipping Point and another $30 million coming from Marc Benioff, the billionaire CEO and founder of Salesforce, the customer relations software giant.[16]

The San Francisco Coalition on Homelessness, a nonprofit organization, led a campaign to fund housing and services with a special tax on San Francisco businesses that gross more than $50 million annually.[17] At first, few believed the measure, put before voters in the form of Proposition C, could pass. CEOs of other high-revenue tech companies in San Francisco, including Patrick Collison of Stripe and Jack Dorsey of Twitter, opposed Prop C, as did Mayor Breed. And the Coalition on Homelessness didn't have the money to pay for large-scale advertising and other costs of a citywide campaign.

But then Benioff donated millions of dollars to the campaign for Proposition C. "What I see is a crisis of inequality in San Francisco," he said. "We have 1,200 homeless families, each with two kids. . . . We have 70 billionaires here in our city. That's incredible."[18]

Benioff criticized the high-tech companies opposing Prop C. "Square [is] worth $30 billion," he said. "Twitter [is] worth $20 billion. Stripe, $20 billion. . . . These are immaterial amounts to us. $10 million doesn't mean anything. That's less than the private plane that [Twitter founder and CEO] Jack Dorsey is going to fly around on."[19] Benioff added, "You're either for the homeless and for the kids and for the hospitals or you're for yourself."[20]

Benioff gave a $30 million grant to Dr. Margot Kushel at the University of California, San Francisco to study homelessness.[21] "We've always known that most homelessness is a result, pure and simple, of poverty," she said.[22] One of the biggest myths is that it is "caused by mental health and substance use problems," Kushel explained. "We know that most homelessness is driven by economic forces."[23]

A study by the real estate website Zillow and the University of New Hampshire found that when median rent exceeded 22 percent of median income, the number of homeless people in a city grew, and rose especially rapidly at 32 percent. The median San Francisco renter pays 39 percent of his or her income in rent.[24]

Some Bay Area reporters agree. "The convenient narrative about homeless people is that they're lazy, mentally ill or drug addicts," wrote one *San Francisco Chronicle* columnist. "But that's not true."[25] Survey data collected by the city, many pointed out, shows that one-quarter of homeless cited job loss as the primary cause of their homelessness, 18 percent cited substance abuse, 13 percent eviction, and 8 percent mental illness.[26]

While all big cities struggle with homelessness, the West Coast cities of the San Francisco Bay Area, Los Angeles, and Seattle struggle more. The change over the last fifteen years has been dramatic. Between 2005 and 2020, the estimated number of homeless people in San Francisco increased from 5,404 to 8,124. The estimated number of *un*sheltered homeless rose from 2,655 to 5,180.[27]

The San Francisco Bay Area as a whole saw sheltered and unsheltered homeless increase by 32 percent between 2015 and 2020, with the share of unsheltered homeless rising from 65 percent to 73 percent.* Total

---

* The San Francisco Bay Area includes the counties of Alameda, Contra Costa, Marin, Napa, San Mateo, Santa Clara, Solano, Sonoma, and San Francisco.

homelessness more than doubled in Alameda County, which includes Oakland and Berkeley, between 2015 and 2020.[28]

Meanwhile, homelessness declined in the nation as a whole, and in other big cities, over the last decade and a half. Homelessness nationwide declined from 763,000 to 568,000 between 2005 and 2020. In the same fifteen-year period, the homeless populations of Chicago, Greater Miami, and Greater Atlanta declined 19 percent, 32 percent, and 43 percent, respectively.[29]

While it is true that New York City saw an increase of 62 percent in its homeless population between 2005 and 2020, over 99 percent of New York's homeless have access to shelter. In San Francisco, just 43 percent do.[30]

Against Benioff's suggestion that San Francisco's homeless population is heavily comprised of families with children, the research finds that far more homeless in the San Francisco Bay Area are adults without families than in other parts of the United States. Whereas families make up 32, 53, and 65 percent of the homeless in New York City, Chicago, and Boston, they make up just 9 percent of the Bay Area's homeless population.[31]

San Francisco has a much higher share of unsheltered homeless who are "chronically homeless" than other cities. The US Department of Housing and Urban Development (HUD) defines chronically homeless as those who have been homeless for a year, had four episodes of homelessness totaling twelve months in the last three years, or those who are too disabled to work.[32] Of the roughly 5,200 unsheltered homeless people in San Francisco, 37 percent in 2020 were chronically homeless, in comparison to the 34 percent, 19 percent, 17 percent, and 16 percent chronically homeless in New York City, Greater Phoenix, Greater San Diego, and Boston, respectively.[33]

San Francisco's mild climate alone cannot explain why it has more homeless people than other cities. Miami, Phoenix, and Houston have year-round warm weather and far fewer homeless than San Francisco per capita. Per capita homelessness in San Francisco, Greater Miami, Greater Phoenix, and Greater Houston in 2020 was 9.3, 1.3, 1.6, and 0.8 per 1,000 residents, respectively. And Greater Miami, Greater Phoenix, and Greater Houston saw their per capita homeless population decline from 2005 to 2020 by 39, 17, and 74 percent while San Francisco saw its rise 30 percent.[34]

Nor can housing prices explain the discrepancy. Palo Alto and Beverly Hills have mild climates and expensive housing but don't have San Francisco's homeless problem. As for the Zillow study that was reported to find a correlation between rising rents and homelessness, a deeper look at the research reveals a more nuanced finding. Homelessness and affordability are correlated only in the context of certain "local policy efforts [and] social attitudes," concluded researchers.[35]

Other cities, including Chicago, Houston, and the Greater Miami area, saw typical rents *increase* 24 percent, 32 percent, and 35 percent and the number of homeless *decline* 20 percent, 57 percent, and 9 percent between 2011 and 2019, which are the years covered by the Zillow study (2011–2017), plus 2018 and 2019. In Nashville, the number of *chronically* homeless fell 54 percent in the same period.[36]

While the homeless are poor, few poor people live on the street. Nearly 90,000 people in San Francisco live in poverty but just over 8,000 are homeless. The vast majority of people, including very poor people who are priced out of San Francisco's expensive rental markets, move out of the city or move in with friends or family. Vanishingly few decide to pitch a tent on the filthiest sidewalks in America.

O ver the last decades there were many visible signs that homelessness was about much more than poverty and housing. Between 2010 and 2020, the number of calls made to San Francisco's 311 line complaining of used hypodermic needles on sidewalks, in parks, and elsewhere rose from 224 to 6,275.[37] In 2018, footage of dozens of people slumped over in an entrance to a Bay Area Rapid Transit (BART) station, many with needles in their arm, went viral.[38] "We call it the heroin freeze," said one local. "They can stay that way for hours."[39] Said another, "It's like the land of the living dead."[40]

For decades researchers have documented much higher levels of mental illness and substance abuse among the homeless than in the rest of the population. It's true that just 8 and 18 percent of homeless people point to mental illness and substance abuse, respectively, as the primary cause of their homelessness, but researchers have long understood that such self-reports are unreliable due to the socially undesirable nature of substance abuse, and the lack of insight that often accompanies mental illness. Using other methods, San Francisco's Health Department in 2019 estimated that 4,000 of the city's 8,035 homeless, sheltered and unsheltered, are both mentally ill and suffering from substance abuse. Of those 4,000, about 1,600 frequently used emergency psychiatric services.[41]

The same is true in other cities. In 2019, the *Los Angeles Times* analyzed government data and found that two-thirds of homeless in Los Angeles struggle with either addiction or mental illness.[42] Against the insistence among some progressives that homelessness is strictly the result of poverty and housing prices, researchers for decades have documented not just the prevalence of mental illness and substance abuse among the homeless, but also their role in creating homelessness in the first place.[43]

A large, 5,406-person study of US veterans published in 2021 found that the major personal characteristics of the unsheltered homeless were "unmarried status, criminal justice problems, weak social support, medical diagnoses, drug (but not alcohol) problems, low income, and inability to afford basic needs." Wrote the authors, "where weather was warmer, or rents were higher, the number of personal risk factors mattered more." Homelessness, noted the authors, reflects "the interaction of person and place."[44]

Some things have gotten better. After negative publicity, the San

Francisco city government signed a $1 million per year contract to clean up the needles and install more public toilets.[45] As a result, complaints to the city's 311 line about needles on the sidewalks declined nearly 34 percent from 2018 to 2020.

But other things got worse. More people called the city demanding action to clear away bulky items in 2020 than in 2019.[46] In 2020, the city received 29,162 requests to remove "Human or Animal Waste," and 6,275 needle complaints.[47] As for the new toilets, they did not eliminate public urination and defecation. "The city has installed five portable bathrooms for the hundreds of unsheltered people in the Tenderloin," noted the *New York Times* in 2018, "but that has not stopped people from urinating and defecating in the streets."[48]

In the past, governments and nonprofits had sometimes required homeless people to earn an apartment unit through sobriety, work, and, when appropriate, compliance with taking their psychiatric medicine. This is called the "contingency" approach, linear approach, or staircase approach, since one must earn the next step through good behavior.

"When we first started," said Margot Kushel, "people believed that to provide housing, people needed to go through steps. First, a shelter. Then, if they 'behaved well' (didn't use drugs, took medicines, etc.), they could get to transitional housing. If they did everything 'right' then they could be offered permanent housing. As a result, only a tiny proportion of people with behavioral disabilities became housed.

"Housing First turned that upside down," she explained, "recognizing that when people were homeless, they couldn't attend to their mental health or substance use needs (or anything else). This has been enormously successful, housing about 85 percent of the most complex folks. There is overwhelming and incontrovertible evidence that this works—people are housed successfully, and then the other things follow."[49]

Utah garnered widespread media attention after state officials claimed a 91 percent decline in chronic homelessness because of its adoption of Housing First.[50] The *Los Angeles Times* declared, "Utah is winning the war on chronic homelessness with 'Housing First.'"[51] Said *NBC*, "Utah is battling homelessness by giving the needy shelter first and then aiding them with job placement, and it's working."[52]

Housing First provides housing without conditions. There is "no empirical support for the practice of requiring individuals to participate in psychiatric treatment or attain sobriety before being housed," wrote founder of Housing First Sam Tsemberis.[53] Kushel agreed. "You hear people saying things like, 'You can't just house people who have addiction problems.' You can, and you must."[54]

The George W. Bush administration made Housing First federal policy. It helped cities and states create plans to end chronic homelessness in ten years through permanent supportive housing, and provided money after they had done so. By 2009, more than two hundred cities and states had done so.[55]

At a local TV news station's roundtable discussion in 2017, elected officials and top homelessness advocates from each of the Bay Area's counties were adamant that Housing First was the *only* solution to homelessness. "Housing is the solution to homelessness," said San Francisco's top homelessness official. "Housing First is the solution to ending homelessness," said Berkeley's mayor. And, stressed San Jose's mayor, "We ultimately all agree that the only real solution is permanent supportive housing."[56]

From 2005 to 2020, San Francisco experienced an astonishing 95 percent increase in unsheltered homelessness as the number of permanent supportive housing units offered by the city rose from 6,487 to 10,051.[57]

Today, San Francisco has the greatest quantity of permanent supportive housing units per capita of any major city in the United States. It has 11 permanent supportive housing units per 1,000 people, which is nearly three times as much as New York City (4 per 1,000 people) and Chicago (4 per 1,000), and over six times as much as Miami-Dade County (1.7 per 1,000).[58]

All of that, and yet the unsheltered homeless population of New York City, Chicago, and Miami fell 11, 10, and 50 percent, respectively, between 2005 and 2020, while San Francisco's rose 95 percent.[59] Why was that?

The mind behind Proposition C was Jennifer Friedenbach, executive director of the San Francisco Coalition on Homelessness. A Silicon Valley native who rebelled against her parents' middle-class, conservative lifestyle, Friedenbach has taken a small salary and dedicated her life to working on homelessness since the 1990s.[60]

Friedenbach and other advocates for the homeless attribute the rise of homelessness to President Ronald Reagan. "The reason we have mass homelessness," she said, "is the federal government's fault. They divested or disinvested from funding housing in the early eighties by 78 percent."[61] A permanent supportive housing provider in the Tenderloin told me, "It's absolutely undisputed that the homeless crisis in America began after severe cuts to federal affordable housing funds."[62] And an ACLU expert said, "The Reagan administration slashed the budget for our federal affordable housing programs by eighty percent."[63]

But public spending on housing barely changed under Reagan, going from $41.8 billion to $40.6 billion between 1981 and 1989, in constant 2019 dollars.[64] Reagan did oversee the end of public housing construction, but this was in the context of a shift away from federal housing projects toward rental subsidies which began under Presidents Gerald Ford and Jimmy Carter, and for good reason.[65] In the late 1960s there was growing unhappiness with public housing, particularly high-rise apartment complexes for the urban poor. They had been built with the greatest of progressive and liberal intentions: to provide former residents of poor neighbors with modern apartment units. But they became infamous for concentrating poverty, crime, and violence.[66]

In the wake of that and other well-publicized failures, Congress sought better solutions, ultimately embracing rental vouchers, or Section 8 certificates. Under Section 8 of the Housing and Community Development Act of 1974, Congress created vouchers to pay the difference between a tenant's rent and 25 percent of his or her monthly income, for fifteen years. The reforms proved more efficient. It cost half as much to house someone with a Section 8 certificate as it did to subsidize construction.[67] And low-income families greatly preferred the freedom to choose their own housing rather than be assigned to a public housing project.[68]

Crack was a major factor behind the emergence of homelessness as a problem in the 1980s. Boona Cheema, a former homeless service provider and advocate in Berkeley, estimated in the early 1990s that 85 percent of the homeless in her Oakland shelter had recently used crack, and that "there are almost no family ties" left among them.[69] Crack radically reduced the price of cocaine, along with the duration of the high, making it available to the poor and working class. The cost of crack declined from $10 to $3 for a single hit between the mid-1980s and early 1990s.[70]

The conventional wisdom holds that the increase in homelessness in the 1980s resulted, in part, from the *loss* of low-cost, often substandard housing, but it was San Francisco's *preservation* of such housing, and conversion into housing for the homeless, which helped make the homeless addiction problem so much worse than in other cities. Most of San Francisco's low-cost housing came in the form of single resident occupancy hotels, where residents had a single room and usually shared a kitchen and bathroom. The number of single resident occupancy units per capita declined by two-thirds in New York City and Chicago from the mid-1970s to today. San Francisco, which started with nearly twice as many units per capita, lost only one-third during the same period.[71]

Advocacy for the preservation of single resident occupancy hotels occurred within the broader progressive movement. Democrats until the late 1960s were pro-development, and had led efforts to demolish slums, build public housing, and revitalize the inner city. But starting in the late 1960s, Baby Boomers and the New Left turned against redevelopment. They were inspired by an influential 1961 book, *The Death and Life of Great American Cities* by Jane Jacobs, which blamed redevelopment, like that which had occurred in the Fillmore neighborhood of San Francisco, for destroying neighborhoods with freeways and high-rises, evicting low-income residents, and making them unlivable, as compared to highly walkable neighborhoods like Greenwich Village.

But redevelopment occurred in Greenwich Village whereas the city of San Francisco increasingly subsidized housing for the homeless in the Tenderloin's single resident occupancy hotels, which have for decades been dominated by a culture of heavy substance use and prostitution. "Of the people in supportive housing in San Francisco, 93 percent have a major mental illness that we can name," said a housing policy maker. "That is very, very high. Eighty percent use cocaine, speed, or heroin every thirty days, or get drunk to the point of unconsciousness."[72]

Tom Wolf, a former Salvation Army caseworker and a member of San Francisco's Drug Dealing Taskforce, says the city's supportive housing facilities are themselves a major market for illegal drugs. "Go down the street to the Camelot Hotel on Turk Street," said Wolf. "Almost everyone that I've seen in those hotels are using. The last front desk guy that was working there got busted because he was selling crack. The actual guy that works in the single resident occupancy hotel is selling crack! It's insane, man."[73]

According to many homelessness researchers, the defining characteristics of chronic homelessness are addiction and "disaffiliation," or estrangement, from friends and family. "What causes homelessness among these skid row dwellers?" asked a leading researcher in the early 1990s.

"Addiction and the lack of a support system."[74] Said Tracey Helton Mitchell, who wrote a memoir about her heroin addiction in the Tenderloin, "When I left my hometown, I cut myself off from my support system, both emotionally and financially."[75]

In November 1991, San Francisco voters elected a former police chief mayor on a promise to move the homeless off the streets and crack down on nuisance crimes, like littering, camping in parks, and aggressive panhandling.[76] He also offered housing and services, subsidized 2,000 moderate- and low-income housing units, and sent outreach workers to offer shelter and drug treatment.[77] And the new mayor fought against the expansion of funding for single resident occupancy hotel rooms, which he viewed as a magnet for hard drug users, triggering protests organized by the nonprofit housing and service provider organizations.[78]

Four years later, Willie Brown, a powerful former state legislator from San Francisco and the highest-ranking African American in the state, was elected mayor. Brown seized on the perception among progressive Democrats in San Francisco that the city's approach to homelessness was cruel. "In my administration," Brown promised, "police will spend their time going after crack dealers, thugs, aggressive panhandlers, and other predators, rather than rounding up people whose only crime is being poor."[79]

But Brown never stopped the sweeps of the homeless and increasingly sounded like his predecessor. "If you put together really aggressive and attractive programs," he said in 1996, "you begin to establish an identity where advocates may become a source of supply for your population."[80] The San Francisco Coalition on Homelessness and other progressives felt betrayed. "I don't have the answer," Brown said. "I'm not working toward anything at this moment except the maintenance of current programs, but that's not a solution." Brown called off a homelessness summit, saying, "I couldn't get the advocates to believe that we were sincere about trying to find solutions."[81]

In 2001, San Francisco supervisor Gavin Newsom proposed a new ballot measure, "Care Not Cash." Its main feature was the diversion of General Assistance (welfare) cash payments into housing, but its broader goal was to shift funding from shelters to permanent supportive housing.[82] Newsom was motivated in part by evidence that people were coming to San Francisco for its generous cash welfare payments. San Francisco at the time gave homeless individuals between $320 and $395 per month, while Oakland gave just $24. Newsom proposed cutting the San Francisco payments to $57 per month and diverting the money saved to housing, mostly single resident occupancy units.[83] Homeless activists savaged the measure. "The Newsom plan is heartless, ruthless and basically immoral," said a Roman Catholic nun who provided homelessness services. But Care Not Cash passed with 60 percent of the vote.[84]

While Care Not Cash modestly reduced General Assistance costs, just 15 percent of the single homeless population was able to secure basic housing.[85] And so, after his election as mayor in 2003, Newsom put together a task force including labor unions, businesses, and the Coalition on Homelessness to create a Ten Year Plan. "The focus," said the task force leader, "is permanent supportive housing for the 3,000 or so chronically homeless, out of the 15,000 general homeless populations."[86]

Spirits were high. Under the new plan, task force leaders claimed, the city would spend just $16,000 per year per chronically homeless person on housing and care, which was dramatically less than the $61,000 city officials estimated that San Francisco was already spending in the form of emergency services, incarceration, and other costs.[87] "I think a 10-year plan is absolutely workable and absolutely doable," said the task force leader, "and don't let anyone tell you that it's not." While some may have doubted that San Francisco would completely solve the problem of chronic homelessness within ten years, few could have predicted just how much worse it would get.[88]

2

Pleasure Island

Progressives have long defended the right of the homeless to camp in public places. In 1983, activists mobilized hundreds of homeless people to march on San Francisco City Hall shouting, "Don't be a louse! Give me a house!"[1] A 1989 earthquake forced some five hundred people to evacuate their city-subsidized single resident occupancy hotel rooms, and nearly two hundred of them, and others, camped out at Civic Center Plaza. Nearby residents and businesses complained about their presence. The city's progressive mayor, a former social worker, refused to move the homeless from Civic Center until replacement housing was available nine months later. By the early 1990s, advocates for the homeless were hosting seminars where they taught people how to camp out in the city.[2]

San Francisco voters sometimes demand greater public order. In 2004, the city passed a ballot initiative that banned aggressive and intimidating panhandling, such as near ATM machines or inside buses. In 2010, San Francisco voters approved an ordinance that made it illegal to sit or lie on sidewalks between 7 a.m. and 11 p.m. And in 2016, voters banned camping on sidewalks.[3]

Progressive homelessness advocates fought these initiatives. One member of the Coalition on Homelessness compared measures like the ban on people lying and sitting on sidewalks to Jim Crow racial segregation laws in the South.[4] "Sitting is not a crime" was the headline for one advertisement ahead of the election, which showed a picture of African

American activists desegregating a lunch counter in the 1950s.[5] In 2013, some progressive merchants in the Haight allowed the homeless to flout the law and sit on sidewalks. "I'm a vet," said an empowered homeless man drinking beer on the sidewalk. "I'll sit anywhere I want!"[6] The homeless know they are supported by progressive elected officials, advocates, and citizens. "This is [San Francisco] downtown! Anyone has the right to be downtown!" another homeless man said. "Whatcha think this is, Palo Alto?"[7]

Progressives give homeless people the equipment they need to live on sidewalks. After Occupy Wall Street protests were held in Oakland's City Center in 2011, protesters gave their tents to the homeless and money to buy more.[8] Five years later, a graphic designer in San Francisco purchased and gave away $15,000 worth of camping tents. "Other organizations were giving them out as well," noted the city's head of homeless services in 2016, "and now we've got 80 encampments."[9]

San Francisco remains significantly more generous in its cash payments to homeless, and other spending to serve them, than other cities. For example, San Francisco's maximum General Assistance cash welfare monthly benefit for the poor is $588, as compared to $449, $221, and $183 for individuals in San Diego, Los Angeles, and New York City, respectively.[10] While New York City, Chicago, Phoenix, and San Diego spend 3.5, 1.1, 0.9, and 2.5 percent of their budget on homelessness services, San Francisco spends 6 percent.[11] When local, state, and federal funding are accounted for, San Francisco spends $31,985 per homeless person just on housing, not including General Assistance, other cash welfare programs like Temporary Assistance for Needy Families, and other services. By contrast, New York City spends $11,662 and Los Angeles spends $5,001.[12]

Even with restrictions on cash welfare payments to some homeless people, San Francisco still gives significantly larger cash benefits to the poor in comparison to other cities. San Francisco gives $709 per capita of total cash welfare payments to the poor as compared to $195, $120, and $0.34 in New York City, Chicago, and Phoenix, respectively. Including overhead, San Francisco spends $15,583 per recipient where New York City spends $7,129 per recipient through its cash welfare program.[13]

There is a provision in Care Not Cash that allows recipients to get full payment if they agree to work for a nonprofit homeless service provider. "If you identify as homeless, you only get $60 per month plus food stamps because of Care Not Cash," noted Tom Wolf. "But if you volunteer at a non-profit for twelve hours per month, you get full General Assistance payment. You collect three months before they kick you off and you never volunteered."

That's what Tom did. "[The homelessness nonprofits'] whole intention is to keep more people in this cycle," he said, "because they're getting money for it."[14]

Tom had himself lived as a homeless addict in the Tenderloin, surviving on the city's cash welfare payments. "I got $581 a month in General Assistance and $192 in food stamps," he said. "I could get a free breakfast at Glide [Memorial Church] and a free lunch at St. Anthony's, which allowed me to use all of my General Assistance money for heroin and then sell my food stamp card to a merchant in Chinatown who would pay me 60 cents on the dollar for it."

According to a 2019 survey conducted by the homeless advocacy group Tipping Point, just one-fifth of San Francisco's homeless said they were born in the city and only half had lived in the city for over ten years. In a different survey, nearly one-third of San Francisco's homeless said they were homeless before coming to San Francisco. And among the 70 percent who said they became homeless after moving to San Francisco, we don't know how long many of them had lived in the city. For some, it could have been as brief as a month, which is the time it takes to become eligible for General Assistance.[15]

Helping the neediest can create perverse incentives. "They love getting in the most fucked up folks out here," complained a homeless man who believed homeless people from out of town were getting into a new and more desirable shelter before him. "I'm just not fucked up enough."[16] Said one young homeless woman, "it's better than being in Oakland. It definitely has more services for homeless people. We have more places where they feed you and help you get into a shelter if you want."[17] "When I was first homeless," said a homeless man in the late 1990s, "I stayed around the [Tenderloin], you know, because that's where the food was, the shelters was."[18] The reputation stuck. In 2019, a homeless man told a reporter that he came from Iowa to San Francisco because he heard "social services are plentiful, anyone is welcome and the weather is pleasant."[19]

But the biggest reason many people come to San Francisco is for the cheap and abundant drugs and the lax law enforcement. "I didn't want that straight life," said a thirty-two-year-old homeless man from Alabama. "I was after the candy—getting high, easy money, freedom, ladies, getting high some more."[20] "Some of these small towns, you stick out straight-away and they come for you. Someone makes a call and the cops get on your tail. You could be just walking down the road like anyone else, no cart, nothing, and they pick you up."[21] Said another, "Some of the things allowed to happen in San Francisco would never be permitted back home in Boston."[22]

Jacqui Berlinn is a mother whose son, Corey, is homeless and addicted to fentanyl and living on the streets of the Bay Area. "My son tells me San Francisco is where he most readily gets what he needs. He calls it 'Hell,' and compared it to Pleasure Island in the Disney film *Pinocchio*.

"On one side of the street are people giving you food and clean needles," Corey told her. "On the other side of the street are all the drug dealers. It's like getting all the candy and treats that you think you want. You think you're having fun. But little by little it's taking away your humanity and turning you into something you were never meant to be, like how the kids start turning into donkeys in *Pinocchio*, and then end up trapped and in cages."[23]

"We watched the movie when he was a boy," said Jacqui, "and so it totally made sense to me that he felt like one of the poor donkeys trying to break free, with the drug dealers giving them treats and enslaving them and taking away their humanity and they had no way to escape."

Others agreed. When I asked a major provider of housing for the homeless in the Tenderloin, Randy Shaw, whether people come to San Francisco for the drugs he said, without hesitation, "Yes, one hundred percent. No doubt about it. We have the worst overdose rate of any city in the country." Matt Haney, the San Francisco supervisor who represents the Tenderloin, told me, "Undoubtedly there are some people who come here because they are sick with addiction. This is a place where you can access drugs more easily."[24]

In 2016, San Francisco opened a new shelter, which attracted homeless from different neighborhoods within the city, according to University of California, Los Angeles sociologist and homelessness researcher Chris Herring. "Unfortunately, after the first few months it became clear that the navigation center [homeless shelter] was not resulting in fewer encampments," wrote Herring, who works closely with the San Francisco Coalition on Homelessness. "Instead, the number of camps increased, as did complaints and policing. This was not due to the shelter's failure of meeting the needs of the unhoused, but rather its success in doing so."[25]

When people arrive in San Francisco, they often discover there isn't room in the shelters for them. "People come from all over the United States, thinking it's some sort of spa here," said a homeless man, "some sort of nirvana here. And they find out that it's very expensive to live here."[26] The same was true in Los Angeles. "For the first time in 13 years, Los Angeles opened its housing voucher wait list last year," said Dr. Margot Kushel. "The city drew 600,000 applicants for 20,000 slots, highlighting the enormous unmet need."[27] And more services attracted more people to Seattle. "I do think we have a magnet effect," said Seattle's former homelessness chief. Nearly one-quarter of the homeless in King County, in which Seattle is the biggest city, said they became homeless outside of Washington State.[28]

Mayor Breed said she opposed Proposition C because she feared that spending yet more on homelessness services, without any requirement that people get off the street, would backfire. "We are a magnet for people who are looking for help," she said. "There are a lot of other cities that are not doing their part, and I find that larger cities end up with more than our fair share."[29]

After San Francisco started offering free hotel rooms to the homeless during the 2020 coronavirus pandemic, first responders reported that people had come from across the state. "People are coming from all over the place—Sacramento, Lake County, Bakersfield," said the city's fire chief. "We have also heard that people are getting released from jail in other counties and being told to go to San Francisco where you will get a tent and then you will get housing."[30]

When a television reporter asked Bay Area mayors why there was so much homelessness in Bay Area cities but not in affluent communities east of the Bay Area, the Berkeley mayor answered, "I assume [it's] the fact that our cities have such robust social services and shelter, as well as just the environment, the climate, a city that is inviting and welcoming to people."[31]

A Los Angeles homelessness service provider emphasizes the extent to which the homeless shop around from city to city seeking the best housing and benefits and avoiding the law. He wrote, "for a majority of people they move from community to community, looking for food, shelter, and services. Keeping one step beyond the arm of the law or moving from others who might harm them."[32]

While some homeless are attracted to San Francisco for housing and services, many of San Francisco's most visible homeless people don't use them. When I visited the Tenderloin with Tom Wolf, he pointed to the doorway to a building. "I slept here," he said, "because I was such an addict that I didn't want to walk the five blocks to the shelter. I wanted to be right near the dealers."[33]

In the context of cities with permissive attitudes toward drugs, like San Francisco, many homeless people stay in encampments to use illegal substances more freely and easily than they can in the shelters. Many policy makers understand this. "I went out with a team twice to have conversations with people to get an understanding of what they're dealing with," said Mayor Breed in 2020. "It was absolutely insane. Most of the people did not take us up on the offer [of shelter and services]."[34]

Even people who would prefer to live in sober environments say they do not want to quit their addictions. "When we surveyed people in supportive housing in New York," said University of Pennsylvania homelessness researcher Dennis Culhane, "almost everybody wanted their neighbors to be clean and sober but they didn't want rules for themselves about being clean."[35]

In 2016, after the city of San Francisco broke up a massive, 350-person homeless encampment, dozens of the homeless refused the city's offers of help.[36] Of the 150 people moved during a single month of homeless encampment cleanups in 2018, just eight people accepted the city's offer of shelter.[37] In 2004, just 131 people went into permanent supportive housing after 4,950 contacts made by then-mayor Newsom's homeless outreach teams.[38]

Homeless people in Oakland successfully prevented the breakup of their camp in a public park by erecting barricades made of trash and furniture. Unable or unwilling to force the homeless to move, the city granted them a different place to live, where they will be able to camp and "co-govern" their new land with a local nonprofit.[39]

After a major homeless encampment was broken up in 2017, reports of low-level crimes rose throughout the city.[40] Some residents started taking matters into their own hands. In 2019, a group of residents arranged for large boulders to be placed on the sidewalks in front of their homes to prevent camping by homeless people. Another group built a wall to block access to a walking path that had become a homeless encampment.[41]

"What ends up happening with a lot of progressive liberals in San Francisco," said Tom, "is they get to go home to their nice house in Noe Valley and six-figure job and kids in private school. They can afford to vote progressively for social justice because they don't have to walk their kids through the Tenderloin and play hopscotch over the feces and needles."[42]

Homelessness advocates often level serious charges at people who disagree with their view of the problem and the solution. In the early 1990s, a Harvard sociologist who wrote a book on homelessness noted, "those who see the homeless as passive victims of circumstances beyond their control often react to [the evidence of service refusal] with a mixture of fury and disbelief."[43]

Advocates of shelters, said Friedenbach, don't really care about the homeless. "There's this thought that [shelters] are an easy, quick solution and we get people off the streets, and the neighbors stop complaining," she said. "It really comes from a perspective of, 'How do we keep the neighbors happy.' They don't want to have to look at homeless people anymore. 'So, let's shove them into a shelter so we don't have to look at them.'"[44]

In 2001, the San Francisco Coalition on Homelessness wheat-pasted posters of a fake front-page *San Francisco Chronicle* across town. Just beneath the masthead a large headline read "Fuck the Homeless!" right above a picture of San Francisco mayor Willie Brown laughing. Below his photo was the headline "Save the Tourists."[45]

Progressives level the same charges at people thirty years later. "Because of some of the stuff I say," said a community activist in Seattle's historically black Capitol Hill neighborhood, "people say, 'Oh, she's not for them.' But I have a heart for homeless and mentally ill. Most of my family works with the mentally ill."[46] Noted a *Chronicle* journalist in 2017, "Inevitably, homeless advocates and others will say, 'You're not compassionate,'" in response to stories about homeless encampments.[47] "They called me a racist," said Tom. "They accused me, a guy who used to be homeless, of demonizing the homeless, because I'm asking for accountability."[48]

I found myself similarly accused. In 2019, after I published an article for *Forbes* about the homeless crisis, a progressive homeless activist accused me on Twitter of having written my article to "make money off of a fear tactic" of "fueling hatred [and] even increasing violence against homeless people."[49] After I asked the former San Francisco supervisor for the Tenderloin neighborhood, former mayoral candidate Jane Kim, how such a progressive city ended up with so much suffering, she said, "My concern, Michael, just to be very honest, is that when that kind of messaging goes out, violence against people who are unhoused goes up."

I was shocked and horrified by what she seemed to be suggesting.

"It sounds like you're worried that I'm going to write something that would cause violence against people who live on the street," I said.

"No," she said. "It's just the initial summary of 'all the misery on the streets of San Francisco' is aligned—gets used a lot. 'And in such a progressive city.' I don't think even political consultants are trying to increase violence against those people who are unhoused. I don't think that that's anyone's mission. But it is what happens."[50]

But there is no evidence for what Kim claimed. In fact, the number of reported attacks on the homeless declined nationwide between 2008 and 2017 from 106 to 29, according to a study by a homelessness advocacy organization, even as concern over homelessness rose from 38 to 47 percent.[51]

The main perpetrators of violence against the homeless tend to be other homeless people, or drug dealers, according to people who have lived on the streets. "There wasn't a day that went by without violence on the street," said Tom about his time living homeless in the Tenderloin. "Someone getting in a fight. Beat up. Shot for drugs. One of the Hondurans [drug dealers] would whip out a machete and chop at a guy's arm because he had used a counterfeit five-dollar bill. That doesn't get brought up at the community meetings. The only people talking to the Board of Supervisors are Harm Reduction Coalition and homeless advocates who paint this very different picture of the homeless being victimized. They point at the politicians saying, 'You're all victimizing them!' with the sweeps."[52]

Said Jacqui, whose son, Corey, compared San Francisco to Pleasure Island, "My son has also been hospitalized twice from being stabbed. One time he almost died. I didn't even know he was in the hospital until he was well enough to call me. After that I bought him a medic alert bracelet with my info on it. He eventually lost it, of course. So I planned to have my phone number tattooed on his chest—he agreed but because of COVID, tattoo parlors are closed."

I soon discovered in my research that I was hardly the first person that progressive elected officials and homelessness advocates had accused of fomenting violence against unhoused people. Many others had been criticized for far worse over the years, including San Francisco's highest elected officials.

"The criticism [by progressive homelessness advocates] was heavy, political and personal," wrote former mayor Willie Brown in his 2008 memoir. "People accused me of abandoning the problem when I was working daily to try and get a solution going. It was brutal. . . . I had become demonized, and my own efforts belittled."[53]

It is notable that the result of such personal attacks is to frighten off people seeking to change, and perhaps improve, the situation. "The problem" of homelessness, concluded Mayor Brown within nine months of entering office, "may not be solvable."[54]

3

The Experiment Was a Success but the Patients Died

"Why can't we help the homeless?" asked HBO comedian Bill Maher in 2019. "If you look around [Los Angeles] you'd think that either the homeless problem is getting worse, or camping isn't what it used to be."

The audience laughed, and Maher pivoted to make a serious point.

"You know, after World War II there was a huge housing shortage in LA when the vets returned home and had nowhere to live," he said. "So the government found some empty space and in a matter of months built Quonset huts for 6,000 people, all for a total cost of what in today's dollars would be less than $18 million. Well, that was then."[1]

What Maher didn't mention, or perhaps know, was that the leading advocates for the homeless often oppose shelters.

In 2011, a reporter asked Jennifer Friedenbach, "What's the solution?"

"The solution," she said, "is making sure that we give every human being in San Francisco a permanent affordable house."

"You can't just give everyone a house," the reporter replied.

"You certainly can," said Friedenbach.

"No, you can't," he said.

"Every human being has a right to housing," she said.

"Hold on," he said, "that's where we differ. But the fact is first, you wanted shelters, and now the street people will not go to shelters."

"No," clarified Friedenbach, "we never called for shelters."[2]

The reason, Friedenbach explained to me, is that "if you ask unhoused people, they're not screaming for shelter. They're screaming for housing."[3]

In the spring of 2021, Friedenbach published an op-ed opposing a proposal considered by the San Francisco Board of Supervisors to create, within eighteen months, sufficient homeless shelters and outdoor "Safe Sleeping Sites" for all of the city's unsheltered homeless. "One can simply take a look to New York City," she wrote. "Their department spends about $1.3 billion dollars of its budget on providing shelter for their unhoused population while thousands remain on the street. . . . As a result, New York has a higher rate of homelessness than San Francisco."[4]

Housing First advocate Margot Kushel of the University of California, San Francisco agreed. "The problem with New York—and I spend a lot of time with people working in the system in New York—is that they spend an estimated $30,000 for each person per year to keep them in shelter. That's not what we want to do. Because if you create the shelter and you don't create the housing, then people are just in shelter forever."[5]

Housing First advocates oppose shelter in Los Angeles. "Why haven't we solved homelessness?" asked Housing First creator Sam Tsemberis. "Because [Los Angeles mayor] Eric Garcetti [has] Andy Bales [saying,] 'You need emergency housing.' 'These people need to be cleaned up.' 'They need to be sober.' 'They need Jesus before they'll be ready for housing.' I said, 'People should be housed and then maybe they'll get sobriety and Jesus and the rest.' We're definitely on polar opposites of the whole thing."[6]

Advocates for the homeless at the national level similarly oppose more shelters. "I don't agree that we should be building more transitional housing," said the head of the National Alliance to End Homelessness.[7]

While some homeless people reject shelter, others seek it, particularly if it is of high quality. "In typical nonpandemic times there are these huge lines that I would wait in with folks, sometimes up to eight hours," said University of California, Los Angeles homelessness researcher Chris Herring, describing San Francisco's newest shelters. "Folks end up sleeping in chairs. Night after night, unable to get a bed. You have a hundred people there trying just to get a one-night bed."[8]

Most homeless people would prefer a studio apartment to living in a shelter, and many would prefer living outside to living in shelter, but people in shelters tend to suffer far lower rates of drug problems, severe chronic pain, psychological distress, and death than people on the street.[9] "As a woman," acknowledged Friedenbach, "if I was suddenly homeless, yes, I'd absolutely rather be in a shelter than out on the streets, surrounded by a bunch of other women. I would feel a lot safer about that. . . . I do think that there is a role that the emergency shelter system plays, but it should be a small component."[10]

But funding permanent supportive housing over shelters has meant that San Francisco lacks shelter capacity and suffers far higher levels of *un*sheltered homelessness than other cities with more shelter. Greater Phoenix has 700 fewer homeless people than San Francisco but has 500 more shelter beds. Miami, a rare city that has had consistent success at reducing homelessness over the last fifteen years, has 75 percent more shelter beds per homeless person than San Francisco.[11] New York City today shelters 95 percent of its homeless after increasing its shelter population by 31,000 since 2005.[12] In 2020, San Francisco had 3,530 shelter beds for 8,124 people experiencing homelessness.[13] There were more than 1,200 people on the wait list for a shelter bed on any given day in 2019. It took one to two months to reach the top of the list. And a bed is only good for ninety days.[14]

San Francisco's leaders have thus deliberately chosen to leave a significant portion of the homeless *un*sheltered rather than sheltered, viewing shelters as a diversion of resources that could and should go to permanent supportive housing. "New York [City] has made the decision that everyone should have an exit from the street," noted Rafael Mandelman, a supervisor. "San Francisco has consciously chosen not to make that commitment. And the conditions on New York's streets versus San Francisco streets are somewhat reflective of what that means."[15]

Progressives in San Francisco have opposed creating sufficient shelter space for the homeless since at least 2004, when then-mayor Gavin Newsom's homelessness task force proposed a phaseout of emergency shelters in lieu of permanent supportive housing.[16]

Housing First homeless advocates have similarly contributed to the shortage of homelessness shelters in Los Angeles. "The mayor is unwilling to put out bridge shelters because of backlash from some homeless advocates," said Skid Row shelter provider Rev. Andy Bales, referring to Tsemberis. He added that Housing First activists insisted on building a smaller number of expensive apartments instead of building cheaper temporary shelter units faster, with the $1.2 billion in tax-financed bond funding that voters approved in 2016.

"In the [Los Angeles] bond measure we passed in 2016 to build housing for the homeless, each unit was projected to cost $140,000," noted Maher. "And now that we're actually building these apartments, the cost for each unit has risen to $531,000. . . . About 40 percent of that cost goes to something the city calls 'soft costs' and I call 'bullshit costs.'"

As a consequence, by 2025, just 7,000 units will be built for the roughly 41,000 homeless people in the city of Los Angeles.[17]

"[Housing First] is a dogmatic philosophy," said Bales. "I've lost friends. One of my closest friends is attacking me for pushing for housing that costs $11,000 instead of $527,000 per person. He can't get that we can't provide a $527,000 to $700,000 apartment for each person on the street. I've been in planning meetings where people said, 'Everybody deserves a granite countertop.' But that isn't going to work for 44,000 people."[18]

In November 2018, Proposition C passed over the opposition from Mayor Breed and many of the city's tech leaders. Salesforce's Marc Benioff's financial contribution and public advocacy for the initiative made the difference, according to researcher Chris Herring.[19] As a result, San Francisco saw the amount it spends on housing and homelessness increase 84 percent, from $364 million annually in fiscal year 2019–20 to $672 million in 2021–22.[20]

During the campaign, the San Francisco Coalition on Homelessness and its allies claimed that Proposition C "would house about 4,000 people over five years," in the words of the *Chronicle*.[21] "The proposition would fund 4,000 new permanent housing units," reported *SF Curbed*.[22] "Prop C funds would house up to 5,000 and prevent the eviction of another 30,000," claimed *Vox*.[23]

"The goal is four thousand?" I asked Friedenbach of the Coalition.

"Yeah, four thousand exits that are permanent," she said.[24]

Ah, I thought. *Exits*, not housing units. While Friedenbach called them permanent, San Francisco helped over 11,000 people "exit homelessness" between 2013 and 2018 even as the number of homeless people on the streets increased. While just over half received permanent housing or "Rapid Re-Housing," a rental subsidy, the rest were given a bus ticket to return to families and friends.[25] And after a year of rental subsidies, some of those people became homeless again.[26] It is unknown how many who had left returned.

In mid-2021, city officials announced that the $1.1 billion would be used for 1,000 new shelter beds, 825 new housing units, 650 rental subsidies, 200 tents, and more outreach. As a result, the city's shelter bed capacity will rise from 2,875 to 3,875, which could reduce San Francisco's total unsheltered homeless population of 5,180 by 19 percent but only if the newly sheltered aren't replaced.[27]

In other words, the reason that there are so many homeless people on the streets in San Francisco is that both progressive and moderate Democratic elected officials, and the city's most influential homelessness experts and advocates, have for two decades opposed building sufficient shelters. And that is unlikely to change even after San Francisco starts spending hundreds of millions more per year on the problem and might even get worse.[28]

In 2018, a reporter asked Marc Benioff if Prop C would create a magnet effect. "It seems like one of the things that you guys are doing is you're creating a magnet for people to come to the city and be homeless," she said, "because it's not a hostile environment. Everybody has talked about seeing people out on the street openly shooting up."[29]

"That's just not true," said Benioff. "I can tell you that's clinically not true. Our University of California at San Francisco, we've got the clinical studies to show you that when you give homeless people a home, their lifestyle does change."[30]

The study found that for the duration of two and a half years, 86 percent of the participants who received subsidized housing stayed for nearly the whole time.[31] "It works," Kushel told the *San Jose Mercury News*. "It improves people's lives. It keeps people housed. . . . It ends homelessness. Full stop."[32] The newspaper's headline read, "'It works.'" Wrote the reporter, "Groundbreaking data proves success of Santa Clara County homeless housing program." The *Mercury News* reported that the "researchers say these findings are groundbreaking because they show that permanent supportive housing—which provides subsidized housing paired with counseling, mental health, addiction and other services—is helping the county's most difficult cases."[33]

But there was a twist. The Housing First intervention did not reduce the rate of deaths. There were 37 deaths out of 199 participants in the control group and 33 deaths out of 224 in the experimental group. Though the samples weren't large, it was still a surprising, and sad, finding. "It was deeply traumatic for the team that was directly working with the folks that were dying, for sure," said Jennifer Loving, the San Jose homelessness leader who advocates for permanent supportive housing. "You want to believe that there's a happy ending."[34]

The high death rate was demoralizing to permanent supportive housing staff. "Theoretically [if] people are getting housing and wraparound services, you should have a major decrease in death," said Louis Chicoine of Abode Services. "We're asking ourselves, 'Why so much death when people are getting what they want?' We have over sixty programs. We're the largest permanent supportive housing provider of this sort of service in the Bay Area now. We had trouble keeping staff because the people we attract to this sort of job really care deeply and got invested in people's lives, sort of like a life coach for people with an incredible list of problems. And then they die on you, even when you house them?"[35]

Housing First founder Sam Tsemberis said he wasn't surprised. "That happens," he said. "People are ill. I think the people would have died whether they were housed or not. They happened to be housed. They had a few comfortable months before they died, but it's not like the housing kills them. Like they were going to die. Anyway, they happened to be randomized into the housing group. And now we know that they were, we know about them. I get it, but people come in with very complicated illnesses."[36]

"I think it's great for people to be able to die a decent death," I said. "But if we're selling this as improving people's outcomes, doesn't that kind of undermine it a little bit?"

"No," said Tsemberis. "People would die anyway. It's just housing. It's not a miracle. People die. If they're homeless, people die, if they're housed they die."

"So we should not expect permanent supportive housing to lower the mortality rate?" I asked.

"Not given the preconditions that people come in with," he said.

The evidence for Housing First turns out to be significantly weaker than its proponents suggest. For example, the much lauded initiative to reduce homelessness among veterans was only four percentage points more successful than the overall decline in homelessness, when accounting for age, which is necessary to accurately estimate what is due to policy and what is due to demographic changes.[37] As for Utah, its legislative auditor general concluded in 2018 that the 91 percent number was wrong, based on a sloppy use of incorrect methodologies. Before 2015, Utah had annualized its homeless count, meaning that researchers counted the homeless at a single point in time and multiplied the data by some factor. But after 2015 the state used raw point-in-time counts, causing a precipitous drop in the official population counts. Over the same period, the state also narrowed its definition of chronic homelessness in several ways, resulting in further apparent reductions.[38] In reality, the homeless population in Utah increased by 12 percent between 2016 and 2020.[39]

An experiment with 249 homeless people in San Francisco between 1999 and 2002 found those enrolled in the city's Housing First program, Direct Access to Housing, used medical services at the same rate as those who were not given housing through the program, suggesting that the Housing First program likely had minimal impact on the participants' health.[40] Wrote a team of researchers, "obtaining housing does not necessarily resolve other issues that may impede one's housing success," pointing to the lack of significant improvements in substance use and psychiatric symptoms over the twelve months that people were housed (the share of patients with severe substance use actually saw a modest increase).[41]

The problem with Housing First stems from the fact that it doesn't require that people address their mental illness and substance abuse, which are often the underlying causes of homelessness. Several studies have found that people in Housing First–type housing showed no improvement in drug use from when they were first housed.[42]

In 2018, the National Academies of Sciences, Engineering, and Medicine published a review of the scientific literature of Housing First. "On the basis of currently available research," the report's authors wrote, with some surprise, "the committee found no substantial evidence that [permanent supportive housing] contributes to improved health outcomes, notwithstanding the intuitive logic that it should do so and limited data showing that it does do so for persons with HIV/AIDS."[43]

Tsemberis said he was not surprised by the findings of the National Academies. "It's not like housing creates improved health," he said. "You have to have a relationship with a nurse. You have to be educated on what your health problems are. You have to have a team that engages you and makes you an active participant in your own health care. I don't even know if that would stop the number of deaths."[44] And, at least in the study funded by Benioff and conducted by Margot Kushel, which had those services, it did not.

Housing First may even increase addiction and overdose deaths and make quitting drugs more difficult. Warned a multiauthor review in 2009, "One potential risk [of Housing First's harm reduction approach] would be worsening the addiction itself, as the federal collaborative initiative preliminary evaluation seemed to suggest." The authors pointed to an experiment that had to be stopped and reorganized after the homeless individuals in the abstinence group complained of being housed with people in the control group, who didn't stop their drug and alcohol use. "They claimed that they preferred to return to homelessness rather than live near drug users."[45]

There is evidence that privacy and solitude created by Housing First make substance abuse worse. A study in Ottawa found that, while the Housing First group kept people in housing longer, the comparison group saw greater reductions in alcohol consumption and problematic drug use, and greater improvements to mental health, after two years. "One reason for the surprising results," wrote the authors, "may be that aspects of the Housing First intervention, such as the privacy afforded by Housing First and harm reduction approach, might result in slower improvements around substance use and mental health."[46]

Researchers have found ways to use housing to reduce addiction. Between 1990 and 2006, researchers in Birmingham, Alabama, conducted clinical trials of abstinence-contingent housing with 644 homeless people with crack cocaine addictions. Two-thirds of participants remained abstinent after six months, a very high rate of abstinence, compared to other treatment programs. Other studies found that around 40 percent of homeless in abstinence-contingent housing maintained their abstinence, housing, and jobs.[47]

In a randomized controlled trial, homeless people were given furnished apartments and allowed to keep them unless they failed a drug test, at which point they were sent to stay in a shelter. Sixty-five percent of participants completed the program.[48] Three similar randomized controlled trials also found moderate to high rates of completion. And participants in abstinence-contingent housing had better housing and employment outcomes than participants assigned housing for whom abstinence was not required.[49]

. It turns out that over longer periods of time, Housing First may not even outperform contingency in terms of keeping people housed. In the spring of 2021, a team of Harvard medical experts published the results of a fourteen-year-long study of chronic homeless placed into permanent supportive housing in Boston. Most studies of permanent supportive housing, including the Kushel study conducted in Santa Clara, only study the newly housed homeless for a span of around two years. The study found that 86 percent of the homeless, who were referred based on length of time living on the streets, suffered from "trimorbidity"—a combination of medical illness, mental illness, and substance abuse. The authors found that after ten years, just 12 percent of the homeless remained housed. During the study period, 45 percent died. The authors concluded that, because the chronically homeless had such higher rates of physical and mental illness, "the supportive services, essential to the PSH model, may not have been sufficient to address the needs of this unsheltered population."[50]

I asked experts and advocates, "How do we know that the homeless population won't replace itself if provided with housing?" Said Randy Shaw, the Tenderloin permanent supportive housing provider, "The question you're raising is one that never gets discussed. Somehow, there's this sense that San Francisco is under the obligation that anyone who comes here we have to suddenly house. There is an underlying logic that San Francisco doesn't really ever want to talk about."[51]

Said Chicoine, the permanent supportive housing provider for the Kushel study, "I don't have a solution. I will acknowledge what you're saying. I'm not going to be a bullshit advocate who says, 'Oh you should just ignore that.' It's real. There's so many stigmas and stereotypes that some of us in the industry were scared of telling the truth."[52]

I asked Steve Berg of the National Alliance to End Homelessness in Washington, D.C., a similar question. "Let's say we build one hundred thousand apartment units. What's to prevent another hundred thousand people from going from doubling-up and couch-surfing to become homeless and ask for housing?"

"That will definitely happen," said Berg. "And it's not 'What if,' it's 'That will definitely happen.' If you don't deal with the reasons people are losing their housing then the system will never be able to keep up.

Communities did really well getting people off the streets but they haven't really thought about the inflow of people."[53]

Some longtime Housing First advocates suggest the movement has become too dogmatic. "Advocates are mostly former [homelessness housing and service] providers," noted University of Pennsylvania's Dennis Culhane. "They don't understand what professional social welfare systems look like around the world. I tell the advocates that I am not ideological about Housing First and they should not be, either."[54]

4

The War on the War on Drugs

No matter how many times you've heard the statistics, they never lose their power to shock: the United States is home to less than 5 percent of the world's population but has 25 percent of its prisoners.[1] Today, the United States incarcerates five times more people than it did in 1970. The total number of people incarcerated in state or federal prison rose from 200,000 to 1.6 million between 1972 and 2014.[2] California's incarceration rate quintupled, from about 100 for every 100,000 residents to nearly 500. Between 1984 and 2005, the state opened twenty-one prisons.[3]

The reason, according to Michelle Alexander in her bestselling 2010 book, *The New Jim Crow*, was drugs. "In less than thirty years, the US penal population exploded from around 300,000 to more than 2 million, with drug convictions accounting for the majority of the increase."[4] Between 1980 and 2012, there were an astonishing 43 million drug arrests.[5] The "uncomfortable reality," writes Alexander, "is that arrests and convictions for drug offenses—not violent crime—are the single most important cause of the prison boom in the United States."[6]

But a closer look at the data reveals that just 3.7 percent of state prisoners are there for nonviolent drug possession, and that 14.1 percent of state prisoners are locked up for any nonviolent drug offense. Forty-seven percent of inmates in federal prisons are in for nonviolent drug convictions, but there are just 172,000 people in federal prisons and 1.3 million in state prisons.[7] Over half of all prisoners in state prisons are there for violent offenses like murder, rape, and robbery.[8]

During the 1990s and 2000s, an estimated 50 percent of the increase in state prisoners came from those convicted of violent offenses.[9] Twenty percent of those serving time for drug charges said they had used a firearm in a previous crime, and 24 percent had a prior conviction for a violent crime, found a 1997 national survey of state prisons.[10]

It's true that the share of drug offenders in prison rose from 6.5 to 22 percent between 1980 and 1990, growing from 20,000 in 1980 to nearly 250,000 by 2010.[11] And nonviolent drug offenses were as responsible for prison growth in the 1980s as violent offenses.[12] But only 20 percent of prisoners in all jails and prisons are there for drugs.[13]

Today, incarceration rates in the United States are at a thirty-year low. In 2019, the state and federal imprisonment rate of 419 prisoners per 100,000 US residents was the lowest it had been since 1995, and was a 17 percent decrease from 2009.[14]

The number of people in prisons for drugs alone was never very large. In 1997 just 1 percent of all prisoners were in for a first or second nonviolent drug offense, and 4 percent of state prisoners were drug "kingpins," people at the mid-to-high level of drug organizations.[15] The offenses that tend to result in prison time, manufacturing and sales, fell steadily from 350,000 to 208,000 during the same span of time.[16]

Of the people convicted of drug offenses, 62 percent never went to prison and one-third never went to prison or jail.[17] And while 43 million drug arrests between 1980 and 2012 sounds like a lot, over the same period there were 445 million total arrests, making drugs less than 10 percent of all arrests.[18]

In her preface to the 2020 edition of *The New Jim Crow*, Alexander acknowledges that drug offenses are not why most people are in prison but implies that shorter sentences for drug convictions result in a greater churn of people through the prison system than their total numbers would indicate. But that wasn't the case, either. During the 2000s, the number of people passing through prison for drug crimes for a single year was only slightly higher than the number of people in prison for drug crimes on any one day.[19]

Parole violations are less the result of nonviolent possession and failed drug tests, and more the result of reoffending parolees. Two-thirds of those sent back to prison for violating parole had committed a new crime, 60 percent of which were violent or property crimes, not nonviolent drug crimes. Less than 10 percent of prisoners surveyed said they had returned to prison for failing a drug test, 6 percent for possession, and 2 percent for missing a test.[20]

Even radical change to drug laws would not significantly affect racial disparities in the prison population. "If we released everyone in prison in 2013 whose top charge was a drug offense," notes criminologist John Pfaff, "the white percentage would rise by one point (from 35 to 36 percent), the black percentage would fall by one point (from 38 to 37 percent), and the Hispanic percentage wouldn't change." While racial disparity may explain some of the difference in enforcement between white and black people, the disparity between white and Latino people is driven by Latinos tending to deal outdoors.[21]

Violence, not stricter drug sentences, drove mass incarceration. New York is proof. For ten years after Governor Nelson Rockefeller and the state legislature increased penalties for drug use beginning in 1973, the number of people in prison for drugs hardly changed. Then, in 1984, the number of people incarcerated for drug crimes started to rise sharply due to violence associated with the crack epidemic. More than a decade later, in 1997, total inmates in New York prisons for drug offenses peaked and began their long decline, mostly because of a reduction in violence. It was only in 2004 and again in 2009 that the state legislature reduced penalties, and the declining rate of incarceration for drug crimes didn't change after those two years.[22]

And those who put many of the stricter drug laws into place did so because they were under pressure to protect African American communities suffering from violence associated with gang warfare over open-air crack markets.[23] Notes Pfaff, "when prosecutors weren't too concerned about drug crimes, they simply ignored the Rockefeller Drug laws, whether during the rising-crime 1970s or the falling-crime 1990s and 2000s."[24]

Rising incarceration rates reflected rising rates of violent crime. From 1990 to 2010, two-thirds of the increase in inmates nationwide came from people convicted of violent offenses. Some of those convicted of nonviolent offenses may also have committed violent acts, or been with others committing violent acts, but had the charge plea-bargained away, notes Pfaff.[25]

America's high incarceration rate of African Americans resulted in large measure from concerns among black Americans about rising crime and violence starting in the 1960s. By 1971, African Americans were two-thirds of all people arrested for homicide and robbery, despite being less than 10 percent of the population.[26] In 1975, black people were murdered at a rate nearly seven times higher than white people.[27] The Congressional Black Caucus worked with then-senator Joe Biden, President Bill Clinton, and Senator Bernie Sanders to pass the 1994 crime bill.[28]

"[H]ow racist can a law be which the Congressional Black Caucus vigorously supported and even considered too weak?" asked Columbia University professor John McWhorter. "If we had asked these black congresspeople in 1986 why they supported these laws, they would have said that they were aimed at breaking the horror of the crack culture, which had turned inner cities into war zones by the mid-1980s."[29]

D rug overdoses are today the number one cause of accidental death in the United States as a result of America's historic addiction and overdose epidemic.* Overdose deaths rose from 17,415 in 2000 to 93,330

---

* Most drug overdose deaths (about 88 percent) are accidental; 7 percent are suicides, 4 percent are of undetermined intent, and 0.2 percent are homicides. (Numbers do not add up to 100 percent due to rounding.)

in 2020, a 536 percent increase.[30] Significantly more people die of drug overdoses today than of homicide (13,927 in 2019) or car accidents (36,096 in 2019).[31]

The overdose crisis is worse in San Francisco than in other cities. In Seattle, Phoenix, and Chicago, there were 23, 46, and 48 overdose deaths per every 100,000 people, in 2020. In San Francisco, there were 81.[32] Overdose deaths rose from 196 in 2015 to 713 in 2020.[33] Just over half occurred in the Tenderloin, the Inner Mission, and South of Market.[34]

There are about twenty-five thousand injection drug users in San Francisco, a number 50 percent larger than the number of students enrolled in the city's fifteen public high schools.[35] San Francisco gives away more needles to drug users, six million per year, than New York City, despite having one-tenth the population.[36]

When you walk through the open-air drug scenes in the Tenderloin in San Francisco, Skid Row in Los Angeles, and the Blade in Seattle, you see people of all races and ages injecting and smoking fentanyl, heroin, meth, and other hard drugs right there on the sidewalk near where they bought them. This has been the case to some extent since the 1990s. "In the Tenderloin, drugs were everywhere," said Tracey Helton Mitchell, who moved from the Midwest to San Francisco to, in part, maintain her addiction. "There was crack on one street, people high on meth on another. . . . People slept anywhere and everywhere on the street."[37] Like many women addicted to hard drugs, Mitchell turned to prostitution. "I never thought I would have sex with anyone for money. Heroin made it so easy."[38]

But things have grown worse over the last decade. "It's the Wild West," said a man who lived in the Tenderloin in June 2020. "You hear screams in the night and the sounds of power tools cutting through bike locks all day . . . the alley has long been a magnet for homeless people and petty drug dealers, but it's never as bad as it is now."[39]

The number of people combining opioids and stimulants has grown. "I did crack and heroin both," said Tom Wolf. "The amount of people using meth and fentanyl at the same time is growing."[40] The combination is known as a "goofball."[41] Indeed, the number of opioid-using Americans who also used methamphetamine rose 83 percent between 2011 and 2017, from 18.8 percent to 34.2 percent.[42] Other studies find similar results.[43]

Heavy drug and alcohol use degrades the health of homeless people. Drug overdose is the leading cause of death among the homeless.[44] Skin infections and disease are more common due to injecting drugs like heroin and meth. Respiratory diseases are common due to smoking tobacco, crack, heroin, fentanyl, and meth.[45] And about two-thirds of the time of hospital emergency departments in San Francisco is spent serving the homeless.[46]

Social scientists who study the homeless in San Francisco describe lives that revolve around addictions. British anthropologist Teresa Gowan published a rich study of San Francisco homeless men who collected and sold aluminum cans and glass bottles for recycling in the mid-1990s and early 2000s. "Most of the [homeless men who worked as] recyclers were indeed heavy users of alcohol or drugs, and they quickly spent their earnings on their cravings," she noted, "smoking crack, nodding on heroin, or, in a minority of cases, drinking themselves into a stupor."[47]

Those who recover from their addictions no longer see homelessness the same way. "Once I started to heal myself," said a formerly homeless man, "I knew I had to work with this so-called homelessness problem, to get some of those people suffering out there into treatment and help them turn their heads around."

"So-called?" asked Gowan.

"Ain't no homelessness problem in my opinion," the man replied. "The problem is addiction, period. Even those people that have schizophrenia or something else like that, generally you find they have a big problem with addiction as well."[48]

F ew have done more to alter America's drug and crime policies than
Ethan Nadelmann. I first met Ethan in the mid-1990s when I helped
promote decriminalization and harm reduction. It is more due to Ethan
than any other individual that America's most progressive cities and
states, including California, Washington, and Oregon, have legalized drug
possession and phased out mandatory drug treatment.

As an undergraduate at Princeton University, he began studying the
globalization of drug trafficking and law enforcement. In 1988 Ethan
published a long article in *Foreign Policy* arguing that the war on drugs
was causing more harm than good. He published a 1993 book, *Cops Across
Borders*. "Around the same time, the *Economist* magazine for the first time
came out saying the same thing," he told me in 2020. "Then we're on
the Donahue show and I'm on Larry King debating [former US senator
from New York] Al D'Amato. The front page of the *New York Times* and
Washington Post and my picture's in *Newsweek*. I thought it was going to
die down, but in fact, it just kept banging away."[49]

Over the next several years, Ethan developed the scholarly case for
decriminalization and harm reduction. In 1992 he organized eighteen
leading scholars to coauthor a major piece in *Daedalus*, the journal of the
American Academy of Arts and Sciences. Ethan started "bringing together people involved in marijuana legalization, psychedelics, the racist
aspects of the drug war, mass incarceration, including people on the European and Australian side," he said.[50]

Then the movement was infused with new funding. "Around the
summer of '92 I get a phone call from George Soros," Ethan said. "We
had lunch and hit it off. He didn't know what harm reduction was. He
was coming at this because he saw how open society ideals were being violated. As a businessperson and economist he saw the absurdity of
trying to ban a popular commodity." Soros, whose many philanthropic

initiatives include drug policy reform, gave Ethan millions in funding to change laws around the country.[51]

My interest in harm reduction and decriminalization grew after the November elections of 1996 when Californians, myself included, voted to legalize marijuana for medical use. The more I read on the topic the more I came to feel that drug prohibition was failing for the same reason alcohol prohibition in the United States failed in the 1920s and 1930s. People addicted to substances would use them even if it meant prison. And prison is the wrong way to deal with what is essentially a disease.

Law enforcement had obviously failed to make drugs less available. In the twenty-five years after 1980, cocaine prices fell by two-thirds, in inflation-adjusted terms, even though the number of people arrested and incarcerated increased tenfold.[52] From 1981 to 2012, heroin and meth prices in the United States fell 86 and 72 percent, respectively.[53] Since 2007, heroin street prices have hovered around $300 per gram, in constant 2017 dollars, while wholesale prices have declined from $84 to $53 per gram.[54] The price of meth fell from $10,000 per pound in 2010 to $1,200 to $1,400 per pound in 2019. Meth users in the Central Valley can buy two doses for as little as $2.50 to $5.50.[55]

The problem has long been the functionally endless supply of poor farmers in Latin America and Asia willing to produce cocaine and opium poppies, and aspiring criminal entrepreneurs willing to transport and sell it. As such, no amount of law enforcement short of dramatic curtailments to civil liberties and commerce in the form of radical border controls, warrantless surveillance, and various other interruptions to daily life could significantly dent supplies.[56]

If drugs were legal, and if we treated addiction as a health rather than criminal problem, there would be far less violence and no mass incarceration, I thought. There are no open-air drug markets for insulin. There are no turf wars for antidepressants. Nobody gets shot over a bottle of chardonnay and a pack of Camel Lights. We would still have problems but they wouldn't be nearly as widespread as during alcohol prohibition in the United States from 1920 to 1933.

Alcohol and tobacco are far more harmful than many drugs and yet they are legal, I reasoned. In the United States, 88,000 people died from alcohol-related causes in 2018, which is significantly higher than the 72,000 who died from illegal drug overdoses that year.[57] And tobacco is responsible for 480,000 annual deaths in the United States.[58]

As President Bill Clinton in the late 1990s considered whether to lift federal restrictions on giving clean needles to drug users, including the homeless, to prevent the spread of HIV and other blood-borne pathogens like hepatitis B and C, I worked with Representative Maxine Waters, a Democrat who represents Watts, a mostly African American and Latino neighborhood in Los Angeles, to organize civil rights leaders to urge President Clinton to lift the restrictions.

For decades, harm reduction and decriminalization advocates have pointed to Portugal as a model, noting that it decriminalized drugs and expanded drug treatment. In 2013, Portugal's drug-induced death rate was sixty-six times less than that of the United States.[59] The number of people in treatment increased by 60 percent between 1998 and 2011, with three-quarters receiving an opioid substitute like methadone or Suboxone, the brand name of buprenorphine.[60] Drug use among 15- to 24-year-olds actually *declined* after decriminalization.[61] "All drugs have been legalized," explained Monique Tula, executive director of the Harm Reduction Coalition. "Their focus is on giving people tools, like job apprenticeships, and the means to support themselves."[62]

Progressive cities and states, including California and Washington, have reformed drug laws. In 2000, California voters passed Proposition 36, a ballot initiative that changed the law so that eligible nonviolent drug offenders could be sentenced to drug treatment and probation instead of jail, prison, or probation without treatment.[63] In 2014, California voters passed Proposition 47 to make three grams of hard drugs for personal use a misdemeanor instead of a felony. Proposition 47 also ended jail sentences for people convicted of many nuisance crimes, including possession of three grams of hard drugs and shoplifting under $950 worth of property. In June 2020, San Francisco's Board of Supervisors voted to allow nonprofits to operate supervised injection sites where people can use heroin and other hard drugs safely.[64] Several other US cities have sought to create supervised injection sites in recent years, though such facilities remain illegal under federal law.[65]

I, like many advocates of harm reduction, compared the death toll from alcohol to deaths from drug overdoses, but the comparison was misleading. Most of the 95,000 people who die from alcohol annually tend to do so after decades of use, while the 93,000 annual drug overdose and poisoning deaths occur within a matter of minutes or hours. Only 2,200 of those annual alcohol deaths occur immediately through acute alcohol poisoning.[66]

Much of what I had believed about prohibition was wrong. There is little evidence that it increased the murder rate because the rise in gang violence was offset by fewer non-gang drunken murders.[67] Plus, there were one-third fewer deaths from cirrhosis of the liver during prohibition, and probably less domestic violence.[68] Urbanization increased violent crime for reasons having nothing to do with prohibition. And, during prohibition, more cities and counties started reporting homicides for the first time.[69]

The fact that the United States has about four times as many alcohol abusers as abusers of all illicit drugs put together is further evidence that liberalization increases use.[70] One reason the homeless until the 1980s mostly abused alcohol was that illegal drugs like heroin and cocaine were far too expensive for many of them.

As for Portugal, it never legalized drugs. It only decriminalized them, reducing criminal penalties but maintaining prohibition. Drug dealers were still sent to prison even after the 2001 decriminalization. And Portugal does not let people addicted to hard drugs with behavioral disorders off the hook like progressive West Coast cities have done. It's true that Portugal massively expanded drug treatment, but people are still arrested and fined for possession of heroin, meth, and other hard drugs. And drug users are typically sent to a regionally administered "Commissions for the Dissuasion of Drug Addiction," composed of a social worker, lawyer, and doctor who encourage, push, and coerce drug treatment.

"Portugal is a conservative culture where drug use is looked down upon," said Stanford University psychologist and addiction expert Dr. Keith Humphreys. "All of these cities [San Francisco, Portland, Seattle] are libertarian in their views about drugs and alcohol. In Portugal they put pressure on people to go into treatment. It's social pressure and pressure toward making people change their behavior."[71]

And decriminalization doesn't end drug violence. "Even if trafficking enforcement decreased, like it did in Portugal," said criminologist John Pfaff, "illegal drug markets would still be forced to rely on violence to resolve disputes."[72] Indeed, prostitution and violence are ever-present in the open-air drug scenes in San Francisco, Los Angeles, and Seattle. "We are seeing behaviors from our guests that I've never seen in thirty-three years," said Rev. Andy Bales, who runs the largest homeless shelter on Skid Row in Los Angeles. "They are so bizarre and different that I don't even feel right describing the behaviors. It's extreme violence of an extreme sexual nature."[73]

People are not dying from drug overdose deaths in San Francisco because they're being arrested. They're dying because they *aren't* being arrested. Decriminalization reduces prices by lowering production and distribution costs, which increases use.[74] This was also the case for alcohol consumption. It increased after prohibition ended in the United States.[75] Even in Portugal, drug overdose deaths and overall drug use rose after decriminalization.

Overall illegal drug use rose sharply over the last two decades in the United States. Heroin use and abuse rose significantly. The number of adults who had ever used heroin rose fivefold from 2001–02 to 2012–13, to 3.8 million, found a study of nearly 80,000 people published in the *Journal of the American Medical Association*. The share suffering addiction rose threefold to 1.1 million.[76]

Other studies find the same results. RAND Corporation found the number of heroin users nationally rose from 1.6 to 2.3 million, their spending on heroin rose from $31 to $43 billion, and heroin consumption rose from 27 to 47 million metric tons, between 2006 and 2016.[77] "Heavy users drive this market," a senior RAND analyst told me. "Eighty percent of consumption comes from twenty percent of the users, which is similar to alcohol."[78] RAND calculates the total US illegal drug market at around $146 billion per year, which is about the same size as the total US market for alcohol.[79]

Experts are unsure how many heroin users there are in the United States and estimates vary significantly, but studies find that there has been a significant increase in usage of heroin and other opiates over the last two decades. The estimated share of 18- to 25-year-olds suffering prescription opioid use disorder, or addiction, rose 37 percent from 2002 to 2014, and the odds of heroin use rose fourfold among adults ages 18–25 illicitly using prescription opioids, and ninefold among adults 26–34 illicitly using prescription opioids, over the same period.[80] The National Survey on Drug Use and Health found heroin use disorder doubled between 2002 and 2019.[81]

Drugs put a severe burden on society, through increased crime, policing, and prisons. Crime rises with drug use, in part because addiction makes it hard to maintain a job, and because addicts turn to crime to maintain their habit.[82] Researchers in 2017 estimated the cost of heroin addiction alone to be $51 billion annually, or $51,000 per heroin user, an amount calculated by looking at the loss of productivity from death or incarceration, as well as negative health effects associated with hero-in.[83]As for heroin maintenance, it is only recommended by experts as a last resort for the tiny subset of heroin addicts for whom methadone or Suboxone does not work.[84]

Vicki Westbrook was born in Alabama in 1966 and became the first from her family to graduate from college in 1991 at the age of twenty-five. San Francisco beckoned. "A friend of mine from [Georgia] Tech had moved out to California. One of my IBM friends and a bunch of other friends of mine from high school had moved also to the Bay Area." A few years later, on New Year's Eve, Westbrook took the club drug MDMA, popularly known as ecstasy, with her friends. After the death of her twin, she started to use meth. "I drank some in college, maybe smoked some weed," she said. "That was pretty much it. When I came to California, I discovered acid and hallucinogenics. And then I discovered speed. At the beginning of 1994 I had just started working at [tech com-pany] Sybase. I'm using this whole time. I was just crazy. You do crazy stuff when you're an addict, dude. I would be snorting meth off my badge in the bathroom."[85]

From the 1990s onward, meth use rose dramatically. Hospital ad-missions from methamphetamine abuse spiked from over 40,000 cases in 1995 to nearly 130,000 in 2015.[86] In 2017, an estimated 1.6 million Amer-icans used methamphetamine.[87] In 2019, 12.6 million US adults took pre-scription amphetamines, 4.5 million of whom either didn't follow their physician's guidance or used the drug illegally.[88]

San Francisco saw a similar big increase in meth. I asked Kelly Kru-ger, a San Francisco police sergeant who oversaw the city's responses to psychiatric emergencies, including drug-related ones, for twenty years before retiring in 2021, "Is it just a lot more meth and heroin than there was back in the 1990s?"

"Very much so," she said. "Every ten years the drug of choice changes. In the sixties it was amphetamines. Right now we have a lot of them. 'Bath salts.'" When they do them, they become aggressive and psychotic."

Kruger said harder drugs had attracted a harder crowd. "There was a sense of community among the people on the street in the eighties and nineties," she said. "They looked out for each other more. They camped out in Golden Gate Park and there were family things. That doesn't seem to be happening as much, as far I can see." Kruger described a homeless man who was abandoned by his friend after overdosing. "His heart stopped and [he survived but] was brain-dead," she said. "The [other] guy didn't stick around to say his name or anything. I got called by the ICU to do fingerprinting to find the family before they pulled the plug. That used to be rare."[89]

Homelessness researcher Chris Herring agreed things had worsened. "It's just so frightening," he said. "It used to be, when I started, that people were really distinct with their drug use. Now it's like everyone's using everything. It all feels more chaotic. And now with the dropping price of meth, it's really becoming huge on the street."[90]

From 2008 to 2020, meth overdose deaths rose 500 percent in San Francisco, and half of psychiatric visits to San Francisco General Hospital are related to meth.[91] In 2019, meth was the most common drug in California overdose deaths.[92]

"Being high on meth looks just like bipolar mania," explained a former psychiatric emergency room doctor. Half of all patients whom he saw at San Francisco General Hospital had both severe mental illness and drug addiction. "Things like methamphetamine and cocaine stimulants will make you psychotic, and so it looks just like bipolar mania," he said. "I mean, it's indistinguishable."[93]

" Synthetic cathinones, also known as "bath salts," are a type of lab-made stimulant similar to meth.

Said Kruger, "You probably figured out that folks who are substance abusers are folks who have mental illness and they end up in crisis. In the emergency department they'll say, 'He's a speeder.' He'll be psychotic but labeled a speeder because he's doing meth. The Mental Health Department says, 'We don't have to deal with him because he's on meth.' But you still need to deal with him."

I asked her what speeders are like. "It was always insects, snakes, conspiracy theory, and good or evil," she said. "One guy came in and he thought a snake was going up his penis. Another guy torched his car because the snakes were trying to go up his pant leg, and he had to torch the snake. And another guy tried to kill his wife because he thought his wife was having sex with the devil."[94]

Proposition 47, which in 2014 decriminalized up to three grams of hard drugs including meth, exacerbated addiction, say drug dealers and law enforcement alike. A meth dealer who had just finished selling to several homeless people in Fresno showed his remaining meth to a reporter while standing on a city sidewalk. He said why he didn't need to be careful: "If the cops came right now and found that, all these drugs on us right now, none of us would go to jail. They'd give you a ticket and send you on your way. They'd leave you with your meth. They don't even take it."[95]

Though meth's negative health impacts are sometimes sensationalized by the media, they are real. "I didn't have any teeth," said Vicki. "My teeth are only from here, see the bottoms?" We were on Zoom. "All my back teeth on the top and bottom were gone from meth."

Today, San Francisco has the fourth-highest drug overdose death rate of any major city in the United States.[96] In 2020, 713 people died of accidental drug overdoses, a 61 percent increase from 2019.[97] San Francisco's overdose deaths rose from 11 per 100,000 people in 1985 to 81 per 100,000 in 2020, an over sevenfold increase.[98] Today, drug overdoses are the leading cause of death for non-elderly San Franciscans, accounting for 29 percent of deaths of residents under sixty-five in 2019.[99]

S an Francisco has a long tradition of tolerance toward drug use. During the Gold Rush of the 1840s, Chinese immigrants opened rooms for smoking opium. Authorities sometimes broke them up starting in the mid-1860s, but San Francisco's leaders did not ban opium dens until 1875. Opium smoking in San Francisco continued well into the twentieth century but was gradually supplanted by heroin. "San Francisco had twice as many alcohol outlets per capita compared to the national average going back at least until the late nineteenth century," said Stanford's Keith Humphreys.[100]

In the 1930s, a stockbroker and a surgeon, both alcoholics, created the twelve-step program for achieving and maintaining sobriety that would later become the foundation of Alcoholics Anonymous and Narcotics Anonymous.[101] From this emerged the Minnesota Model of the 1950s. Its most important innovations were to have former addicts help others with their recovery, to see addiction as a kind of disaffiliation and spiritual alienation, and the creation of individualized treatment plans with the active involvement of families over a twenty-eight-day inpatient drug and alcohol treatment.[102]

Insurance companies began to reimburse addiction treatment starting in 1964 and by 1987, the American Medical Association (AMA) had declared addiction to be a disease. Local governments, including San Francisco's, created "drug courts" that allowed judges to sentence many addicts to treatment as an alternative to jail.[103]

Drug culture in San Francisco reached a new level during the Summer of Love in 1967. On January 14, 1967, former Harvard professor Timothy Leary and others organized a "Be-In" of between twenty thousand and thirty thousand people in Golden Gate Park to take LSD and have a spiritual experience. Allen Ginsberg, whose 1955 poem, *Howl*, is today considered one of the greatest American poems, reminisced that "people were walking around in the crowd handing out these tiny white tablets, the most professional-looking and also the strongest LSD tablets yet."[104]

The Be-In inspired young people from across the United States to travel to San Francisco for the Summer of Love a few months later. Many of the seventy-five thousand young people who flocked to San Francisco that summer experimented with drugs, including marijuana, LSD, cocaine, and heroin.[105] Where most of the white, educated, and upper-middle-class youth left San Francisco after the Summer of Love, poorer and more working-class youth stayed behind and struggled with addiction, crime, and homelessness.[106]

Ginsberg may have detected that all was not right at the 1967 Be-In. Looking like a "cross between holy man and Jewish mother," at forty-one years old Ginsberg played the role of wise elder to Baby Boomers half his age. As Ginsberg surveyed from the stage the young people in the crowd all taking LSD, he turned to his friend and asked, "What if we're wrong?"[107]

In the 1970s progressives advocated decriminalization as a middle approach between drug prohibition and drug legalization. President Jimmy Carter in 1977 came out for the decriminalization of marijuana and for drug policies to not "be more damaging to an individual than the use of the drug itself."[108]

The pendulum swung back toward prohibition in the 1980s, particularly among Baby Boomers, many of whom were settling down and starting families, and among women.[109] President Ronald Reagan increased the US government funding and focus on law enforcement responses to drug dealing. First Lady Nancy Reagan launched the "Just Say No" campaign urging children not to use drugs. Efforts in the 1980s to crack down on drugs were partly motivated by the crack cocaine epidemic, which led to increases in addiction, open-air drug markets, and violence by dealers defending their turf.

In the 1990s, harm reduction and drug reform advocates began to argue that doctors were unnecessarily underprescribing pain medications and exaggerating the risk of addiction.[110] Over time, doctors began to view the risk of addiction as overblown.[111] "With addicts, their quality of life goes down as they use drugs," one pain doctor told *New York* magazine in 2000. "With pain patients, it improves. They're entirely different phenomena."[112] Big pharmaceutical companies went far beyond what was medically sound by promoting opioids for chronic, not just acute, pain.[113]

Beginning with California, states exempted doctors from lawsuits for prescribing opioids as long as their prescriptions were within the practice of responsible health care.[114] Doctors prescribed opioids in 20 percent of all patient visits with pain symptoms in 2010, nearly double that of 2000.[115] Opioids became the most prescribed class of drugs, surpassing blood pressure, cholesterol, and anxiety medications. Americans, who represent less than 5 percent of the world's population, were consuming 80 percent of the opioids supplied and 99 percent of the supply of hydrocodone, an opioid pain medication also commonly used as a cough suppressant.[116]

After the federal government put in place regulations to restrict pharmaceutical opioids, many users turned to heroin, which was far cheaper. The National Institute of Drug Abuse found in one study that the number of heroin users who had previously taken nonmedical pain relievers was nineteen times higher than those who did not.[117] A study of young, urban injection drug users in 2012 determined that 86 percent had taken opioid pain relievers nonmedically before using heroin.[118]

The shift from opioids to heroin can be seen in overdose deaths. The nationwide death rate from prescription opioids was roughly the same in 2019 as in 2010, while the death rate from heroin overdoses soared 430 percent. Kentucky reported a 278 percent increase in the rate of heroin deaths from 2010 to 2019, compared to a decline of 31 percent in prescription opioid deaths. Ohio reported heroin deaths had increased approximately 400 percent from 2010 to 2016, before falling to 146 percent of the 2010 heroin death rate in 2019.[119]

While many rightly blamed greed on the part of pharmaceutical companies, and laziness and corruption on the part of government regulators, the overprescription of opioids was equally due to naïve or unskeptical compassion on the part of doctors and the wider society. Harm reduction advocates didn't create the opioid epidemic, but they were part of the same movement starting in the 1990s urging the softening of restrictions on drugs, including hard ones.

In addition to his funding agreement with Soros, Ethan Nadelmann raised money from other wealthy Americans including Laurance Rockefeller; John Sperling, the creator of the for-profit University of Phoenix; and Peter Lewis, the founder of Progressive Insurance. In 2017, Soros agreed to give $50 million over the next ten years to Drug Policy Alliance.[120]

In 2000 drug reformers led by Ethan successfully campaigned for the passage of California Proposition 36. The Probation and Treatment for Drug-Related Offenses Initiative passed with over 60 percent of the vote.[121] The initiative allowed people convicted of nonviolent drug possession to receive probation and drug treatment instead of incarceration.

In 2008, the University of California, Los Angeles published a report about the initiative. Researchers found that Proposition 36 had saved millions of dollars, and that violent crime had declined more in California than nationwide in the preceding eight years. But the difference in the decline of violent crime was small, 12 percent in California versus 9 percent nationally, and could not be attributed to Proposition 36. Moreover, the study found that drug treatment was mostly *ineffective* with hard drug users and that arrests for drug and property crimes were higher among Proposition 36 participants than a comparison group of pre–Proposition 36 drug offenders.[122] A study several years later found that Proposition 36 participants, while initially more successful on discharge, were more likely to recidivate within a year than those who had treatment mandated by drug courts.[123]

Housing First worsened addiction starting in 2009, say some service providers and law enforcement. It was then that California cities stopped making housing conditional upon sobriety. "The 'Housing First' harm reduction people said, 'Recovery doesn't work,'" said shelter provider Andy Bales. "But it was after that when homelessness exploded."[124]

After the passage of Proposition 47 in 2014, police could no longer keep meth-intoxicated speeders in jail for a few days to come down. "Now we're not having those be crimes where people can be in jail for a couple of days to take a chill," said Kruger. "Instead, they're out breaking into cars and robbing people."[125] "Our guests went from twelve to seventeen percent addicted to fifty percent addicted or higher," said Bales.[126]

Said Tom Wolf, "In 2015, when Proposition 47 took effect, there were 115,000 people homeless in the state of California. Today, there are 165,000. I believe that there's a direct correlation between the two. People that would have maybe cycled through the justice system for committing smaller crimes—like running into Walgreens, filling your backpack full of makeup, and running out, because you're a drug addict—might actually have found some help."[127]

Between 2016 and 2021, Walgreens closed seventeen of its stores in San Francisco due to shoplifting.[128] When a reporter in 2020 asked a clerk where all the merchandise from the empty shelves had gone, he said, "Go ask the people in the alleys, they have it all."[129]

Said one homeless man recently, "San Francisco needs to stop sending the message out about the Summer of Love because the Summer of Love is over."[130]

5

"We Can't End Overdoses Until We End Poverty and Racism"

Tom Wolf was married with two children and worked a good, if mundane, job with San Francisco city government when he got hooked on opioid pain pills. His doctor had prescribed them after foot surgery. In the spring of 2017, after Tom's prescription ran out, he googled where to buy opioids and discovered that he could do so on "Pill Hill," which is the intersection of Hyde and Golden Gate Avenue in the Tenderloin. To maintain his addiction, he sometimes spent his entire paycheck on drugs and stopped paying bills, including the mortgage, and stole his wife's debit card. He estimates he spent a total of $100,000 on pills. Eventually he switched to heroin, which is much cheaper than pills, snorting it in the bathroom at work and passing out on his desk. He stopped going to work. Pacific Gas & Electric turned off the power to his house. He fled the house for an eleven-day bender in the Tenderloin. His wife filed a missing person's report, and a police officer found him.

Tom's wife gave him an ultimatum to either get drug treatment or leave the family. He decided to abandon his family and become homeless. "Addiction is the only disease that I know of that actually tells you to make it worse," he told me. "I remember sitting in my garage after I had bought a bunch of OxyContin and thinking, 'Fuck it, I'm just going to be an addict.'"[1]

For the next six months Tom lived on the streets. He smoked fentanyl. He woke up beside people who had overdosed and died. He saw people develop skin abscesses from shooting low-grade heroin. At one point he was hospitalized for six days for sepsis after missing veins while injecting. "And that still wasn't enough for me to stop," he said.

Tom became desperate. After he had been arrested multiple times by the police, the drug dealers would no longer use him as a mule to hold the drugs they sold. He started shoplifting from drugstores and selling the merchandise. The last time he was arrested, in June 2018, he had promised his son he was going to an AA meeting. He smoked crack instead and cried with shame. Later, even though he was wearing a court-ordered monitor around his ankle, and was supposed to stay away from the Tenderloin, he went there anyway. Notified by his ankle monitor that he was in the area, the police arrested him.

Tom's abandonment of his family isn't unusual. People often end up homeless after losing their jobs and relationships with friends and family in a desperate effort to support their addictions. "I had a very good friend," a meth dealer told a reporter. "I knew her husband and I knew her kids. Her kids were still small at the time. I smoked her out [with meth] and smoked her out and smoked her out and she started buying it from me here and there. About seven months later she gives her kids to her mom and starts hauling her pussy out on the street. . . . I know people say 'God forgives you' and 'Time heals all,' but I know I'm [going to] have to answer for that one."[2]

A round 2013, Adam Mesnick, a chef and restaurant owner in San Francisco, got to know some of the homeless people who hung around his restaurant, the Deli Board. "I was in there because I wasn't trying to violate their trust or piss them off . . ." he told me. "I was pretty much just hanging out smoking pot with them."

"So when Deli Board closes, you go out, smoke a couple [of pipe] bowls [of marijuana], and they were shooting up and you just chitchat with them and hang out?" I asked.

"I had to understand what the heck was going on," he said. "I didn't really understand. I didn't understand it. Now I get it."

"What did you get?"

"They just come here to die," said Adam. "That's it. They come here to shoot up, nod, and die. That's it. This is not any other place but to come to die. They'll all tell you that. They've all told me that—"

"They say 'die'?" I asked.

"Of course, they do," Adam said. "You can see it in some of my interviews. [Homeless fentanyl user] Jessica tells me on the camera exactly how it is. She smokes fentanyl. She tells you, 'Everyone's here to die.' She tells you, 'Everyone ODs.' She tells you, 'Everyone boosts.' She'll tell you everything."

"But is 'die' slang or literal?" I asked.

"I don't know," he said.

"But they say that explicitly?" I pressed. "'I come here to die'?"

"They explicitly say that," he said. "Look at Jessica's interviews. Jessica's telling me about how she died seventeen times from doing fentanyl and then they Narcaned."[3]

Addiction disaffiliates. "When I was an addict," said Vicki Westbrook, "I had lost touch with all of my spirituality. To me, spirituality is the connectedness that we all are with each other, with nature, with everything, right? I had lost that. When I tell you that addiction is very isolating, it's so much more than the fact that people want to use by themselves and go in some cubbyhole, right? They're disconnected from everything, right? Themselves, other people, the world, the environment. Even if they're around people, there is isolation and disconnection."[4]

Adam says witnessing the effects of addiction on his homeless friends has taken its toll on him. "It cannot be healthy for me to see what I see," he said. "I couldn't tell you a day when I didn't see someone either smoking fentanyl or shooting up or taking a shit on my block. And it wears on you. I'm sort of not kidding when I say that the city owes me an apology."[5]

I asked Chris Herring how he coped psychologically. "My advisor is more of, 'You got to tough it out.' Other advice is, 'You've got to just start drinking more.' I couldn't explain this away, or become numb to it, in the sense that you're not the primary traumatic. You're not the one who is directly experiencing the trauma. But that proximity really wears on you."[6]

Vicki Westbrook went on and off meth. "When it was time for me to go back to work, I got a job with another company in tech support, and started using again. I'd be in my office with the door closed, smoking dope [meth], listening to phone calls to see if they were doing what they were supposed to. I eventually got fired, not because I was smoking dope, but because I had those things that also come with being an addict. You have no self-esteem, but you're also arrogant."

After she lost her job, Vicki made the fateful decision to start selling drugs. "One of the people that I had been selling to moved to Michigan, and she needed somebody to be a distributor. It was sweet. I could ship drugs to her, make hella more money than I could make here. Real easy, right?" But she was soon arrested. "They intercepted her package. The feds picked her up, and she rolled over on everybody. My kids went to school one day and around nine o'clock the feds knocked on my door. I was like, 'God.'"[7]

No state in America has taken more aggressive action to reduce the public's exposure to chemicals, and to secondhand smoke, than California. California banned the sale of flavored tobacco, because it appeals to children, and the use of smokeless tobacco in the state's five professional baseball stadiums. It prohibited the use of e-cigarettes in government and private workplaces, restaurants, bars, and casinos. San Francisco in late 2020 banned cigarette smoking in apartments.[8] In the fall of 2020, California outlawed companies from using in cosmetics, shampoos, and other personal care products twenty-four chemicals it had deemed dangerous.[9]

And yet breathing secondhand smoke and being exposed to trace chemicals in your shampoo are hardly sufficient to kill. By contrast, hard drug use is both a necessary and sufficient cause to kill, as the 93,000 overdose and drug poisoning deaths of 2020 show. And yet, where the governments of San Francisco, California, and other progressive cities and states stress the remote dangers of cosmetics, pesticides, and second-hand smoke, they downplay the immediate dangers of hard drugs including fentanyl.

In 2020, San Francisco even paid for two billboards promoting the safe use of heroin and fentanyl, which had been created by the Harm Reduction Coalition. The first had a picture of an older African American man smiling. The headline read, "Change it up. Injecting drugs has the highest risk of overdose, so consider snorting or smoking instead." The second billboard's photograph was of a racially diverse group of people at a party smiling and laughing. The headline read, "Try not to use alone. Do it with friends. Use with people and take turns."[10]

When I asked Kristen Marshall of the Harm Reduction Coalition, which oversees San Francisco's overdose prevention strategy, about the threat posed by fentanyl, she said, "People use it safely all the time. This narrative that gets it labeled as an insane poison where you touch it and die—that's not how drugs work. It's not cyanide. It's not uranium. It's just a synthetic opioid, but one that's on an unregulated market."[11]

Said the harm reduction services director from Glide Memorial Church, "People have used [fentanyl] for years and not come to harm. We can't be shaming, stigmatizing, sensationalizing. We just have to educate people that overdoses are reversible."[12] Glide is one of San Francisco's largest homeless service providers and had $4.8 million in active contracts with the city in 2020.[13]

In 2020, when the city government put homeless people in hotel rooms to prevent the spread of COVID-19, it also pursued a harm reduction approach. That approach included delivering residents prescription drugs, medical marijuana, and alcohol bought by private donors. Tom Wolf tweeted about it, and the program made national news.[14] "When you walk inside those [single resident occupancy] hotels for the homeless they have all kinds of drug paraphernalia for you to use," Tom said. "Most people think, 'Oh, clean needles and tourniquet.' But giving away crack pipes and foil?"[15] Smokers of fentanyl sprinkle the substance on small strips of aluminum foil and heat the foil with a lighter until the fentanyl turns into smoke, which they inhale with straws.

"There's a criticism of harm reduction," acknowledged Marshall, "that sometimes we even give them the drugs, but it's part of a much bigger picture." The roots of the problem, said Marshall, are "displacement, poverty, and structural racism."[16]

When I asked homelessness advocate Paul Boden whether he thought it was okay for taxpayers to subsidize meth pipes, he suggested I was being hypocritical for not questioning the tax deduction that corporations claim for providing health care to their employees.

"It sounds like you're suggesting that providing meth pipes for people is the same as providing health care," I said.

"Providing meth pipes *is* the same as providing health care," he said. "I think people are killing themselves with these drugs and anything that we can try, anything that we can do. . . . And if it doesn't work, do something else, try something else. But I'm not going to sit there and throw rocks at a group."[17]

Not everybody I interviewed was aware of how much drug overdose deaths had risen. That included Bill Zimmerman, the political consultant who helped pass the 1996 medical marijuana ballot initiative, the 2000 drug treatment instead of incarceration initiative, and the 2004 initiative that taxed millionaires for mental health. I worked with Bill on drug decriminalization, the death penalty, and criminal justice reform in the late 1990s, and we have remained on friendly terms ever since. We spoke by phone in late 2020.

"So, you know," I said, "drug overdose deaths increased from about seventeen thousand to over seventy thousand in the last twenty years."

"Oof," said Zimmerman. "That's horrible."

"Had you heard that?" I asked.

"No," he said. "I had not."[18]

I asked Monique Tula of the Harm Reduction Coalition, "Is there a national, state, or city strategy anywhere to reverse the rise in overdose deaths?"

Without hesitating she said, "No." She then added, "One of the things we'll be working on next year is pulling together a coalition to create a national harm reduction strategy."[19]

In late 2020, I asked Supervisor Rafael Mandelman if San Francisco had a strategy to deal with rising overdose deaths. "Not that is clear to me," he said.[20]

Today, when San Francisco, Seattle, and Los Angeles firefighters or police rescue someone from overdose with Narcan, the person is often put right back into the open drug scene, and not offered drug treatment. "The way our city is doing harm reduction does not work," said Vicki Westbrook. "It's not like they give you clean needles and works and talk to you about what it could look like to be clean or get your life back. Harm reduction is like life support. It keeps people alive, but it doesn't give them their life back."[21]

Tom says that while harm reduction workers gave him the equipment for using heroin, nobody once offered him drug treatment. "If I had walked in off the street to get rehab, there was maybe a twenty percent chance that I could have gotten a detox bed that day and an eighty percent chance that it could take me up to three weeks to actually get into treatment," said Tom. "If I get turned away that day back to the street, and in those three weeks, who knows what's going to happen? Possibly overdose and death."

A detox bed is merely the first step to getting clean. Because opiates in particular can have dangerous withdrawal symptoms, medically assisted detox is recommended to slowly wean an addict off of them. The process requires close medical supervision and can take over a week. After detox, recovering addicts need two to six weeks of transitional support services, before living in a recovery home, formerly called halfway houses, for three to six months.

Tom said there were about fifteen sanctioned beds for detox made available by the Department of Public Health. "The Salvation Army has detox beds available," he said, "but the city actually discourages you from going to the Salvation Army because it's a faith-based organization. So there's really nowhere to go for treatment."[22]

Is the reason for the lack of drug treatment that the United States does not have a single-payer health-care system like Medicare for All, or the Canadian system? There may be good reasons for such a system. But Canada has a single-payer system, and yet the West Coast province of British Columbia has seen overdose deaths increase 74 percent, from 984 deaths in 2019 to 1,716 deaths in 2020.[23] Like San Francisco, Seattle, and Los Angeles, British Columbia's most populous city, Vancouver, embraced decriminalization, harm reduction, and Housing First. And most homeless addicts in the United States are destitute and thus already eligible for government-funded Medicaid, so a single-payer system might not have mattered.

Despite skyrocketing overdose death rates, none of the country's leading advocates of harm reduction are rethinking their advocacy of decriminalization and harm reduction. Instead they focus on things like promoting Narcan. "It's really about getting emergency responders to carry [naloxone/Narcan]," said Ethan. "The guy who was a real pioneer in all of this was a guy named Dan Bigg out of Chicago. He really took this issue by the horns in the early 2000s."

What happened to him?

"He himself died of an overdose a few years ago," said Ethan.

Bigg's death in 2018 attracted national media attention. "The substances found in his body included heroin, two benzodiazepines . . . methadone, fentanyl, and acetyl fentanyl," wrote a journalist for *Vice*. "The cause of Bigg's death, however, in no way repudiates the cause to which he devoted his life."[24]

Leaders of the Harm Reduction Coalition agreed. "We can't end overdoses until we end poverty," said Kristen Marshall, "until we end racism, and until we end homelessness."[25]

For several years in the early 2010s, a UCLA sociologist named Neil Gong studied two very different drug treatment programs in larger Los Angeles. One was in Skid Row in downtown and the other in Malibu, an affluent coastal community just north of LA. The Skid Row treatment center was funded by the 2004 Mental Health Services Act, which taxes the state's millionaires and raised nearly $2 billion in 2019 alone.[26] The Malibu drug treatment facility was privately funded.[27]

Gong discovered something surprising: the Malibu drug treatment program was far harder on its elite clientele than the Skid Row program was on the downtrodden. On Skid Row, wrote Gong, "the public providers offer some 'difficult' clients a surprising level of freedom to refuse medication, continue substance use, or act in socially deviant ways."[28] Gong found fatalism at the Skid Row treatment "characterized by an acceptance that rehabilitation is unlikely."[29]

Social workers gave private rooms to addicts if they were difficult, effectively rewarding bad behavior. "Clients deemed too difficult for other agencies or who had done poorly in structured settings were offered independence and a surprising freedom," he wrote, "to engage in ostensibly problematic behaviors."[30]

Psychiatrists have long warned against giving money to the mentally ill homeless addicted to drugs, and yet that is what San Francisco,

Los Angeles, and other progressive cities do. "It is not only clinically incorrect," said the director of psychiatric services at San Francisco's Haight-Ashbury Free Clinic, "but almost sadistic to give money on a regular basis to people who have a demonstrated inability to handle cash funds."[31]

Gong found that leniency toward drug and alcohol abuse could result in death by overdose. "One day [social worker] Carlos confided in me that they had wanted to schedule [a longtime street drinker in her fifties] for more visits, to try and connect with her and encourage her to drink less," wrote Gong. "Carlos feared he would find her dead, and indeed, a year after my fieldwork, they found her unresponsive."[32]

Many people in recovery from addiction say they would have died had they not been forced to accept treatment. "I don't recommend it as a way to get your life together," said Vicki, "but getting indicted by the feds worked for me. I wouldn't have done this without them. I didn't go to treatment to get clean. I went to treatment to get out of Santa Rita [jail]."[33]

After the police came for her in a Tenderloin hotel, Tracey Helton Mitchell hid under the stairwell. "I didn't need much room," she said. "Starved by daily drug use, I was a walking skeleton. Underneath my three T-shirts you could see all my ribs. I pushed my body into the crawl-space. As I crouched in the enveloping dust, trying not to cough, a rat ran past me. . . . I was done."[34] Even so, she said, "They had to drag me into recovery in handcuffs. If I did not complete the program, I would automatically be sentenced to three and a half years in state prison."[35]

"What's happened in these places [San Francisco, Seattle, and Portland] is just the removing of all pressure," said Keith Humphreys. "The thinking was, 'Oh, people will just show up automatically and go into treatment.' But that doesn't happen very often in addiction. Usually there's pressure."[36]

Research finds that many addicts need mandatory treatment, and that it works nearly as well as voluntary treatment. Noted a team of researchers, "patients who have been forced to enter a substance abuse treatment have shown during and posttreatment results that are quite similar to those shown by supposedly 'internally motivated' patients."[37]

Other research finds that mandated drug treatment through specialized "drug courts" aimed at addressing the underlying cause of crime, addiction, is effective in reducing drug use and recidivism, or repeat offending. One study concluded that people sentenced through drug courts were two-thirds less likely to be rearrested than individuals prosecuted through the normal criminal justice system.[38] Another study found that a group of participants in drug courts had its rate of recidivism lowered from 50 percent to 38 percent.[39] Researchers estimated that every dollar allocated to drug courts saves approximately $4 in spending on incarceration and health care.[40]

Today, many progressives advocate for the decriminalization of all drugs, including heroin, meth, and fentanyl. They propose that cities build special facilities where people can inject or smoke heroin, meth, and fentanyl. Said Glide's director of harm reduction, "we're not going to get beyond the opioid deaths until we get to safe consumption sites. There's really no downside, except for people who see it as a moral failing and they're morally outraged."[41]

But the people who have recovered from addiction aren't so sure. "How compassionate is it to let somebody just shoot dope the rest of their life?" asked Vicki. "If you hold people accountable, but you don't give them an opportunity to change their life, that's just punitive. But if you give them opportunities without holding them accountable, which is what we do now, that's not going to work, either."[42]

Legalization, they fear, would result in even more overdose deaths. "If they [had] legalized drugs or they decriminalized everything," said Tom, "and made it a lot easier to get fentanyl on the street when I was on the street in 2018, I would be dead, because there would have been no real compulsion for me to stop."[43]

In early 2021, Penguin published a book by a Columbia University professor of psychology describing, defending, and to some extent advocating his recreational use of heroin, titled *Drug Use for Grown-Ups*. The author, Carl L. Hart, argues that he and others should have the freedom to use heroin and meth without restriction, and that fears of heroin are overblown.

Keith Humphreys disagrees. "I would ask any person to sit down and graph the overdose rate for heroin and the overdose rate for cannabis," Humphreys said, "and struggle for more than a nanosecond with why they are different."

After thousands of years of usage, there is no recorded case of a person dying from overdose of marijuana.

Meanwhile, noted Humphreys, "We're having funerals all over the country for heroin."

I tried to represent Hart's argument. "But they would say, 'Okay, but if heroin were legal—'"

"Like OxyContin?" said Humphreys.

"Like alcohol," I said. "Some would say, 'Maybe at a safe injection site to avoid contaminants.'"

"If it is really true that the problem is contaminants," said Humphreys, "that opioids are not being made and distributed under tight regulation by legal manufacturers, then no one would ever have died from OxyContin. It is weird to me to hear people who think of themselves as leftists slinging a line that the most shameless corporate attorney for Purdue Pharma would be embarrassed to raise in court. Because that was what they said, right? 'OxyContin's not dangerous.' 'Give it as much as you want.' 'There's no risk of addiction or overdose' That is just the same rhetoric over again!"

Humphreys stressed he favored harm reduction, when appropriate, but that it wasn't the only response required to addiction. "The first statement by any White House that naloxone [Narcan] should be widely distributed was written by me when I worked for President Obama," he said. "That's harm reduction. And there's no contradiction between that and saying, I don't think a heroin industry would be a good thing. I'm all fine and good for harm reduction. I don't want anyone to die. I work in health care for a reason. I don't want Purdue Pharma to sell cocaine because I am for harm reduction."[44]

6

Let's Go Dutch

In early 2019 I traveled to the Netherlands at the invitation of a member of parliament, Dilan Yeşilgöz, to give a talk at the Delft University of Technology. Afterward, Dilan and her husband, Rene Zegerius, gave me a ride back to Amsterdam. Rene is a former second division men's professional soccer player in his late fifties who looks like the British action film actor Jason Statham. Rene had worked as a nurse, social worker, and drug policy expert for the Dutch government since the 1980s.

"What's the secret?" I asked him. "Amsterdam has decriminalized marijuana and many other drugs but I haven't seen any homeless. What is San Francisco doing wrong?"

Rene said that in the 1980s, the Zeedijk neighborhood in Amsterdam was a lot like the Tenderloin today. There was open-air drug use, particularly of heroin, and needles strewn about, as well as crime. People started to flee the neighborhood, worsening its slum conditions. Homeless people squatted in abandoned buildings. "We had ghettos where it was not safe to go," said Rene, who started working in the neighborhood as a nurse in 1985. It was considered a "no go" zone. "We had a lot of people from abroad who came to Amsterdam because our heroin was so good. But our heroin was so good that they died from it."

At first the city tried a "helping approach" exclusively, offering addicts clean needles, methadone, and other forms of help without any law enforcement, but it didn't work. "In the eighties we just wanted to help people," said Rene. "We started with methadone programs and medical treatment. We did a lot of work without much of a carrot and a stick. It was really a disappointment. They just used the methadone to stay addicted. They dealt drugs and committed other crimes. They lied and cheated about it. We were just supporting a different kind of market. We had to learn the hard way.

"We started as very motivated caretakers," Rene said, "but at some point, with drug addicts, you have to change your attitude. You can't help with just giving. I always watch Dr. Phil with my wife"—here Rene did his best impersonation of Dr. Phil—"'*It's not working for you*,' he would have said. And it wasn't."

The police and helping services didn't work together. "There were two separate worlds because doctors did not talk with police officers," said Rene, "and we had a lot of people dying on the streets. It didn't work and it didn't feel good as well because our [jail] cells were bad and the street was still filled up with a lot of people who were addicted and who committed a lot of crimes."

The Amsterdam City Council asked the Amsterdam Municipal Health Service to develop a strategy to deal with "unmotivated drug users." Said Rene, "it took until the beginning of the nineties to work something out in collaboration with the College of Police. They thought that we were some silly nutcases who were only good for the flu or whatever. And we thought that they only saw the bad side of people. You need people to change that. I was fortunate in that I had to work with some police colleagues who I still see. They convinced me and I convinced them. At some point, we started making house calls together."[1]

The police broke up the open-air drug scene and health workers were on hand to offer methadone, treatment, and shelter. The police broke up gatherings of more than four or five users, but did not treat personal and private use as a crime. Officers ticketed violators, and if users did not pay their fines, which was frequent, the courts ordered arrests, and sentenced individuals to follow a treatment plan or face incarceration.[2]

"For every individual homeless person, we make a plan," said Rene. "We made tens of thousands of those plans." Plans are overseen by a caseworker and a team that may include a psychiatrist, shelter provider, service provider, judge, employer, parole officer, and police officer. "You need people in the police and health department working together," he said.

What Amsterdam did was the same as other major European cities. Lisbon, Frankfurt, Vienna, and Zurich all dealt with their open-air drug markets, using a combination of law enforcement and social services. Crucially, Amsterdam and other European cities prevented services from being concentrated in a single neighborhood, since their concentration often enables an open-air drug scene to thrive.

Today, Rene says, Dutch police officers are sometimes *too* soft. "Sometimes they say, 'Please don't punish them, you have to help them.' And I have to make sure that they do punish them, because otherwise it can't help. I have to motivate those police officers to stick to the program. If you only do it with care it's not going to succeed. It's about carrots and sticks. At some point there are some people who do not want to or are not able to listen. For them there are psychiatric examinations. And some people are just bad. Those people go to jail. Not forever. But if they do bad things they go to jail and they have to know that they go to jail."

The efforts worked. "We had several thousand people who were addicted to heroin in the eighties and nineties," said Rene. "Many died. Today we have four or five hundred people addicted to methadone. And we have about 120 in Amsterdam who we supply heroin to on a medical basis because methadone doesn't work for them. They have to use heroin."[3]

It is reasonable to ask whether a small European nation like the Netherlands is a relevant or useful model for California. California has slightly more than twice as many people (39 million) and far more ethnic and racial diversity than the Netherlands, which has a restrictive immigration policy compared to the United States. Most European nations, including the Netherlands, after all, have universal health insurance coverage, which makes drug treatment and psychiatric treatment more available, and the Dutch government subsidizes more housing. Finally, the Netherlands' big success was with heroin, which has effective pharmacological substitutes, methadone and Suboxone, not with meth, which lacks anything similar.

But there may be fewer obstacles than appear. The Netherlands has a private health-care insurance system similar to that of the United States and covered the people who needed health care in ways similar to Medicaid and the Affordable Care Act, which significantly expanded access to drug treatment, including medically assisted treatment, in the United States.[4] San Francisco subsidizes a significant quantity of housing, as we have seen. While California is larger than the Netherlands, the population of Amsterdam (872,000) is nearly identical to San Francisco's (882,000).[5] And while California's population and geographic area are larger and more difficult to manage than those of the Netherlands, California also has significantly greater wealth and resources, constituting in 2019 the fifth-largest economy in the world.[6]

And the approach to breaking up open drug scenes, treating addiction, and providing psychiatric care is fundamentally the same whether in five European cities, Philadelphia, New York, or Phoenix. Working together, law enforcement and social service agencies have in recent years broken up open-air drug camps in Philadelphia and Seattle, and dispersed homeless populations across a larger area. In the Philadelphia neighborhood of Kensington, known as the "Wal-Mart of heroin," police in 2018 broke up an open-air drug market. Research shows that police visibility can deter crime.[7]

Miami, too, reduced its homeless population 57 percent, from a peak of 8,258 in June 2001 to 3,560 in January 2020, by adopting policies similar to those used in the Netherlands.[8] Miami broke up the open-air drug scenes, provided free psychiatric care and drug treatment to the homeless, and expanded both shelters and supportive housing.[9] "The three things you got to have," said the head of Miami's top homelessness non-profit, "is a plan, money, and leadership."[10]

The Department of Justice has even published a handbook for cities to use to break the markets up using both social services and law enforcement. It notes that open-air drug dealing damages public safety and undermines the shared community of parks and sidewalks. It acknowledges that breaking up open-air drug markets will not end drug dealing but will push it indoors, making drug dealing less of a public nuisance and increasing costs.[11] There is little unique in how the Netherlands ended its open-air drug scene. It just happened to be one of the first nations to realize that it needed to use both law enforcement and social services because either one alone was insufficient.

America's fragmented drug treatment system is an obstacle to breaking up the drug markets, reversing the overdose crisis, and reducing addiction. Studies show that outpatient drug treatments of less than three months are more likely to result in relapse than longer treatments.[12] One study found that, over an eight-year period, half of all people who are sober for a year stay sober. Of those who are sober for five years, just 15 percent relapse within eight years.[13]

"Everything's on Medi-Cal now," said Vicki Westbrook. "So you get thirty days with two chances of thirty days extension, so ninety days of treatment. They're kicking people to the street when their triggers and cravings will be at their highest. It doesn't make sense to not provide serious aftercare. Treatment needs to be longer."[14]

Treatment providers and the public both support making treatment mandatory for those convicted of crimes. Eighty percent of treatment providers say they support short jail stays to motivate treatment compliance.[15] "If you don't want to send them to prison, make them go to treatment," said Vicki. "Not everybody's going to take. Some people will bounce. Some people will end up having warrants. Okay. But they still go away and sit down for a minute and actually have some new thoughts in their heads, see the world in a different way, see themselves in a different way."[16]

"The left's idea is that everyone who's addicted really wants to change if we just give them the right services," said Stanford's Humphreys. "But look at how much money addicted people spend on drugs every year versus how much they spend on treatment. That tells you what they want. If you can afford to keep a heroin habit you could afford to go see a psychiatrist. Why don't you? There isn't this massive, spontaneous kind of 'I want to self-actualize' demand for drug treatment. And so even if you opened up lots of beds, you would still have tons of people saying, 'That's great that I could have that, but I don't want it.' That is part of the reality of drugs. They're intensely rewarding in the short term."[17]

Social pressure by an assertive caseworker like Rene can do a lot before resorting to law enforcement. "Even strongly dependent users seem to be able to quit without formal treatment services under the right kind of pressure," noted the late drug policy researcher Mark Kleiman.[18]

Inpatient treatment, where addicts stay in a residential facility for several months, is more effective than outpatient treatment, where addicts return home at the end of the day. Addicts who received inpatient resident treatment under California's Proposition 36, which allowed drug treatment to be used in place of incarceration, were more than twice as likely to complete the program successfully as those in outpatient. The problem was that just 12 percent of Californians sentenced under Proposition 36 ever received a residential placement.[19]

Part of the reason that it's important to break up the open drug scenes on the Tenderloin, Skid Row, and the Blade is to end the visibility and availability of such dangerous temptations. Researchers find that it is easier for people to quit drugs when they aren't being constantly offered or exposed to them, which recovering addicts say "trigger" their cravings. In a famous study of American soldiers who returned from Vietnam addicted to heroin, most of the men quit without almost any professional help, in part because they weren't constantly exposed to it, as they had been overseas.[20]

Part of what drug dealers and drug users like about large, highly visible drug scenes in neighborhoods like the Tenderloin, Skid Row, and the Blade is precisely the fact that they do trigger users. Recall that Corey, Jacqui Berlinn's son, compared the Tenderloin to Pleasure Island in *Pinocchio*. Their very existence advertises drugs.

Open-air drug markets also reduce costs by eliminating the time-consuming process of dealers and users having to find each other. Kelly Stamphill, whose son, Morgan, is addicted to fentanyl and lives homeless on the streets of the Tenderloin, said, "When Morgan lived in San Diego, he had to spend eight hours a day finding drugs, whereas here it's too easy."[21] Breaking up open-air drug markets may not deter "serious and addicted users," notes the Department of Justice, but "casual and novice users would be discouraged from buying and therefore the market would be constricted."[22]

In late 2020, I asked Monique Tula of the Harm Reduction Coalition if drug treatment should ever be mandatory as a sentence for when people commit a crime.

"No," she said. "Bodily autonomy."

"Does that go for everybody?" I asked

"Yeah . . . I don't think that mandated treatment for substance use disorders is something that works because it doesn't get at the root of the issues," said Tula. "You know, people are using for a reason. They're trying to mitigate something, and that's the thing that we should be focusing on first. What is underneath that to try to take somebody's coping mechanism away as the first intervention?"

"But let's say a guy had for the fifth or tenth time overdosed in public,"

I asked, "and a judge were like, you know, 'We're going to sentence you to thirty days in jail, or you can have mandatory treatment.' Would you still oppose mandatory treatment under that circumstance?"

"I don't think that that should be the option," she said. "I don't think the courts and criminal punishment system should be involved in the choices that somebody has around mental illness and substance use."

"If the number of overdose deaths were significantly higher," I asked, "would you change your mind?"

"No," she said.

It was then that she asserted that Portugal had legalized all drugs, which, as noted above, is incorrect.[23]

I heard something similar from two representatives for the American Civil Liberties Union (ACLU), which is the most influential organization in progressive cities and states on issues relating to crime, drugs, and mental illness.

"What about the open-air drug markets?" I asked them.

"We are not aware of open-air drug markets as a concrete formal thing that law enforcement is concerned about," said the ACLU's director of litigation, Jamie Crook. "But we are deeply concerned by the use of nuisance ordinances to crack down on drug offenses that are enforced in racially disparate ways. In addition, forcing people out of their homes is a way to put them onto the street."

"But if it's not an open-air drug market," I asked, "what is it? And how would you deal with it?"

"No one would disagree that there is a problem of drug sales," she said. "But the Housing First model is to get people off the streets and get them into housing where they can get their lives in order."[24]

Some progressives I talked to embraced the idea of breaking up the open drug scenes. "Open-air drug markets make as much sense as open-air alcohol markets," said Bill Zimmerman, the political consultant who helped liberalize drug laws. "We strictly regulate the sale of alcohol because we recognize that it is a dangerous and highly addictive substance. Similar strict regulation should be applied to drug sales. You need a license to sell bourbon; you should need a license to sell heroin."[25]

I asked San Francisco's political leaders whether we should break up the open-air drug markets in the Tenderloin and other neighborhoods. "I think we have to try to do it," said Supervisor Rafael Mandelman. "But it is a flash point."[26] Supervisor Matt Haney said, "There should be an emergency response that is of the size and scale of the crisis we are facing."[27] But Haney also discounted the importance of law enforcement in achieving those goals. "I don't know what the answer is on the drug market. I hear a lot of people who want to incarcerate a lot of people, and America tried that," he said. "Also there isn't really an appetite for it with judges and juries in San Francisco anymore."[28]

Such talk frustrates Stanford's Keith Humphreys. "I get the same requests exactly from San Jose, San Francisco, Portland, and Seattle," he said. "All of them have large numbers of people with untreated mental illness and addiction, high housing prices, lots and lots of property crime, and a political culture that stops them from doing anything about it."[29]

Mandelman noted that some of the city-funded nonprofit service providers in the Tenderloin had just published an open letter decrying efforts by the city attorney to impose civil penalties on the drug dealers whom the district attorney refuses to prosecute. "There's a sort of, I don't want to say knee-jerk, but there is a strong reaction against law enforcement," he said. "I think sometimes it is counterproductive. The politics at City Hall remain dominated by the ACLU and the Democratic Socialists. There is an anxiety in San Francisco about stirring up the far left on these issues. You have a ready-made constituency that will oppose that. And it's a powerful constituency in San Francisco."[30]

The problem is that they face opposition from well-organized and well-financed constituencies. Said Humphreys, "Anytime a person says, 'Maybe the police and the health care system could work together?' or,

'Maybe we could try some probation or low-level arrests,' there's an enormous outcry. 'No! That's the war on drugs! The police have no role in this! Let's open up some more services and people will come in and use them voluntarily!' "[31]

Many parents of addicted homeless children want mandatory treatment. "I think Corey might need mandatory intervention," said Jacqui Berlinn. "I get a lot of pushback. It's the old adage of, 'You can't force them,' and to some extent I believe that. But honestly everybody's different and my son's rock bottom is death. Unless he's sober and thinking clearly he is too scared of withdrawal. He needs to be able to focus in a controlled environment so he can think straight. As long as he's on the street, he can't think straight. Some people do, but many can't think straight because they are constantly under the influence, or sick. For some people there needs to be a level of 'you need to be forced to do this.' "[32]

Some former addicts, and advocates for the homeless, agree. "Addicts cannot get clean," notes Tracey Helton Mitchell, the former heroin addict, "if they are dead."[33] Said Steve Berg of the National Alliance to End Homelessness, "If you completely reject criminalization, you just end up with lots of people with addictions dying on the street."[34]

Many policy makers recognize that most homeless people addicted to hard drugs won't quit unless they are required to. "The problem of homelessness is not going to be solved," wrote former San Francisco mayor Willie Brown, "until one major drastic change takes place in public policy: we have to be able to impose help and treatment on people."[35]

Humphreys agreed. "A lot of people are addicted and don't want to change until it hurts. It's hurting now, but it's going to have to hurt a lot more until they realize this isn't working. A lot of people are going to suffer and die because the political culture won't let [policy makers] be like Portugal, and won't let them try evidence-based tactics that involve using something other than just offering people more services."[36]

There are some signs of change. After the billboard advertisements promoting the supposedly safe use of fentanyl came to public attention, the city took them down.

But by the spring of 2021, Tom Wolf was more frustrated than ever. "I know 8 people that overdosed and died from illicit fentanyl since 2018," he tweeted. "3 of them I witnessed or woke up to dead next to me on the street."[37]

I asked Deli Board owner Adam Mesnick if the problem was that San Franciscans were just too liberal. "What's happening is not even liberal," he said. "It's not realistic. It's fantasy land. This is a severe drug addiction crisis that needs greater intervention or everyone's just going to die from fentanyl."[38]

7

The Crisis of Untreated Mental Illness

When you ask progressives who remember the 1980s why there are so many people on the street, many blame former California governor and president Ronald Reagan. "In the 1970s we never saw homeless people on the streets," said Democratic political strategist Bill Zimmerman. "After Reagan shut down the mental hospitals, we saw people. Most of those people appeared to be mentally ill rather than addicted to drugs."[1] Susan Mizner, a senior attorney for the American Civil Liberties Union, agreed. "The degradation of our affordable housing and mental health and behavioral health services started in the 1980s with Reagan's cuts to HUD, decimating the amount of money that was available for subsidized and supported housing."[2]

Others point to the fact that Governor Reagan in 1972 signed the Lanterman-Petris-Short Act, which aimed to significantly reduce involuntary hospitalization of the mentally ill.[3] California's mental hospitals closed and by 2019 there were 93 percent fewer patients in California's mental institutions than their peak, sixty years earlier, when adjusted for population growth.[4] The rest of the United States saw a similar decline.[5] If the United States still hospitalized its mentally ill at the same rate it did in 1955, its mental health institutions would house almost 1.1 million people any given day. Instead, they house fewer than 50,000 patients.[6]

Many of the mentally ill discharged from state hospitals went to live in neighborhoods like the Tenderloin, where they mixed with people with serious alcohol and drug problems.[7] On a single day in late June 1972, Agnews State Hospital released over 3,800 patients into the San Jose area, creating a "mental health ghetto." Local mental health service providers were forced to quickly convert vacant buildings into supportive housing.[8]

About one-fifth of the homeless on Skid Row in Chicago were mentally ill. The "new," post-1980 homeless had 50 percent more chronic mental illness than the old homeless. Based on a review of multiple homelessness studies from major US cities, one researcher estimates that one-quarter of the homeless had been patients in mental hospitals and one-third showed signs of psychosis or affective disorders.[9]

While it is true that, as California's governor, Reagan oversaw the closure of mental hospitals, he didn't start deinstitutionalization. It began nationally in the 1930s, mostly to save money.[10] The closure of California's mental hospitals began in earnest in the 1950s, more than a decade before Reagan became governor.[11] The emptying of state mental hospitals continued at the same rate between 1959 and 1967 under a Democratic governor as it did under Reagan. By the time Reagan took office in 1967, nearly half of the patients in California's state mental hospitals had already been released.[12]

As for the Lanterman-Petris-Short Act, it was a creation of civil libertarians, mental health professionals, and anti-psychiatry activists, sponsored by two Democrats, and passed in a 77–1 vote. It would have passed even had Reagan vetoed it.[13] And while Reagan, as president, cut over 300,000 workers from Social Security Insurance and Social Security Disability Insurance, he reversed his cuts just a year and a half later, and by the end of his presidency, nearly 200,000 had won back their benefits.[14]

In reality, it was a Democrat who got the deinstitutionalization of psychiatric hospitals rolling. President John F. Kennedy proposed and successfully advocated a crucial 1963 reform that required the federal government to fund community mental health centers but leave it to the states to fund mental hospitals.[15]

In 1963 President Kennedy argued that medical advances would enable "most of the mentally ill to be successfully and quickly treated in their own communities and returned to a useful place in society."[16] The Kennedy White House recommended shifting funding away from mental hospitals to community-based treatment. Experts argued that hospitals were "superfluous" institutions, sites of "therapeutic tyranny," and "merely a symptom of an outdated system that is crying for a complete remodeling" and that should be "liquidated as rapidly as can be done."[17]

California Democrats were active in efforts to close the mental hospitals. "I saw Senator [Dianne] Feinstein speak about this," said Michelle Tandler, a San Francisco native who worked as an intern in Feinstein's office in 2006. "She was like, 'We really need to solve this. We need to come together.' She was saying all the right things. 'We have a real problem because you see people wandering around in traffic talking to themselves. It's like what are you going to do with that person? Are you going to put them in an insane asylum?'"

"I used to visit the insane asylums back when I was a supervisor," Feinstein said, according to Tandler. "I used to visit them. I remember I would go into the kitchen at every single insane asylum and I would open the fridge door, and I would usually just see a big stack of potatoes. And then you'd look outside in the yard, people are being walked around on leashes. We can't go back to that."[18]

When Paneez Kosarian arrived at her condominium in downtown San Francisco around 1:40 a.m. on a Sunday morning in the late summer of 2019, she discovered a man blocking the entrance. His back was turned, and he was staring inside. The man, twenty-five-year-old Austin Vincent, said to Kosarian, "I'm the only human left." And, "Everybody else is a robot." He then said, "What can I do to earn your trust? I'll kill anyone. I'll kill the robot to earn your trust." By "robot," Vincent was referring to the woman working at the front desk.[19]

A security camera captured what happened next. Kosarian's building entrance has two large glass doors with L-shaped steel handles, common for new buildings in her neighborhood. On both sides of the doors are large windows. The man's back is pressed directly up to where the two doors meet.[20]

Kosarian attempts to enter the building, but Vincent pulls her away from the doors. A struggle ensues. As Kosarian tries to escape, he fights to open the door, and they both tumble to the sidewalk. We see the female security officer at the front desk calling the police. Vincent pulls Kosarian on top of him. Kosarian tries again to get away. The security guard runs to the door, phone still in hand, and opens it for Kosarian. But Vincent doesn't let go. "I want to save your life!" he says.[21]

Vincent gets up and pushes the door closed before Kosarian can escape. Once again, she tries to get past him. He lunges at her until she falls and crawls through the door. But just inches before the two women are able to close the door behind them, Vincent grabs the door and, overpowering them, forces his body into the entranceway.

The two women have their hands on the door handle and are furiously pulling it closed. There is no sound in the video, but Vincent can be seen shouting something at both women, an enraged look on his face. Then, while still holding on to the door handle with her right hand, Kosarian releases her left hand from the door, sending her yellow-encased iPhone flying behind her, and strikes the man.

It does the trick. We see Vincent let go long enough for the two women to yank the door behind them. We see Vincent shout at them. Kosarian shows Vincent her middle fingers, runs her left hand through her hair, and walks away. The security guard holds on to the door handles a few seconds longer, watching as Vincent walks away before returning to her station. She gets back on the phone with the police. Kosarian picks up her iPhone, stares out at the street, and walks behind the front desk. She puts her back to the wall and slowly slides down it as she starts to cry. Now sitting, Kosarian scoots farther behind the front desk, as though trying to make herself invisible.[22]

While about 52 million people in the United States suffer from a mental illness such as anxiety and depression, just over 13 million adults are seriously mentally ill.[23] The category includes schizophrenia, severe bipolar disorder, mood and thought disorders, and serious depression.[24] Serious mental illness is disabling, preventing people from engaging in normal work or family life. Adults with serious mental illness are more likely to suffer from substance use disorder as well as numerous general health conditions such as heart disease, diabetes, and respiratory conditions, complicating their care needs.[25]

Approximately 121,000 mentally ill people are conservatively estimated to be living on the streets.[26] In 2012, an estimated 35,000 were in state hospitals, while an estimated 356,000 people with serious mental illness were in jails and state prisons at any given time.[27]

The San Francisco Department of Health estimates that 4,000 of San Francisco's homeless have a history of both serious mental illness and substance abuse disorder.[28] "And of those 4,000 individuals," said Mayor London Breed, "41 percent frequently use urgent and emergency psychiatric services. Ninety-five percent of those folks suffer from alcohol use disorder. Thirty-five percent are African Americans despite the fact that we have a less than 6 percent population of African Americans in San Francisco overall."[29]

People with serious mental illness are more likely to be homeless, interact with drug dealers, and be raped, beaten, or otherwise victimized than the general public.[30] According to the World Health Organization, serious mental illness reduces life expectancy by ten to twenty-five years, primarily due to chronic physical health conditions but also due to suicide.[31] The mentally ill are up to ten times more likely to be incarcerated than hospitalized.[32]

The problems surrounding the homeless mentally ill have only grown worse since the 1980s. A psychiatrist who worked in San Francisco General's emergency psychiatric ward for twenty-five years compared parts of the city in 2018 to an "open-air insane asylum."[33] The problem is similar in Los Angeles and Seattle. There are over 11,000 people with serious mental illness living unsheltered on the streets in Los Angeles.[34] A *Los Angeles Times* reporter described LA's Skid Row as "a dumping ground for hospitals, prisons, and other cities to get rid of people with nowhere else to go."[35]

There is frequent violence within the psychiatric emergency departments. "One day someone was swinging a pipe, someone was swinging a bat, and someone was swinging a bicycle," said psychiatrist Paul Linde to the *San Francisco Chronicle*. "These are often people who are intoxicated on intravenous methamphetamine and/or psychotic from either untreated bipolar, untreated schizophrenia, and oftentimes both. Maybe a third of the patients brought in immediately need to be medicated and sometimes even placed in four-point restraints."[36]

Seventy-eight percent of homeless inmates of the San Francisco County Jail system who suffered serious mental illness also suffered from addiction to alcohol or drugs, according to a study in 2000. Inmates who suffered both mental illness and addiction were more likely to be homeless and to be charged with violent crimes.[37]

Most people Linde saw suffered both mental illness and substance abuse. "Only about a quarter have psychiatric illness with no substance use problem. And then, frankly, there's another 10 to 20 percent that really only have the substance use disorder."[38]

Vincent, the man who attacked Kosarian, may well have been suffering meth-induced psychosis. "I got contacted by someone who seemed to be an ex-friend of his," Kosarian told me in early 2021, "who said he had the same problems in New York. He ran away from home at an early age, had been in rehab in Orange County but got fired and still had addiction problems."[39]

Much of what we call "deinstitutionalization" was really trans-institutionalization.[40] The Los Angeles County Jail has more mentally ill people than every hospital in the country and nearly more than any other institution.[40] In the jail, "thousands of men in pods live behind Plexiglas under the constant surveillance of cameras monitored by guards perched in elevated posts," noted psychiatrist Ken Rosenberg in his 2019 book, *Bedlam*.[42] "If you think seeing a mentally ill person homeless is bad," said a street doctor who treats the homeless, "a mentally ill incarcerated person is five times worse because they're in there for full-blown psychosis, and they're not accepting resources. That just kills me."[43]

In California, just under one-third of those in prisons and jails have mental illness.[44] In the Los Angeles County Jail, about 25 percent of the men and 40 percent of the women need mental health care.[45] Eighty-nine percent of the remaining 12,000 patients in California's state mental hospitals in 2018 were there for criminal cases.[46] Prisoners with a serious mental illness are two to three times more likely to be reincarcerated as other prisoners. The high rate of recidivism creates the cycling of people between the streets, hospitals, and jails or prisons.[47]

"The reason that it's hard to see those costs is because they're buried in the hospital budget, they're buried in the police budget, they're buried in the courts, they're buried in ambulance budgets, so the cost of homelessness tends to be hidden," said retired University of California, San Francisco psychiatrist Dr. Robert Okin.[48]

Things often end badly when mentally ill people are forced into the criminal justice system. One study estimates that around one-quarter of the people shot and killed by police in any given year in the US have an untreated severe mental illness. Those with an untreated severe mental illness are thus sixteen times more likely to be killed in an encounter with the police than those without one. California had 162 such incidents in 2017. In San Jose, every police shooting in 2017 involved someone with mental illness, according to news reports.[49] A 2016 *San Francisco Chronicle* analysis found that 60 percent of all fatal shootings by police in the city since 2010 had involved people who had a mental illness or were acting erratically.[50] And at least thirty-seven people with mental illness died in California jails between 2011 and 2017 because staff left them languishing.[51]

Shortly after police arrested Vincent for attacking Kosarian outside her waterfront condo, the San Francisco police released his mug shot. In it, he is arching his head backward, his eyes are wide open, and his face stretches into a wide, unnerving smile.

The following Wednesday, after the preliminary hearing, a judge at San Francisco's superior court let Vincent go free. "The court determined that Mr. Vincent was not a threat to public safety," said the defense attorney. The judge ordered Vincent to stay away from Kosarian and required that he check in with a caseworker to "assess his mental health needs and assist him in navigating the complex legal process ahead." But the judge did not require that he wear an ankle monitor, and so Vincent was free to return to a life of meth, psychosis, and violence.

Kosarian was shocked by the news. "I'm scared. Terrified." After all, Vincent knew where she lived. "I don't understand what more it takes for the city and the judge to understand that this man is a danger," she said.[52] She tweeted at Governor Gavin Newsom, "Please watch this video of me getting attacked at my front door less than 72-hrs ago. The man who attacked me was released this morning because the judge, Christine Van Aken[,] believes that this man is not a danger to our community. PLEASE SAVE OUR CITY!!"[53]

Kosarian's tweet went viral, and within a matter of hours, Breed, Supervisor Matt Haney, and the police officers' union condemned the judge for releasing Vincent. "I think the court's decision to release him while he awaits trial was clearly wrong," said Breed. "This man needs to be receiving mental health services under observation, not back out on the street."[54] The San Francisco Police Association urged the reassignment of the judge to traffic court.[55]

Two days later, the judge held another hearing in which she ordered Vincent to wear an ankle monitor, which allows police to monitor the movements of people under court order. The judge said she had only seen the video later on television, in the media coverage of her initial ruling. "When I saw the video, I was frankly alarmed at the level of violence," she said. "It altered my assessment of the public-safety risk of this case. I take public safety very seriously."[56] The judge implicitly blamed the district attorney's office for not having shown her the video, to which the district attorney's office replied that videos are not typically played at arraignments and that the algorithm that assesses whether a person might re-offend recommended that Vincent remain in custody.

After they saw Vincent's mug shot on television, three other victims came forward to say he had threatened them, too. One person said that Vincent, armed with a knife, had threatened to kill a group who had just left a restaurant and were waiting for an Uber ride, five months before he attacked Kosarian.[57]

San Francisco's treatment of Vincent wasn't unusual. In 2019, a homeless man told a twenty-eight-year-old woman walking to work in downtown San Francisco, "I just want to smell your flowers," grabbed her, and then pushed his nose into her breasts, and tried to rip off her dress and bra. "I screamed and said, 'Get the fuck off me!'" said the woman later. After she threatened to call the police, the man laughed and said, "The cops aren't going to do nothing."[58]

Vincent and others who assault women reportedly boast of their immunity from the law. "He kept saying, 'What are you going to do? Call the cops? They don't care. They're not going to do anything to me,'" said Kosarian. "And he kept repeating that to me."[59] After a fifty-six-year-old woman reported being punched in the back of her head by a man, a police officer told her, "You can press charges, but the judge will probably drop it. It's not going to go anywhere." So she dropped it. "It's a beautiful city," she said, "but there's something broken somewhere."[60]

Kosarian says the most unusual aspect of Vincent's assault on her was simply that it was filmed. "I have ten girlfriends who were punched in the face," she told me in early 2021. "There are too many girls in the city of SF who are vulnerable and getting attacked left and right. Right before I walked to the door there were three guys who walked in. Vincent didn't mess with them. If you're a woman, you are more vulnerable to being attacked."[61]

P art of the problem is that patients outside of institutions stop taking their medications, become psychotic, disaffiliate from their support systems, and end up on the street. It is similar to the process of disaffiliation that occurs in people suffering from drug or alcohol addiction. Some are sent back to prison, which is often the only way the seriously mentally ill get the medical care they need.[62]

"And then, when they're let out of the jails, they're let out with fifty bucks in their pocket and no place to go," said San Francisco psychiatrist Dr. Robert Okin. "It's like these institutions of government are conspiring to create homelessness at the same time that they're trying to eradicate it."[63]

Mentally ill homeless people are less likely to receive care from service providers. "It is very difficult for us to serve someone who has three-, four-, or five-day-old feces on them," said a San Francisco service provider in 2020.[64] California has more than one million individuals with a serious mental illness, according to estimates, and on any given day in 2019, as many as half were untreated. They cycle in between the streets, jails, hospitals, and halfway houses, and there are often few openings in any of those places.[65]

In early 2020 I went to Los Angeles to shadow a Skid Row street doctor, Dr. Susan Partovi. Susan has a warm hippy vibe and is nonjudgmental, making her popular with her patients. In early 2021, the actress Marcia Gay Harden announced on Instagram that she was playing Susan in a forthcoming film.[66] After watching her treat patients in her office on Skid Row, I followed Susan around Los Angeles as she treated people living on the street.

We visited a man who was lying on a mattress near a bus stop. "We call him liquid legs because so much blood and pus come out of them," a homeless outreach worker told us. The man's hair and beard were matted, and his face was red and marked with sores. A small bottle of what appeared to be hard alcohol was next to him on the mattress.

Susan talked with and cared for the man. He had been sleeping when we arrived. She spoke in a sweet and nonthreatening voice. I kept my distance to avoid frightening him. After a few minutes, she persuaded him to let her look at his legs. The man yelped in pain as he removed his socks. I had to turn away after seeing, and smelling, his legs. Susan dabbed lightly at them with hydrogen peroxide. Then the man took the bottle from her and poured the peroxide over his lower legs. He winced in pain. Susan and her two assistants wrapped the man's legs in bandages. After about forty-five minutes, they had finished.

While Susan was treating him, a man who appeared to be in his forties, with a tattoo on the back of his bald head, walked by us and shouted, angrily, "He should be in a hospital!" About fifteen minutes later he walked by again and said, in a normal voice this time, "He's been there for months and the cops won't take him to the hospital." He sounded sad. "Nobody's doing anything."

One block away, as we were leaving, I gave Susan a hug and asked, "What was that all about?"

"That was all about us engaging him so that we can eventually persuade him to come in for treatment," she said. "We started by asking him if we could just treat the dry skin until he finally let us treat the rest of his legs."

But my question was more existential, not practical.

"Why do we let mentally ill people live like that?" I asked.

She rolled her eyes. "Don't ask me. It's your job to figure that out."

California has long been an international psychotherapeutic and psychiatric leader, and voters have repeatedly voted to fund treatment of the mentally ill, including in 2004, when voters passed a ballot initiative that now raises over $2 billion a year for their treatment. The conferences of the main psychological and psychiatric associations are frequently held in San Francisco. The University of California, San Francisco is world-renowned for its psychiatry department. And after World War II, California in general, and the San Francisco Bay Area in particular, became the center for humanistic, post-Freudian psychotherapy.

And yet the numbers of, and trouble with, the homeless mentally ill have risen dramatically. San Francisco General Hospital evaluates 6,100 annually for psychiatric holds, one-third of whom are homeless, but only admits 20 percent of them. While some of them just need to get sober, many of them would benefit from being hospitalized, even if briefly, say experts.[67]

I asked Kelly Kruger, the former San Francisco police sergeant who oversaw the department's psychiatric crisis unit before retiring in 2021, why the city was still failing to treat homeless mentally ill people. "When I was here in the eighties," Kruger said, "St. Mary's [hospital] had an adolescent and children's unit, a geriatric ward, and so did [Sutter Health's California Pacific Medical Center]. [University of California, San Francisco] had an acute, non-acute, geriatric, and children's unit. St. Luke's had an inpatient psych unit where you could get people hospitalized, and that is huge."[68]

Neither San Francisco nor California has enough psychiatric beds. The California Hospital Association recommends having a minimum of 50 beds per 100,000 people, yet the state has less than half that. The European Union has 73 beds per 100,000 people.[69] As of 2020, the San Francisco Bay Area as a whole needed over 2,500 more psychiatric beds to meet the California Hospital Association's goal of 50 inpatient beds for every 100,000 residents.[70] San Francisco General saw its acute inpatient psychiatric beds decline from 88 in 2011 to 19 in 2013. They have not risen since.[71] Across California, the number of psychiatric beds per 100,000 people declined from 30 in 1995 to 17 in 2017.[72]

What's causing the shortage? "Money," said Kruger. "It's always money."[73] John Snook, a researcher and advocate for the mentally ill, agreed. Snook is in his mid-forties and speaks in a measured, almost pastoral tone, even when frustrated. "Homeless guys are not where the money is," he said. "The spine center pays more."[74] California insurance providers pay a lower-than-average reimbursement rate to psychiatrists.[75] It is thus a statewide problem. "There's really not a lot of options for people who need long-term psychiatric treatment or assisted living," said Susan. "Even 'board and cares' [residential group homes] have been like dropping like flies because they only get thirty bucks a day for their residents. And that wasn't sustainable."

Between 2012 and 2019, more than one-third of the board and care group homes in San Francisco that served people under the age of sixty closed their doors. It was more valuable to sell the homes than to be reimbursed by Medi-Cal and Medicare, which was only $1,058 per person per month.[76] The same is occurring nationally. The United States lost 15,000 board and care beds between 2010 and 2016.[77]

California voters in 2004 passed historic legislation, the Mental Health Services Act, Proposition 63, which raises and disburses to the state's

fifty-eight counties over $2 billion per year for the treatment and preven-
tion of serious mental illness. The initiative was promoted to voters as a
way to address untreated mental illness among the homeless. The initiative placed a 1 percent tax on incomes over $1 million, affecting roughly
30,000 taxpayers. It increased the state's spending on mental illness by
nearly one-third. It passed with particularly strong support from Democrats, people in cities, and people in counties with high rates of homelessness.[78] Since its enactment, Proposition 63 revenues have more than
doubled, from $900 million in fiscal year 2005–06 to $2.4 billion in California's fiscal year 2021–22 budget.[79]

California has a 30 percent higher rate of mentally ill people in jails,
and a 91 percent higher rate of mentally ill people on the streets or in
homeless shelters, than the nation as a whole, despite spending $7,300
per patient on mental health services, which is 50 percent more than the
national average.[80]

"There's a shitload of money," said the mental health advisor to Governor Gavin Newsom, psychiatrist Dr. Thomas Insel, who served as the
director of the federal National Institute of Mental Health from 2002 to
2015. "We think $11 billion goes into California's state mental health
budget every year. That makes California the number one in per capita
spending in the United States. No state spends as much as we do. And yet
when you look at the rankings by Mental Health America, and NAMI
[National Alliance on Mental Illness], we're not in the top half. We're 26
for Mental Health America but for children we're number 38. That's not
great."[81]

San Francisco in 2019 spent record amounts on mental illness and
substance abuse, $370 million, of which about two-thirds was spent on
the homeless, and half on homeless who suffer both mental illness and
substance addiction. In December 2019, the Board of Supervisors passed
a measure aimed at extending mental health care to all uninsured or homeless San Franciscans,[82] and in 2020, voters approved a bond measure that

earmarked another $207 million for mental health care, substance abuse treatment, and homelessness services.[83]

"California spends more than most places," said Snook, "and yet it came in near the bottom while Arizona, which spends significantly less, came in near the top. When you look at the amount of money being spent, and then you hear the argument that we need more money, you have to ask, 'How much more?' Right now it's just good money after bad."[84]

Why is that?

8

Madness for Decivilization

For much of human history, people with mental illness were thought to be possessed by gods or devils. Madness, as it was called, was believed to be supernatural, not natural. Some Greeks, including Plato, viewed mental illness as a kind of spiritual gift, a portal into new ways of seeing. Many believed that madness revealed hidden intuitive and mystical knowledge.[1] The idea that mental illness was in fact a way toward wisdom could still be found in the writings of medieval Christian visionaries.[2]

This may have been how people viewed thirteenth-century Catholic Saint Francis of Assisi, after whom San Francisco is named. Francis is known for renouncing his family's wealth and caring for lepers. But he also preached to birds and animals in a state we might today call psychotic, and suffered from what some scholars believe was mental illness.[3] When his parents intervened, possibly by trying to appoint a legal guardian to manage Francis's finances, the local bishop ruled that Francis could have his freedom as an "ecclesiastical person" if he renounced his family and inheritance.[4]

Over time, people came to see madness as a physical illness that interfered with rational thinking and not as a divine blessing or demonic curse.[5] In ancient Greece the physician Hippocrates proposed a naturalistic explanation, and biologically based medicine returned to Europe from the Arab world during the Middle Ages.[6] This view gave rise to mental hospitals and asylums to treat the mentally ill. The English started the first one, Bethlehem Hospital, near London in 1247, or "Bedlam" for short.[7] It was a grim place. "On the second floor is a corridor and cells like those on the first floor," noted a visitor, "and this is the part reserved for dangerous maniacs, most of them being chained and terrible to behold."[8]

In the early eighteenth century, some in Britain condemned madhouses as infringing on rights.[9] The English writer and journalist Daniel Defoe, famous for his novel *Robinson Crusoe*, wrote a pamphlet denouncing the upper-class men who used mental institutions as a way to be rid of their sane wives so that they could more easily indulge in infidelity. Defoe argued that the institutions themselves made women of sound mind fall into madness.[10]

In 1818 the French monarchy hired a researcher to investigate the conditions under which the mentally ill were kept. His report shocked the nation. He described patients kept in tiny, infested, and dark cells where they were barely clothed and had only straw to insulate them from their cold and damp surroundings. The madhouses were so wretched, he concluded, that the French monarchy would not subject their prized wild beasts to the same conditions.[11]

It was a similar story in the rest of Europe. In eighteenth-century Ireland, mentally ill family members were locked in holes five feet beneath their cottage floors, a space too small for most to stand. In Germany, one teenager with mental illness was shackled in a pigpen for so long that he lost the use of his legs; in England, the mentally ill were chained to the floors of workhouses; and in one Swiss city, one-fifth of the mentally ill were restrained constantly.[12]

Mental health found its first great American reformer in Dorothea Dix, who had encountered the nascent mental health reform movement during a visit to Great Britain. Dix crusaded to pull the seriously mentally ill out of abusive and degrading conditions in jails, homes, and poorhouses, and put them in hospitals. She pushed for hospitals to phase out brutal practices like physically restraining patients. Ultimately, her work led to thirty-two asylums being opened. An 1880 survey found that about the same number of mentally ill were living at home (41,083) as lived in hospitals (40,942) while 9,302 were in almshouses, charitable housing that sometimes included basic care services. Only 397 were in jail, making the mentally ill just 0.7 percent of the total jail population.[13]

Dix's humanism was felt in California. San Francisco's Marine Hospital opened in 1850 to care for sick sailors and the mentally ill.[14] Previously, a ship called the *Euphemia* had served as a makeshift mental hospital and jail, where individuals determined to be insane were shuttered in the hold alongside criminals deemed too dangerous to hold on land. Conditions were cramped, with six to eight men crowded into each of the tiny cells.[15] In response, the California legislature one year later established three general hospitals, including the Sacramento State Hospital, which served as a general hospital as well as for the treatment of the mentally ill.

In 1853, the Insane Asylum of California became the first publicly funded mental health facility west of the Missouri River. The resident physician required his attendants to refrain from violence or flashes of anger when caring for patients. He encouraged a sense of self-respect.[16] In 1875, California opened Napa State Asylum, where inmates raised poultry, vegetables, dairy cows, orchards, and other crops.[17]

But over time, state mental hospitals abused their power to involuntarily hospitalize people and grew overcrowded. People were committed for reasons including "excessive masturbation," being "kicked in the head by a mule," and "habitual consumption of peppermint candy."[18] Women who defied social mores were diagnosed with "hysteria."[19] In the 1940s a visitor to one hospital described 250 naked men simply milling about in a large room. "Patients squatted on the damp floor or perched on the window seats. Some of them huddled together in corners like wild animals."[20]

Life magazine in 1946 published an exposé of state mental hospitals. "Hundreds are confined in 'lodges'—bare, bed-less rooms reeking with filth and feces—by day lit only through half-inch holes in steel-plated windows, by night merely black tombs in which the cries of the insane echo unheard from the peeling plaster of the walls."[21]

In response, Congress in 1946 passed, and President Harry Truman signed, the National Mental Health Act, which created the National Institute of Mental Health (NIMH). Congress's intention was for NIMH to focus on "diseases of the nervous system which affect mental health."[22]

But reformers increasingly believed that addressing mental health required much broader societal changes. Many reform leaders viewed mental illnesses like schizophrenia and bipolar disorder as the result of class, racial, and other forms of inequality and oppression, and not the result of biology.[23] Political action was thus necessary to create "mentally healthy" environments, organize tenants, and fight landlords. "The changes I am talking about," said a leader at the new National Institute of Mental Health, "involves a redistribution of wealth and resources."[24]

The big idea was to replace public mental hospitals with 1,500 privately owned, community-based mental health centers. But fewer than half were ever built.[25] Part of the problem was that the leaders of community mental health clinics were unable to impose involuntary care. It is thus partly understandable why they tended to serve the easiest-to-treat.

It is true that Kennedy had envisioned better funded community health centers, and that, over the years, various administrations cut the budgets for this program. But the centers also abused their mandate, sometimes building tennis courts, swimming pools, and rooms for fads like "inhalation therapy" that did nothing to help the people who most needed care.[26] "The people who run the mental health industry are not bad people," emphasized one advocate. "But their goal is no longer to help those with serious mental illness."[27]

The tragic irony is that many of the people who had drawn attention to the poor conditions in mental hospitals had hoped to mobilize the public to increase funding for better care in them, not shut them down entirely.[28] The hospitals had been underfunded because of the Great Depression, and understaffed because of World War II. The population of state mental hospitals had increased from 150,151 to 423,445 between 1903 and 1940. Meanwhile, around half of the hospitals' professional staff worked on the war effort.[29]

Idealism and ideology had triumphed over pragmatism and reason. Between 1948 and 1962, the mental health center that reformers had pointed to as the model had not prevented a single case of mental illness or even treated a single individual with schizophrenia or other major psychiatric disorders.[30] As a result, notes a historian, "The majority of lives were little different than they had had while hospitalized . . . and a significant number were considerably worse off."[31]

Some mental health reformers regretted what they had done. "The deformed creature that has developed from the original community mental health center movement," said one of them, "does not arouse much enthusiasm in any of us who had some more grandiose visions."[32]

In 1961, the French historian Michel Foucault published a book, *Le folie et la raison*, which was translated into English in 1965 as *Madness and Civilization*. The book made Foucault one of the most famous intellectuals in the world, and enormously popular in California, where he taught as a guest lecturer during the mid-1970s. Foucault's book had a major impact on how we treat, and don't treat, the seriously mentally ill.

Foucault argued that the supposedly humanistic treatment of the mad as suffering from mental illness was, in fact, a more insidious form of social control. Before 1500, the mad wandered freely in Europe, Foucault argued. After 1500, Europeans began to medicalize madness, treat it like an illness, as a way not just to control the mad but also to establish what was rational, normal, and healthy for the rest of society. Mental hospitals emerged at a time, Foucault argued, when the state was seeking to impose rational order on societies. And that started with policing the boundary between sane and insane.[33] Foucault even criticized a humanistic asylum in England whose pioneering psychiatrist no longer used physical restraints, which the mentally ill today testify are terrifying and even constitute a kind of torture, on his patients. Said the psychiatrist, "these madmen are so intractable only because they have been deprived of air and freedom."[34]

Foucault wasn't alone in his attack on psychiatry and mental hospitals. In 1961, an American sociologist, Erving Goffman, published an influential book, *Asylums: Essays on the Social Situation of Mental Patients and Other Inmates*, which compared mental hospitals to concentration camps. That same year, a psychiatrist named Thomas Szasz published *The Myth of Mental Illness*, which argued that psychiatrists and others invented the concept of mental illness, with no biological evidence, in order to punish people who were different from the norm.

The anti-psychiatry movement became a cultural phenomenon in 1962 with the publication of Ken Kesey's bestselling novel *One Flew Over the Cuckoo's Nest*. It revolves around a socially deviant but nonetheless sane man who feigns mental illness so he can go to a mental hospital rather than prison. He is drugged, electro-shocked, and eventually lobotomized. The novel was adapted as a Broadway play and an Oscar-winning 1975 film starring Jack Nicholson.

Szasz formed an alliance with the ACLU, which began to crusade politically, and litigate through the courts, for an end to involuntary treatment of the mentally ill.[35] Because psychiatrists were no more reliable at diagnosing mental illness than flipping coins, argued the ACLU's most influential attorney on the matter in 1972, they "should not be permitted to testify as expert witnesses."[36] Said another leading civil rights attorney in 1974, "They [the patients] are better off outside the hospital with no care than they are inside with no care. The hospitals are what really do damage to people."[37]

In early 1973 the journal *Science* published an article, "On Being Sane in Insane Places," by a Stanford sociologist, David Rosenhan, who claimed to have sent research assistants into several mental hospitals where they were misdiagnosed with mental illness. "We now know that we cannot distinguish insanity from sanity," he concluded.[38] The study received widespread publicity and "essentially eviscerated any vestige of legitimacy to psychiatric diagnosis," said the chairman of Columbia's Department of Psychiatry.[39] "Psychiatrists looked like unreliable and antiquated quacks unfit to join in the research revolution," wrote another psychiatrist.[40]

Rosenhan's study became one of the most read and reprinted articles in the history of psychiatry, but a journalist in 2019 published a book describing so many discrepancies that she questioned whether it had ever even occurred. She only found one person who said he had participated in the study, and he said he was treated well by the hospital and had been discharged simply because he asked to leave.[41]

The psychiatric hospitals disappeared, but the anti-psychiatry stigma remained. "I experience stigma every day as a psychiatrist," said one in 2016. "The profession to which I've dedicated my life is the most denigrated and distrusted of all medical specialties. There's no anti-cardiology movement that's trying to stamp out cardiology. And there's no anti-oncology movement that's trying to ban cancer treatment. But there's a very violent anti-psychiatry movement that claims there's no such thing as mental illness and wants to eliminate psychiatry."[42]

That same year, when the chief medical officer of the federal Substance Abuse and Mental Health Services Administration under the Department of Health and Human Services quit her post, she criticized the anti-psychiatry movement. "Unfortunately, SAMHSA does not address the treatment needs of the most vulnerable in our society," she said. "There is a perceptible hostility toward psychiatric medicine; a resistance to addressing the treatment needs of those with serious mental illness; and a questioning by some at SAMHSA as to whether mental disorders even exist."[43]

Liberals and progressives had gone, thanks in part to the ACLU, Foucault, and *One Flew Over the Cuckoo's Nest*, from advocating humanistic psychiatric care to opposing it. Part of the reason progressives demand proof of mental illness in the form of violent assault, murder, or suicide is that they have lost faith in our capacity to recognize it and at times even denied its existence.

9

Medication First

There are two main ways to require long-term psychiatric care in California: conservatorship and assisted outpatient treatment. Under conservatorship, which is called guardianship in other states, a judge appoints a relative or other qualified person to make financial, legal, and other key decisions on behalf of a person deemed "gravely disabled" by a qualified physician. But California courts have been reluctant to apply conservatorships, and so in 2002 the California legislature passed "Laura's Law," named after a college student who was killed by a mentally ill man who had refused psychiatric treatment, to allow for assisted outpatient treatment. Under assisted outpatient treatment, courts can require mentally ill people who do not comply with their treatment plans to be held for up to seventy-two hours to determine if they meet the standard for involuntary hospitalization.[1]

There is good evidence from California and other states that assisted outpatient treatment reduces homelessness and incarceration. Nine of the ten assisted outpatient treatment programs studied in California reduced criminal justice involvement. Six out of seven programs significantly reduced homelessness.[2] Research finds that similar assisted outpatient treatment laws in other states reduced homelessness by up to 74 percent and arrests of the mentally ill by up to 83 percent.[3]

And yet progressive elected officials and civil liberties leaders use strong language to oppose expanded use of either conservatorship or assisted outpatient treatment. "Conservatorship is the biggest deprivation of civil rights aside from the death penalty," said Susan Mizner, an attorney for the American Civil Liberties Union.[4] "We're still coming to grips with the forced sterilizations that went on in our hospital," said Los Angeles County supervisor Sheila Kuehl. "My community, young people in my community, were regularly put away in institutions because being gay was a mental illness. This is different, of course, and the families who say this is different, I respect them and I understand. But, I always worry, as the line goes in *The King and I*, 'Might they not protect me out of everything I own?'"[5]

Opposition to involuntary hospitalization is also behind the failure of California's Mental Health Services Act, Proposition 63, passed in 2004. None of the $2.4 billion raised through Proposition 63's tax on millionaires can be used for involuntary treatment. Twenty percent of MHSA money is allocated by the state to spend to "prevent mental illness from becoming severe and disabling." But much of this money has been spent on ostensibly therapeutic activities for people with milder mental illness, including exercise classes, gardening, and "creative learning circles," rather than on preventative psychiatric treatment of the seriously mentally ill.[6] In 2015, the Little Hoover Commission, an independent oversight body, reported that the "state still cannot definitively quantify who has been helped by Proposition 63 spending and how."[7] The result is that the most difficult mentally ill and addicted homeless people end up becoming the responsibility of the police and criminal justice system.[8]

Where 4 to 5.5 out of every 10,000 people are under conservatorship in neighboring counties, fewer than 1 person per 10,000 San Francisco residents is.[9] The number of people in San Francisco referred to conservatorships actually declined by 143 between 2012 and 2018.[10]

In 2019, San Francisco's Board of Supervisors debated legislation to expand conservatorship to people suffering mental illness and drug addiction. The current law permits California counties to do so only if someone is a chronic user of alcohol or has a serious mental health crisis. The legislation would have changed the law to include people who use drugs or have been 5150'd and taken to Psychiatric Emergency Services eight times in one year.[11] "There are about 100 to 150 people who are clearly mentally ill and who are cycling through the system and who need to be forced into conservatorship," said Mayor Breed. "We know all of them." She noted that 12 percent of people who use services provided by the San Francisco Department of Public Health account for three-quarters of the costs.[12]

The ACLU and progressives on the board fought the measure.[13] San Francisco supervisor Matt Haney, who represents the Tenderloin, opposed the measure because "5150s involve law enforcement. . . . A big focus we've been moving toward is to alleviate negative interactions with law enforcement in the community."[14] "Lots of people came out to oppose it. It was a huge ideological fight," said Rafael Mandelman in 2020. As a result, the final legislation was extremely weak. "The passive form is very hard to implement. It has still not been implemented even in one case in San Francisco."[15]

Opposition by the ACLU and progressives is also behind California's failure to apply for, and receive, federal funding to pay for more psychiatric beds. An obscure provision, the "Institutions for Mental Disease (IMD) Exclusion," prohibits Medicaid from reimbursing states for adults with mental illness who receive long-term care in a psychiatric hospital with more than sixteen beds. The provision requires states to pay 100 percent of the cost of care for the seriously ill who need long-term hospital care, as compared to 50 percent for those treated in the community.[16]

"There's a provision that says Medicaid will now pay for beds in psychiatric hospitals," explained Snook. "Medicaid (Title 19 of the Social Security Act) is a federal health care program for the poor that reimburses states [for] about 50 percent of the cost of care for people enrolled in it. It is an important source of revenue for useful outpatient programs and provides $30 billion to help the mentally ill. It's a no-brainer, but California is hemming and hawing. They don't want to involuntarily hospitalize. But it's self-defeating because you end up with mentally ill [people] in jail because a bed isn't available."[17]

Snook said that applying for the waiver was somewhat complicated, but at bottom the failure of California to do so had more to do with ideology than paperwork. "There are legitimate pieces that have to be figured out," said Snook. "But there's this bullshit stuff of, 'There's no such thing as mental illness,' 'Can you imagine hospitalizing people!' and 'Jails are better than hospitals.'"[18]

Psychiatrists say that's absurd. "I have been in both places and can assure you that the fate of psychiatric patients in prison dungeons is much worse than was their plight in snake pit hospitals," wrote a psychiatrist, in response to such claims. "I have seen cell after cell smeared with excrement and mentally ill prisoners shouting their lungs out or drugged into stupor. And, our patients are especially vulnerable to physical and sexual abuse. They are disproportionately represented as victims of the 200,000 rapes that occur in prisons each year."[19]

Lack of legal tools to impose involuntary care has made some parents of the seriously mentally ill desperate enough to support the arrest of their children. "[The officers] said, 'Do you want to press charges?' And I said 'Absolutely,'" said one mother. "It's the only way. If they're not willing to go for help, there's nothing you can do."[20]

But since San Francisco, Los Angeles, and other progressive cities have largely stopped enforcing the laws against public defecation and open-air drug use, the police do not make those arrests and often do not investigate violations of the law by potentially mentally ill homeless people, as I discovered after calling the police on more than six separate occasions in between late 2020 and early 2021 to report people who were psychotic and a potential danger to themselves and others. In one instance, a half-naked man crashed into the glass windows at the front of our retail offices in Berkeley, collapsing outside the Italian restaurant next door. In another, a highly intoxicated man wandered into traffic wearing dark clothes and was nearly hit by a car.

LA street doctor Susan Partovi contrasts our society's treatment of psychosis to our treatment of dementia. "My mom has dementia now," she said. "Serious Alzheimer's. She would have been homeless had I not been around. We don't have a problem telling our demented family members, 'You need to go to home care and take this medicine.' And eventually they do. Why is that different than a psychiatric illness?"[21]

Today, the problem facing the mentally ill homeless in California is the exact opposite to the one Foucault worried about, concluded UCLA sociologist Neil Gong. The way social workers on Skid Row in Los Angeles care for the homeless mentally ill "does not aim at the deep internalizations of norms, as in a Foucauldian model," wrote Gong. "It is driven primarily by the dynamics of legal liability, as workers must both try to prevent danger and avoid violating patient rights." Therapy is oriented toward very modest goals like trying to get a woman to stop banging her head against the wall, according to Gong.

As such, the criminalization rather than hospitalization of the mentally ill represents a triumph of the anti-psychiatrists. "Recall that US thinkers like Szasz," writes Gong, "advocated a radical libertarianism that saw criminal trial as fairer than hospitalization, and in some sense the American criminalization and social abandonment of mad people resembles this model."[22]

In his memoir, former San Francisco mayor Willie Brown writes, "I discovered factors—some bureaucratic, some political—working in a kind of evil synthesis with each other that really prevented the long-term homeless from entering the system. Backing this up was a collection of so-called activists with heavy political clout who absolutely believed (and still believe) that homeless people should have a right to live on the street. They believed that homeless people had an absolute right to do everything they were doing, no matter how harmful to themselves or to the rest of the citizenry."[23]

Susan agrees. "California is really one of the worst states when it comes to taking care of seriously mentally ill," she said. "I think a lot has to do with civil liberties. It's really ingrained in the culture."[24]

At a shelter in Amsterdam, during my second trip in the fall of 2019, I watched Rene Zegerius argue with an intelligent man with severe Asperger's who was refusing to attend a work placement opportunity that was waiting for him, and with a mentally ill woman whose daughter had been taken from her custody by the government. He told them both they would get better housing if they followed their plans. After Rene offered the woman an apartment of her own if she took her medication, she stormed out in a rage. She sat in the courtyard of the shelter and smoked a joint. I watched the expressions of Rene and the two other social workers. They seemed strangely calm.

"That's okay to let her smoke marijuana like that?" I asked.

Everyone kind of shrugged. Rene said that marijuana was better than other drugs, including alcohol.

"Could you offer to reunite her with her daughter," I asked, "if she took her meds?"

"That would have been the next thing I would have offered," he said.

By offering better housing in exchange for behavior change, Rene was practicing contingency management, which, studies over the last three decades find, results in the largest and most long-lasting reductions in alcohol and drug use of all kinds of treatment,[25] and works well for people with serious mental illness.[26]

In a major recent review of the literature, out of 176 controlled studies, 151 of them, or 86 percent, found contingency management to be effective for treating addiction, with the average effect size ranging from moderate to large. On average, a small but significant effect remained even after incentives were discontinued.[27] It significantly increased participation in therapy, a key component of addiction recovery.[28] Contingency management can also reduce psychiatric hospitalizations, improve financial management, and raise the quality of life for the mentally ill suffering substance abuse disorder.[29]

A large, randomized controlled trial among the seriously mentally ill, two-thirds of whom were homeless, found that the participants who received the contingency management intervention were 2.4 times more likely to be abstinent than the control group. Contingency management had a very low cost compared to other forms of drug treatment, just over $100 per week per participant. Those receiving contingency management were one-fifth as likely to be hospitalized for psychiatric reasons. And "abstinence persisted after treatment was discontinued," researchers found, which has been replicated by many subsequent studies.[30]

Contingency management harnesses well-established psychological principles, which is likely why it works for such a wide number of people and such a large spectrum of drugs, including both opioids and stimulants. Contingency management is based on the psychological theory of operant conditioning. It emphasizes the need for concrete and immediate reinforcements, such as housing or a gift card, in exchange for good behavior, including abstinence, work, and compliance with psychiatric medicines. Contingency management swaps one set of rewards, such as meth and heroin, for another set of rewards, such as gift cards and apartment units.

Operant conditioning was called "behaviorism" in the sixties and seventies. It gained a bad reputation when some people took it too far and viewed humans purely as animals driven by instinct. But, since then, psychologists have demonstrated that humans are significantly motivated by tangible, real-world rewards, and that operant conditioning can be used humanely.

Despite the evidence in favor of contingency management, it remains rarely used in the United States. Part of the reason is that it has been unpopular with some policy makers and practitioners, who are skeptical that it makes a difference over the long term. But contingency management has been included in the National Registry of Evidence-Based Programs and Practices, adopted and implemented by the Department of Veterans Affairs, as well as by the governments and medical establishments of the United Kingdom, Brazil, and China. Hundreds of studies, meta-analyses, and reviews published in the world's leading scientific journals conclude that contingency management works as well as, and often better than, any other drug treatment.[31]

One concern is that people need internal motivation to stay abstinent and cannot depend on external reinforcements because once the external reinforcements are gone, their self-destructive behaviors will return. But there is evidence that external reinforcements build internal strength over time.[32] And even if contingency management only kept people externally motivated, that might be okay, given the high cost to society of addiction and the cost savings from abstinence.

Assertive case management is critical to keeping the mentally ill out of jails and prisons, said Rene. He told me about helping a man with schizophrenia. "His mother came to me twenty-five years ago, when he was twenty-five," said Rene. "He was on the streets. He didn't have contact with anyone. He didn't want to go to a shelter. I got in contact with him. We connected." Rene paused. "Sometimes you do something that you're not supposed to do, but [that] you have to do. I did not do anything wrong. But two times I grabbed him and said, 'If you do not listen, you get in trouble with me.' I don't know what kind of trouble, but that's just . . . That's just something that I said.

"So, I went with him to a shelter with a lot of different sort of patients, and with a room for himself. We made sure that he blended in with all the other crazy people. He stayed there for a few weeks, and then I wanted to take him the next step, which would be medication. He didn't want to take it. So with the police I admitted him against his will to the psychiatric hospital. I did that twice.

"Later on, I had the opportunity to get him to [the] next level of sheltering, et cetera, et cetera. Now he's living on his own with a car and a job. He calls me every Friday to say how he did that week. He uses Leponex [clozapine], which is a lot. He's still psychotic, but he can discuss it with me. One time he said, 'I think there are people in my garden watching me.' I said, 'Please close the curtains.' He does so and then says, 'Okay. It worked.'"[33]

In early 2020 I asked two ACLU representatives about their organization's position toward involuntary psychiatric treatment as an alternative to incarceration for the mentally ill who break the law. "We support the Housing First model, not involuntary treatment," said ACLU attorney Jamie Crook, "which has proven to be ineffective and has violated liberties without keeping people off the streets."[34] Said her colleague Eve Garrow, "All of the research to date shows that coercive or involuntary outpatient treatment is no more effective and sometimes less effective than voluntary treatment. We're very much against it."

But comparing voluntary to involuntary treatment isn't an apples-to-apples comparison. Two different groups of people are being compared, those who admit they have a problem and those who do not. Everybody would prefer 100 percent voluntary treatment. But the fact that involuntary treatment may be less effective than voluntary treatment is not an argument against it, since it might be a better alternative than incarceration, homelessness, or crime.

"Do you think people are living in tents on Skid Row because they are too poor to afford an apartment?" I asked.

"The root cause," said Garrow, "no matter how a person falls into homelessness, the root cause is always the scarcity of affordable housing."

I asked the ACLU's lead attorney on the issue, Susan Mizner, why the ACLU opposed conservatorship for people suffering psychosis but not for people with dementia. "What's the difference? Is it because one is about aging and the other about mental illness?"

"The biggest difference," she said, "is that dementia tends to be more constant and deteriorating whereas psychiatric disabilities are more episodic and responsive to treatment."

"I think a fair number of psychiatrists would say that untreated psychosis is degenerative," I said.

"I said 'responsive to treatment,'" she said.

"So because it's responsive to treatment, less coercion is merited?"

"Because it's responsive to treatment and because coercion in treatment hasn't been shown to be more effective."

"So let's say somebody defecates ten times on the sidewalk, is finally arrested and brought to the courts. Would you favor a situation where that person would have the option of getting psychiatric care as an alternative to prison or jail?"

"I would favor the option of them not being arrested in the first place. That whole scenario is problematic."

"So what do we do about people with psychosis who defecate in public? Who shoot drugs in public? Should they be treated any differently than somebody who is not showing signs of mental illness?"

"We should be using more models like full-service partnerships where we have persistent and patient outreach that develops relationships with the individuals and meets them where they are, so that the trust develops and then moves them into housing and treatment," she said. "A case manager or a social worker needs to build [rapport] with someone to overcome that individual experience and the psychosis."

"So which laws, specifically, should we not enforce?" I asked. "Because what you said is that we should not enforce the law against public defecation. Is that the only one or are there other laws that we, in your view, should not enforce?"

"I'm not saying we shouldn't enforce them, period," she said. "If a frat guy gets too much to drink and decides to use my driveway as his bathroom, I've not only said I would get him ticketed, but I've made him come and clean it up. There's a different level of capacity involved when the homeless guy who's talking to himself is in my driveway. I go and talk to him and bring him something to eat and ask him if he has a place to stay and try and develop a relationship with him."

"I'm dealing with people defecating, not urinating," I said. "I'm not sure it's my job to evaluate whether the person is mentally ill or just a drunk frat boy."

"I don't want to say that what they're doing isn't harmful," she said, "but you have to have *mens rea* to be committing a crime."

Mens rea is a legal term. It is Latin for "guilty mind," and refers to a person's awareness that what he is doing is wrong and illegal. The standard is usually that a person knows, or should know, that what they are doing is illegal.

"The frat guy knows he should not be pooping in your driveway," she said. "The guy who's psychotic may not know."[35]

In other words, for Mizner and the ACLU, the mentally ill are too impaired to be held accountable for breaking the law but not impaired enough to justify the same kind of treatment we provide to other people suffering mental disabilities, such as dementia. Understanding this, and the power of the ACLU in progressive cities and states such as San Francisco and California, goes a long way toward understanding the addiction, untreated mental illness, and homelessness crisis.

I told John Snook about my conversation with the ACLU. "[Progressives] say there isn't enough treatment, but it's the only place they make that argument," he said. "They never flag the fact that it's because of their work shutting down the mental hospitals in the past, and that California would have the Medicaid waiver if it were not worried about what the ACLU had to say."[36]

The ACLU's continuing political power to prevent psychiatric treatment of the seriously mentally ill upsets retired University of California, San Francisco psychiatrist Dr. Robert Okin. "Civil rights lawyers," he said, "were more interested in people's civil rights than their lives."[37]

While the ACLU is powerful, there is a growing movement for reform comprising natural, if seemingly unlikely, allies: psychiatrists, street doctors, police officers, and civil rights leaders. Relationships are emerging between doctors and police. And there is growing bipartisan support in both liberal and conservative states for getting the seriously mentally ill the care they need.

Dr. Thomas Insel, Gavin Newsom's mental health advisor, said that New York provided better mental health services and that doing so was enough to overcome ACLU opposition to greater use of involuntary care. "In New York they said, 'Take your medicine, but we're also going to provide you with eighteen different things that will give you a reason to take your medicine and a reason to care.'"[38]

"Was opposition from the ACLU easier to overcome," I asked, "because New York had a proper system of care?"

"Yeah, that's right," said Insel. Even so, he said, the radical antipsychiatry movement remained opposed to expanding conservatorships. "[Sacramento mayor] Darrell [Steinberg] has put together these forums on conservancy and how to change current regulations. I've sat in on one or two of them. They're pretty frustrating, frankly. It's been hard to find common ground."

Insel felt that federal reforms would eliminate the requirement that

California apply for the special exemption to receive Medicaid money to treat the mentally ill, and noted that 2021 federal stimulus was "pumping a ton of money into this." The problem, said Insel, is that "[t]he people who are running this [in the federal government] don't even know who to deal with in California because there is no state department of mental health the way you have in other states."

In their reflective moments, I found that many progressives agreed that more involuntary treatment is needed. I asked progressive Berkeley homelessness advocate Boona Cheema, whose son was mentally ill and committed suicide, if we used conservatorships enough. "No, we don't," she said. "Somebody comes in who has been walking naked in the streets and is manic, and you take them in and then you let them out two days later. Come on. They haven't even been stabilized!"[39]

Said homeless housing provider Louis Chicoine, "Last year, we went to a concert and on the way back, this woman's on the [BART train] platform and is just out of it. I mean it's hard to imagine someone more out of it. She had a crack pipe. She was most likely seriously mentally ill and self-medicating. I want to protect people's rights, but how are we protecting this woman's rights when she's five feet from falling on the tracks and being run over?"

Continued Chicoine, "I could call someone, and they'd tell me they can't do anything about it because she's not literally a threat to herself or someone else. We're careful about saying this publicly because we want to stay allied with the people we serve. But there's a truth in the need to remove from some people the right to do whatever the hell they want when they have absolutely no control of themselves."[40]

Insel said he felt the people of California would come around once they understood the problem. "I started from a civil libertarian perspective," he said. "But at the end of the day, I don't want to see people die with their rights on. That's not the solution."[41]

Susan Partovi expressed hopes for a long-acting anti-psychosis medicine. "I've gotten four people on injectable, once-a-month anti-psychotic treatment," she said. "People have proven that they can't take medications on their own, but they're willing to take the injection. It's night and day. Now they're able to think clearly and accept resources. One of them refused to be with a roommate, but now she's got a place to stay with a roommate. She's off the streets going to homeless health care for her drug treatment program. I'm almost thinking now that for some people, it's not Housing First, it's Medication First."[42]

10

Not Everyone's a Victim

When Jabari Jackson was a teenager growing up in the Mission District of San Francisco in the 1980s, he started losing friends. "We went camping up in Lake Sonoma, and Kermit drowned. He was the baby of the crew. We all grew up together. A year after that, Gerald got shot in the head. Then this guy Kala got killed. A couple of other people got killed. It was like somebody was dying every month."

As Jabari told me about his experience turning to drugs and alcohol, he spoke with the matter-of-fact tone of a man who had confronted his demons. "My addiction started when I was like sixteen," he said. "I was smoking weed and drinking." Soon he switched to crack cocaine. By his mid-thirties Jabari was using heroin. The result was, he said, "multiple times of incarceration, homelessness, crime, theft, violence, and drug abuse." Jabari said he sometimes stayed awake for many days at a time while high. He sometimes slept on the street, standing up, and sometimes in cars that he stole. "It was to a point where all my money I get, I'll spend it on dope. I mean, I would sit in the house and not eat. I was just really full-blown into my addiction at that point in time. I came down with congestive heart failure, and I got hospitalized. My body was breaking down on me."[1]

While just 6 percent of San Francisco residents are, like Jabari, African American, 37 percent of the homeless are.[2] "When we look at the homeless population, we see an over-representation of African Americans," said Jennifer Friedenbach of the San Francisco Coalition on

Homelessness. "We see everyone who is facing oppression reflected in the homeless population."[3]

Domestic violence and child abuse contribute to homelessness. "The loss of your network safety net is really what tips people into homelessness in general. People are desperately poor all the time," said Housing First advocate Jen Loving, "but what is the thing that creates the tip? Domestic violence."[4] Said Vicki Westbrook, who spent two years in prison for dealing methamphetamine to support her addiction, "We tend to have more substance abuse and more mental health issues, more trauma, and our trauma is usually sexual trauma. A lot of times, we end up in prison because of toxic relationships."[5] "A lot of the kids on the street have the same type of story," said Adam Mesnick, the San Francisco restaurant owner. "There was some sort of mental or physical abuse. There were addictive personalities and addicted parents."[6]

It's a myth that people are on the street by choice, say advocates for the homeless. "Homeless people didn't create homelessness," said Paul Boden, cofounder of the Coalition on Homelessness. "It was not a lifestyle choice where, in the early eighties, a bunch of us sat around and said, 'Oh fuck this. I want to sleep in the street.'"[7] Said Kristen Marshall of the Harm Reduction Coalition, "The vast majority of people experiencing homelessness did nothing to be out here other than lose their housing, get traumatized, live with over-policing, come from generations of poverty, and not have access to jobs or stability."[8]

The US government has cut welfare and housing subsidies while subsidizing middle- and upper-middle-class homeowners, advocates for the homeless say.[9] Welfare reform in 1996, which reduced the number of people receiving cash benefits from 12.3 million to 4.4 million between 1996 and 2011, resulted in a 130 percent increase in the number of households with children that survive on less than two dollars per person per day.[10]

People dehumanize the homeless, perpetuating their victimization. "When we look at newspaper articles, when we look at how homeless people are talked about, they're often referred to as trash, they're referred to as junkies, they're referred to as basically less than human," Frieden-bach said.[11] Around the United States, cities have criminalized camping, lying, and sitting on sidewalks. One-third of America's largest 187 cities have citywide bans on camping, and half have bans on camping in particular public places. Citywide bans increased 60 percent between 2011 and 2014.[12]

In 2016, a start-up founder in San Francisco sparked outrage after he published an open letter where he called the homeless "riff-raff," lamented that he shouldn't have to see the homeless on his way to work each day, and demanded San Francisco's leaders do something about it.[13] His letter attracted attention from the international news media. "In an open letter to the city's mayor Ed Lee," wrote the *Guardian*, "entrepreneur Justin Keller said he is 'outraged' that wealthy workers have to see people in pain and despair." The reporter referred disparagingly to the man as a "tech bro."[14]

For about forty years, from 1930 to 1970, black families were denied loans and channeled into renting rooms, whereas white families were encouraged to buy homes.[15] The Home Owners' Loan Corporation, a federal agency, designated some neighborhoods as "hazardous" for lenders before the Fair Housing Act of 1968, and the segregation caused by this policy is still measurable today in many cities.[16] And exclusionary housing policies didn't come to an end, scholars argue; they simply took the form of opposition to new homes and apartment buildings for "quality of life" and environmental reasons.[17]

Racism contributes to homelessness, addiction, and overdose, argue progressives. African Americans suffered 25 percent of overdose deaths in 2020.[18] Half of the inmates of San Francisco's county jails are African American, and 75 percent suffer from substance addiction, serious mental illness, or both.[19]

"My friend who I worked with for years, who did not use drugs, but was homeless, got hit by a car," said Marshall. "And because he was a black man who fit some stereotype for medical providers, they sent him home with ibuprofen. What are you going to do? You're going to find something that makes you feel better. If it would have happened to me, I would have been given whatever I needed. But because he was black, and used heroin, he passed away. And so instead of being regulated, so you know what's in those pills, to get relief from being hit by a car, you're going to say, 'Just say no'? You're going to blame him for not being in pain?"[20]

But if poverty, trauma, and structural racism cause addiction, why did addiction worsen over the same period that poverty, trauma, and racism declined?

Trauma from child and partner violence is at its lowest level in decades and perhaps hundreds of years. Crimes of violence against children, including rape, assault, and robbery, declined by one- to two-thirds between 1992 and 2010.[21] Total reported child abuse during the same period declined 62 percent. And the number of children who were spanked or otherwise received physical discipline declined by one-third between 1975 and 2014.[22]

Few nations have achieved a higher material standard of living than the United States. Just 2 percent of Americans who graduate from high school, live in a family with at least one full-time worker, and wait to have children until after turning twenty-one and marrying, in what is known as the "success sequence," are in poverty. According to research by the Brookings Institution, 70 percent of those who follow the success sequence enjoy middle-class or higher incomes, defined as at least 300 percent of the poverty line.[23]

In the fifty years between 1970 and 2019, per capita income in the United States rose from $18,719 to $39,156 in 2019 dollars. True, white and Asian per capita incomes were higher at $41,374 and $44,880, respectively, compared to black and Latino incomes of $27,024 and $23,289. But per capita income still rose 84 percent among Hispanic people and 145 percent among black people.[24] And a declining share of incomes today go to many basic necessities, allowing for far greater material wealth. In 1960, the average American family spent 24 percent of its income on meals at home. In 2019, it spent just 6 percent.[25]

US government programs have proven remarkably effective at reducing poverty. By 2012, social programs had lifted 40 million Americans out of poverty, which was fifteen times more than they had in 1967. Progressives point out that pretax inequality today is far higher, which is true. But the social safety net today is also much more effective. Government programs in 1967 reduced the would-be poverty rate by only 1.3 percentage points. By 2012, government programs, including welfare and the Earned Income Tax Credit, reduced poverty from 29 percent to 16 percent.[26]

It's true that the backlash to the overprescription of opioids has in many cases resulted in doctors undertreating pain, particularly of black patients, but such undertreatment also appears to have saved over 14,000 black lives, according to a *New York Times* estimate based on peer-reviewed research.[27] The psychiatrist Sally Satel notes that most patients have no trouble with opioids, with estimates of pharmaceutical opioid addiction or abuse ranging from 1 to 8 percent of patients. The patients most likely to abuse opioids suffer from a mental health condition, in particular depression. More careful screening, patient education, and follow-up can help.[28] But achieving the right balance between treating pain and avoiding addiction is complex, difficult, and not reducible to simplistic claims about discrimination.

One thing everyone can agree on is the need to reduce the *need* for opioids. And when it comes to physical suffering from accidents, we have. Although preliminary estimates show a spike in traffic fatalities in the pandemic year of 2020, the rate of fatality and injury from car accidents has still declined long-term. The latter saw a decline of 36 percent in the last thirty years, from 1,305 injuries per 100,000 people in 1990 to 835 per 100,000 people in 2019, the latest year for which numbers are available.[29]

It was wrong that the federal government channeled black families into rental apartments and white people into subsidized homeownership after World War II, but few argue that racism *increased* since then, and on many measures it declined significantly in the period that addiction worsened. The 1964 Civil Rights Act mandated desegregation by institutions that received federal money. In 1968 the Fair Housing Act closed loopholes on discriminatory lending. And governments, universities, and firms have used affirmative action programs to promote people of color to positions of power within organizations since 1965.

America's social safety net has expanded dramatically over the last half century. New programs included Supplemental Security Income (SSI) program (1972); the Women, Infants, and Children (WIC) nutrition program (1972); Pell Grants (1972); the Earned Income Tax Credit (1975); the child support program (1975); Low Income Home Energy Assistance Program (1981); Children's Health Insurance Program (1997); Medicare Part D subsidy for low-income Americans (2003); and the Affordable Care Act (2010).

The disabled have gone from being treated as subhuman a mere century ago to being treated with more dignity and generosity than many thought possible. Federal financial support for people with disabilities, both physical and mental, has grown nearly fourfold, from $40 billion in 1978 to $149 billion in 2019, adjusted for inflation.[30]

Before the passage of welfare reform in 1996, Congress and President Bill Clinton significantly expanded the Earned Income Tax Credit, which gives money directly to low-income workers, and disability payments in the form of Supplemental Security Income. The Earned Income Tax Credit transferred $66 billion in 2017, which is nearly three times as much as it redistributed in 1992 (in constant 2017 dollars).[31]

And, in early 2021, Congress passed and President Joe Biden signed into law a $1.9 trillion pandemic relief plan that could reduce the number of Americans living in poverty by a third, raising nearly 13 million Americans out of poverty. The package expands the Child Tax Credit, the Earned Income Tax Credit, and the child and dependent care tax credit. It also provides $1,400 stimulus checks to millions of Americans, including to the homeless. "This legislative package likely represents the most effective set of policies for reducing child poverty ever in one bill, especially among Black and Latinx children," said a policy expert at Georgetown University.[32]

Women have never been freer, richer, or more powerful. In 1970, just 4 percent of women earned more than their husbands;[33] today, 29 percent earn more than their male spouses.[34] Today, girls match or outperform boys in education in the developed world.[35] Spousal homicides have declined since the 1960s thanks to better policing as well as more protections for victims, such as restraining orders, shelters for victims, and automatic arrests of suspects of domestic violence.[36]

Few minority groups have achieved more progress in a shorter amount of time than the lesbian, gay, bisexual, trans, and queer communities have. In 2015, the US Supreme Court required states to grant same-sex couples the right to marry. Afterward, Americans' approval of rights for same-sex couples soared. Support for same-sex marriages rose from 27 percent to 70 percent in the span of twenty years. Between 1977 and 2019, Americans' belief that gay people should have equal job opportunities and the ability to adopt climbed from 56 to 93 percent and from 14 to 75 percent, respectively. [37]

While people still say dehumanizing things about the homeless, doing so certainly isn't good politics. Quite the opposite. Over the last decade, the governor of California and the mayors of San Francisco, Los Angeles, and Seattle have made helping the homeless a centerpiece of their election campaigns. All have expressed great compassion and sympathy for the homeless. And all have significantly expanded the amount of money they spend on housing, shelter, and services.

As for the San Francisco technology entrepreneur who supposedly dehumanized the homeless, the *Guardian* took his words out of context. The man did not say he was outraged "that wealthy workers have to see people in pain and despair"; that was simply how the *Guardian* reporter spun it. In fact, the man expressed, however poorly, the sadness, anger, and disgust that the vast majority of us feel when we see people suffering mental illness and severe drug addiction living, defecating, and shooting drugs on the sidewalk. And he explicitly recognized that the homeless were in "pain, struggle, and despair," and noted that we all share in the responsibility to address the problem.

It is worth putting today's treatment of the homeless in historical context. California's constitution in 1879 authorized local governments to arrest beggars, vagrants, and the poor if they were Chinese. In 1941, California defended before the US Supreme Court a law that resulted in a man being incarcerated for six months simply for bringing his homeless brother-in-law into the state. The US Supreme Court rejected California's argument, and struck the law down, saying "poverty and immorality are not synonymous."[38]

Over the last fifty years, public attitudes, laws, and the courts have all grown significantly more liberal. In 1972, the Supreme Court strongly restricted the enforcement of vagrancy laws, which in some states had targeted African Americans.[39] In 1993, a federal court ruling prevented New York City from banning panhandling because, it ruled, begging is a form of protected free speech.[40] In 2006, the Ninth Circuit Court of Appeals blocked Los Angeles from enforcing a 1968 law that outlawed sleeping on sidewalks.[41] And in 2020, the Supreme Court upheld a 2018 ruling by a lower court against the city of Boise, Idaho, which found that cities cannot impose or enforce camping bans unless "shelter" were "practically available."[42]

During the pandemic, the federal government gave cities funding to pay for hotel rooms for many homeless to stay in, free of charge, for most of the pandemic, and when it received the coronavirus vaccine, San Francisco and most other cities vaccinated its homeless population early in the process.[43] The city spends a share of its budget that is 50 percent larger than the share spent by New York City and six times more than the share spent by Chicago on homelessness. San Francisco increased its spending on homelessness from $157 million to $567 million between 2011 and 2022.[44]

While it's true that people on the street suffer higher rates of eviction, trauma, and abuse than people who don't live on the street, it's also true that the vast majority of people who lose their housing, get traumatized, live with over-policing, and come from generations of poverty *aren't* living on the street, or addicted to heroin, fentanyl, and meth. The choices that evicted, traumatized, and over-policed people make must matter, otherwise the number of homeless would be far higher.

L ate one night, while out on the town in the mid-1990s, when Jabari Jackson was in his early twenties, his girlfriend wanted to go home, but his friends wanted to drive around.

"Come on, baby," she said. "Let's go home. Let's go home. Let's go."

Jabari didn't want to. He ignored her.

"No, no, let's go," she pled.

"Ah, fuck that," he said. "I'm going ridin'. I'm going to do this. I'll call you later."

"No, come on," she begged, pulling on his arm. "Let's go home. Come on, let's go home."

But she couldn't change his mind. Jabari hopped in the car with his friends and drove off to Twenty-Fourth and Shotwell in the Mission District.

Jabari grew up middle-class, not poor, in the Mission, and went to

Catholic school. "I went to good schools," he said. "After grammar school, I went to Riordan, an all-boys Catholic school."

Jabari rebelled. "The big homies in the neighborhood was either in and out of prison, sold dope, pimping, gangbanging, and so those was the people that I idolized. Those were the guys that I saw every day. Those are the ones with the gold chains and the money and the girls and the cars. And I'm sitting out there like, 'I want to be like these guys right here.'"

Jabari is, like all of us, a product of his environment, but he emphasizes, "The streets didn't choose me, I chose the streets. I was excited by gangbanging. I was excited about dope dealing. I wanted to be a part of that lifestyle. I wanted to be that guy on the corner. I wanted to be that guy with the money in my pocket. I wanted to be a part of the nightlife. I wanted to be the guy with the girls all around me with the jewelry. I want to be this person with the gold chains, the beeper, the fly clothes, the money in the pocket, all the girls standing by the cars."

Jabari started dealing drugs in the open-air market around Twenty-Fourth Street and Hampshire Street in the Mission District. "Drinking, hanging out on the block, coming home late. Around this time I started dabbling with cocaine, snorting cocaine. Drugs were always a part of the thing because all my friends was drug dealers. We all sold dope, we all hustled on the block. Then it was just crazy after that. Boom: girlfriends, buying cars. I'm out there selling dope."

Jabari was arrested the night his girlfriend urged him to go home. He jumped out of the car when he and his friends saw two men walking down the street. "We hit one of the guys, got the money, jumped back in the car, went to the gas station," Jabari said. But then Jabari and his friends did something dumb. "Instead of going home then, we decided to go back and drive around the place where we just committed this crime."

Police pulled them over. Jabari and his friends fit the description. Officers found the stolen money and a gun. The district attorney's office charged Jabari with strong-armed robbery, assault, and battery. Prosecutors added a hate crime charge because the two men they had assaulted turned out to be gay.

But the day Jabari was scheduled to stand trial, a woman walked into the courtroom, whispered something to Jabari's attorney, and the judge dismissed the jury. "Mr. Jackson, this is your lucky day," the judge said. "We're just going to put you on probation, credit time served. We're going to let you go."

It turned out that Jabari's father's best friend was close with the district attorney. "My dad worked some kind of magic for me," said Jabari. By contrast, the other men involved in the mugging were sentenced to prison or to Walden House, a men's residential treatment facility.

Jabari was arrested many times over the next two decades but was given relatively short sentences. Finally, in April 2018, San Francisco police arrested Jabari and eleven other people for a string of sixty burglaries in the Bay Area. According to police, the thefts were being committed by serial burglars and netted eleven stolen firearms, hundreds of pieces of jewelry, US and foreign currency, credit cards, and passports altogether worth an estimated $3 million. Police arrested Jabari for possession of stolen property, vehicle theft, and stolen credit cards.

Looking back now, Jabari doesn't play the victim. He says he had no one to blame but himself. "That was my punk-ass way of justifying all I did to everybody," he said. "Because deep down inside I was a really selfish motherfucker, man. You know what I mean? I had no rhyme or reason or remorse for nobody. It was me, me, me, you know what I mean? And if I messed anything up, I can beg that, 'Oh, I'm sorry. It's going to be okay. I'll never do it again.' Just like a spoiled child."[45]

When I told Tom Wolf that Jabari had ascribed his addiction and life of crime to being spoiled, not traumatized, he laughed.

"There's similarities between him and me," said Tom. "I was kind of spoiled."

I asked him why he laughed.

"Because the narrative on Twitter, and with addiction doctors, is all about being 'trauma-informed,'" said Tom. "But it's not like everybody who got hooked on drugs did so because they experienced trauma. I can't tell you how many stories I've heard of, 'I was at a party and I had a beer and it changed how I felt and who I am, and then it became an addiction.'"[46]

The criminal justice system failed Jabari not because it was too hard on him but because it wasn't hard enough. Time and again, Jabari was arrested and either let go or given an extremely light sentence. Ultimately what stopped Jabari was his failing health, after decades of cocaine and alcohol abuse, not the criminal justice system.

University of Minnesota anthropologist Teresa Gowan discovered that many homeless men reject the victim identity. "[Del] adamantly refused to play the victim. To do so would violate the core of his way of seeing," she notes.[47] "Ray had become uncomfortable with the idea of being classed as a victim of homelessness," she writes.[48] And "Lee fiercely rejected the victim role. He never referred to himself as homeless, for example, and in fact used 'homeless' as a term of abuse for those unable to 'keep themselves together.'"[49]

They identified as hustlers, not victims. "Del would construct every interaction with healthcare or service agencies as an opportunity to display his hustling craft," explains Gowan.[50] Some homeless men Gowan befriended expressed relief at not having to play the victim in front of her. "'Seriously, it's cool with me, this research deal,'" said one of the men. "'To be honest, it is a big relief to drop the bullshit. Just be *real*, you know. I can get kinda down out here.'"[51] Some homeless express gratitude for their relative privilege. "I'm not one of these homeless people that thinks everybody owes him something," said one man who suffered from addiction, "because I still eat better and live better than probably 95 percent of the world's population."[52]

Others evince a discernment bordering on entitlement. "Ever since I arrived in Berkeley three years ago, after previously living on the streets in New Orleans, Oakland and San Francisco," a man wrote in a letter to the editor of a Berkeley news site, "several shelters have disappointed me, particularly when I wanted to take a shower . . . several of the ones I've stayed at also required you to sit through an hour of a 'praise God, halle-lujah, soul-saving' service."[53]

And many acknowledge that, for some homeless people, being home-less is indeed a choice. "To say that people choose to become homeless seems indecent," noted a Harvard sociologist in the early 1990s. "But the homeless are not just passive victims. They make choices, like everyone else."[54]

A formerly homeless man who lived in shelters and in a tent in Seat-tle's Pioneer Park told me in early 2021, "For a lot of people here, being homeless is a choice." Said the father of a recent high school graduate who died from fentanyl poisoning in 2020, "She was homeless on purpose. She chose to be there [in Echo Park, Los Angeles]."

"To camp out and do drugs?" I asked.

"Yeah," he said. "I guess, better than living at home, and she was out there feeling her oats. It was what she chose to do."[55]

Even Paul Boden, who was once homeless himself, grudgingly ad-mits that the unsheltered homeless have *some* amount of choice. "Well, if your only other option is a gospel mission," he said, "fuck yeah, I'm there by choice."[56]

Until the early 1980s, many people described the homeless as "bums," "hobos," and "vagrants" who chose their lifestyle and were unde-serving of help. "It was advocates who coined the phrase, 'homeless,'" said the University of Pennsylvania's Dennis Culhane. "They're the ones who thought 'homeless' would be a soft, fluffy term for the public to be sympathetic to."[57]

The term was used as a way to advocate for public subsidies for housing. "The anti-homelessness movement chose the term 'homelessness,'" wrote Gowan, "as opposed to 'transient,' 'indigent,' etc., for its implication that the biggest difference between the homeless and the housed was their lack of shelter."[58]

Words are powerful. The word "homeless" not only makes us think of housing, it also makes us *not* think of mental illness, drugs, and disaffiliation. The word directs our attention to things perceived as outside of a person's control, such as the high cost of housing, and away from things perceived as in their control, such as working, parenting, and staying sober.

The news media have framed homelessness as poverty since the 1980s. "It hasn't been this bad since the Great Depression," claimed KQED, San Francisco's main public broadcaster, in 1983. "Yet the stock market is booming. Venture capitalists are making millions of dollars overnight in Silicon Valley video games. For a few, it's the best of times. For many more, it's the worst."[59]

It was a grossly misleading statement. The poor farming families like the Okies who fled to the Bay Area in 1933 were utterly unlike the crack-, heroin-, and alcohol-abusing single homeless men of San Francisco in 1983. The two groups were homeless for completely different reasons and needed completely different things to improve their lives. As for unemployment, it declined dramatically, from nearly 10 percent in 1982, the year when the national news media started to heavily cover homelessness, to just over 5 percent in 1989.[60]

Few were more influential than homeless advocate Mitch Snyder, who was played by the actor Martin Sheen in a 1986 made-for-TV movie. Snyder had become famous in 1982 after claiming that the number of homeless had grown to two to three million, based on little evidence and wild extrapolations.[61] Experts at the time said that the number was wrong but news media used it to conflate homelessness with poverty and attribute it to mass unemployment and the economic policies of Reagan.

Media attention and advocacy resulted in sweeping new federal legislation. In the spring of 1986, five million people attempted to form a human chain from California to New York to raise $24 million for the "Hungry and Homeless."[62] Thanks in part to the heavy media attention, progressive advocates for the homeless were able to turn out 40,000 demonstrators to march in Washington to demand "Housing Now!" in the fall of 1989.[63] The year before, over one hundred of the nation's leading editorial cartoonists and comic strip creators, including *Doonesbury* creator Garry Trudeau, created cartoons aimed at "raising awareness."[64] In response, Congress passed the McKinney Act, which provided federal money for homeless shelters and transformed homelessness support services from the independent agencies of the 1980s into what is today referred to pejoratively as the "homeless industrial complex."[65] The number of government agencies increased tenfold, from 1,500 in the early eighties to over 15,000 a decade later.[66]

But the warning signs were all there, including with Mitch Snyder, who ran a dangerous homeless shelter. "That place was an insane asylum," wrote a *Washington Post* reporter later, "with people fighting and vomiting and urinating on themselves. After 15 years of trying to help such people, almost anyone would be depressed."[67]

A rresting and prosecuting the homeless for things like defecating in public, injecting fentanyl publicly, and living on the sidewalk is unethical, say a growing number of progressive political candidates and elected officials, because the people doing those things are victims of racism, poverty, and trauma. When he ran for office in 2018, San Francisco district attorney Chesa Boudin announced, "We will not prosecute cases involving quality-of-life crimes. Crimes such as public camping, offering or soliciting sex, public urination, blocking a sidewalk, etc., should not and will not be prosecuted."[68] Enforcing the law contributes to further victimization, says Boudin. "Jails do nothing to treat the root cause of crime," read his campaign platform.[69] In early 2020 Boudin said, "There are people who are harmed by the addiction crisis in this city, by open-air drug use and drug sales." But, he added, "those are technically victimless crimes."[70]

From 2019 to 2021, the number of crimes Boudin decided not to enforce grew. In 2020, Boudin announced that he was not going to prosecute street-level drug dealers because, in part, they are "themselves victims of human trafficking."[71] Defendants often receive plea deals and stay-away orders that are easily ignored. "It's common for the defendant to return to the same corner anyway, get arrested again and be sentenced by a judge to probation," noted a *Chronicle* columnist. "Defendants are almost always out in the community as their cases wind their way through the courts."[72]

In May 2021, a San Francisco Superior Court judge refused to grant stay-away orders for four defendants who had been charged multiple times with drug dealing offenses, ruling that such orders would "violate the defendants' constitutional rights." The ACLU applauded the ruling, saying the judge had rejected the city's "attempt to scapegoat four individuals for its own policy failures to address real needs in the Tenderloin."[73]

In 2020 a Seattle city councilor introduced legislation to order the district attorney to stop enforcing laws if they are committed by the poor, the mentally ill, or people with substance use disorders. "Stalking, harassment, vehicle prowls, sexual exploitation, property destruction, hit-and-run, threatening someone with a gun," noted the *Seattle Times*, "would be minimized and easily defensible."[74]

But even if we were to accept that everyone on the street has been victimized, and even if we were to agree that victimization has grown worse, does that mean we should give them the identity as victims, and make them immune from the law?

In 1928, a twenty-three-year-old psychiatrist in Vienna, Austria, named Viktor Frankl created youth counseling centers to address rising suicides among adolescents. The innovative psychotherapy he created was so effective that by 1931, not a single student in Vienna had taken his or her life. Throughout the 1930s Frankl treated depressed patients, as well as other people with mental disabilities, and saved many of them from the Nazis who sought to exterminate them.[75]

Frankl demanded that his depressed patients find a reason for living. He would even ask them, somewhat shockingly, "Why do you *not* commit suicide?" He wasn't encouraging them to do it. Rather, he knew that by asking the question they would be forced to identify and specify their purpose, which was often tied to personal relationships or some kind of work.[76]

Frankl asked challenging questions to provoke individuals to take responsibility for, and gain power over, their lives. Where Freud wanted people to orient toward the past, toward their childhood traumas, Frankl wanted people to orient toward their future, toward their goals. Where Freud emphasized how we are shaped by our environments, Frankl emphasized how we can control our experience. When people have a powerful reason to live, Frankl argued, and are aware of what it is, and pursue it, we can be free.

Frankl married his girlfriend in December 1941, one month before the Nazis rounded up Austrian Jews, split him from her and from his parents, and shipped them to different concentration camps. A prisoner, Frankl realized that if he were to survive he would need to put his theory of human motivation to work. He decided to concentrate on his reasons for living, which were so he could be with his wife and parents again, as well as to write a book about how he survived the death camps.

When the war ended and Frankl was released from the Nazi

concentration camps, he learned that his wife and parents had all been killed. The goal of seeing them again had saved his life; now that goal was gone. So he turned to his other goal, to write a book about his experience, and added a new one, remarrying. He wrote the book quickly and saw it published in 1946. The original title in German was *Nevertheless Saying "Yes" to Life*, and the original title in English was *From Death-Camp to Existentialism*, which was eventually renamed *Man's Search for Meaning*. It became one of the most influential books of the twentieth century, with translations into two dozen languages and over 10 million copies sold.[77]

Frankl's books and lectures helped give rise to self-help culture, first in progressive cities, and then in the rest of the United States, starting in the 1960s. Frankl loved the San Francisco Bay Area and was enormously popular here in the 1960s and 1970s, visiting several times, and giving lectures to very large audiences. In 1978 a scholar in Berkeley, a fellow survivor of the concentration camps, started the Viktor Frankl Institute of Logotherapy. Progressive psychologists and psychiatrists who are familiar with Frankl's work, in my experience, revere him, as do the many progressive high school, college, and university teachers and professors who still assign his book today.

However, the very same progressives who promote Frankl's philosophy as a guide for living, either directly or indirectly through Dr. Phil, Oprah, and other self-help gurus, condemn similar self-help thinking in political life as "blaming the victim." Why is that?

11

The Heroism of Recovery

After World War II, a long-standing philosophical debate over whether we have free will or are just the products of our environments gained real-world significance. Former Nazi officers on trial defended themselves by saying they were not responsible for their actions, including the operation of gas chambers, because they were following orders. Courts ruled that this was not a valid defense, and philosophers including French existentialist Jean-Paul Sartre gained worldwide fame in his emphasis on individual responsibility. "Man is condemned to be free," he writes. "From the moment he is thrown into this world he is responsible for everything he does."[1]

Michel Foucault disagreed. Following the philosopher Friedrich Nietzsche, Foucault felt that individual responsibility was a myth used by powerful people to punish and discipline others for things they could not control. None of us chose our brains and bodies, our families and communities, or our places in time and space. How could we be said to have "free will" at all?

The problem with this line of thinking is that people appear to behave far better when they take responsibility for their actions than when they don't. Subjects primed to disbelieve in free will are, for example, more likely to engage in aggressive behaviors.[2] Disbelief in free will even seems to impair some cognitive processes.[3]

One way to think about free will is that it exists only as a belief. The more we believe in free will, the more it exists. The less we believe in it, the less it exists. "If you do call free will an illusion, it's a useful illusion, right?" said Cory Clark, a professor of social psychology who is doing innovative research into how we think about freedom and responsibility. "Thinking through, 'If I do X, Y will happen,' is an important part of the process that leads to making better choices. If people thought they didn't have to do that, they might not make good choices anymore."

But perhaps what's behind Clark's view is a desire to punish people who break the law?

"I'm one of the least punitive people that I know," she said. "I do feel for prisoners. At the same time, I'm not prepared to relinquish the idea of responsibility."[4]

The lesson for anyone who cares about expanding human freedom, as opposed to trying to control others, is that we should be communicating to people that they have far *more* freedom, not less freedom, than they realize. The more you play the victim, the more of a victim you'll become.

That was Jabari Jackson's experience. After he was arrested for the robbery, he blamed everyone else but himself. "I was mad," he said, "and after a while you start believing the shit you tell yourself. In my mind I was the victim. My ways was nowhere close to being why things are happening is happening. 'I'm the victim, I'm the victim. I played no part in this. You all are just taking this shit out on me.' And after a while you start believing your own bullshit."[5]

In the mid-1960s, psychologist Eric Berne wrote a book that observed the ways in which we all unconsciously adopt roles in our relationships, whether with friends, family, or colleagues. Many dramas require a victim. One person plays the Victim, another the Persecutor, another the Patsy (that is, a person who is fooled), and still another the Rescuer.

Crucially, we tend to develop role-playing patterns in our relationships, but we also switch roles as the situation changes.

In a game Berne called "Alcoholic," he described the interactions between an alcoholic husband and his wife, who would role-switch. At night, she played "the Patsy, undressing him, making him coffee, and allowing him to beat her. In the morning, [she played] the Persecutor, berating him for the evil of his ways; and in the evening the Rescuer, pleading with him to change them." Our motivation in playing these roles, felt Berne, is praise and recognition, which he called "strokes."[6]

Notes Clark, "When society says, 'Oh, these people who've had these bad things happen to them are victims, and we should feel sorry for them, and should do everything we can to help them,' people come to learn that playing the role of the victim gets them favors."[7] Scholars call such excessive compassion "pathological altruism," defined as "behavior in which attempts to promote the welfare of another, or others, results instead in harm that an external observer would conclude was reasonably foreseeable."[8]

The related idea that all white people are Persecutors and all black people are Victims locks all of us into terrible roles, argue some scholars. "It is a formula that binds the victim to his victimization by linking his power to his status as a victim," wrote Shelby Steele in his 1990 National Book Award–winning book, *The Content of Our Character.*[9] "[T]here is, lying at the heart of modern black American thought," wrote Columbia University linguist John McWhorter in his 2000 book *Losing the Race*, "a transformation of victimhood from a problem to be solved into an identity in itself, and as an identity to be nurtured."[10]

It is today common, socially acceptable, and even rewarding for progressives to put others, and themselves, down, for being white, male, and straight, and sometimes Asian, while elevating those in supposed victim categories to higher social, moral, and even spiritual status.

Frankl, a victim of biology-based identity politics, attacked the notion of collective guilt after the war. "In 1946," he said, "I lectured in the French occupation zone of Austria. I spoke against collective guilt in the presence of the commanding general of the French forces."[11] Frankl insisted on individual not group responsibility. We are responsible for our behavior, not the behavior of all black or white people, women or men.

For many progressives it is taboo to suggest people are on the street for any reason other than poverty. "Journalists need to not frame this problem as people with meth addiction," Housing First advocate Margot Kushel said to me, sternly, at the end of our call.[12] Part of the reason, as we have seen, is a determination to ensure that societal resources are spent on housing, rather than addiction. But another motivation appears to be to downplay the notion that even victims can have responsibility for and control over their behavior.

There are many versions of the Persecutor-Victim-Rescuer game when it comes to homelessness. In the mind of many progressives, the homeless person is the Victim, the police is the Persecutor, and the social workers and activists are the Rescuers. But sometimes the Victim plays the Persecutor, the Persecutor the Victim, and finally the Victim the Rescuer.

In the fall of 1993, as I was walking up Sixteenth Street toward Mission Street, in San Francisco, a man who appeared to be homeless gripped the neck of a woman, holding her head against a wall and punching her in the face. Every time he did her head slammed against the wall behind her. She was bawling and bloodied. I stopped about fifteen feet away from them and stared, unsure what to do. Several people walked quickly by me without stopping.

"Hey!" I shouted.

"What the fuck do you want!" the man screamed at me, never taking his hand off her neck. He appeared significantly stronger than me. "Fuck off!"

At that moment, a coworker, who is both taller and stronger than me, came up behind me and said, "Hey, you grab him from behind and I'll grab him from the front." Before giving me a chance to respond he swung his tote bag full of books at the man's stomach. Without thinking, I bear-hugged the man from behind, pinning his arms against his body, as hard as I could, while my friend grabbed the man by the lapels.

But as soon as we did, the woman started screaming at us to let the man go. I was struck by how quickly she switched from Victim to Rescuer, recasting her Persecutor into our Victim. "Fuck both of you then," said my friend, switching from Rescuer to Patsy, as he let go of his shirt. I, too, then released the man and joined my friend in walking away, the couple still screaming obscenities at us after we turned the corner.

In the fall of 1978, a relatively conservative member of the San Francisco Board of Supervisors, Dan White, resigned from his post. He felt disappointed and discouraged from constantly losing battles to Harvey Milk and the emerging progressive majority on the board. White had also grown to resent the significant pay cut that he took from leaving his job as a firefighter to become supervisor. He was under stress from both him and his wife working side jobs, and resigned abruptly from the board without consulting or informing his supporters in advance. After they reacted negatively to his decision, White tried to withdraw his resignation, but it was too late. White's resignation gave Mayor George Moscone the chance to appoint a progressive and for them to have a majority. Milk urged him to seize it.

Angry and spiteful, White snuck into City Hall and shot and killed both Milk and Moscone. The murders were premeditated. White had overheard Milk lobbying the mayor to replace him. White used hollow-point bullets, to maximize damage to the body, and carried extras so that he could reload. He fired into the heads of both Moscone and Milk at point-blank range, splattering their brains against the floor and wall.

Before White shot Milk he sounded like a child. "Why do you want to hurt my name, my family?" he said. "You *cheated* me!"[13]

The jury found White guilty of voluntary manslaughter and acquitted him of first-degree murder, which meant he would be released from prison in under five years.[14] The reason for the light sentence was a combination of prejudice and compassion. In court White claimed he had been in a state of diminished mental capacity due to stress and junk food. He was, he claimed, a victim.

The jury appeared to pity White. What seemed to be particularly influential was a recording of White breaking down in tears during his confession to the police. "My wife's got to work long hours," he said, sobbing, "fifty and sixty hours, never see my family." White described how mean Milk had been. Cried White, "he just kind of smirked at me, as if to say, 'Too bad,' and then I just got all flushed, an', an' hot, and I shot him."[15] Said a homicide detective, "When I heard that confession, I said, 'This better be tried right in the courtroom, because if not, he'll walk.'"[16]

Playing the victim, or what researchers call victim signaling, appears to be working better than ever. Society's definition of trauma and victimization is broadening, researchers find. As a result, there are more people who identify as victims today, even as actual trauma and victimization are declining. Researchers find that people are increasingly "moral typecasting," or creating highly polarized categories of "victim" and "perpetrator."[17] And they find that people who portray themselves as "victims" believe they will be better protected from accusations of wrongdoing.[18] In one study, participants judged how responsible an imaginary car thief was for his actions. One group was told that he had a genetic oversensitivity to pain. The other group was not given that detail. The people in the group who were told that the man was oversensitive to pain held him less responsible for his action.[19]

Victim signaling is more common among those with the so-called Dark Triad personality traits of narcissism, Machiavellianism, and psy-

chopathy. In one study, participants who strongly identified with statements of victimization like "I have fewer opportunities presented to me
than other people" were more likely to lie about whether they correctly
guessed a coin flip, a lie that they knew would reward them one dollar.
They were also more likely to agree with statements like "If I knew I
could never get caught, I would be willing to steal a million dollars."[20]
And, researchers find, groups using victim signaling are more likely to
seek retribution in violent conflicts.[21]

Victim signalers are more likely to boast of their victim status after
being accused of discriminating against others, or of being privileged.[22]
And so-called virtuous victims, people who broadcast their morality,
alongside their victimization, are more likely to gain resources from
others, researchers find, and display Dark Triad personality traits, than
victim signalers who did not signal their virtue.[23]

Nobody in the gay community rejected victimology more than Harvey Milk. Before running for office he owned and managed a small
camera shop in the Castro neighborhood. But his passion was community
organizing and he became known as "the mayor of Castro Street."

Publicity of open and sometimes flamboyant homosexuality in places
including the Castro in San Francisco, West Hollywood in Southern
California, and Greenwich Village in New York City was met with a
backlash. In 1977, a beauty queen, singer, and television pitchwoman for
orange juice successfully repealed a gay rights law in Florida, inspiring
antigay activism nationwide.[24]

The same year, Dan White ran for the Board of Supervisors on
a morality platform. He had become famous as a firefighter after saving a mother and baby from a burning building. White condemned the
"cesspool of perversion" in San Francisco. "I am not going to be forced
out of San Francisco by splinter groups of radicals, social deviates [*sic*],

and incorrigibles."[25] The next year, 1978, a California state senator put an initiative on the ballot to ban gay teachers from California's schools. He called San Francisco "the moral garbage dump of homosexuality in this country."[26]

In the summer and fall of 1978, as Milk and his allies campaigned against the initiative, violence against gay and lesbian people rose. Young men started attacking gay people in the Castro neighborhood with knives and fists. In the summer of 1977, four teenagers jumped a gay couple walking to one of their apartments. A nineteen-year-old man pinned one of the men to the ground and stabbed him repeatedly in the chest with a fishing knife while screaming "Faggot, faggot, faggot!"[27]

In the Castro, gay men started carrying whistles to sound the alarm in case someone tried to attack them.[28] When Milk heard a whistle blow one night, he ran toward it. Milk, a veteran of the US Navy, saw the perpetrator, chased him, and tackled him. The man begged Milk not to hurt him. Milk growled at the man, "Tell all your friends we're down here waiting for them." On another occasion, Milk asked a reporter, "Do you think gay people are going to go with their heads bowed into the gas chambers? I mean, I'll go kicking and screaming before I go with my head bowed."[29]

Milk's work paid off. He and his allies mobilized thousands of people for grassroots outreach. With Mayor Moscone, Milk persuaded Governor Jerry Brown to oppose the proposition. Jerry Brown got President Jimmy Carter to oppose it, and so, too, did Ronald Reagan. In the end, the initiative was defeated, 58 to 42. Milk and his burgeoning movement appeared to have played the decisive role.[30]

The Sixteenth Street BART stop in San Francisco was an open-air drug scene in the late 1990s. Young heroin addicts, almost all white, would sometimes ask me for money as I walked by. I was often struck by how genuinely friendly they sounded when asking me for money, and also how hostile they became as soon as I said, "Sorry," and shrugged my shoulders. They were only playing the Victim in the hope that I would play the role of Rescuer.

Homelessness researcher Teresa Gowan discovered the same dynamic. "Many panhandlers, especially white panhandlers, presented themselves as helpless victims of homelessness, trying to get themselves together," noted Gowan. "In effect, they had learned to use sick-talk in a purely instrumental way, evoking depression, HIV, and various physical injuries as their primary obstacles to a normal life."[31]

The anger of many homeless often lies just beneath the surface. "Panhandling? . . . it wasn't easy," a homeless man told Gowan. "You get to hate the people marching past. . . . I used to give people this intense look, just say, 'Please, anything helps.' I figured people should like that, showing you're not fussy, you'll take the pennies. . . . The thing is, after a while, you hate them, you hate everyone, and they feel it, they know."[32]

The "game" puts the homeless in the role of the Child and the rest of society in the role of Parent. "The [homeless] kids were telling us overwhelmingly, 'We want you to bring the services to us,'" said one San Francisco homeless service provider. "So we had a couple of supplies on us and would go up to kids and offer them. In a way, it was utterly natural: 'How are you doing? Do you need some socks tonight? Do you need a snack tonight?'"[33]

Such helping-only strategies provoke a strong reaction from people in recovery from addiction.

"Every time I hear somebody say, 'Well, I just want to help people,' I want to punch them in the face," said Vicki Westbrook. "Those are the people that are usually harming the people the most."

"How so?" I asked.

"Because they're the ones that let people off the hook or they just want to make sure they have everything they need, but they're not giving them their life back. Thank you for keeping them alive. I'm sure they need to eat. Give them some clean clothes and some clean socks and keep them warm. Can you do something that will really help get their life back? Is this what we're helping them do? Live on the streets for the next twenty years till they die? What kind of life is that?"[34]

Stanford University addiction specialist Keith Humphreys agreed. "There's a lot of people who have been really hurt by addicted people," he said, "and people in the addiction field haven't wanted to cope with this. Sometimes the field screams at people, 'How dare you have negative feelings about addicts?' But people are thinking, 'I buried my child and I'm supposed to apologize?' or 'My nose had to be reset three times until I got a restraining order and you want me to feel bad for the guy who did it?' We don't honor that rage and pain and the addiction field doesn't, either. They just say, 'You're not allowed to feel this way' and 'If you understood the neuroscience, it wouldn't bother you that your nose was broken three times.'"[35]

Toward the end of our conversation, I asked San Francisco's overdose prevention coordinator, Kristen Marshall, "What do you say to people who say it's been made too easy to use hard drugs in San Francisco?" Marshall chuckled ruefully. "Depends on what you mean by 'easy,'" she said. "People who ask questions like that have very little understanding of what life is like in poverty and trauma and generations in poverty. Those critiques are coming from the people who haven't lived any semblance of the life of the people we've served."[36]

Except that they're not. In fact, some of the harshest critiques of radical harm reduction and drug decriminalization are coming from people like Tom Wolf, Vicki Westbrook, and Jabari Jackson, who suffered from and overcame trauma, addiction, and homelessness.

In the spring of 2016, I visited a very poor community in Delhi, India, whose residents made their livelihoods by picking through garbage for recyclable materials. Even wearing a mask, I could not spend more than a few minutes near the large dump where the people spent hours without masks. My guide was a former schoolteacher in her mid-thirties named Anindita. When we arrived at the community, a circle was formed around a boy who appeared to be about twelve years old. He looked glum. Anindita talked to somebody in Hindi, and then walked over to the boy. She spoke to him in a stern voice, like she was scolding him. She then walked out of the circle and back to me.

"What was that all about?" I asked.

"His mother died of tuberculosis last night," she said.

"Oh, that's terrible!" I said. "But why were you scolding him?"

"He didn't go to school," she said.

While shocking to me, such harsh discipline was common in the United States and other developed nations one hundred years ago. Sociologists date changes to parenting styles to the transition from farm to city life in the nineteenth and twentieth centuries. Urban couples needed far fewer children and indeed could not take care of as many children as when they lived on farms. The quantity of chores expected of children declined dramatically, and has continued to decline.[37]

Concerns that parents were spoiling their children rose after World War II. Mothers mostly stayed home to engage in parenting, and parents, teachers, and others who work with children became significantly softer and gentler with them. Spanking and other forms of corporal punishment declined. Child-rearing expert Dr. Benjamin Spock taught that "children should be permitted to develop at their own pace, not pushed to meet the schedules and rules of adult life." Eventually, the "overprotective mother" became a stereotype.[38]

The philosophical roots of coddling culture lie in the 1762 book *Émile*, by Jean-Jacques Rousseau, which argued that children are born good and that their education should be largely self-directed.[39] The philosophy was a break from the older Christian idea that we are born with original sin and must develop the internal discipline required to resist our sinful desires. His idea was embraced in the 1960s by the new bohemians. They believed in "salvation *by* the child," which held that we can only realize our full potential by getting back in touch with what some called our innocent "inner child," changing our child-rearing, and changing our educational system.[40]

Parents today follow the thinking advanced by Rousseau without knowing it when they treat their children as natural, pure, and fragile, requiring as little discipline or strictness as possible. "The hippie ideology was premised on being *kind*," wrote University of California sociologist Henry Miller. "They wanted to love and be loved."[41] Some parents in the Haight in the sixties followed the Summerhill method of child-rearing, which advocated a Rousseauian, hands-off approach. In its most extreme form, hippie parents let their children be in the house without diapers because that was supposedly their natural state.[42] As the children grew older parents encouraged them to "follow your bliss," telling them that they could grow up to be and do "anything," giving enlarging self-importance but also increasing their need for affirmation, admiration, and recognition.[43]

Today, researchers studying families around the world, from Italy and Sweden to Samoa and Peru, find that American families are outliers in how much they spoil and coddle their children. "In other societies, school-aged children are expected to be vigilant and see what needs to be done around the house, and they routinely do chores without being asked," said the lead researcher of one study. "But here, in middle-class mainstream households, you can't ask kids to do anything."[44]

In the 1990s, parents started giving out participation trophies to members of the losing sides of youth sports teams so they wouldn't feel sad. "As children receive trophies and praise for mere participation rather than achievement," noted researchers, "they value these rewards less, perform worse and are more likely to suffer from depression."[45] And many young men took longer to grow up, which some psychologists describe as the "primary neurosis" of our time. We give the phenomenon names like "man-child," and "Peter Pan syndrome," and "apathy."[46]

Additionally, children today spend less time on self-directed creative play, as opposed to time spent with electronic devices, or in structured activities organized by adults. Less free play means children are "deprived of opportunities to 'dose themselves' with risk," notes a psychologist. "Instead of enjoying a healthy amount of risk, this generation is more likely than earlier ones to avoid it."[47] The number of adolescents who agreed with the statement, "I get a real kick out of doing things that are a little dangerous," declined from over 50 percent to 43 percent between 1991 and 2015.[48]

One can grow up coddled, go to an elite university, and land in a job, all without much suffering or risk, and even with a significant amount of pampering. "These institutions keep them insulated from much of the world, and the next thing you know, they're a senior person in their field," noted one entrepreneur. "They have resources. They have influence. But they've never actually worked outside of a pretty sheltered context."[49] Now, with the rise of remote work and delivery apps, many of us do not even need to go into the office and can live like only the superrich a generation ago could live, with workers delivering groceries, meals, and consumer products to our doorstep.

The culture of coddling contributed to the opioid epidemic, some believe. Patients suffering pain felt more confidence demanding opioids while refusing to accept responsibility. Noted one author, "patients were getting used to demanding drugs for treatment. They did not, however, have to accept the idea that they might, say, eat better and exercise more, and that this might help them lose weight and feel better. Doctors, of course, couldn't insist . . . [and] patients didn't have to take accountability for their own behavior."[50]

OxyContin was seen as vastly more effective than existing painkillers.[51] Across the United States, unscrupulous doctors set up "pill mills" to give out prescriptions for opioids to people who didn't need them.

Companies used deceptive marketing. They convinced doctors, regulators, and patients that the prescribing of opioids to treat chronic pain long term was a safe and effective treatment.[52] Until the scale of the problem became clear, it was difficult for doctors to refuse to prescribe opioids to patients who expected instant pain relief. Though the newly popular opioids carried little risk of addiction for most patients, they could have devastating effects on those already in the habit of self-medicating their emotional pain with other substances. And patients who did not become addicted themselves sometimes stored their medications in places where those more vulnerable to addiction, particularly teens, could find them.[53]

The problem is that creating a good life for one's self, one's family, and one's community requires denying or delaying gratification. Getting an education and maintaining a job mean setting aside pursuing immediate happiness in favor of investing in satisfaction later. Raising children, particularly for parents who attempt to establish discipline, is hard. Somewhere along the way, many parents and the wider society stopped passing this message on to their children.

Lack of discipline to delay gratification makes people fragile. The social workers told Vicki, "We don't want to push them too much and then they fail. Then they're going to think about failing." Too few social workers have the right attitude, says Vicki. "I can't tell you how many arguments I've gotten into with case managers, especially if they're licensed clinicians, because they're 'client-centered, client-driven.' They say things to me like, 'Well, you know this person has substance use.' That's the end of their sentence. I'm like, 'Okay. And? What's next?' That can't be the end of the story."[54]

The politics of victimology undermines our freedom and threatens us all. "Losing faith in your own willfulness and capacity to act, you eventually lose freedom," noted an early critic of victim culture. "That was one lesson of totalitarianism, which succeeded by organizing masses of the disaffected, politically inactive, self-centered people who felt helpless and victimized, believed that they didn't matter and sought 'self-abandonment' in the state."[55]

It also makes more victims. By not prosecuting the drug dealers whom District Attorney Boudin describes as "victims of human trafficking," he ends up allowing the victimization of people of color, the poor, and the mentally ill, who are the very victims that progressives claim they want to protect.

Thinking back to Anindita's scolding of the boy who lost his mother, do we think her behavior was cruel? By today's progressive standards, yes. If a Berkeley mother behaved similarly toward a twelve-year-old boy who had just lost a parent, she would be ostracized. The boy would be viewed as doubly victimized. However, a boy who gives up on school in that community of trash-pickers practically dooms himself to breathe toxic garbage for the rest of his shortened life. By scolding the boy, and making him as afraid of her as he was sad about his mother, Anindita did the compassionate thing.

In Amsterdam, in the fall of 2019, after my morning with Rene Zegerius, I visited the Rijksmuseum. I was struck by the juxtaposition of art in two separate rooms. One was full of large, action-oriented paintings of Dutchmen in gunboats at war with their enemies. The other room was of paintings of tranquil family life. I was captivated by one painting in particular of a very wealthy family with classic round Dutch heads, each person holding a musical instrument. The Netherlands was the first country in the modern world to become fabulously wealthy. That wealth, and the great city of Amsterdam itself, were only possible through military security and force, which is something we tend to forget when we are making music with our families at home.

I met a Dutch friend for tea that evening. I told him about my experience with Rene, his insistence on balancing carrots and sticks, and the contrasting rooms at the Rijksmuseum. He smiled and nodded. "We have an expression," which he said in Dutch. "It means"—here he paused and looked up—"'Soft doctors make wounds stink.' Does that make sense?"

"Do you mean doctors who are so afraid to hurt their patients fail to properly clean wounds, and they become infected and stink?"

"Yes," he said. "Do you have that expression in the US?"

I told him we didn't but that perhaps we should.

Jabari, Tom, and Vicki all stressed that great social workers are both loving and tough. "My drug treatment specialist in prison was too much," said Vicki Westbrook. "She was a [correctional officer] before she was a treatment counselor. I did not like this woman. But I'll tell you what, I hear that woman in my head. When I'm doing something and I'm like, "Oh my God, this sucks.' I hear her go, 'Vicki, that's where the growth is. Get excited. That's where the growth is.' I'm like, 'Okay. That's where the growth . . .' You know what I'm saying? I love that woman because of the things that still go on in my head because of that."[56]

People need help setting the right goals, and creating a plan to achieve them, which is what empowered caseworkers using assertive case management would do. "The problem isn't setting the bar too high and not meeting it," said Vicki. "It's setting it too low and meeting it. People can't imagine what's possible for them."

When homeless men pursue their goals through hard work, they express happiness. "I know this sounds weird," said Spike, one of the homeless men Gowan followed, "but I am happier doing this shit [collecting bottles and cans for recycling] than I have been in years. You get such a sense of achievement out of it. Set off in the morning with nothing, then you find all this cool stuff, and people even appreciate what you're doing half the time. It's like I get high from it, a real buzz. But it is a buzz that lasts, not some quick high. It puts me in a good, mellow mood all day, especially when the weather is good. . . . I'm starting to see what I've been missing out on in my life."[57]

It wasn't until Vicki's partner, Raven, didn't have Vicki to depend upon that he pulled his own life together. "By the time I got out of prison, his landscaping business was thriving," Vicki said. "He has contracts with apartment complexes and has a team, a crew, and a truck. I feel like that happened partly because I wasn't around because he would have been more dependent on me to take care of stuff. I still do some of his stuff, but as far as taking care of the business, invoicing, and putting in bids and things like that, that's all him. I think it was a struggle for him at first, too."[58]

Becoming a hero means taking responsibility for what one did in the past. "I've just destroyed people's lives with some of the actions that I've done," Jabari told me. "It's not cool, man. It's not cool, because if somebody did that to me and mine, I'd be ready to kill somebody for doing that to me and mine. Who the fuck am I to walk around here and gloat, that I did that to the next person? With every action comes recourse from it, and I understand that."[59]

Vicki felt the same. "I was really ashamed of what I had done to my community. I sold drugs to people that weren't really taking care of their kids. I would justify it. Their kids could come to my house and eat. I was so good. But, 'Bitch, you shouldn't have been selling drugs to them! That was taking food out of'—you know what I'm saying? That's that thing you do when you're an addict. You make justifications and twist things around to make it look like what you want it to look like."[60]

For Jabari and Vicki, learning different forms of psychotherapy was liberating. It gave them awareness and a sense of control over their trauma. I asked Jabari if his recovery was focused around the twelve-step program.

"You know what?" he said. "I'm a sponge. I do twelve-step. I do attack therapy. Because different ones work for me in different ways."

"What's 'attack therapy'?" I asked.

"Attack therapy is behavioral modification," he said. "It's not harm reduction. They'll call you on your shit. They're going to tell you when you're doing wrong. When you're trying to minimize stuff and manipulate something, they're going to call you on it. If people continue to call me on my shit, yeah, it breaks me out of that mode and that habit."[61]

Vicki said her drug recovery, including her time in prison, improved her life in ways beyond sobriety. "My life was bigger in prison than it had been when I was out on the streets using and dealing," she said.

"What do you mean by 'bigger'?" I asked.

"More expansive," she said. "Possibility. Experience. I had a job in prison. I was doing all these classes. I was a leader in my treatment community. I was helping other women, so much more robust of a life than I had then. That never would have happened if I kept using."[62]

Over time, Paneez Kosarian overcame the physical attack. "I went through a very dark year," she said. "PTSD [post-traumatic stress disorder] is dark. I was blocking feelings. I couldn't do anything for a long time. I had to learn to not let that incident define who I am. I learned that this is life. Things happen. It's in the past. I survived."

"It almost sounds like you're saying the attack made you a better person," I said.

"I am a better person now," Paneez said. "I understand and appreciate life more. I was a little shallow. I was a little spoiled. I appreciate what I have more. I understood that leading with love suits me better, regardless of what they do to me. I became more spiritual. More calm. More centered. There are a lot of things I can't control. I can only control my actions. And now I know that if, God forbid something bad happens again, I won't be as affected."[63]

Heroism is not the absence of victimization but the overcoming of it. Thanks to his intense commitment to recovery, including honesty with himself, Jabari Jackson today is in a healthy romantic relationship.

"Today, for the first time in my life, I have a wonderful, beautiful, healthy relationship," he said. "I have a woman in my life that filled the needs of my life that I hadn't even imagined that I needed. And it makes this journey all the way easier than it was before. It makes me realize things of who I am and who I want to be."

Jabari is taking responsibility for a child he didn't know he had. "I found out that I have a ten-year-old daughter who was conceived through my times out there in the field," he said. "I found out through the DMV because child support was trying to come get me. She's beautiful. Me and her mother are best of friends. And my [romantic] girl has a thirteen-year-old son and so we have a family, now."

The psychotherapeutic philosophies and techniques that belonged to a tiny elite of psychotherapists in the 1960s are today so prevalent that they constitute the positive alternative morality to victimology.

"I like the [twelve-] steps [program] because the steps helped me get closer with my spirituality," said Jabari. "And I like to hear the stories of other people. It builds a community."[64]

The twelve-step program and other drug recovery efforts help people accept the ways in which they were initially shaped by their parents, neighborhoods, and other circumstances but then overcame them. "You let that shit go when you work the twelve steps, if you do it right," a former addict told Gowan. "It's no good looking outside of you, and it's no use blaming. For me, I had to accept that my *mother* was an addict, and *I* have always been an addict, since I was a little kid."[65]

Toward the end of our interview, Jabari struck a similarly stoic note. "I don't want nobody to go through the shit that I've been through," he said. "I'm not disgraced and I'm not ashamed of the shit I've done. I don't condemn myself anymore. If I wouldn't have got past them times, if it wasn't for those things, I wouldn't be where I am today."[66]

All of us must evolve beyond the "helping only" or "incarceration only" approach toward a more balanced "tough love" and goals-setting one. "If you just give a carrot," said Rene, "you get spoiled people. If you give an addicted person just the carrots you'll be addicted. But if you treat them both ways, it gives them space to change. It gives them space to recognize their problems and to see that there are ways to solve those problems."[67]

Jabari today has achieved peace with his past. "I truly, truly feel that my experiences are life lessons," he said. "If I could turn around and tell my life lessons to the next person so they don't go through this shit that I've been through, that's all what matters to me, man. Because it's time for me to give back to the family, friends, and the community that I've taken so much from, that I've destroyed."[68]

Vicki's time in prison, particularly her psychology training and her personal journey, allows her to see through the lies her substance-abusing clients told her. "They couldn't run game on me because I had already been there," she said. "I would have young dealers coming in trying to make changes and they come into my office suited. I'm like, 'Dude, I got you your job. I know how much money you make. This is not twenty bucks an hour. Stop doing that. You can't have a foot in both worlds.' They're like, 'No, Mom. Not doing it.' Then, I don't know, a week and a half later, I'd find them somewhere slinging dope in the city. I was like, 'Man, you don't got to lie to me. You got to make a decision.'

"I worked with people on a very different kind of level than I think they were used to sometimes," said Vicki. "I don't deal in, 'This is right' and 'This is wrong.' I deal with like, 'Tell me where you want to go, and I'm going to tell you what supports that goal and what doesn't. If it doesn't support that goal, then you're either lying to me or yourself, or you need to knock it off and let's do something to get to where you really want to go.'"[69]

Said Humphreys, "The only people who get the hurt caused by addiction are the twelve-step people. They all get that part of getting better is atoning for the shit things you did, [against] this sort of lefty view that no one should have to apologize. The twelve-step people know that if you pass out at your daughter's twelfth birthday and humiliate her, and she gets made fun of for the next five years, you have to apologize. They get that. You can't just say, 'It's a brain disease, honey. Stop being angry.' But there isn't a more broad way to let people atone without punishing them horrifically. And so we handle it by throwing them in prison and ruining their lives, which doesn't make us feel better, either."[70]

12

Homicide and Legitimacy

Victoria Beach was born in Seattle in 1959 and raised in the historically black Capitol Hill neighborhood downtown. "We have five generations here now in Seattle," she said. "My grandfather was an activist. He went to jail because they said he was a communist, which he wasn't. Dad was somewhat of an activist, too." Vickie remembers protests in the early 1970s. "I remember driving through a riot with the Black Panthers and getting teargassed," she said. "My dad took all of us home—we lived a few blocks away and went back to fight the fight."*

Vickie grew up hating the police. "My dad was an alcoholic and would beat up my mom," she said. "We would call the police. They would come and beat the crap out of my dad in front of us. Every single time. Back then they could get away with stuff like that. And so, I hated them." The violence continued when Vickie was a teenager. "One night my brother and sister were going to go to the store and we pushed the car to get it to start. Somebody called and said the car was being stolen. The police came and they beat the crap out of my brother. My twin sister was screaming at them. 'You're going to kill him!' And they took her, beat her up, and arrested both of them. Some of our white friends were doing the same stuff but they weren't addressed at all.

---

* Victoria (Vickie) Beach of Seattle is a different person than Victoria (Vicki) Westbrook of San Francisco. To avoid confusion, I will only refer to them by their first name when it is clear which one is being discussed.

"I went up to the [police] car window to talk to my sister just to tell her, 'I'm going to call Mom. Don't worry.' They threw me down and handcuffed me for talking to her. We kept saying, 'We're kids!' And they were like, 'No, you're not. You're going to jail.' The whole ride down there being called n*****. It was like, 'They can't do that. They can't call us those names!' But it was like, 'Who's going to help? Nobody's going to do anything about it.'"

Police violence against Vickie's family was intergenerational. "My daughter is twenty-five now, but when she was five, she was in an incident," said Vickie. "I used to work graveyard and so I would come home and sleep when her dad got home. My nephew was fixing the brakes in front of our house. A white friend of his and my ex-husband came up and said, 'We need to get a part for the car. We're going to leave. And I'm taking Maya with us.' And so, they get up.

"I'm not too far from the East Precinct. They get close there and they're surrounded on every side by police cars with their guns pointed at them. My daughter and ex-husband were sitting in the backseat. Over the loudspeaker [the police are] saying, 'One by one, get out with your hands up!' And they're all yelling, 'We have a five-year-old in the backseat!' [The police] didn't care. They go, 'Get out with your hands up!' One by one, they get out and they're told to lay on their bellies.

"They all got out except my daughter. And when they got to the car, of course she wasn't going to get out. She had her hands up. A five-year-old with her hands up! And they had guns pointed at her. She wasn't crying. Eventually they said, 'You can sit with your dad in the backseat.' But he's handcuffed.

"She was so traumatized by that," said Vickie. "She had to sleep with us. She said, 'They're going to kill us. They're in our basement!' We had her in counseling forever."[1]

———

In the spring of 2020, a white police officer in Minneapolis kneeled on the neck of a black man named George Floyd for eight minutes and forty-six seconds. A bystander filmed the event on her smartphone.[2] Twenty times Floyd said he could not breathe. Floyd pled for his mother, saying, "Please, please, please," and "You're going to kill me, man." Floyd knew he was dying. "Mom, I love you. Love you. Tell my kids I love them." He then said, "I'm dead."[3]

Within a few hours the video had gone viral, triggering some of the largest protests in American history. In Washington, D.C., in 2020, protesters painted giant yellow letters on the street that spelled out, "Defund the police."[4] In mid-June 2020, more than 1,000 protesters marched peacefully under the banner of Black Lives Matter from Mission High School to City Hall in San Francisco to demand the defunding of the police department. They shut down several freeway entrances, the Golden Gate Bridge, and the Bay Bridge.[5] In Berkeley a large crowd marched and chanted, "Abolish police," with drivers honking their support. "We want to disband police," said one organizer, "by any means necessary."[6]

Police in the United States kill at a rate of three people per day, for a total of nearly 1,000 deaths per year. Canada has the second-highest rate of police killings in the world at a rate one-third that of the United States.[7] Black Americans are killed at between two to three times the rate of white Americans, according to a *Washington Post* analysis of police killings between 2015 and 2020.[8] A total of 15,699 men aged 15–34 died at the hands of law enforcement between 1960 and 2010, found researchers publishing in *Harvard Public Health Review* in 2015. Of those men, 55 percent were white and 42 percent were black. In that fifty-year period, African Americans were killed by police at a rate three to four times higher than white Americans, according to the study.[9]

Higher rates of police killing cannot be explained by higher rates of violent crime by African Americans.[10] And studies find that white people killed by the police are 57 percent more likely to be armed, and 13 percent less likely to be a threat to law enforcement as black people.[11]

A team of Harvard University researchers found in 2020 that police were 53 percent more likely to use nonlethal physical force on an African American than on a white American. They analyzed 5 million police encounters with civilians in New York City and a database of 1,316 police shootings of civilians between 2000 and 2015 in localities in California, Texas, Florida, and Colorado.[12] But since that number was based on police reports alone, the actual number could be higher.

A national survey found that black Americans were 350 percent more likely to have police use physical force on them than white Americans. "This is true of every level of nonlethal force," said Harvard economist Roland Fryer, who led the team, "from officers putting their hands on civilians to striking them with batons. We controlled for every variable available in myriad ways. That reduced the racial disparities by 66 percent, but black people were still significantly more likely to endure police force."[13]

One reason suggested for this is African Americans resisting arrest more than white people, but Fryer found that black people whom police recorded as compliant were still 21 percent more likely to suffer police violence. "This was perhaps our most upsetting result," said Fryer. "Compliance does make you less likely to endure a beat-down—but the benefit is larger if you are white."[14]

Aside from police killings, there is abundant evidence that the criminal justice system treats black people differently from white people. African Americans are more likely to not be told by police why they were pulled over, be treated with less respect by law enforcement, and have their cars searched after traffic stops, even though such stops turn up fewer weapons than do stops of white people.[15] A 2020 study in *Nature* looked at 100 million traffic stops and found black people were more likely to be stopped during the day, when their race was visible, than at night, an indication of racial bias.[16] Black adults are five times more likely than white people to say police have unfairly stopped them because of their race or ethnicity.[17]

African Americans are more likely to be wrongly convicted of murder, rape, and drug crimes, to be incarcerated longer for the same crimes, and to be convicted to life without parole for nonviolent offenses, than white Americans.[18] Black people are more likely to receive higher bail requirements for the same crime, to be offered plea bargains that include jail time, and to be incarcerated while waiting for trial, than white people.[19] And African Americans are more likely to be charged with low-level offenses, fined for jaywalking, and have their probation revoked, than white people.[20]

Between 2010 and 2019, 79 percent of homicides with white victims were solved, compared to just 60 percent of homicides with African American victims.[21] One-third of US states have never had a black state supreme court justice, black judges are more likely be overruled than white judges, and 95 percent of prosecutors and 85 percent of attorneys are white.[22] One in ten black men with a high school diploma was, by 2010, in jail or prison, while an astonishing 37 percent of African American men who dropped out of high school were.[23]

There is significant unpunished racist conduct among police, an alarming prevalence of white supremacy in departments, and many reports of racism.[24] Police unions often exert undue influence over local politicians, including demands for qualified immunity from prosecution for police shootings.[25] And the "blue wall of silence" in many departments eerily reflects the culture of "no snitchin'" within many inner-city communities.[26]

Police unions have made it difficult for cities to hold officers accountable. Established in a backlash against the riots of the 1960s, unions added obstacles to disciplinary action in the form of binding arbitration, appeals processes, and an officers' "bill of rights."[27] A 2017 investigation by the *Washington Post* found that while 1,881 officers had been fired since 2006 for offenses including fraud, sexual assault, and unjustified shootings, over 450 were reinstated after appeals required by union contracts.[28] A *New York Times* review of about one hundred controversial police killings found that departments did not discipline or publicly disclose discipline in the majority of cases, with some departments refusing to answer basic questions or release records.[29]

One surprising finding by Harvard's Roland Fryer was that he and his research team *didn't* find racial differences between the use of *lethal* force by police after they accounted for whether the shootings or killings were "justified" or "unjustified," which is something that the databases created by the *Washington Post* and other media organizations did not do. In Fryer's data, around 20 percent of police shootings could be considered "unjustified" because the person did not attack, draw a weapon, or otherwise make the officer feel at risk of bodily harm.[30]

Fryer found no evidence of higher rates of police shootings of African Americans than white people, when the suspect is stopped by police.[31] "When using the simple statistical framework that economists have used for more than a half century to analyze racial differences on myriad dimensions—from wages to incarceration to teen pregnancy," wrote Fryer, "the evidence for [racial] bias disappears."[32]

The findings of Fryer might be easier to dismiss if he weren't black and doing research in service of reducing police violence. "For all of us who are frustrated about decades of racial disparities that have gone unchecked," wrote Fryer, "this is our Gettysburg. Yet we do ourselves a disservice in the battle against racial inequality if we don't adhere to rigorous standards of evidence, if we cherry-pick data based on our preconceptions."[33]

Others, using different data sets, came to similar conclusions. The nonpartisan Center for Policing Equity found that police killings are rare, that black Americans face higher rates of *non*lethal force, and that racial disparities are smaller in *lethal* use of force.[34] And the authors of the 2015 *Harvard Public Heath Review* study concluded, "We cannot, based on the limited data available, address debates over whether our findings reflect racially biased use of excessive force."[35]

A big part of the reason social scientists can't say whether police unjustly kill black Americans at higher rates than others is that police departments lack a uniform protocol for reporting victim demographics and encounter characteristics. Fryer notes that "[u]ntil recently, data on officer-involved shootings were extremely rare and contained little information on the details surrounding an incident." Violent interactions with police and civilians are "rare events." On average between 2000 and 2020, 1,481 people were killed nationally by police per year (about 0.5 per 100,000). Those numbers for the police departments of New York City, Los Angeles, and San Francisco were 17, 24, and 4, respectively. Among those killed whose race was known, 29 percent were black and 71 percent were nonblack, compared to 13.6 percent black and 86.4 percent nonblack in the general population.[36]

That African Americans are disproportionately killed by police is evident from these numbers alone. What is more difficult to discern is whether this reflects the reality that black people are more likely to end up in a situation that involves lethal force, or whether it reflects racial bias, a targeting of black people above and beyond the requirements of just policing and public safety. A rigorous measure of racial bias would require regulated and more transparent incident reporting by police departments. In the end, Fryer could only use data from Houston to measure racial bias and differences in justified lethal force. "Racism may explain the findings, but the statistical evidence doesn't prove it," said Fryer.[37] Other studies have attempted to analyze differences across US counties, using whether suspects were unarmed as a shortcut for estimating whether force was unjust, but have still failed to find differences in shootings of white and black Americans that hold up in margins of error.[38] The bottom line, notes Brandon Vaidyanathan of Catholic University, is that "none of the data on police shootings can tell us whether racial bias is a motivating factor."[39]

In 2019, Chesa Boudin won an underdog campaign against opposition from the city's police union, the Police Officers Association, to become San Francisco's district attorney. "I was consistently the furthest left candidate in the race," said Boudin. "And a lot of other folks said, 'Well, this is not going to work.' The POA is going to spend money again. They spent $700,000 attacking me in a ten-day period at the end of the race . . . as much as we spent the whole year on our campaign."[40]

Boudin is today one of the leading voices for a progressive approach to criminal justice. "Right now, we have a criminal justice system that's really, really good at punishing people," he said in 2020. "It's really bad at healing the harm that crime causes and it's really bad at preventing future crime. In fact, it perpetuates cycles of crime. I know that because I grew up visiting my own parents in prison. I've been impacted my whole life."[41]

The election of Boudin is the culmination of work by a criminal justice movement that has, alongside the movement against the war on drugs, sought to draw attention to the disparate impact of America's criminal justice system on people of color, particularly African Americans, a cause I have long cared about. In 2000 I committed civil disobedience at a protest organized by criminal justice advocate and, today, CNN talk show host Van Jones at an Oakland police station. The initiative we were protesting, Proposition 21, increased the punishment of juvenile offenders by expanding the circumstances where juveniles can be tried in adult court, reduced the discretion of probation departments, and increased sentencing length for gang-related crimes. It passed with 62 percent of the vote.[42]

But much of what I believed back then turned out to not be true, or at least wasn't the whole truth. We already saw that just 14 percent of state prisoners are nonviolent, low-level drug offenders, that 90 percent of all prisoners in the United States are in state, not federal, prisons, and that many trends are going in the right direction. That also goes for police violence. Police killings of African Americans declined from 217 per year in the 1970s to 157 per year in the 2010s in the 58 largest US cities. Police killings of all races in New York City declined dramatically, from an average of 59 per year between 1970 and 1975, to an average of 12 per year between 2015 and 2020, even as its population increased. In San Francisco and Oakland, the rate of police killings per year increased slightly, going from 2.7 and 2.8 per year, respectively, in the 1970s, to 2.4 and 3.9 per year in the 2010s, but police killings *per capita* in the two cities *declined* by 8.3 percent.[45]

While many police departments need to do a better job, it is also the case that police departments have improved markedly over the last fifty years. Racism in police departments persists, but there is now more representation of black Americans among officers and commissioners. And many police departments have seen significant reforms in recent years. Use of force by the San Francisco Police Department declined by nearly half between 2016 and 2020. In 2020, the *New York Times* described San Francisco as a place "where police reform has worked" to reduce killings.[46] "What we're talking about is significant cultural change in the department," said a former lawyer for the American Civil Liberties Union.[47]

While racial disparities persist, racism in police violence is today heavily outweighed by other much larger factors, such as the degree to which police have been properly trained and managed, and the power of police unions to block necessary reforms. In fact, there is wide variation between American counties when it comes to racial disparities in the rate of police shootings, and those differences could not be attributed to different crime rates.[48] "Does racism play a role?" asks Frank Zimring, a criminologist who has been studying and writing about homicides for more than fifty years. "You bet. Is it the dominant force in explaining American lethal violence by police? No."[49]

Why then did so many of us come to believe that police killings were rising and that racism was the main motivation behind them? Smartphones and the Internet, combined with the fact that videos of white police officers and black victims are more likely to be shared than ones of black officers and white victims, appear to be a big part of the reason.

The problem with such videos is that they aren't representative of police use of force. "Our analysis tells us what happens on average," noted Fryer. "It isn't average when a police officer casually kneels on someone's neck for 8 minutes and 46 seconds."[50] The impact of such videos is strong, especially among people who have had negative experiences with the police. "I wish to God I didn't watch that video," said Vickie about the George Floyd video. "When stuff like that happens, I flip so quick back to the other side where I hate police. It's just, 'Oh, I hate them. I'm not going to help them.'"[51]

Carmen Best was born in Tacoma, Washington, in 1965 and joined the Seattle Police Department after two years in the military. She loved police work. "I liked it if I caught a car prowler," she said. "Or, if it was gang activity, knowing who the players were, where their homes were. Being able to help people in domestic violence and child protective situations."

In 2018, Best interviewed for the job of chief of police. The hiring committee, selected by the Seattle City Council, seemed hostile. "It felt like the committee really just did not want me to be the chief. It felt unfair, but I was like, 'Okay, well, it wasn't meant to be, I'm just going to move on.'" A member of the search committee told a local reporter that they wanted a candidate from outside the police force.[52]

But when Seattle residents, both black and white, found out that Best would not get the job, they organized politically. "Community members came from everywhere and just would not accept it," she said. "The next thing I knew [the hiring committee said], 'Hey, we'd like you to put your name back in as a contender for the job.'" Best had a mandate to expand and diversify the police department. "The community really wanted more cops," she said. "At least three City Council members campaigned on more cops. They wanted better response times."

And so Best created a plan with the former mayor and previous chief to increase the number of officers "but also to really try to have a lot more diversity with our hiring, for women and people of color both. We got to about almost forty percent of either minority or women representation as new hires."

Then 2020 arrived. "There was a mass shooting in downtown Seattle," she said. "Eight people injured, two deceased." It was a battle between rival gangs to control the open-air drug market. "Just when we were working through all of that, COVID hit. Seattle is one of the first major agencies to have to deal with it. It was eighteen-hour days for days on end. There wasn't no road map. We just had to work through it and figure it out. Then, the killing of George Floyd happened."[53]

Because of COVID-19, Best said, "A lot more people had the availability to come out and to engage in what happened to George Floyd, which was quite beautiful." But a small group of people within the crowd started to behave violently. "Within that large group of people who were there peacefully protesting there were groups there to create mayhem, throw rocks, bottles, and incendiary stuff, and point lasers at the officers."

Vickie confronted violent protesters after she saw them light a car on fire and vandalize stores. "I got in the faces of all these white kids writing

'Black Lives Matter,' breaking windows at Nordstrom's, spray-painting. My daughter was like, 'Mom, they're gonna beat you up!' But I told them, 'This isn't what we're about! Why are you doing this?' It was a lot of white kids and I was just like, 'The black community is going to get blamed for this!'"[54]

Then, in June, somebody removed a police barricade that had prevented demonstrators from protesting in front of the East Precinct downtown. "It was decided," said Best, "I'll put it that way, to remove the barricade and to allow the demonstrators to fill in the street in front of the precinct. We didn't want to give up the precinct. I have to tell you it was not my decision." Police officers inside the East Precinct building feared the protesters would throw Molotov cocktails through the windows and set the building on fire. And so they began removing items from the precinct in case it caught on fire or was overrun by protesters.

"The next morning there were these folks out there armed with long rifles, telling the officers who responded that it was their 'sovereign land,'" said Best. "What 'sovereign property' are they talking about? Well, they're talking about Twelfth Avenue." She laughs. "We had never experienced anything like that. And therein began CHAZ, the Capitol Hill Autonomous Zone." Later, the organizers would rename the area CHOP, for Capitol Hill Occupied Protest.[55]

The anarchist leaders invited hundreds of Seattle's homeless residents to move into the occupied zone, and many did. When asked, Seattle's mayor insisted that everything would work out fine.

"How long do you think Seattle and those few blocks looks like this?" CNN's Chris Cuomo asked Seattle's mayor.[56]

"I don't know," she replied. "We could have a summer of love!"

"After she called it 'Summer of Love' is when all hell broke loose," said Vickie. "That's when they took over. And it was a battle every single night. . . . They had hundreds of tents on the street and were living in front of the police department. Women were raped in there more than once. Two young black men were murdered up there. It was crazy chaos up there. I can't believe more people didn't die."

Guns were in the wrong hands. "A lot of mentally ill people had weapons," Vickie said. "There was one guy who had three guns, an assault rifle and two handguns. He was bat-shit crazy. He wanted to shoot somebody. Every black person that I saw come up there was like, 'They don't represent us. They're not representing Black Lives Matter. This is a whole other whatever. This has got to end.' The [CHOP] crowd was 98 or 99 percent white. They don't even live in Seattle! They hit a police officer in the back of the head with a baseball bat, and the one who did it goes, 'I wish he didn't have a helmet on.'"

As a representative of the Capitol Hill community, Vickie felt compelled to stand up to the anarchists. "You're not going to do this in my neighborhood!" she shouted. "How dare you disrespect George Floyd and his family! We don't protest like this. Stop using Black Lives Matter to tear up the city." Vickie at one point shoved a protester. "I got to my breaking point where enough was enough," she said. "A girl flipped me off and called me a few names and I lost it. I just shoved her. I'm not proud of that action, but I'm not sorry, either."[57]

Afterward, Vickie learned from sources that the anarchists were targeting her for violence. "I got a phone call from a woman and she goes, 'There's a bull's-eye on your back.'" Seattle's mayor told Vickie that the police were monitoring potential threats to her life.

Best started reading about anarchism to understand what she was dealing with. "In some of the literature on anarchy," she said, "they talk about having autonomous zones. Very soon it was a lawless area. They were barricading themselves in. I went there myself, twice on my own. I walked in and somebody tried to stop me. She said, 'What are you doing?' I was in uniform. She's like, 'Where do you think you're going?' And I said, 'I'm going to walk down the street. And that's what I'm going to do.' I mean, it was just like the craziest thing ever!"

Some of the city staff were talking to the occupiers. "But that really wasn't working well, either, because they were enablers, bringing in porta-potties, handing out hand sanitizers, letting them tear up the park to build a vegetable farm . . . memorializing the graffiti. All of it seemed counterproductive to public safety."

Soon the police started to get reports of crimes. "We were getting reports of rape, robbery, assault. I wasn't making it up," said Best. "These things were happening in a zone where it was very dangerous. There were people there who were armed. There's video out there. You can see them shooting up in there. I don't know what the Wild West was like, but it couldn't have been any worse than that."

Best and her team saw other ominous signs. "We knew many of them were armed. We'd seen them practicing, linking arms around the facility to try to keep officers out. We fully expected there to be a significant amount of resistance to moving people out of that area. Some of the [CHOP leaders] haven't always been winners in life. Now they've got CNN and Fox interviewing them. They've got a mission. They suddenly feel connected to this area and in a way that [they] probably never in their lives had been, which meant that they were probably going to try quite hard to hang on."

Seattle's mayor and City Council started to change their tune after "the first person was murdered," said Best. "They realized, 'Oh, maybe this isn't as safe as we thought it might be.' Then, everybody was panicking. I was like, 'I've been telling you for weeks we need to get this thing shut down. It was bad.'"[58] Best told reporters the police would retake CHOP. "Two African American men are dead, at a place where they claim to be working for Black Lives Matter. Enough is enough. We need to be able to get back into the area."[59]

Any meaningful effort to protect black lives should aim to reduce homicides overall, not just homicides by police officers. Thirty times more African Americans were killed by civilians than by police in 2019. San Francisco's homicide victimization rate from 2009 to 2019 was on average 6 per 100,000 and was 49 percent black and 19 percent white non-hispanic. In the same ten-year period, Oakland's homicide victimization rate averaged 23 per 100,000 and was 74 percent black and 10 percent white non-hispanic.[60] No one should be satisfied with those numbers and yet there is remarkably little debate over how to lower them.

It is reasonable to ask whether homicides are really a concern given declining homicide and prison rates over the past two decades. The total US prison and jail population peaked in 2008 and has declined ever since. Between 2008 and 2019, the total US and California incarcerated populations declined from 2,304,000 to 2,165,000, and from 273,000 to 192,000, respectively. The incarceration rate of the United States and California declined from 762 per 100,000 to 643 per 100,000 and from 742 per 100,000 to 487 per 100,000, respectively, between 2008 and 2019.[61]

But the United States has the highest rate of homicide of any developed nation. The homicide rate in the United States is four times as high as that of France and Britain and more than five times higher than Australia's.[62] Scholars have studied racial disparity in homicides for as long as it has existed. In Philadelphia between 1948 and 1952, scholars found black men died from homicide at twelve times the rate of white men.[63] A national survey found the same difference in 1950.[64] Today, black Americans are seven to eight times more likely to die from homicide than white Americans.[65] In 2019, the homicide rate for white people was 2.3 per 100,000 whereas it was 17.4 for black people.[66]

And in 2020, in the wake of summer protests against police violence, the homicide rate increased on average by more than one-third in America's 57 largest cities. Homicides rose in 51 cities and declined in just 6 of them. Homicides rose 35 percent in Los Angeles, 31 percent in Oakland,

74 percent in Seattle, 63 percent in Portland, 60 percent in Chicago, and 47 percent in New York City.[67] The coronavirus pandemic may have played a role. "Gangs are built around structure and lack thereof," noted a Fresno, California, police officer. "With schools being closed and a lot of different businesses being closed, the people that normally would have been involved in positive structures in their lives aren't there."[68]

But there had been a similar spike in homicides in 2015 when there was no coronavirus pandemic. Back then, as in 2020, a disproportionate number of victims and suspects were black men under thirty from poor, inner-city neighborhoods. "Rivalries among organized street gangs, often over drug turf," noted two *Times* reporters in 2015, "and the availability of guns are cited as major factors in some cities. . . . But more commonly, many top police officials say they are seeing a growing willingness among disenchanted young men in poor neighborhoods to use violence to settle ordinary disputes."[69] After the spike in homicides in 2020, some pointed to higher gun sales, which rose in March, at the beginning of the pandemic. But homicides in 2020 only started to rise in June, not March.

In truth, young men, street gangs, and large numbers of handguns have existed in American society for hundreds of years, and over periods where homicides declined, such as in the early 1990s. And there was little evidence to suggest that any of those variables had changed suddenly or dramatically enough in 2015 or 2020 to account for the homicide spikes. What, then, was going on?

13

When the Law's Against the Laws

Violent crime including homicides rose precipitously starting in 1965. By 1980, violent crime rates overall were 250 percent higher than they had been twenty years earlier, while property crime rates were 200 percent higher. Following a brief lull in the early eighties, violent crime rose again in 1984 and peaked in 1991 at over 400 percent of the 1960 level, which many scholars attribute to the rise of crack cocaine and battles between dealers for turf.[1] By the early 1990s, violent crime in the United States had never been worse, while property crime remained almost as high as it had been in 1980.[2] Then, between 1993 and 2018, homicides declined 47 percent and violent crime overall declined 49 percent in US cities.[3]

While the rise of crack increased violence, historians believe that previously high rates of violence in inner-city African American neighborhoods attracted the drug dealing more than the drug dealing introduced violence.[4] Evidence for this comes from the fact that the black homicide rate declined 20 percent from 1970, when Nixon declared a "war on drugs," to 1990, the height of crack-related violence. The relationship between drug dealing and violence suggests that many of those incarcerated on drug charges during the more violent 1980s and 1990s would have been imprisoned regardless of the war on drugs.[5]

In his 1999 book, *Why They Kill: The Discoveries of a Maverick Criminologist*, the Pulitzer Prize–winning historian Richard Rhodes goes beyond statistics to describe how individuals become murderers. The biographies of killers often show evidence of a disturbing intergenerational process. Violence begets victimization begets more violence. Without intervention, this process of "violentization" is self-perpetuating.[6] But what, then, explains why violence declines?

Over the last twenty years, scholars and journalists have tried to pinpoint what causes homicides to rise and fall, with little success, argues historian Randolph Roth in his 2009 book, *American Homicide*. Researchers have attempted to attribute declining homicides to the removal of lead, a neurotoxin, from gasoline, under the theory that it makes exposed children more violent when older; the legalization of abortion, under the theory that unwanted children are more likely to commit crimes; and changes to the death penalty, gun laws, and unemployment. But such efforts miss the wider picture, Roth argues. The reason, he says, "is that it is impossible for researchers to hold historical circumstances constant while they study the influence of a single factor."[7]

To avoid reductionism, Roth developed the most comprehensive set of homicide data. It covers four hundred years of American history. "There is only one way to obtain reliable homicide estimates," he writes, "and that is to review every scrap of paper on criminal matters in every courthouse, every article in every issue of a number of local newspapers, every entry in the death records, and every local history based on lost sources, local tradition, or oral testimony."[8] Roth believes his method is more reliable than homicide counts based on court records alone, which he argues can be too low by a third or more, especially during wars or revolutions.[9]

In his analysis, Roth finds little evidence to support the claim that "root causes," like poverty and structural racism, cause crime rates to rise and fall. African American crime rates were lower during the 1940s and 1950s when segregation was legal, poverty more widespread, and discrimination more overt than between 1965 and 1990. Indeed, homicides among African Americans shot up despite the passage of the 1964 Civil Rights Act. It's true that homicides rose during the first few years of the

Great Depression. But they then declined in most major cities afterward. And crime rates, including for homicide, kept declining even after the 2007 financial crash and resulting recession, the worst since the Great Depression.

The underlying drivers of homicide are related to subjective conditions like ideology and politics, says Roth. Social conditions like poverty, oppression, and unemployment do not drive violent acts, as people suffering from these conditions have varied rates of violence throughout history. Homicide is irrational and emotional, not a natural and predetermined response to personal setbacks.[10] Roth views the public's belief in the legitimacy of "the system," as well as things like patriotism and "fellow feeling," solidarity with one's fellow citizens, as the most important factors when it comes to homicide.

Roth finds that the government's monopoly on legitimate violence is fragile, even in an established modern nation-state like the United States, and that the rate of unlawful killing reflects changes to perceived legitimacy. Public trust in government, Roth argues, impacts the prevalence of violence in a way that transcends the immediate impact of short-term economic and social regulations. As such, the "New Deal, World War II, and the Cold War may have reduced homicide rates," Roth writes, but "the crisis of legitimacy in the 1960s and 1970s (especially in the eyes of African-Americans) may have contributed to soaring homicide rates."[11]

Homicide rates among unrelated adults in the United States follow closely the proportion of the public who trust their government to do the right thing and believe that most public officials are honest. As trust in government fell in the late sixties and early seventies, homicides increased. When trust in government rose in the fifties and mid-nineties, homicides decreased.[12]

Roth's research is supported by Steven Pinker 2011 book, *The Better Angels of Our Nature*. In it Pinker describes how violence has declined broadly since the dawn of civilization and specifically in recent American history. Pinker finds downward trends in wars, sectarian violence, anti-woman violence, and child abuse, which he suggests flow from historical trends like industrialization and urbanization. Pinker argues that these historical trends reduced the emotional and practical need for violence, which has given way to the "better angels" of our personalities, traits like empathy, self-control, and reason. Like the philosopher Thomas Hobbes and sociologist Max Weber, Pinker describes the rise of the modern state, which monopolizes the *legitimate* use of violence, as a primary cause of radical declines in violence from pre-modern times.[13]

California was a national leader in taking a progressive, rehabilitative approach to prisoners starting in the 1940s, building on the humanistic tradition that began in the eighteenth century. In 1855, guards at the San Quentin prison still flogged inmates and suspended them from the ceiling by their wrists. The governor banned torture three years later and began a very gradual move away from punishment toward rehabilitation.[14] In 1947 San Quentin hired a world-class librarian to oversee a Great Books program for inmates and its world-class book collection.[15] The warden and librarian were optimistic about the prospects of books, sports, and religion to rehabilitate. By 1956, 90 percent of San Quentin prisoners were reading books from the library as compared to just 18 percent of the American people.[16]

In 1975 Michel Foucault published *Discipline and Punish*, which made a similar argument against reformist prisons like San Quentin that he had made against humanistic mental hospitals. Just as so-called reformers caused more harm than good when they treated the mentally ill in hospitals, rather than leave them to wander in the streets, prison reformers only made punishment more insidious and sinister, Foucault felt. The prison reform agenda of "more kindness, more respect, more 'humanity,'" argued Foucault, was a ruse. In reality what the prison, schools, and other societal institutions did was control individuals without them knowing it.[17]

The goal of the state is to "neutralize [the prisoner's] dangerous states" of mind and create "docile bodies," argued Foucault.[18] Rehabilitation was thus more oppressive than torture because it was more insidious. It made prisoners actually *want* to rehabilitate themselves.[19] For Foucault, torture and execution had the benefit of being less insidious than the psychotherapeutic approach that replaced it, which established norms of behavior that were powerful precisely because they were taken for granted and accepted without question.[20]

Radical thinkers during Foucault's time and today still point to the use of anti-vagrancy laws,[21] the lack of enforcement of laws against corporations and powerful elites,[22] and lower rates of crime in the Western Europe nations that are more socialist than the United States, as evidence of how the criminal justice system protects capitalism, not the people. Equal justice under the law is thus a myth, they argue, because wealthy people can hire skilled attorneys and others to avoid or reduce punishment. Crime is thus a rational response to the high levels of inequality created by capitalism.[23]

Foucault and the radical prison movement challenged the legitimacy of the state.[24] The prison offered a powerful metaphor for doing so. Radical prisoners questioned the notion of guilt itself.[25] By his own admission, Foucault's goal was not to make prisons more humane by expanding privileges like better toilets or more visiting time. Instead, he aimed to blur the moral divide between innocence and guilt.[26]

Black prisoners were incarcerated because they were black in a racist country, progressives argued. As such, black prisoners incarcerated at San Quentin for rape and robbery convictions were no different from the civil rights activists arrested for sitting at soda counters in North Carolina. "That's what America means: prison," said Malcolm X at a 1963 rally.[27] "The system in this country cannot produce freedom for an Afro-American," he said in another speech in 1964. ". . . It's impossible for a white person to believe in capitalism and not believe in racism. You can't have capitalism without racism."[28]

Progressives looked to black radical prison activists for leadership. "Prisoners are the revolutionary vanguard of our struggle," declared the progressive National Lawyers Guild. "When prisoners come out, they will lead us in the streets."[29] The Weather Underground, a radical left terrorist group that killed two police officers in 1981, was "determined to plug themselves into the black revolution," noted a *Times* reporter, "whether the black revolution wanted them or not." Idealizing radical black prisoners was a way for white people on the radical left to free themselves from guilt they felt for being white, she argued. "White-skin privilege," she wrote. "Rich bitches. Spoiled kids. Bourgeois liberals. The young radicals of the Vietnam era set out to prove that such phrases did not apply to them."[30]

The radical prison movement peaked in 1970 during the murder trial of a prisoner named George Jackson. Jackson promoted violence, writing, "give the brother a flame-thrower . . . give him also two comrades in arms, one equipped with an M60 machine gun, the other an anti-tank rocket launcher."[31] Jackson assaulted a bailiff during his trial and had to be subdued. Even so, many progressives maintained that George Jackson was entirely innocent.[32] The Grateful Dead, Pete Seeger, Jane Fonda, and other celebrities raised money for his defense. Foucault coauthored the foreword to the French translation of Jackson's book.[33]

Foucault described crime in positive terms, claiming in *Discipline and Punish* that "the existence of crime happily manifests 'an irrepressibility of human nature'; it is necessary to see in it, not a weakness or a disease, but rather an energy that is straightening itself out, a 'striking protestation of human individuality.'"[34]

A radical prison advocacy organization that Foucault supported in France helped trigger more than two dozen prison revolts between 1971 and 1973.[35] In 1972, a security guard at a Renault factory shot and killed a worker protesting outside the factory gates. Foucault joined his Maoist comrades in a protest, where they clashed with the police. "At the height of the battle," recounted Foucault's biographer, "witnesses glimpsed the gleaming skull of the great professor at the Collège de France absorbing blow after blow from the truncheon of a police officer."[36]

For Foucault and others on the radical left, the ends justified the means. "When the proletariat takes power," said Foucault, it may "exert toward the classes over which it has triumphed a violent, dictatorial, and even bloody power. I can't see what objection one could make to this."[37] The problems created by the new nihilism weren't academic. "We had the means of terrorism," recalled another French radical left leader. "Some of us were on the way to that kind of action. And you must know that when Foucault was speaking, he was speaking to people who were in the mood of terrorism."[38]

In the United States, the radical political rhetoric served as cover for drug dealing and other criminal activities. "I came charging out [of prison] in 1970 expecting to find a Red Army ready for revolutionary war," wrote one black prison radical. "What I found was a handful of red criminals with the same world view I'd had as a poolhall hustler, reinforced with heavy doses of ideology and drugs. . . . So being a 'revolutionary' consisted mainly of . . . snorting coke and puttin' on the style in Oakland." It was later revealed that the entire California's Prisoners' Union, the largest and most heavily funded of the organizations, had become a front for dealing drugs and running prostitutes.[39]

Black Panther Party cofounder Huey Newton spent the last twenty years of his life out of prison shaking down liquor stores in a protection racket, running prostitutes, and dealing cocaine to support his addiction. "Huey Newton is on drugs," said a San Quentin prisoner in 1989. "He became corrupted. When they started off, I don't think they actually thought it would become as big as it became. When it became as big as it became, a lot of money became involved." A few weeks after the interview, somebody fired three bullets at point-blank range into Newton's head, apparently after a cocaine deal went bad.[40]

The chaos, political radicalism, and rising crime in the late 1960s provoked a desire among all races and both political parties for greater
law and order. The California legislature in 1976 passed the Uniform
Determinate Sentencing Act, which transformed the sentencing process
from one focused on rehabilitation to one focused on punishment. Prior to
the new law, there was "indeterminate sentencing," which granted judges
great latitude in determining sentences. An armed robbery could result in
a few years or a life sentence. After a prisoner had served the minimum
sentence, a parole board would review their case and decide the remaining sentence length. The Uniform Determinate Sentencing Act replaced
arbitrary sentencing with set prison terms mandated by the legislature.
Offenders were now given sentences of a standard period of time, with no
ability for a parole board to modify punishments.

The aim of indeterminate sentencing was to encourage rehabilitation
by inmates. But the radical prison movement viewed indeterminate sentencing as discriminatory and paternalistic, while conservatives viewed
indeterminate sentencing as too soft on criminals.[41] And so the legislature
set long, fixed sentences. Over the next twenty years it passed nearly one
hundred laws to increase sentences.[42] The number of prisoners in California quadrupled between 1980 and 1990, adding over 100,000 inmates.[43]

Meanwhile, through ballot measures, voters enacted tough-on-crime
policies. In the 1980s, California voters approved over $3.6 billion in
bonds for prison and jail construction and maintenance.[44] Voters passed
Proposition 4, which expanded the denial of bail, with 82 percent of the
vote.[45] They also backed Proposition 8, the "Victims' Bill of Rights,"
which granted victims a constitutional right to restitution, increased
prison terms for repeat offenders, and reduced the cases where defendants
could plea-bargain.[46]

Throughout the 1980s and 1990s, voters, policy makers, judges, and prosecutors pursued steeper charges and longer sentences. Crimes that had before led to little if any jail time began to fill prisons and jails. For example, the number of people imprisoned for less serious types of theft rose 565 percent between 1980 and 1990.[47] In the 1990s, the California legislature and voters enacted other tough-on-crime measures. They included expanded application of the death penalty,[48] the use of hearsay evidence in preliminary hearings in cases of rape,[49] and, most notoriously, the "three strikes you're out" law, which imposed a mandatory minimum sentence of twenty-five years to life for three-time felony offenders.[50]

The year 2000 marked the transition from tough-on-crime policies to softer policies. Voters in 2000 passed Proposition 21, which I fought and failed to defeat, which expanded the circumstances whereby juveniles can be tried as adults.[51] But California voters also passed a ballot initiative, Proposition 36, created by Ethan Nadelmann and funded by George Soros, which permitted offenders convicted for the first or second time for a nonviolent, low-level drug possession offense to receive probation and community-based drug treatment instead of jail or prison. It was the first of a series of measures passed over the next two decades that gradually reduced the consequences for using, and then for dealing, hard drugs.[52]

14

"Legalize Crime"

Christopher Young is a Seattle Police Department detective and twenty-five-year veteran of the police force who describes himself as a "progressive who wants to decriminalize drugs and advance the welfare state" and as sympathetic to the goals of Black Lives Matter.[1] But Young was so disturbed by Seattle's ceding of the Capitol Hill neighborhood to anarchists that he, like Vickie Beach and former police chief Carmen Best, has started speaking out publicly about the episode. "The anarchists had always been a cosplay clown joke," he told me in early 2021. "On May Day they would come and fight the police and break some windows. We'd be like, 'Okay guys, go back to your mother's basement.'"[2]

Then, after the election of Donald Trump as president in 2016, the anarchists rebranded themselves as anti-fascists, said Young, and that increased their legitimacy in the eyes of Seattle's progressive voters. "They said, 'We're here to fight the racists and fascists.'"

Over the years, anti-police rhetoric and policies became increasingly mainstream in progressive cities. At the election night party for Chesa Boudin in 2019, progressive San Francisco supervisors Matt Haney, Hillary Ronen, and former supervisors Jane Kim and David Campos joined Boudin on the dais and gave rousing speeches. Another progressive supervisor, Sandra Lee Fewer, held up the middle fingers of both hands and led the crowd in a chant against the Police Officers' Association, or POA. "Fuck the POA! Fuck the POA! Fuck the POA!"[3]

Oakland mayor Libby Schaaf was elected in 2014 on a promise to increase the police force to eight hundred, but, in the summer of 2020, the Oakland City Council voted 5–1 to cut $15 million from the police department. The vote of opposition came from a member who felt the cuts weren't deep enough.[4] One African American police task force member in Oakland told the *Chronicle* that, while he thought the police budget was too high, he cringed when "100 new white folks" spoke at a recent City Council hearing to argue that police are "harmful to Black and brown people."[5]

Of every major city in America, progressives are most powerful, and most advanced, in achieving their goals in Seattle. "CHOP/CHAZ didn't happen by accident," said Young. "That's the goal. They don't believe in the legitimacy of any government. They are dead serious about getting rid of police, prisons, and jails. There are [anarchists] in the prime of their life going to federal prison for five years because they want to set the police department on fire. And it's not fringe. It's high-profile people. Even [former American football player] Colin Kaepernick is publishing essays quoting Michel Foucault and saying he wants to abolish all police. Which means that the Antifa would be the police."[6]

Armed residents of the CHOP shot two teenage boys just before it was shut down. The shooting killed Antonio Mays Jr., a sixteen-year-old, and left his fourteen-year-old companion in serious condition. It appears that on June 29, 2020, Mays and his companion "trespassed" in the CHOP in a Jeep and provoked its "security." Some residents of the CHOP opened fire on the Jeep. After looking in on the boys bleeding inside the vehicle a CHOP member could be heard saying, "Yo, you wanna get pistol-whipped?" Due to the CHOP's autonomous nature and habit of preventing law enforcement from entering, no one could arrive on the scene until hours afterward. By then, Mays was dead.[7]

Radical left-wing protesters also created an autonomous zone in Portland in December 2020 after a black family was evicted from their home for defaulting on a second mortgage. Occupiers took over several blocks, including the house, in protest. In response, the mayor of Portland authorized the police to use "all lawful means" to end the occupation and declared, "There will be no autonomous zone in Portland." Police violently clashed with protesters but failed to take back the city blocks. Finally, the city cut a deal with the protesters and paid to let the family stay in the home. Said one occupier, "This isn't like what we've seen before. It's a negotiation and a win, and that is something we're just not used to."[8]

In the spring of 2021 anarchists created yet another autonomous zone, this time in Minneapolis, at the intersection near where George Floyd was killed. Local black-owned businesses suffered because customers were unwilling to enter the zone.[9] Many of the occupiers were not from the community that had been taken over. Some weren't even from the city. Two white occupiers prevented a television news crew from entering. After a local African American resident, and member of the local church, saw the segment, he was outraged, and invited the news crew to accompany him into the zone. But once again, anarchists threatened them and told them to leave. "This is supposed to be sacred ground, not ground to push people out," said a local African American church leader upset by the anarchist rule, "but ground for all of us to come together."[10]

Then, as in Seattle, two men were shot. The anarchists prevented first responders from coming into the zone, and one of the men died. The mayor of Minneapolis initially said police would not move to break up the zone until the trial of George Floyd's killer is completed but then reversed himself.[11]

Some have protested elected officials at their homes. In San Francisco, radical left activists protested Mayor Breed in front of her home. Breed said the protesters were "all white people. But that didn't bother me as much as the taunting of me coming outside with firework torches in their hands looking like what used to happen when the KKK would show up to black people's houses to burn their houses down."[12]

San Francisco police sergeant Kelly Kruger described the anti-police violence she and her colleagues experienced in 2020. "After the protests after the Floyd killing, they threw fecal matter on us and chanted 'Save a life! Kill a cop!' and threw urine," said Kruger. "I thought it was horrible about Floyd, and it was not okay, and any reasonable cop is going to be ashamed or sad about that."[13]

The same occurred in other progressive cities. Marchers set fire to the Oakland Courthouse, smashed police station windows, and chanted "OPD [Oakland Police Department], back the fuck up," pointed lasers at the eyes of Oakland police officers, threw rocks, and punched officers, one of whom was injured.[14] One man was arrested for concealing a machete in a protest sign.[15] In Seattle, protesters urged police officers to commit suicide, and threw rocks, fireworks, and Molotov cocktails at them.[16] And others made death threats against Seattle's mayor, called her a white supremacist, and protested her at her home. On December 7, 2020, Jenny Durkan announced she would not run for reelection in 2021.[17]

During California governor Jerry Brown's time in office, voters passed several reforms aimed at reducing the size of the prison population. In 2012, voters passed a change to the Three Strikes law so that the third strike imposes a life sentence only if the new felony was serious or violent.[18] In addition to lowering punishments for drug possession, Proposition 47, which voters passed in 2014, redefined shoplifting, forgery, petty theft, and receiving stolen property as misdemeanors when the value in question does not exceed $950.[19] In 2016, voters approved a proposition that shortened the time it took for some nonviolent offenders to be eligible for parole and which released nonviolent offenders into drug treatment and rehabilitation.[20]

Property crimes rose in San Francisco starting in 2012. Larceny, which is shoplifting and other petty theft, rose 50 percent, from roughly 3,000 incidents per 100,000 people in 2011 to about 4,500 in 2019. Property

crimes as a whole, which include larceny, motor vehicle theft, and burglary, rose from 4,000 incidents per 100,000 people in 2011 to 5,500 in
2019. [21] One study suggests that Proposition 47 increased the rate of auto
theft 17 percent and the rate of larceny (non-auto property) theft 9 percent,
but discerning between causation and correlation may not be possible. [22]

Upon taking office in January 2020, Boudin followed through on his
campaign promises. Instead of prosecuting and incarcerating people for
breaking car windows to steal money and other items from inside, Boudin
proposed creating a $1.5 million fund to reimburse car owners. But there
were over 25,000 car break-ins reported in 2019. [23] If every break-in cost
just $250 in repairs, the fund would need four times that amount. And
what would prevent people from falsely claiming to have been robbed in
order to get city money?

Boudin's main goal is deincarceration. "The challenge going forward," said Boudin, "is how do we close a jail?" [24] Many believe that most
in jail are there for nonviolent offenses but the most recent available data
shows that two-thirds of the people in San Francisco's jail were there for
violent crimes or weapons possession, not petty, nonviolent, or "victimless" crime. Just 4 percent are there for drug crime. [25]

San Francisco residents needed to understand that some amount of
crime was inevitable given the city's wealth, said Boudin in 2020. "We
have some of the richest people in the history of the world in this city.
Fortunes never imaginable ten or twenty or fifty years ago. . . . When we
have those extremes in close proximity, there's going to be some level of
property crime. That's a reality." [26]

Boudin opposed efforts by the mayor and the city attorney to prevent drug dealers who had already been arrested from entering the Tenderloin. "Until the city is serious about treating addiction and the root
causes of drug use and selling," said Boudin in a statement, "these recycled, punishment-focused approaches are unlikely to succeed at doing
anything more than making headlines." [27]

Home burglaries rose in early 2021 in San Francisco. Homeowners started posting on Twitter videos from their security cameras of people breaking into homes and garages. "When I first moved here we had a car break-in problem," said Michael Solana, a writer who works for a venture capital fund. "Now we have a home invasion problem. These things are wearing on people."[28] Boudin attributed the rise of burglaries in San Francisco to the decline of tourism and "people in desperate economic circumstances." Progressive supervisor Hillary Ronen agreed. "We know that [economic insecurity and inequality] is one of the root causes of property crimes specifically," she said.[29]

But Tom Wolf and others argued that the robberies were, like the shoplifting, done by people seeking money to buy drugs and feed their addictions. "The drugstores have been shoplifted to death and that's all because of drug use," said Tom. "I know. I used to do the same thing when I was out there. That's what you do. You 'boost.' And then you go and you sell your stuff down at UN Plaza," an open-air drug scene.[30]

In a May 2021 city supervisors' meeting, a representative from CVS called San Francisco "the epicenter of organized retail crime in the country" and claimed that 85 percent of the shoplifting is committed by organized theft rings.[31] Police broke up one such ring in October 2020 and recovered $8 million of stolen merchandise.[32]

The problem goes beyond property crime. Boudin declined to prosecute two men who went on to kill people. One man had been repeatedly arrested for stealing cars, despite having just been released from prison earlier in the year, and appeared to be abusing meth. On New Year's Eve, 2020, the man killed two people while driving intoxicated. Police found inside of his car a semiautomatic handgun and twenty-three grams of methamphetamine. On February 4, another intoxicated driver killed a pedestrian in a stolen car. The San Francisco police had arrested him in October 2020 for possessing a stolen car, a tool for stealing cars, and what appeared to be meth. Boudin chose not to pursue charges. In December, the California Highway Patrol arrested the man again for driving a stolen vehicle under the influence.[33] Again he was not prosecuted.

The accident victim, an immigrant from Kenya, and his wife had moved to San Francisco two weeks before the fatal crash. "I blame the DA," said the widow of the victim. The suspect, she said, "was someone who was out in the public who shouldn't have been in the public. It was completely avoidable."[34]

Tom said he could feel the difference on the streets. "Drug dealing is unabated and it's not one guy, it's fifty guys dealing fentanyl and meth," he said. "And it's going unabated because the district attorney says, 'These are the nonviolent, quality-of-life crimes,' and 'I'm not going to prosecute them.'"

In October 2020, San Francisco police officers discovered a body on fire in a neighborhood frequented by heavy drug users. "Officers on patrol saw a fire, thought it was a debris fire," said an officer. "They came up and saw it was a person."[35]

Said Deli Board owner Adam Mesnick, "It makes no sense that the district attorney will tell you that he has more fear of a Honduran dealer's family having challenges than a local family whose kid OD'd on fentanyl. I mean, it's absurd. This guy protects dealers."[36]

District Attorney Boudin was offering weaker sentences than even defense attorneys were requesting, according to Vicki Westbrook of San Francisco. "There's a defense attorney who said, 'It used to be that I would argue for this deal in court with the DA but now I don't say anything because the DA is going to offer me a deal better than what I would have suggested. Somebody shot up the street with an automatic weapon. The first offer was six months in jail or time served plus two years of probation or something. And then [the DA] said, "How about thirty days in jail?"'"

Vicki laughed. "You really can do anything in San Francisco," she said. "If you do get arrested, chances are you're going to be out of jail in less than thirty days for damn near everything except maybe killing somebody and maybe even then, too. It's hard to say at this point."[37]

The situation was similar in other progressive West Coast cities. "It's a free-for-all here in Seattle," said Vickie Beach. "You can commit crimes and not get in trouble. I don't even know if we can get back to what it used to be, especially with the law they're trying to pass saying that if you're homeless and mentally ill and commit a crime you don't get in trouble."[38]

In early 2021, a San Francisco resident posted on Twitter a photo of a bare mattress propped up against a building on a sidewalk intersection in the neighborhood of Diamond Heights. The words "Legalize Crime" were scrawled on it. "In case anyone is confused about why SF is crazy," the person tweeted, to which people replied, "it's pretty much legalized as it is," "few are confused," and "that's Chesa's handwriting!"[39]

In 2014, the police chief of St. Louis described less aggressive policing and more empowered criminals as the "Ferguson effect." Three months earlier, a white police officer in nearby Ferguson had killed an unarmed eighteen-year-old black teenager. "I see it not only on the law enforcement side," said the chief, "but the criminal element is feeling empowered by the environment."[40]

In 2015, the US Department of Justice asked one of the country's leading criminologists, Richard Rosenfeld from the University of Missouri–St. Louis, to investigate whether homicides had, in fact, risen after Ferguson. At first, Rosenfeld was skeptical. He noted that homicides in St. Louis had already started rising before 2014. But after looking at the evidence, he changed his mind. "The homicide increase in the nation's large cities was real and nearly unprecedented," he wrote in his 2016 report. Rosenfeld had found a 17 percent rise in homicide in the nation's largest cities, between 2014 and 2015.[41]

Rosenfeld describes the experience from the point of view of African

Americans living in the inner city. "When the police are called to respond to a crime, they arrive at the scene late or not at all. They do not follow up with vigorous and thorough investigation, even of the most serious crimes. They harass innocent youth. And, too often, they use force unnecessarily and indiscriminately. What matters is not the factual accuracy of these beliefs in every instance; what matters is that they can metastasize into a pronounced 'legal cynicism,' especially in disadvantaged African-American communities."

Rosenfeld subscribes to the concept of legitimacy, the public's belief in police and the broader criminal justice system. He cited the research of Randolph Roth and others. "When people believe the procedures of formal social control are unjust," noted Rosenfeld, "they are less likely to obey the law."[42]

Other researchers found that negative publicity about the police has a powerful impact on police officers, making them more likely to believe that the public's attitude toward them has worsened and that their legitimacy is being questioned. And it makes them more fearful of having false allegations leveled against them.[43] Viral videos of police brutality demoralize police departments, found Roland Fryer, who then retreat from the kind of policing that prevents crime. In investigations preceded by an incident of deadly force that went viral, said Fryer, there were 893 additional homicides and 33,472 more felonies than would have been predicted without the viral video. "In Chicago alone after the killing of Laquan McDonald," reported Fryer, "the number of police-civilian interactions decreased by 90% in the month the investigation was announced."[44]

In 2020, then–vice presidential candidate Kamala Harris tweeted, "America has confused having safe communities with having more cops on the street. It's time to change that."[45]

But there is good evidence that more police, and more policing, can reduce crime. In 2009, President Obama's stimulus package funded nearly a billion dollars in police hiring grants to struggling American cities. A Princeton professor used statistical methods to find that cities that qualified for the grant had increased policing by 3.2 percent and experienced a 3.5 percent decline in crime. The effect of more police was statistically significant for "robbery, larceny, and auto theft," he noted, "with suggestive evidence that police reduce murders as well." And the investments were cost-effective, with every $95,000 spent on police salary preventing $350,000 in crime.[46]

A similar study of federal grants made to local police departments in the 1990s also found that they reduced crime rates for assault, robbery, burglary, and auto theft in cost-effective ways.[47] Researchers find $1 invested in policing results in $1.63 in crime reduction benefits.[48] In a 2019 paper a scholar concluded that crime rose by 7 percent when police patrols in Houston declined by 10 percent.[49]

The lack of sufficient police may have made communities more vulnerable to the spikes in homicides seen in 2015 and 2020, as police were redirected to deal with anti-police protests. Since 2008, the number of cops per capita has retreated from the post-crime-wave peak, thanks both to state and local austerity and to growing agitation against policing. Some experts believe that the declining police presence caused or contributed to the plateauing of the crime decline, and costs millions of dollars and thousands of lives every year.[50]

I asked Chief Carmen Best about the homicide spike.

"When you have your officers and detectives every night on the front line dealing with demonstration after demonstration after demonstration," she said, "they are not engaging with community members. They are not talking to young people. All of that is not happening because the focus now is on the nightly demonstrations."

Rosenfeld said there is evidence to support Best's theory. He pointed to community policing in Oakland, which is tied to social services, as effective.[51]

"There's a dynamic relationship between police and criminals, isn't there?" I asked Rosenfeld.

"Of course," he said. "They know each other. When you get on the ground, the cops have a sense of who the big troublemakers are. And you can't do your business slinging drugs or waiting to rob dealers when the cops are around so you have to keep your eyes on the cops."

Police killings and overall homicide rise and fall together, both nationally and at the state level. Roth found that the number of police-involved homicides, where the police may be assailants or victims, followed the number of general homicides.[52] And Best says that potential criminals know when the police aren't around. "People start figuring it out. The cops aren't really around, and there was a level of frustration about the discussion around policing and what they can and can't do. And then you do that in the middle of a pandemic and people are frustrated about other things, too."[53]

In New York City, effective policing helped reduce homicides dramatically between 2000 and 2020. Where Oakland's homicide rate over the last thirty-five years failed to drop below 17 per 100,000 people, and averaged 18 per 100,000 between 2015 and 2019, New York's homicide rate was around 4 per 100,000 from 2015 to 2019.[54] New York may thus show a way forward for Oakland and other high-homicide cities.

Neither greater incarceration nor demographic changes can explain the dramatic declines in homicides and other crimes in New York. An 11 percent increase in people locked up correlated with a drop in killings five times as large. Street crime fell 80 percent without a significant change in population structure, age distribution, or incarceration, which undermines the belief that those factors cause crime.[55] By 2009, over three-quarters of the young men who would have gone to prison if New York had followed the national trends did not. Good policing had prevented over-incarceration.[56]

University of California, Berkeley criminologist Frank Zimring attributes much of the decline to the hiring in 1994 of William Bratton as commissioner of the New York Police Department. Bratton introduced the CompStat process, which changed the police's central performance measure from arrest count to crime reduction.[57] He made removing guns from the street a high priority. Bratton made officers more accountable for their performance.[58] And Bratton prioritized breaking up open-air drug scenes, just like European cities had. That included breaking up the large and infamous one in New York City's Times Square.[59] By the late 1990s, public drug markets disappeared, and the number of drug-related killings fell 90 percent.[60]

The same approach has worked in other parts of the United States. In High Point, North Carolina, police targeted three neighborhoods with persistent crack cocaine dealing. There, police officers, accompanied by local community workers, met with dealers in person, asked them to stop, and offered job training, tattoo removal, and help restarting their lives.[61] The officers gave the dealers unsigned arrest warrants, three-ring binders of the evidence against them, and video proof of their crimes. These interventions broke up the market, which hundreds of arrests over two decades had failed to do.[62]

The New York success is supported by research that finds that greater police visibility decreases crime. It does so by convincing would-be criminals that they are more likely to get caught, known as deterrence.[63] The same research into deterrence also finds that longer sentences do not deter crime and may in fact increase it. Probation is also shown to prevent crime and decrease recidivism, while imprisonment is not.[64] This suggests that an effective way to reduce crime and mass incarceration would be shorter, swifter, and more certain prison sentences, with the money saved redirected to more and improved policing, including policing capable of handling the severely mentally ill.

Other programs show how the criminal justice system can incentivize positive changes by being present in people's lives. There is evidence that probation programs that are "swift, certain, and fair" reduce arrests, recidivism, and drug use in probationers, in contrast to traditional programs, which tend to be arbitrary and slow with punishments.

One such program is Hawaii's Opportunity Probation with Enforcement. It incentivized offenders to follow probation rules by applying guaranteed, immediate, and short jail time for parole violations like failing a drug test. One study found that HOPE reduced drug use by 72 percent, future arrests by 55 percent, and incarceration by 48 percent.[65] One researcher summarized the benefits of the program, saying, "HOPE actually gets people to change their behavior by setting up a circumstance where their natural behavior moves in the right direction. They don't want to be arrested and go to jail, so they stop using. That's a profoundly rehabilitative thing to do."[66]

This success spurred other jurisdictions to implement swift, certain, and fair. The state of Washington implemented it for 70,000 of its inmates, which reduced jail stays by two-thirds. One researcher estimated that swift, certain, and fair could halve the United States' prison population.[67] A large study across four different counties in the United States failed to find an effect on arrests, recidivism, or reincarceration from swift and certain punishment, but it contained serious flaws, argued a RAND Corporation analyst. Instead of analyzing each jurisdiction individually, researchers averaged them together. The result masked the differences in implementation between programs. In truth, the localities that implemented swift and certain most like Hawaii did see reductions in repeated crime. And, as important, across all cities attempting swift, certain, and fair, regardless of how faithfully they implemented the Hawaii model, probationers were 60 percent less likely to test positive for drugs.[68]

Progressive cities have not embraced swift, certain, and fair probation programs. Vicki Westbrook had never heard of it, even though she works in reentry for previously incarcerated people in San Francisco. But Vicki said that she thought some people needed probation and regular drug testing to stay sober. She told a story about a man she had become friends with in drug treatment. "I call him my brother even though he's not my brother," she said. "We were both fed clients so he's still on probation. And he's like, 'Yeah, I do better when I'm on probation. I hate my [parole officer]. She's a bitch. She's always giving me a hard time. I hate going to see her. She pops up out of nowhere. But, Vicki, I do better when I'm on probation.' So some people do good on probation because somebody's watching them."[69]

After the two young men were killed in Seattle's Capitol Hill occupation protest, Chief Best developed a plan to take it back from its anarchist occupiers. Her team tried to enlist support from neighboring police departments. "But only one agency, [neighboring city] Bellevue, sent people," she said. "I'm not kidding you. All of the other jurisdictions were like, 'Forget it. We are not going into Seattle. Every time we go there our people get complaints, and they're not supported.'" Best told her officers, "Nobody else is coming, so we're going to have to use our own people to do it. That means getting detectives and patrol officers. That's how it's going to have to be."

There were about three hundred police officers and some agents from the FBI when she took the podium to instruct Seattle's officers how to clear CHOP. "We need to clear out the Capitol Hill Organized Protest," Best said. "It has become untenable, dangerous, and lawless. Do not look behind you because no one is coming. No matter what happens today we absolutely have to finish the mission. It's up to us.

"If one of those people in one of those tents decides to come out shooting and something happens, I will call Force Investigations, but we're going to keep going. Any officer gets shot, we'll get you to the hospital, but we keep going. Somebody barricades themselves in a facility and we got to call the hostage negotiators, we'll do it, but we keep going.

This day doesn't end until we clear that area out. There is no other option. We need to get it done."

She surveyed the room. "The whole world is watching," she said. "We need to get it done. And everybody in here needs to have that sense of fortitude that you're going to stick with it, because this day can get to be very long."

"You're going to get us killed!" shouted an officer from the back of the room.

"If you don't want to go," said Best, "then take off the uniform and go home. I only need people who are going to get the job done."

"It was quite nerve-racking for me," she said. "But as far as I know, nobody left. It felt like my whole life was leading up to that moment. I felt like I was standing by myself on an island. Nobody is listening to me in the city, and nobody's coming to help us."

Best observed the police operation from the fire station one block away. She thought, "If this lasts until night, then we're going to have to make sure we get really bright lights in places so the people can see and continue clearing it out." But just an hour into the operation, a commander radioed Best to say, "We're headed west toward the park to clear the park out."

"'What?'" she thought. "In my mind it was going to be at least eight hours, but within probably two hours it was done. No shots fired. No significant injuries. We were able to clear out the area."

Looking back, Best is bothered that many progressives question whether or not the police should have retaken the neighborhood. "I still find it perplexing. You still hear people saying it wasn't that big of a deal. But it was a big deal because people were getting hurt and no one really seemed to want to address that. There was a large contingent in the city that was trying to give away the precinct."[70]

———

I n August 2020, a few weeks after Chief Best and her officers took back the Capitol Hill neighborhood in downtown Seattle from anarchists, the Seattle City Council voted to cut the budget of the Seattle Police Department.

"That means that all these new people that we hired who are black, people of color, and women will be the first ones to go," she told the City Council. "Because it's first in, first out."

The council said they wanted Best to go through and pick the people to fire. "Let me get this straight," she responded. "You want me to pick the white people to go? Are you crazy? They were highly dismissive. It was the most bizarre thing that I had ever dealt with." After Best called the council's action "reckless" and "dangerous," some members of the council appeared to retaliate.

"Because I said that they were being reckless and dangerous and that people are going to suffer for it," said Best, "the next day, one of the counselors said, 'We need to cut her salary by forty percent.' It wasn't even on the agenda for them to talk about. It was highly punitive and retaliatory."

By the end of 2020, two hundred police officers had left the Seattle police force. "I refuse to work for this socialist City Council and their political agenda," said one officer. "It ultimately will destroy the fabric of this once fine city." Another said the city's progressive City Council "will be the downfall of the city of Seattle."[71]

At least two dozen other police chiefs or senior officers resigned, retired, or took disability leave in America's fifty biggest cities in 2020, while 3,700 beat officers left.[72] Chiefs left cities where police had been involved with highly visible killings of African Americans, like Louisville, Atlanta, and Rochester, New York, but also cities where they hadn't, like Seattle, Dallas, and Tempe, Arizona. The chiefs of Seattle and Dallas happened to be black.[73] Today there are fewer police officers per capita than at any time since 1992.[74]

In 2020, San Francisco had fewer police on the streets than it did a few years earlier. San Francisco's current police staffing in 2019 was already "severely inadequate," according to a city-commissioned study. San Francisco in 2019 had just 1,971 officers but needed 2,176 by law.[75] The number of San Francisco police officers leaving their job grew from 12 officers in 2018 to 26 in 2019 to 31 in 2020. "That might be hard to make up," noted the *Chronicle*, "as the last police academy had only 19 cadets. Most classes are budgeted for 55 people." The head of San Francisco's police officer's union warned, "This is just the beginning. Dozens are actively in the hiring process with other agencies."[76]

As homicides were rising in 2020, New York's mayor, Bill de Blasio, claimed the city was becoming safer. "We now have fewer people in our jails than any time since WWII," he said, "and we are safer for it and better for it."[77]

De Blasio announced the elimination of the department's plainclothes unit, which had been instrumental in breaking up the open drug scenes and getting guns off the street. New York's police force was 7 percent smaller in late 2020 than during the same moment in 2019. The chief of police said the loss of officers was due to "low morale resulting from anti-police sentiment in New York since the death of George Floyd at the hands of Minneapolis officers."[78]

Mayors forced out other police chiefs. Tempe's police chief, who was hired in 2016 as a reformer, said "city officials wanted the department to transform more quickly than is realistic, due to political pressure." The chief was about to start teaching police officers meditation as a strategy for improving police work. "When folks across policing see reform-minded leaders who are also cops' cops being completely discarded without some real foundation as to why, they can't help but question why one would want to tackle the challenge of being a chief," the chief said.

Former San Francisco police officers say they left the city because of the climate of hostility against them. "In San Francisco, everyone was mad," a former officer told the *Chronicle*. "The homeowners would get mad because you didn't move the homeless who were sleeping in front of their house. Then, when you tried to help the homeless, someone would start yelling about police brutality. And everyone had a cell phone camera on you."[79]

Counter to the claims of those who advocate defunding the police as a way to reduce violence, the evidence suggests that fewer cops may mean *more* police misconduct, because the remaining officers must work longer and more stressful hours. Research has found that fatigue predicts a rise in public complaints against cops: a thirteen-hour rather than ten-hour shift significantly boosts their prevalence, while back-to-back shifts quadruple their odds.[80]

The public supports improving, not defunding, the police. In 2020, 58 percent of Oakland residents told pollsters that they wanted to either increase or maintain the size of the police force. In the Oakland neighborhood that has suffered the worst violence, 75 percent of those surveyed wanted to increase or maintain police levels. The survey found greater black support (38 percent) than white support (27 percent) for increasing the number of police.[81]

Experts urge a range of measures police departments can take to reduce violence. They can put in place a rule where if the weapon in question can't kill police officers, police can use other kinds of force, but not shoot. Another is that if an officer suspects that making an arrest will risk someone getting hurt, he should back off. Departments can put in place a "stop shooting" rule where police stop shooting as soon as the target is hit once.[82]

Police departments can build upon past successes and proven practices. The share of civilians killed while fleeing from police declined from 39 percent of all legal intervention homicides in the sixties to just 12 percent by the late 1980s.[83] Some departments need more accountability.[84] City governments, for their part, can demand more transparency in the operation of police departments,[85] and more training for officers,[86] particularly related to working with mentally ill and substance-abusing homeless people.[87]

Rosenfeld felt the Black Lives Matter movement had the potential to improve policing. "It's the existence and persistence and pressure brought about by social movements that keeps these issues on the front burner," he said. "Just as the women's movement and the victims' rights movement kept the issues of the victims of sexual assault and the victims of intimate partner and family violence on the policy front burner."

"But then you need Black Lives Matter to be making a very different demand than 'defund the police,' right?" I asked.

"Of course, you do," he said. "There is a social movement there, and it needs to hoist a banner proclaiming that minority victims' lives matter as well."

"So, you need the moms of the boys who got killed to be like the #MeToo movement?"

"Or Mothers Against Drunk Driving," he added. "In St. Louis and other places every year, there's a march organized by mothers of homicide victims, but that's the extent of it. There's not a sustained political presence of those voices because of the louder voices, running the show. Just look at these Antifa-related groups in Portland. Basically, they're saying, 'Hey, we matter, too!' It's terrible."[88]

In 2019, a Seattle police sergeant asked Vickie Beach to become a block watch captain, an unpaid community role that involves holding meetings once a month for her neighbors to meet and have a conversation with a police officer about crime in the neighborhood.

"I don't know if I want a cop in my house," she told him. "They've always been cocky, arrogant, and rude!"

But Vickie started meeting some police officers she liked. "I would share my story and they didn't say, 'Oh, I don't believe that!' After a few years, I just thought, 'Maybe I can't lump them all together.'"

He said, "Vickie, you know why I want you. You'll call BS on both sides."

Vickie said, "Okay, I'll try it out for a little bit. It's been really hard because my community comes first. But, sometimes, they are in the wrong, just like the police. I want to make a space where there's open dialogue. And in the last four meetings we made progress. I said, 'I want you to be open, real, and raw. Don't hold back. We have got to come together and open ourselves up.'

"I invited my daughter," said Vickie. "She lives in Pasadena and is in graduate school to be a clinical psychologist. She said [the police incident is] one of the reasons why she wants to work with little kids in trauma. Her ex-boyfriend from high school is on social media. He's just constantly bashing the police. His Facebook page was just full of that. And we would get into it sometimes. I had him call me and I said, 'This is what I'm doing. Will you come?' And he said, 'Yeah, I'll come.'

"I was shocked. By the end of the meeting, [he and the police officers] were hugging, exchanging phone numbers. And he said, 'I'm sorry. I get to see you as a black man and not as a police officer.' And these officers are saying, 'We're scared when we see blue lights behind us, too, just like you! They don't know that we're police officers.' It was so moving."[89]

Since then, Vickie has added a new role: mediator between the Black Lives Matter movement and the Seattle Police Department.[90]

What will it take to prevent future occupations like CHOP? Said Vickie, "I think it's going to take the black community to say, 'Go home. You don't represent us. When we protest, we march in a peaceful way with thousands, no violence.'"[91]

15

It's Not About the Money

In 2004, a man named Joel John Roberts published a plaintive book called *How to Increase Homelessness*. In it he pointed out that, for more than thirty years, a large and financially motivated lobby of homeless service providers, homeless housing developers, labor unions, for-profit consultants, and advocacy groups have lobbied at the federal, state, and local level to increase funding for themselves. During that time, homelessness only grew worse. "I do not know of any community plan that actually details how to dismantle the existing homeless service system after homelessness has ended," wrote Roberts.[1] "Maybe, just maybe, we don't really want to end homelessness."[2]

One might be tempted to dismiss Roberts's book as yet another diatribe against the "homeless industrial complex" were it not for the fact that he is an important figure within it. Roberts is CEO of PATH, an integrated housing and services homelessness agency in Los Angeles. He was chairperson of the Los Angeles Homeless Services Authority Advisory Board and a member of LA's Blue Ribbon Panel on Homelessness.

Roberts was saying something similar to HBO's Bill Maher, who described the homeless industrial complex as "Layer upon layer of middle men, inspectors, contractors, lawyers, lobbyists, and—oh, yes—labor unions, too. And until those $531,000 apartments are built, we are putting special porta-potties near the homeless camps, which cost $320,000 each! For porta-potties! That's some good shit!"[3]

The amounts of money are not small. California spent at least $13 billion on homelessness between 2018 and 2020.[4] San Francisco alone will spend $1.1 billion on homelessness over the next two fiscal years. As of spring 2021, the homeless industrial complex was gearing up to seek more money from California taxpayers through legislation that would increase taxes on businesses with more than $5 million in annual revenue and raise over $2 billion more.[5]

The nonprofit service organizations, funded by taxpayers, turn around and advocate for taxpayer funding, a conflict of interest. "The beautiful thing about the way we have it set up," said Kristen Marshall, who runs San Francisco's overdose prevention program, "is that [drug overdose prevention nonprofit] DOPE is funded by the Department of Public Health but we're a program of Human Rights Coalition, so we're not a city agency. We're independent. And that's what gives us the leverage to fight and work the way we do. If we worked in the city system we wouldn't get anything done. We are putting in place restrictions on evictions, reparations for black San Francisco, and showing up every single place and every single time our people are being discussed."[6]

And yet most influential homelessness advocacy organizations are not service providers, and have small budgets. The annual revenue of Jennifer Friedenbach's Coalition on Homelessness, the most influential homelessness advocacy organization in San Francisco, was just $656,892, according to its most recently available tax filing.[7] To put that number in context, consider that the annual revenues of the Nature Conservancy and the National Rifle Association were $1.2 billion and $353 million, respectively, in 2018.[8]

As such, advocates for the homeless would not be so successful in passing ballot measures, raising taxes, and increasing funding for homelessness programs if voters didn't support spending more money on the problem. If voters thought the homelessness industrial complex was causing more harm than good—enabling addiction and overdoses, for example, rather than preventing them—they would not have voted to keep giving them more money over the past thirty years. The problem, in other words, isn't coming from within the homeless industrial complex. It's coming from within ourselves.

Progressive homelessness advocates hold two moral values particularly deeply: caring and fairness. "Across many scales, surveys, and political controversies," notes the psychologist Jonathan Haidt, "liberals turn out to be more disturbed by signs of violence and suffering, compared to conservatives, and especially to libertarians."[9] But in the process of valuing care so much, progressives abandoned other important values, argue Haidt and other researchers in a field called Moral Foundations Theory.

Researchers point to surveys of over 11,000 people over the last twenty years to suggest the existence of six universal values: Caring, Fairness, Liberty, Sanctity, Authority, and Loyalty.[10] Haidt and others note that while progressives ("liberal" and "very liberal" people) hold the values of Caring, Fairness, and Liberty, they tend to reject Sanctity, Authority, and Loyalty as wrong. Because these values are so deeply held, often subconsciously, Moral Foundations Theory explains well why so many progressives and conservatives today view each other as not merely uninformed but immoral.

The values of Sanctity and Authority appear to explain why conservatives and moderate Democrats more than progressives favor prohibitions on things like sleeping on sidewalks, public use of hard drugs, and other behaviors. In a more traditional morality, drug use is seen as violating the Sanctity of the body, and the importance of self-control. Sleeping on sidewalks is seen as violating the value of Authority of laws and thus Loyalty to America. Writes Haidt, "liberals are often willing to trade away fairness when it conflicts with compassion or their desire to fight oppression."[11]

But there is a twist. Progressives don't trade away Fairness for victims, only for those they see as privileged. Progressives still value Fairness, but more for victims, and their progressive allies, than for everyone equally, and particularly not for people progressives view as the oppressors and victimizers. Conservatives and moderates tend to define Fairness around equal treatment, including enforcement of the law. They tend to believe we should enforce the law against the homeless man who is sleeping and urinating on BART even if he is a victim. Progressives disagree. They demand we take into account that the man is a victim in deciding whether to arrest and how to sentence whole classes of people including the homeless, mentally ill, and addicts.

Progressives also value Liberty, or freedom, differently from conservatives. Many progressives reject the value of Liberty for Big Tobacco and cigarette smokers but embrace the value of Liberty for fentanyl dealers and users. Why? Because progressives view fentanyl dealers and users, who are disproportionately poor, sick, and nonwhite, as victims of a bad system.

Progressives also value Authority and Loyalty for victims above everyone else. San Francisco homelessness advocate Jennifer Friedenbach told me that we should "center unhoused people, primarily black and brown folks, that are experiencing homelessness, folks with disabilities. They're the voices that should be centered."[12] She is not rejecting Authority or Loyalty. Rather, she is suggesting that we should have Loyalty to the victims, and that they, not governments, should have Authority.

Indeed, progressives insist on taking orders, supposedly without questioning them, from the homeless themselves. "Drug use is often the only thing that feels good for them, to oversimplify it," said Kristen Marshall. "When you understand that, you stop caring about the drug use and ask people what they need."[13] The San Francisco Coalition on Homelessness has similarly argued that the city must let homeless people sit and lie on sidewalks, and camp in public spaces including parks and sidewalks, if that's what they would prefer, rather than require them to stay in shelters. Once you decide, in advance, to let victims determine their fates, then much else can be justified.

Many progressives do something similar with Sanctity, which is to value some things as sacred or pure. When Monique Tula, the head of the Harm Reduction Coalition, insisted on "bodily autonomy," against mandatory drug treatment for people who break the law to support their addiction, she was insisting upon the Sanctity of the body, not rejecting it. The difference between her definition of Sanctity and the traditional view of Sanctity was what violated it. Where traditional morality views recreational injection drug use as a violation of the Sanctity of the body, Tula, like many libertarians, believes that the state coercing sobriety is.

The germ of the idea that society should be organized around the downtrodden was developed by Karl Marx and Friedrich Engels in the mid-nineteenth century. In *The Communist Manifesto* they argued that it was possible and desirable to build a radically egalitarian society. We would do so from a place of cooperation, not competition. Socialism would take us from our current system of capitalist meritocracy to communist utopia. While Marx and Engels described the worker overthrow of the government in economic and social terms, revolution had a spiritual meaning, too: "the total redemption of humanity."[14]

Marx and Engels thought factory workers, the proletariat, were the people who would make the revolution. They believed that labor, not capital, was the source of economic value. The only way for capitalists to make money was to underpay those who created value for them. Capitalists, mean or nice, had no choice but to do so, in order to compete in the system. While Marx and Engels believed that unemployed, disaffiliated, and often homeless people, whom they called the *lumpenproletariat*, would benefit from life under communism, the *lumpenproletariat* had no special role in creating the revolution, because their exploitation wasn't necessary for capitalism's success.

In the early and mid-twentieth century, socialist and radical thinkers and activists began to realize that the proletariat was too disorganized and weak to achieve revolution. They sought to build a much broader political coalition. In California, the International Workers of the World, an anarchist group founded in 1905, sought to link the economic interests of the working class with those of the homeless, the people Marx and Engels had dismissed as the *lumpenproletariat*. They blamed the government and capitalism for their fate. They recruited hobos, who illegally hitched rides on railroad cars, and migrant farmworkers, as members.[15] Antonio Gramsci, head of the Italian Communist Party in the 1930s, realized, after being imprisoned by Benito Mussolini, that fascists had defeated communists because they had taken over important cultural institutions, like the church, schools, and the military. If communists wanted to have the same influence, Gramsci reasoned, they would need to do the same.[16]

By the mid-twentieth century, many radicals had grown disillusioned with the Communist Party as they watched the moral failures and bureaucratic stagnation of the Soviet Union. In the United States, the trade unions, which were once a bastion of the left, had become "fiercely anti-Communist and patriotic," notes a political historian.[17] In the 1950s, the Marxist American sociologist C. Wright Mills argued that students could be a more revolutionary class than workers, which inspired young Baby Boomers, who infused the radical, anti-modern, and anti-Enlightenment New Left.[18] In the 1960s, some progressives came to believe that black Americans were inherently revolutionary due to their disadvantaged position in society, and that white people could join the revolution by following their lead.[19]

The loosening of traditional morality widened the possibilities available to many people, but it also created a moral and spiritual vacuum. Where major religions had viewed humans as having souls that had some continued existence after the death of the body, the new secularism tended toward the view that consciousness was the result of material processes. Humans had no spirit independent of the biological processes inside the physical brain. Once we died, nothing in us lived on.

Such hard secularism created anxiety. Whereas people on the political right tend to adhere more closely to traditional religions and moralities, whether Christianity, Judaism, or Hinduism, progressives are more secular, atheist, agnostic, and more open to alternative religions. Research suggests that progressives are more existentially anxious, neurotic, and unhappy, which some researchers attribute to lower levels of religiosity.[20] One of the long-recognized benefits of religion is that it helps people to cope with their fear of death. If we follow a certain code of conduct, or morality, religions around the globe say, we can transcend death, and live on in a new world, whether heaven or a future world through reincarnation.

Friedrich Nietzsche in the late nineteenth century predicted that rising disbelief in God, and life after death, would result in new moralities and religions. Some would try to turn science into a religion, he believed, which is today known as scientism. The two great political religions of the twentieth century were fascism and communism. Where Christians believe that the kingdom of God is in heaven, communists believed the kingdom of communism was in the future. And where Christians had believed in the ultimate Authority of God, fascists believed in the Authority of the state as the manifestation of the spirit of the nation, or race.[21] As these two great ideologies lost legitimacy and power in the twentieth century they split and changed into different moralities and ideologies.

In the Marxist story, workers had played the role of hero, overcoming all odds to save the world. They started as mere peasants on a farm before moving to the city and being exploited in the factories. Over time, they and their children learned to read and demanded their rights from the bosses. They organized unions and valued Loyalty to those who were in their same socioeconomic class. They came to understand their exploitation, and their special role in history, which Marx believed they were destined to play for inherent, structural reasons. Similar to enslaved people who revolted, factory workers would one day rise up, take control of the factories, and take control of governments, violently or nonviolently. The workers would embrace technological progress and share its rewards in the form of material wealth and leisure time.[22]

Starting in the 1960s, many on the New Left cast African American prisoners in the role of revolutionary and even spiritual heroes. "For some [New Left] extremists," noted a historian, radical black prisoners "had become nature spirits, self-actualized, noble, violent, sexual primitives."[23] Said a white attorney for radical prisoners, "They are more loving. They have more creative human potential."[24] Wrote the white left-wing editor of radical prisoner George Jackson's books in 1974, "For most middle-class whites like myself, life is a matter of chronic discontent. . . . We say to ourselves that only blacks possess true authenticity."[25] The white attorney's office in Berkeley had massive posters of the black prison leaders on the walls, and a staff of young white women, noted a sociologist at the time. "All of 'em had picked one of 'em as the one that she was worshipping."[26]

All religions and moralities have light and dark sides, suggests Haidt. "Morality binds and blinds," he writes.[27] On the one hand, they bind us together in groups and societies, helping us realize our individual and social needs, and are thus very positive. But religions and moralities can also create giant blind spots preventing us from seeing our dark sides, and thus can be very negative.

The dark side of victimology is how it moralizes power. Victimology takes the truth that it is wrong for people to be victimized and distorts it by going a step further. Victimology asserts that victims are inherently good because they have been victimized. It robs victims of their moral agency and creates double standards that frustrate any attempt to criticize their behavior, even if they're behaving in self-destructive, antisocial ways like smoking fentanyl and living in a tent on the sidewalk. Such reasoning is obviously faulty. It purifies victims of all badness. But by appealing to emotion, victimology overrides reason and logic.

This is not a phenomenon of ignorant people but rather of highly educated ones. It was philosophers, university professors, and journalists after World War II who decided that because the mentally ill had been so badly mistreated they needed to be freed immediately, even though that meant becoming homeless and often incarcerated. The same kinds of people in the 1990s felt that because America had gone overboard with drug prohibition, punishment, and mass incarceration we should not pressure addicts, as they do in Portugal and the Netherlands, to get sober. And it is educated progressives in West Coast cities today who point to centuries of racism as reason for stopping enforcing the laws that make city life possible, including laws against armed gangs taking over whole neighborhoods.

Charity, and acting from altruism more broadly, has long had a dark side. Consider Saint Francis. He was born rich, the son of a prosperous silk trader. After he heard the voice of Jesus say, "Go, Francis, and repair my house, which as you see is falling into ruin,"[28] Francis went home and stole from his father both money and valuable silk cloth. After the priest at the local church rejected his offering, Francis grew angry and made a scene, suggesting that his act was selfishly motivated.[29]

Francis is an extreme character but also a familiar one. Psychological research supports what might seem intuitively obvious, which is that many people behave in more altruistic, generous, and compassionate ways when they know they are being watched.[30] There is nothing necessarily wrong with conspicuous compassion. Philanthropists who have sought to win the altruism game have achieved many positive things, including higher agricultural yields, the elimination of disease, and rights for traditionally victimized minorities. And when they accomplish positive things they deserve recognition.

The problem is when compassion acts as cover for darker motivations. Throughout history people who appear to have the Dark Triad personality traits of psychopathy, Machiavellianism, and narcissism, most famously Stalin and Mao, have successfully manipulated compassionate, idealistic people to support them, even after evidence of their barbarism came to light. What is notable is that they have often done so not by pretending to be altruistic but by being genuinely altruistic. If we are to understand why progressives ruin cities, we need to understand how and why compassion, altruism, and love have created a blind spot, and not just in relationship to foreign despots but also to homegrown ones.

16

Love Bombing

In 1931, one of the worst years of the Great Depression, a young couple in a rural Indiana town had their first and only child. Scarred by the loss of their farmland and the ravages of World War II, they raised their son in a shack without running water. The mother educated her son as best she could. He showed empathy at a young age for African Americans. He read voraciously, showing an early interest in Gandhi, and religion. He argued with his father over race and did not speak to him for many years after he refused to let him bring a black friend into their house. In 1948 he graduated from high school with honors. At Indiana University in Bloomington he was moved by a speech from former first lady Eleanor Roosevelt about the suffering of black Americans. His name was Jim Jones.[1]

Jones married and moved first to Northern California and then to San Francisco with his wife to start a church. He called it the People's Temple. Jones believed he was the leader of a socialist revolution. He warned of nuclear war and claimed black people would be put in concentration camps. He became a hugely charismatic preacher among African Americans, the disaffiliated poor, and young transplants to the city looking for community.[2] Scenes from the era show a remarkably large and diverse congregation smiling and singing. The People's Temple grew and provided services. Jones cultivated two progressive San Francisco politicians, George Moscone and Willie Brown, and mobilized people to volunteer for their campaigns.

Jones had a complicated relationship to race and religion. He adopted several children of different races, naming his African American son Jim Jones Jr. But in 2012, Jim Jones Jr. described his father "manipulating black people" by giving him special treatment compared to Jones's other adopted and biological children.[3] Jim Jones Sr. sometimes referred to himself as "mixed," "Indian," or "black," and appeared to have believed he was a reincarnation of an African American spiritual leader who himself claimed to be Jesus Christ reborn.[4] But Jones became an atheist who rejected religion, including Christianity, as oppressive, and became an apocalyptic Marxist. He ridiculed the notion of God and heaven. He was hedonistic and cruel. Jones coerced young congregants into sex, stole money from African American families, and took both amphetamines and barbiturates.[5]

While Jones thought globally, he acted locally. His son and a San Francisco historian believe he stole the mayoral election for Moscone in 1975. Historian David Talbot, founder of the progressive website *Salon*, points to evidence that Jones committed sufficient voter fraud to account for Moscone's narrow 4,443-vote margin of victory. "We loaded up all thirteen of our buses with maybe seventy people on each bus, and we had those buses rolling nonstop up and down the coast into San Francisco the day before the election," said Jones Jr. "Could we have been the force that tipped the election to Moscone? Absolutely! Slam dunk. He only won by four thousand votes." When federal investigators looked into fraud claims three years later, they discovered that all of the records were missing from the city of San Francisco's registrar of voters.[6]

Jones also boasted of providing Moscone with black women from his congregation for sex.[7] One time Moscone, drunk and "accompanied by a young black woman whom the politician had kindly agreed to drive home," crashed into another car.[8] Another time, Moscone and Willie Brown "were with a black woman in an alley at two in the morning at some restaurant in North Beach," said a local bar owner.[9] State legislator

"John Burton was part of that gang too. They were all using marijuana and cocaine."[10] Said Jones Jr., Moscone would "always be there at temple parties with a cocktail in his hand and doing some ass grabbing." A Temple member overheard Jones speaking to Moscone the day after one of those parties saying, "I want to let you know that the young lady you went off with is underage," adding, "Now don't worry, Mayor, we'll take care of you—because we know that you'll take care of us."[11] Afterward, Moscone made Jones the chairman of the powerful San Francisco Housing Commission.[12]

Jones cultivated progressives with money and favors. He made large donations to the ACLU, the NAACP, and United Farm Workers. Jones and Moscone met privately with vice presidential candidate Walter Mondale on a campaign plane a few days before the 1976 presidential election, and Mondale praised People's Temple shortly afterward. Jones met with First Lady Rosalynn Carter several times. Governor Jerry Brown praised Jones. Glide Memorial Church's Rev. Cecil Williams loved Jones. There is a photo from 1977 of a smiling Williams awarding Jones the church's "Martin Luther King, Jr. Award."[13]

Jones used his perch as chairman of the Housing Commission to fight for housing for the poor. He tried to use eminent domain to acquire the International Hotel, a single resident occupancy hotel. After a court sided with the hotel's owner, Jones mobilized seven thousand protesters to picket it.[14] By mid-January 1977, the situation had become heated. There were rumors that protesters inside the building were armed with guns and Molotov cocktails. Jones lost the legal battle in 1977, and the tenants were evicted.[15] But the drama was a publicity victory for Jones, which burnished his image as a white savior.[16]

A conservative member of the Board of Supervisors who was defeated in the mayoral election by Moscone accused the new mayor, the *San Francisco Chronicle*, and the rest of the city establishment of being blind to Jones's extremism. "There's no radical plot in San Francisco," insisted Moscone, in response. "There's no one I've appointed to any city position whom I regard as radical or extremist."[17]

Willie Brown, a powerful state legislator from 1964 to 1995 before becoming mayor in 1996, "seemed oblivious to Jones' hucksterism and demagoguery," notes a historian.[18] Brown was master of ceremonies at a dinner for Jones in the fall of 1976 attended by an adulatory crowd of the rich and powerful, including Governor Jerry Brown. "Let me present to you a combination of Martin King, Angela Davis, Albert Einstein . . . Chairman Mao," he said, to loud applause.[19] And yet Jones was contemptuous of Brown even as Brown did Jones more and more favors. Jones mocked Brown for his designer suits, sports cars, and women. Once, while Brown was addressing the congregation and Jones was seated onstage behind him, Jones flipped his middle finger up to mock him.[20]

San Francisco's establishment stood by Jones even after a California magazine, *New West*, owned by Rupert Murdoch, published an exposé of Jones's beatings of Temple members and financial abuses in August 1977.[21] The article was written by a *San Francisco Chronicle* reporter and was meant for the *Chronicle* to publish. But the newspaper killed the story because it didn't want to alienate Jones, whom it viewed as central to its plans to expand the *Chronicle*'s circulation in the heavily African American Fillmore District.[22] Jones also managed to avoid investigation and prosecution in part by getting the district attorney to hire as deputy district attorney Jones's longtime attorney and confidant.[23]

Progressives defended Jones against the *New West* article. At a rally in the summer of 1977, Willie Brown said, "When somebody like Jim Jones comes on the scene, that absolutely scares the hell out of most everybody occupying positions of power in the system."[24] Angela Davis sent a radio message broadcast over the cult's compound, Jonestown, in Guyana. "I know you're in a very difficult situation right now," she said, "and there is a very profound conspiracy designed to destroy the contributions which you have made to the struggle."[25] After visiting Jonestown, the attorney to the Black Panthers said, "I have seen paradise."[26]

Harvey Milk, too, was tarnished by his association with Jones. In the fall of 1977, Milk wrote to President Carter's secretary of health, education, and welfare requesting that Social Security checks be sent to elderly Temple members in Guyana. "People's Temple," wrote Milk, has "established a beautiful retirement community in Guyana."[27]

In truth, the cult was disintegrating. Jones separated families and lovers, pitted relatives against each other, and forced neighbors to inform on each other. Jones sent people who violated the rules to solitary confinement in "the Box," an underground cubicle where people were held as prisoners for days on end. Others were drugged. Progressives who had spent thirty years fighting to close prisons and mental hospitals found themselves praising a man who had reproduced their worst practices.[28]

In November 1978 a Bay Area congressman flew to Guyana to investigate human rights violations at Jonestown with NBC News. Jones gave the delegation a formal reception at Jonestown. A Temple member surreptitiously passed a note to one of the delegation members, saying he and another member wanted to escape. They fled the next day after a Temple member tried to stab the congressman. Jones didn't prevent them from leaving but then sent gunmen to fire machine guns at the delegation at the airport, killing the congressman and four others.[29]

A few hours later, 907 inhabitants of Jonestown drank Flavor Aid laced with cyanide and died. Two-thirds of the victims were African American and one-third were children. Jones had told them that if they didn't drink it they would be killed by invading soldiers from a shadowy global military conspiracy intent on imposing fascism and torturing children. As people started crying in grief, Jones scolded them. "Stop these hysterics," he said. "This is not the way for people who are socialists or communists to die." Jones's wife protested the murder of children and had to be forcibly restrained. "We didn't commit suicide," said Jones in a tape recording, "we committed an act of revolutionary suicide protesting the conditions of an inhumane world."[30]

Few were as stained by Jonestown as Willie Brown and George

Moscone. "Even as the bloated bodies of the dead were removed from the jungle and the wounded were airlifted by the U.S. Air Force to hospitals in the United States," wrote a historian, "Brown said he had 'no regrets' over his association with Jones."[31] They repeatedly disavowed responsibility. Said Moscone, "it's clear that if there was a sinister plan, then we were taken in. But I'm not taking any responsibility. It's not mine to shoulder."[32]

After Moscone and Milk were killed, one week later, San Franciscans and other Americans wondered if something fundamentally was wrong with one of the world's great cities. "There must be something evil out there," a visitor from San Francisco was told by a person hearing the news of Jonestown in Washington, D.C. "It's crazy, it's sick," said another person. A *San Francisco Examiner* columnist described San Francisco as "[a] city where tolerance deteriorates into license. A town without a norm."[33]

Leading progressives were blind to the reality of the People's Temple and Jonestown for the same reason cult members were attracted to it: the intense commitment to Caring and the redefinition of Fairness, Liberty, Sanctity, Authority, and Loyalty around victims. The heavy focus on Caring, and the Authority given to the victims, as represented by Jones, left progressives unable to see Jones's behavior, and the very creation of Jonestown, as something deeply problematic and, ultimately, a violation of Caring. "At every stage in its existence, People's Temple outreach programs really did practice what Jones preached," wrote a historian. "Needy people were served. Outcasts from every corner of the community were warmly welcomed. Yet no matter how many people were fed, clothed, helped to find jobs, or rescued from drug addiction by Temple programs, Jim Jones ached for all those who still were not."[34]

Jones and the Temple preyed on compassionate people who were also psychologically and spiritually lost, angst-ridden, and concerned about their social status. Cult members often recruit people by convincing them that they are loved and that the cult leader can answer all the important questions they have. Cult recruiters have sometimes used "love bombing," the showering of affection on the newcomer, as a recruitment strategy on college campuses, even waiting outside counseling centers to target troubled students.[35]

After Jonestown, progressives in the Bay Area sought to distance themselves from cult members. Joining a cult, argued psychologists, was a way for young people to "save themselves from the terror associated with the increasing responsibilities and the progressive independence involved in maturing."[36] Such people were mentally impaired, they argued, and often suffered psychotic disorder, which made them less tolerant of moral ambiguity and more in need of moral absolutes.

But cults are much more common in progressive, secular places like the West Coast than in more traditional and conservative religious places. Researchers find that secularization "stimulates the growth of cults where the conventional churches are weakest," including in the San Francisco Bay Area.[37] In 1980, less than two years after Jonestown, more than half of all high school students in the San Francisco Bay Area reported at least one recruiting attempt by a cult member, and 40 percent reported at least three contacts.[38]

The relatively conservative values of voters in places like Miami, Houston, and Phoenix may explain why those cities have lower rates of homelessness than San Francisco, Seattle, and Los Angeles. Adherents to traditional religion tend to be more conservative and favor policies that reduce homelessness, such as banning public camping, defecation, and drug use, and using more mandatory drug and psychiatric treatment. Indeed, in 2018 scientists found that "measures of religiosity can help explain significant variation in unsheltered homelessness in warm places." Concluded the researchers, "culture or variation in service delivery may play an important role."[39]

Victimology appears to be rising as traditional religions are declining. Social scientists had for many years viewed the United States as a possible exception to the broad trend of secularization in other developed nations. But today, it appears that the United States is secularizing like other nations, even as it remains more religious than many nations in Europe. In 2021, fewer than 50 percent of Americans belonged to a house of worship.[40] The decline of traditional religion has allowed for the rise of untraditional ones.

Unlike traditional religions, many untraditional religions are largely invisible to the people who hold them most strongly. A secular religion like victimology is powerful because it meets the contemporary psychological, social, and spiritual needs of its believers, but also because it appears obvious, not ideological, to them. Advocates of "centering" victims, giving them special rights, and allowing them to behave in ways that undermine city life, don't believe, in my experience, that they are adherents to a new religion, but rather that they are more compassionate and more moral than those who hold more traditional views.

The treatment of victims as sacred and thus good occurs outside of the United States, to equally destructive and degrading effect. In 1979, just a few months after Jonestown, a fundamentalist Islamic faction overthrew the government of Iran, winning support from progressives around the world, including Michel Foucault. He believed it was a triumph of the victims of Western colonialism, and wrote magazine articles praising the new regime. "Again and again," noted his biographer, "he went out of his way to stress that the religious opponents of the Shah were *not*, as they were often glibly portrayed in the Western media, 'fanatics.' The mullahs struck him as creditable megaphones for the popular will" who promised a new "political spirituality."[41] But within weeks of taking power, the mullahs' firing squads were executing gay people.[42]

After Dan White had shot and killed Mayor George Moscone and Supervisor Harvey Milk on November 27, 1978, it fell to Supervisor Dianne Feinstein, president of the Board of Supervisors, to inform the public of the horrible news. Footage of her press conference can be seen in a powerful documentary, *The Times of Harvey Milk*.

"As president of the Board of Supervisors," she said, voice trembling, "it is my duty to make this announcement. Both Mayor Moscone and Supervisor Harvey Milk have been shot and killed."

"Jesus Christ!" a man shouts. A woman's cry can be heard.

"The suspect," said Feinstein, "is Supervisor Dan White."

That night, tens of thousands of people took to the street holding candles, marching quietly toward Civic Center Plaza, in one of the most moving and powerful demonstrations ever captured on film.[43]

At the time of the assassinations, Feinstein had felt her career in politics was over. "It seemed clear to her," noted historian David Talbot, "that she was not the leader that San Francisco wanted—too starched, too middle of the road, too goody-goody." For example, Feinstein had wanted to "clean up the Tenderloin, the city's drugged-out red-light district." But Rev. Cecil Williams of Glide Memorial Church felt she was blaming the victim when she extolled the virtues of good hygiene and hard work to the homeless. "If they had a place to get cleaned up," he said, "most of them would get cleaned up."[44]

A few weeks before the assassinations, Feinstein had been trekking in Nepal, where she caught a bad intestinal illness. After she recovered, she decided to announce her resignation from politics on her return to San Francisco. "I was firmly convinced that I was not electable as mayor," she said later. But now with Milk and Moscone dead, she was mayor, and staring out over the crowd at City Center, preparing to give a speech.

Feinstein told the crowd that she would make sure, as mayor, that San Francisco would continue to seek "human rights, love, and understanding." She received the loud and warm applause that San Francisco audiences had never given her before. "When I am really in crisis," she said later, "things are much clearer to me. I move in a regular way and can just sustain myself through the crisis. . . . I needed that ability when I became mayor, because the city was falling apart."[45]

Feinstein took a balanced approach. She appointed a progressive to replace Milk, seeking to affirm the will of the people who had elected him. "Dianne never had a good relationship with Harvey Milk," said the Milk ally whom Feinstein appointed as supervisor to replace him. "*Her* homosexuals were not *his* homosexuals. But very much to her credit, she put all that aside when she appointed me."[46] Feinstein also increased funding for the police. "I believe safety is the first thing you need to guarantee as mayor," she said.[47]

Feinstein rose to the challenge of the AIDS crisis. When it hit in the early 1980s, many believed it would set back the gay rights struggle, but instead it propelled it forward. Coming out of the closet went from being a nice thing to do to becoming a precondition for building the popular support for funding research and treatment. When Supervisor Harry Britt in 1982 asked Feinstein what should be funded, she said, "Fund everything." Said Britt, "She spent more time visiting AIDS patients in hospitals than I did. She was a giver; she was a very compassionate person. I don't want to say 'queenly,' because that sounds very negative, but she was a good queen."[48]

Feinstein "proved to be the best possible leader for the crisis," concluded Talbot. "San Francisco in November 1978 was a broken vessel on a dark sea. When deliverance finally came, San Francisco owed it large part to an unlikely leader." The reason, said Talbot, was that after the tumult of the sixties and seventies, San Franciscans needed a "grownup."[49]

That was then. Since the beginning of the new century, moderate Democrats have seen their power decline against progressive Democrats, in San Francisco and around the country. Even when moderates are in charge, progressives have exercised their powers in other ways.

Progressive members of the Seattle City Council, Los Angeles City Council, and San Francisco Board of Supervisors, and other political officials, often with the significant support from nonprofit activists funded by local governments, have attacked mayors as uncaring. Growing progressive power culminated in the election of Chesa Boudin in 2019, the Seattle Capitol Hill Occupied Protest of 2020, and demands that the homeless, mentally ill, and substance abusers be immune from prosecution in 2021.

It's true that moderate Democrats control the executive branches of the local, state, and federal governments, but they have little to speak of as an agenda beyond being less radical than the radical left. Progressives have, by contrast, a full agenda: Medicare for All, Green New Deal, and sweeping criminal justice reforms, including defunding the police, deincarceration, and drug legalization. Progressives have been on the rise in San Francisco, Seattle, Los Angeles, and nationally, and openly stand in opposition to the more moderate members of the Democratic Party. While the mayors of Seattle, San Francisco, and Los Angeles are all ostensibly moderate, their agendas have either been progressive or a response to progressive demands on harm reduction, Housing First, and criminal justice.

In 2021, the San Francisco School Board voted to strip Dianne Feinstein's name from an elementary school. Her crime was for allegedly replacing the Confederate flag in an historical flags exhibit in 1981 after it had been temporarily removed. In truth, Feinstein had agreed to replace the flag with one representing Union soldiers. But that didn't appear to matter much to anyone. Everybody seemed to understand that the progressive members of the San Francisco School Board in 2021 were targeting Feinstein for her moderation today, not for her policy toward flag exhibits forty years ago.[50]

Over the decades historians have debunked many of Foucault's claims, including around mental illness in Europe, but we can also fruitfully employ his ideas, particularly about the power of language to manipulate our ways of thinking and feeling. "I would like to know the ways in which our bodies, our daily behavior, our sexual behavior, our desire, our scientific and theoretical discourses," he said, "are linked with several systems of power, which are themselves linked with one another."[51] This started with language. "Study the power mechanisms at work in our speech and our society," he advised.[52]

Consider the power mechanisms at work in the discourses of homelessness and victimology. The demand that we not enforce laws against people defined as victims is an attack on a foundational principle of our democracy, equal justice under the law. What is being proposed is, fundamentally, unequal justice, or perhaps a kind of revenge, something that sociologists detect in the sacralization of victims. "Holding the victim of an offense in higher regard can be a way of reversing the harmful effects of the offense, and even a way of punishing the offender, since one is rewarding the person the offender wanted to harm or punish," wrote two scholars. "And, if victimhood is a virtue, privilege is a vice."[53]

As soon as you use the word "homeless" you find yourself trapped within a powerful discourse, one that manipulates our thinking and feelings. The people that my staff and I interact with every day outside of our office in Berkeley may or may not have homes, relatives, or friends with homes where they could stay. They may or may not have access to shelter. Some do and some don't. But what they all have in common is usually some combination of mental illness, severe or not, addiction, and disaffiliation. Several young men I interviewed were from the area with living, housed parents. They implied that they were on the street because of some combination of addiction and estrangement from their loved ones.

Consider a young man who appeared to be in his early twenties named Daniel. While walking to work one morning, I came across his body stretched out in front of the laundromat. His sleeping bag looked expensive and new. His boots looked of similarly good quality and were sitting five feet away from him on the sidewalk, an empty can of tuna fish, plastic wrappers from chips, and used beverage containers scattered around him. When I woke him up to ask if he was okay, he said he was. He looked fit and strong and in much better shape than the older homeless men and women around our office, like Stephen, whom I first met after he had passed out, facedown, his pants down around his knees, in front of our retail office. Stephen is from Ohio but has been here for nearly two decades. He has few if any teeth and spends his days drinking alcohol while playing a video game on his smartphone. The two men are utterly different. Does it really make sense to lump them into a single category called "homeless"?

Neither Stephen nor Daniel is a single mother seeking shelter and a restraining order against an abusive husband, and yet all are categorized as "homeless" or as "unhoused." But, as we have seen, such labeling stemmed from an advocacy effort aimed at convincing us that the problem is poverty and the solution is spending more money on housing and services for the homeless and not, say, shelter and abstinence-contingent housing. One word, "homeless," entails an entire, insidious discourse that acts unconsciously and subliminally on our hearts and minds, rendering us unable to understand the reality before us.

Perhaps the most tragic and harmful work done by the word "homeless" is the mixing together of people with severe mental illness with people like Daniel and Stephen, neither of whom suffer from any mental illness remotely as severe as the ones from which the two women who often wander past my office suffer. I have seen each over a dozen times in the last year and every time they were in a psychotic or distressed state. One screams accusations of rape and molestation, randomly, at passersby. The other one, missing most of her teeth, rants incoherently at invisible beings. Once, while leaving work at dusk, and locking the door, I had the feeling of being watched. With my hand still on the key, I slowly turned my head 45 degrees to my left to look behind me. The woman was by a trash can, about twenty feet from me, staring at me intently with a big, openmouthed smile. As our eyes locked, she started laughing in a way that sent chills down my back.

I do not spook easily. I have traveled through war zones since the late 1980s, been robbed at gunpoint, and worked and lived in dangerous neighborhoods for thirty years. I believe it is possible to be safe in dangerous places if you have a good idea about what you can expect. But by the spring of 2021, more and more people whom I encountered on the street frightened me due to their unpredictably aggressive behaviors. In one week in February, three psychotic people in separate incidents lunged at me. One man came running and yelling at me from the inside of a darkened garage as I walked along the sidewalk, distracted by a phone conversation, after work. I involuntarily reacted, turning around and shouting back, "Jesus!" instantly causing the man to himself startle and say, "I'm sorry! I'm sorry! I'm sorry! I'm sorry!" in a desperate and pathetic voice. Rattled, and my heart booming, I said, "Okay! Okay! It's okay! It's okay," before walking quickly away.

In the spring of 2021 two colleagues and I went to San Francisco. We first went to check in on the open-air drug scenes in the Tenderloin and United Nations Plaza. It was the usual scenes of people sitting against buildings and injecting drug needles into their necks and feet. There was garbage, old food, and feces everywhere. After a couple of hours, we decided to go out to eat in the Mission. Work was over. We were all looking forward to a relaxing dinner. We were eating ice cream and walking along Valencia Street when a psychotic man, perhaps about thirty years old, began following us and screaming obscenities. When we turned around to look at him, he screamed at us, "What are you looking for, huh! WHAT. ARE. YOU. LOOKING. FOR!" and started walking faster toward us. We walked faster until the man found other people to verbally assault.

I have no unusual fear of mentally ill people and have long felt compassion toward them. My aunt suffered schizophrenia and at an early age my parents, who are psychologists, explained mental illness to me. I did not spend a great deal of time with her but the strongest memory I have of her is positive. She spoiled us like an aunt often does, taking us to McDonald's and giving us M&Ms, which she called "pills." I remember her face being heavily painted with makeup in shades of red and green. She was slightly scary but I could tell that she treasured her time with us, and I cared and worried about her.

But it is also clear that untreated mental illness and addiction in progressive West Coast cities has gone well beyond being degrading to the people suffering from it, and dehumanizing to everyone who witnesses it, to also being a threat to public safety and order.

I asked Daniel if I could help him find help and he declined. He told me he was from Pittsburg, a middle-class city of 71,000 people about forty miles from San Francisco. He implied that he was estranged from his parents. I asked him if his parents loved him and he said they did. I told him that, as a parent, I would be worried sick about him, especially if I knew he had spent the night on such a dangerous street, his boots on the sidewalk, and trash strewn about him. I asked him if he believed in God and he said he did. I told Daniel that God loves him and that I believed He wanted Daniel to live his life to his potential and not stay on the streets or on drugs.

According to the homelessness discourse, I should not have said any of this, because it was embarrassing to Daniel. But shouldn't Daniel feel embarrassed waking up in a sleeping bag on the sidewalk? The question might make us uncomfortable. Just like compassion, shame can be abused to manipulate others or make them feel inferior for things they shouldn't feel ashamed of, such as mental illness. But shame is essential to enforcing social norms, from picking up after your dog, to not being intoxicated in public, to not sleeping on sidewalks with your personal belongings and trash strewn about, without the use of law enforcement or incarceration.

Many would say Daniel should *not* feel shame because he is "homeless," and thus by definition a victim. But just as people who can't feel pain accidentally injure themselves, Daniel will suffer mentally and socially if he isn't allowed to feel shame. And he will suffer if he does not value the things that make our lives meaningful, honest, and fulfilling. "The function of pain is to prevent us from damaging our own tissue," says one psychologist. "The function of shame is to prevent us from damaging our social relationships, or to motivate us to repair them."[54]

It's not a matter of whether we will shame but what we will shame. Progressives preaching the gospel of victimology have nothing against shame. They just shame, and value, different behaviors than others. Consider if I had said, "We must have compassion for Daniel. Imagine what he might have suffered at home to lead him to risk his life sleeping on the street! How lucky we should feel to not share his fate! And yet any of us could, at any moment, end up just like him. Either way, anyone who does not have compassion for Daniel is contributing to his victimization." Saying all of that is shaming those who might see things differently.

Consider if you had asked, in response, "But why was Daniel really out there? How do we know he wasn't just a spoiled boy who had partied too hard the night before? And what about the rights of the people who live and work nearby?" I could have said, "How dare you, a person who lives in a fine home and who enjoys drinking alcohol, judge Daniel? You don't know what he's been through! He could be a victim of molestation! He could be mentally ill! And what—now you want to throw him in jail, which will destroy his life, or make him sleep in a shelter, where he could be victimized further? Why don't you help him, instead? See what he needs?" Such moralizing, which involves both valuing and shaming, is usually all that is required to shut up anyone seeking to defend the right of city people to enjoy clean, safe, and orderly shared spaces, from sidewalks to parks.

These internal conflicts happen because seeing someone in a deplorable state inspires uncomfortable feelings. It's normal for shame to arise when we experience the moral dilemmas, both for him and ourselves, around Daniel's situation. But rather than thinking through those dilemmas, progressives have normalized people's aberrant behavior in their fights to first decriminalize and then destigmatize behaviors that are incompatible with city life. It's not necessarily illegal, after all, for chronically inebriated people to stare at me, scream at me, and scare me. It might be, if they can be viewed as threatening me with violence. But simply saying, "I'm sorry" implies it was accidental, particularly to the progressive judges and juries of San Francisco. Part of the power of the progressive discourse around homelessness is how it has constantly pushed the limits of existing laws to allow for behaviors that are incompatible with civilization. Recall that the ACLU defends the right of floridly psychotic people to break the law because they are too mentally ill to be responsible for their actions but not mentally ill enough to be hospitalized.

When streets, parks, and entire neighborhoods are dominated by homeless encampments and open-air drug scenes, they become frightening, inhospitable, and dangerous. Nobody is proposing to prioritize the enforcement of drug laws against people who want to drink alcohol, smoke marijuana, and even inject fentanyl and meth in the privacy of their homes, causing no harm to others. But when camping on sidewalks, public defecation, and public drug use are permitted they undermine the safety and thus the freedom of others.

The antidote to the misleading homelessness discourse is to use specific words that refer to people in the real world, which is more accurate and more humanizing. Many people on the street are disaffiliated, unemployed, alienated from their parents, and suffering from addiction and mental illness. We do not need the same policy for a mother of two toddlers escaping domestic violence as we do for Daniel, Stephen, or the two psychotic women on the streets near my office. Conflating all these people under one definition of "homelessness" makes it harder to create policies that will help any of them.

We must train ourselves to be alert for misinformation and manipulations of our emotions, including compassion, anger, and shame. The homelessness discourse preys on the public's ignorance of the issues, rising sympathy and compassion in an increasingly secular society, and the emotional distancing that many people engage in to avoid disturbing information. But many of the core premises of the homelessness discourse are misleading and false, as we have seen. Gaining mastery of the facts is essential to gaining mastery over our thinking and feelings.

Foucault's ideas simultaneously weakened and strengthened the progressive commitment to victimology. On the one hand, Foucault rejected reductionism and essentialism, the idea that complex individual people could or should be reduced to a single and supposedly essential trait, like race, gender, religion, or sexual orientation. In his last major book, *History of Sexuality*, Foucault argued that our sexuality is "produced," or socially constructed, and doesn't exist purely biologically. "I believe that the term 'gay' has become obsolete—and indeed, all such terms denoting a specific sexual orientation," said Foucault in 1975. Just because someone was attracted to someone of the same sex did not make them "gay," felt Foucault, and labeling people in such ways was oppressive.[55]

On the other, Foucault argued that any attempt to free ourselves from powerful forces would require other powerful forces that would ensnare us in new ways, no matter our intentions. We were helpless to do anything other than tear down the old institutions and categories. Foucault was thus, in an important sense, encouraging his readers to deliberately limit their political engagement to negative, critical, and destructive actions, namely, attacking social norms and civic institutions. And yet, as we have seen, progressives have insisted that it wasn't them, it was Reagan and Republicans who were responsible for closing the psychiatric hospitals without creating a viable replacement.

Out of the view that inequality is by definition proof of racism and other forms of victimization, progressives in recent years have turned their sights on public schools, particularly ones that still decide student admissions based on merit rather than a lottery. In February 2021, the San Francisco School Board voted to replace merit-based admissions to its most elite high school, Lowell, with a lottery system.[56] The then vice president of the School Board said, "meritocracy based on standardized testing, I am just going to say it . . . those are racist systems."[57] In March 2021, activists in New York filed a lawsuit calling for an end to merit-based admissions to its elite high schools, Stuyvesant High and Bronx Science, because, they said, the meritocratic system of admissions testing perpetuates racism and segregation.[58]

But the progressive board members presented no evidence that they are caused by racism. Rather, they simply pointed to the racial disparities in admissions as proof of bias. During the 2020–21 academic year, Asians, whites, Latinos, and African Americans constituted 42, 25, 13, and 2 percent of freshmen at Lowell.[59]

It is hard not to consider the San Francisco School Board's actions in the context of the city's failure to meaningfully narrow the achievement gap between white, black, and Latino students. Where 69 percent of San Francisco's white students were proficient in math, just 14 percent and 22 percent of its black and Latino students were.[60] As such, the School Board may have been using Lowell consciously or unconsciously, as a scapegoat for the broader societal, parenting, and schooling failures that had allowed racial disparities of this magnitude to persist.

Many San Francisco parents were infuriated by the contrast between the haste with which the board took its action and its relaxed attitude toward resuming in-person classes for children during the pandemic. So, too, was San Francisco mayor London Breed. "What I cannot understand," she said, "is why the School Board is advancing a plan to have all these schools renamed by April, when there isn't a plan to have our kids back in the classroom by then."[61]

Amid the furor, Lowell supporters unearthed a series of tweets written in 2016 by the School Board's vice president, who had called Lowell's merit-based admissions racist.[62] Asians used "white supremacist thinking to assimilate and 'get ahead,'" she claimed in one of them. "Where are the vocal Asians speaking up against Trump? Don't Asian Americans know they're on his list as well? Do they think they won't be deported? Profiled? Beaten? Being a house n****r is still being a n****r. You're still considered 'the help.'"[63] In other words, she was upset that Asians didn't recognize that their race, and society's racism, make them victims, no matter how successful they are.

Her comments upset Tom Wolf. "Both of her kids [are] in a merit-based private school in San Francisco," he said, pointing me to a tweet she wrote referencing the exclusive private school to which she sends her daughters. "My kids are in virtual [public] school and they're struggling," said Tom. Nearly two dozen San Francisco elected officials, including Mayor Breed, called on the School Board's vice president to resign her position and demanded that the board return San Francisco's public schoolchildren to in-class learning as soon as possible.[64] Tom was also bothered by the anti-Asian remarks. "It's really toxic," he said. "My wife is Filipino and my kids are biracial. San Francisco is just really sick right now."[65]

17

"It's a Leadership Problem"

In February 2020, California governor Gavin Newsom dedicated most of his annual "State of the State" address to California's homelessness crisis. "Let's call it what it is," Newsom said, "a disgrace, that the richest state in the richest nation—succeeding across so many sectors—is failing to properly house, heal, and humanely treat so many of its own people."[1]

Between 2010 and 2020, the number of homeless rose by 31 percent in California but declined 19 percent in the rest of the United States.[2] As a result, there were, as of 2020, at least 161,000 total homeless people in California, with about 114,000 of them unsheltered, sleeping in tents on sidewalks, in parks, and alongside highways.

Homelessness had become the number one issue in the state.[3] Half of all California voters surveyed said they saw homeless people on the street five times a week. Three-quarters said the problem had worsened.[4] People close to Newsom told me that he knew he had to make progress on solving homelessness if he were to be a serious candidate for the presidency.

Newsom said he knew from personal experience what worked. "Fifteen years ago, when I was mayor of San Francisco, in the face of long odds and stiff opposition, we established Project Homeless Connect to bring local government services directly to people. It has been wildly successful and adopted in 250 cities. I don't *think* homelessness can be solved," said Newsom. "I *know* homelessness can be solved."[5] After he finished, lawmakers from both parties stood and applauded.

Newsom appeared to make good on his commitment in April 2020 by helping San Francisco and other California cities use federal stimulus funding to rent hotel rooms for the homeless to shelter in place during the COVID-19 pandemic, an initiative called Project Roomkey. Doing so was an obvious win-win-win for hotel owners who could have been bankrupted by the pandemic, for the homeless who were uniquely vulnerable to the spread of COVID-19, and for the public. Jennifer Friedenbach of the San Francisco Coalition on Homelessness praised Newsom, whom she had criticized fiercely over the years, telling National Public Radio, "I'm a big believer in redemption."[6]

Newsom appears to understand that addiction and mental illness are core drivers of homelessness, and to genuinely care about the problem and the people impacted by it. For over twenty years, Newsom has walked the streets of San Francisco and other California cities, deliberated with experts for hundreds if not thousands of hours, and interacted with countless homeless people. Newsom personally escorted psychiatrist Ken Rosenberg into the Los Angeles County Jail to witness the mentally ill inmates in their plexiglass cells. "The state of mental illness in this country is beyond the trite notion of crisis," Newsom told Rosenberg, "it's at a point of comedic absurdity."[7] And in his February 2020 "State of the State" address, Newsom called for more conservatorship, noting that some are "capable of accepting help, to get off the streets and into treatment in the first place," but "[s]ome, tragically, are not."[8]

But he has not been honest with the public and perhaps with himself about the problem. Newsom pointed to a specific San Francisco initiative, Project Homeless Connect, which he claimed was "wildly successful." I frequently saw advocates do the same, pointing to programs they claimed were successful despite the overall problem getting worse. Doing so is understandable. People need to believe in something. But it misses the big picture of what is causing the failure and what will fix it. California's independent Legislative Analyst's Office said something similar when it evaluated Newsom's proposals. "We find the Governor's budget proposal falls short of articulating a clear strategy for curbing homelessness in California," it wrote.[9]

Now, there is evidence that the response to COVID-19 by progressive cities including San Francisco made the addiction crisis worse. Before the pandemic, many street addicts would be occasionally arrested and forced to detox and get clean for a few days or weeks, but during the pandemic many remained intoxicated without interruption, worsening their addictions. "Morgan was really into meth," said Kelly Stamphill, who tracked down her fentanyl-addicted son in a Tenderloin Safe Sleeping Site in March 2021. "When I walked through there it's mind-bogglingly scary. I'm on his Instagram page and saw that he said to one of his friends, 'I'm more addicted than I've ever been.'"[10]

And because Newsom remains committed to Housing First, he failed to seize the opportunity to get addicts into recovery. Instead, he and other California leaders gave away free hotel rooms without asking anything in return.[11] "They've missed so many opportunities," said San Francisco's Vicki Westbrook. "They've had people in these [shelter-in-place] hotels. Why, instead of giving them alcohol and all the drug paraphernalia, not offer them [drug treatment] groups? Like, 'We're giving you these hotels, but we're also going to have case managers come around and talk to you about sobriety.' But no, nothing. And now, of course, [the homeless] don't want to leave these hotels. I get that alcohol withdrawal is a serious thing. But, 'I'm going to put you in a hotel. I'm going to feed you. I'm going to do your laundry. And I'm giving you booze.' Like, who would leave?"[12]

When city workers offered one group of shelter-in-place hotel residents placements in a newly renovated permanent supportive housing facility in early 2021, two-thirds turned down the offer, likely because the hotel rooms were free and had private instead of communal bathrooms.[13]

San Francisco city government had also, during the pandemic, created "Safe Sleeping Sites" where the homeless could pitch tents to social distance. The city spent $61,000 per tent, which is 2.5 times the median rent for a one-bedroom apartment in the city. The program served 262 homeless people.[14] The city turned Civic Center Plaza and several empty lots in the Tenderloin into sites.

In the spring of 2021, Supervisor Rafael Mandelman introduced legislation to require the homeless to stay either in a shelter or, if there is no shelter space available, in a tent at a Safe Sleeping Site. Jennifer Friedenbach of the San Francisco Coalition on Homelessness denounced the proposal as cruel, writing that "the author has often talked about it as a way to justify the criminalization of homeless folks through enforcement of anti-homeless laws such as sit-lie."[15] Progressive supervisor Matt Haney "blasted Safe Sleeping Sites," reported the *Chronicle*, saying they were "a failed approach."

In the end, Mandelman found little support for his proposal, San Francisco reaffirmed its decriminalization of public camping, and progressives remained more in charge of the city's response to crime, drugs, and homelessness than ever before.[16]

What explains Newsom's commitment to a failing status quo? "The people who bear the consequences aren't the same ones who set the policy," said Keith Humphreys. "You can sit in the suburbs and feel smug about the fact that you oppose the war on drugs and have a Black Lives Matter sign in your yard. But you don't have homeless people taking a crap on your front stoop every day or [have] all your packages stolen every single day. When you're in a city, as Gavin used to be, the cost of this stuff is more evident to you than it is from fifty thousand feet. And he would endure great political blowback from lots of people who support him who don't see the downsides and feel very good about the current policy."[17]

The American Civil Liberties Union, the Harm Reduction Coalition, and Housing First advocates exercise significant influence over elected leaders. One of Newsom's homelessness advisors, Philip F. Mangano, told me that the governor feared lawsuits by the American Civil Liberties Union if he sought to expand mandatory treatment of the mentally ill and addicted.[18] "Gavin is a check-the-box kind of Democrat," a political consultant in Sacramento told me. "Crossing powerful Democratic Party interest groups is simply not in the interest of someone who wants to be president."

One important reason homelessness must be addressed at the state level is the high level of transience among the homeless. As we saw, at least 30 percent of San Francisco homeless said they were homeless before coming to the city,[19] and stricter and smaller towns displace difficult populations to larger and more liberal cities. "There is a lack of shelter, housing, and services throughout our country," said Los Angeles service provider Joel John Roberts, "so if a person is forced into another community that is deficient of services, what makes you think they will stay? If they have already found a safe hiding place under a bridge, in the bushes along the freeway, or in a park, they will return to their haven."[20] Said Mandelman, "I don't think it can be solved at the county level."[21] Mental health advocate John Snook agreed. "Every community has been allowed to build smoke screens and pawn things off on the next county. Neither governors nor mayors directly oversee many mental health services and instead give contracts to nonprofit organizations. They are thus unable to hold the mental health system accountable."[22]

A big part of the reason for the failure of the homeless industrial complex has had to do with perverse incentives, progressive resistance to mandatory treatment, and the insistence on permanent supportive housing over shelters. But it also has to do with the neoliberal model of outsourcing services. Instead of governments providing such services directly, they give grants to nonprofit service providers who are unaccountable for their performance. "There is no statutory requirement for government to address homelessness," complained University of Pennsylvania researcher Dennis Culhane. "It's mainly the domain of a bunch of charities who are unlicensed, unfunded, relatively speaking, run by unqualified people who do a shitty job. There's no formal government responsibility. It's only something we dream of. And that is fundamentally part of the problem."[23]

Nobody can even accurately calculate how much money is being spent. The state auditor calculates that California spends $12 billion total on homelessness, and it is not clear how much of that is overlap with other state spending.[24] The Legislative Analyst's Office found many difficulties: "Difficulty assessing how much the state is spending on a particular approach towards addressing homelessness, for example—prevention versus intervention efforts. Difficulty determining how programs work collaboratively. Difficulty assessing what programs are collectively accomplishing."[25] Said Vicki Westbrook, "Sometimes, I think there are too many nonprofits. You don't know which one to go with. Maybe it matters and maybe it doesn't. Maybe they're providing exactly the same services. Maybe they say they are, but they're not doing it in the same way."[26]

Thomas Insel agreed that the state needed to make sweeping reforms. But, he said, "Everybody says the same thing to me: 'You're going to have to change the constitution because the way that we got to where we are was through a series of ballot measures.'"[27] But that's not as daunting a challenge as it may seem. California governors raise money and pass ballot initiatives all the time, as they did over the last two decades when they liberalized drug laws. Why wasn't Newsom doing that?

After Insel somewhat halfheartedly pointed to COVID-19 and the subsequent recall campaign, I scowled. He knew as well as I did that Newsom had been governor for more than a year before the pandemic and had been lieutenant governor and mayor for fifteen years before that. Insel didn't criticize Newsom directly, but when I read the transcript from our interview, I was struck by how often he returned to one theme in particular. "It's been really hard to get any real leadership," Insel said. "I don't think money is the problem. I think it's the leadership . . . we need state leadership. . . . There's no state leadership. . . . We have to create state leadership. . . . I don't think it's a money problem. I think it's a leadership problem."[28]

In 2019 Newsom convened another homelessness task force, pledging to appoint a "homelessness czar" to oversee the program. In early 2021, I asked a member of the governor's task force, Jeff Bellisario of the Bay Area Council, an influential business advocacy group, if it had created a plan to end homelessness.

"No," said Bellisario.

What about a proposal to just shelter people?

"There's a lot of power in Sacramento on the Housing First side," said Bellisario, "and few people talking about shelter. Housing First has taken over a lot of what happens on the ground, whether in the nonprofits or cities and counties. In the end we ended up with nothing."[29]

In May 2021, Governor Newsom unveiled a plan to spend another $12 billion to "confront the homelessness crisis head on," supposedly demanding more accountability and urgency from service providers.[30] But he again missed the point. Newsom's new plan promises to increase housing placements and treatment beds for those with behavioral health problems, but there is no indication of how he will ensure that people use those services. As such, he is doubling down on the exact same solutions that have contributed to the growing homelessness crisis in California over the last decade.

Said Snook in 2020, "I'm always cynical about California. You've had lots of opportunities for this to happen over the last twenty-five years with a lot of the same people."[31]

It is not hard to imagine what an aggressive response from the White House would look like, not just on rising overdose deaths but also rising homicides. The president and vice president would make heavy use of the bully pulpit, meeting with family members of victims, giving speeches, and funding millions of dollars in public service advertising. They would warn of the dangers of fentanyl and other hard drugs, demand national action to reduce violence, overdose deaths, and homicides, and inspire America around a vision and strategy to reverse the rise in overdose deaths and homicides. And they would pressure the states to step up mandatory, medically assisted drug treatment, break up the open-air drug markets, and expand conservatorship and assisted outpatient treatment for the mentally ill.

In early 2021, momentum appeared to be building for the White House to take aggressive action on the drug addiction, overdose, and poisoning crisis. Humphreys and other experts publicly urged President Joe Biden to take strong measures.[32] In July, the Centers for Disease Control and Prevention announced there had been more than 93,000 overdose and poisoning deaths in 2020.[33] In April, President Biden's son Hunter Biden published a memoir describing his crack addiction, which revealed poignant moments between father and son as Hunter spiraled downward.[34]

But by mid-2021 little had been done. "They have just issued expanding rules for MDs as well as [physician assistants] and [nurse practitioners] to prescribe buprenorphine [Suboxone]," Humphreys said, "and they also have $4 billion to give out in grants this year." It is notable that the highest-profile action the Biden White House had taken relating to drugs and crime was to deny employment to some low-level White House staffers who admitted to having smoked marijuana in the past. The decision was viewed by many progressives and conservatives alike as bizarre, given the marijuana and cocaine use acknowledged by former president Barack Obama, and the marijuana use acknowledged by Vice

President Kamala Harris.[35] Noted Humphreys, "there is no confirmed head at [the Office of National Drug Control Policy], FDA, or DEA, and the President has said little about the epidemic to date."[36]

How and why do progressives ruin cities? So far we have explored six reasons. They divert funding from homeless shelters to permanent supportive housing, resulting in insufficient shelter space. They defend the right of people they characterize as Victims to camp on sidewalks, in parks, and along highways, as well as to break other laws, including against public drug use and defecation. They intimidate experts, policy makers, and journalists by attacking them as being motivated by a hatred of the poor, people of color, and the sick, and as causing violence against them. They reduce penalties for shoplifting, drug dealing, and public drug use. They prefer homelessness and incarceration to involuntary hospitalization for the mentally ill and addicted. And their ideology blinds them to the harms of harm reduction, Housing First, and camp-anywhere policies, leading them to misattribute the addiction, untreated mental illness, and homeless crisis to poverty and to policies and politicians dating back to the 1980s.

But progressives are defined in opposition to moderate Democrats and Republicans, and so our explanation is incomplete. To understand why progressives ruin cities we have to understand why they have been able to maintain and increase their political control of them, over the last thirty years, despite the reality on the ground.

Democrats sometimes say progressivism is inextricable from the identities and ethos of California and Washington State. "San Francisco is the center of that progressive liberal ethos," said former San Francisco mayor Art Agnos. "I think it begins with the origins of the city in the Gold Rush."[37] "Washington State's history is marked by a Progressive ethos," wrote a Seattle historian. Movements like "social legislation, labor laws, and woman suffrage," spanning from the state's founding, are all part of Washington's "enduring progressive impulse."[38]

But conservatism and Republicanism used to be so prevalent that California and Washington were both considered swing states. In fact, between 1948 and 1988, both states were more Republican than the rest of the country. Washington State voted for a Democratic candidate in just two presidential elections in those forty years, while California voted Democrat just once, in Lyndon Johnson's landslide 1964 victory. Between 1943 and 1998, Republicans held the California governorship for forty-one years, interrupted only by Pat Brown and his son, Jerry Brown, who had two four-year terms each. The states' legislative branches were more closely contested; Democrats and Republicans handed off control equally in the post–Cold War era.[39]

The move toward progressivism in California and Washington can be explained by shifts in the parties' postures and shifts in voter demographics. After the end of the Cold War, the federal government decommissioned superfluous military bases on the West Coast. As part of this "peace dividend," many military families and contractors, who reliably voted for Republicans, left California and Washington for cheap real estate and new employment in the fast-growing Sun Belt states. Simultaneously, an influx of Latin American immigrants was arriving in California, and many Latinos were put off by Republican governor Pete Wilson's support of Proposition 187, which blocked access to public benefits for undocumented immigrants.[40] At the same time, the nascent tech industry was attracting a new professional class that emerged from the sixties counterculture. To them, the Republican Party was seen as culturally and ideologically tied to establishment. The new class of tech entrepreneurs and engineers instead flocked to the Democratic Party, which increasingly promoted probusiness policies alongside a social and cultural progressivism.[41]

Meanwhile, conservatives ceded the issue of homelessness to progressives. I asked Christopher Rufo, a leading critic of harm reduction and Housing First, why that was. "Most Republican policy makers don't actually care about the issue of homelessness because it doesn't affect their districts," he said. "Any urban district, especially on the West Coast, is pretty much a one hundred percent Democratically controlled area. Republican legislators from the eastern side of California, or rural districts, have a limited, 'Look at the feces-covered West Coast cities, the libs are ruining everything' view. They don't really feel like they need a plan and they don't really care what happens in San Francisco or LA or Seattle."[42]

Some conservatives uncritically embraced Housing First because they had failed to develop their own solutions to the problem. Said the economist Wayne Winegarden, "The left will tell you what the government should be doing, but the right is very squished. 'What is the government's responsibility? Should we be running institutions that help people who have drug addictions and mental illness?' You don't have that debate on the right. It is all about, 'We want less government and lower taxes.' The question is, 'What should we be spending?' and 'What should it be on?' And I think the right, if it's really going to rebuild itself, needs to have definitive answers to those questions."[43]

Part of the power of harm reduction, said Stephen Eide of the center-right Manhattan Institute, is that it can be viewed as conservative. "Some people might say it's just a small government philosophy," said Eide. "Government just can't change behavior, so we should focus on what government can do, which is hand out needles, create supervised injection facilities, and teach sex ed instead of making people be abstinent."[44]

Many on the left and right embraced drug decriminalization and even legalization for libertarian reasons. George Soros told Ethan Nadelmann he opposed drug prohibition because, "[a]s a businessperson and economist, he saw the absurdity of trying to ban a popular commodity."[45]

As a result, in the name of freedom for the victims of mental illness, we have today abdicated our responsibility to properly care for people. A "person's 'choice' to bang her head in a subsidized apartment, to drink himself into a stupor, or to sit idly might easily be reframed," noted the sociologist who contrasted drug treatment in Malibu to that in Skid Row, "as the state's abdication of responsibility for profound need and social defeat."[46]

If California were to provide a $500,000 studio apartment unit to each of its 150,000 homeless people, the cost would be $75 billion. The cost of providing services, at a cost of $25,000 per person, would be an additional $3.75 billion annually. Thus, over a thirty-year period, the total cost would be about $187.5 billion, in 2020 dollars, or $6.2 billion annualized. What if the cost per unit ended up being $750,000 rather than $500,000, as they ended up being in the Bay Area and Los Angeles? The cost would be $225 billion in 2020 dollars over a thirty-year period, or $7.5 billion annualized. Let's say California spent half that amount and spent the other half on lower-cost residential homes and shelters, to bring the cost down to $6 billion. And let's say that the federal government paid for half, to account for the fact that California has half of America's homeless but just 12 percent of the population. That would bring total annual costs down to $3 billion, which is just one-quarter of what California currently spends in a year on homelessness.

Could California afford it? Of course. If the money for housing could not come from existing pools of money, would voters support increasing the total budget by 2 percent, or $3 billion annually, to build the basic shelter and housing for the homeless? It is conceivable. Recall that California as a whole spent $13.3 billion on homelessness between fiscal years 2018 and 2021,[47] beyond the $1.25 billion San Francisco spent on homelessness in the same period. And homelessness remains the number one issue in the minds of voters, who are fed up and want a solution to the problem.

But what can be done to prevent the homeless population from simply replenishing itself? And where, and how, could California build all the new apartments, residential homes, and shelters?

For the last two decades, San Francisco and other progressive cities have sought to become more livable and walkable, including through expansive greenbelts surrounding cities, but without building significantly more housing. Since the 1960s, progressives have criticized suburban housing for breeding conformity and urban redevelopment for displacing poor people of color. They have demanded large, protected areas around cities, where housing is prohibited. And they have demanded greater power at the neighborhood level, empowering not-in-my-backyard (NIMBY) activists across the state.

By 1987 progressives had put twenty-four no-growth referendums on municipal ballots in California. Twenty passed.[48] In Redwood City, south of San Francisco, anti-growth arsonists burned down single-family homes under construction in twenty separate locations after the City Council lifted a moratorium on new home construction.[49] In California, Bay Area cities, including San Francisco, Oakland, and Berkeley, and Southern California cities, including Los Angeles, Santa Monica, and West Hollywood, all imposed rent control. The only major cities in California that rejected it were San Diego and Sacramento.[50] Local governments in California are able to reject new housing even when it complies with the zoning rules. More than 80 percent of all lawsuits filed under the state's 1970 California Environmental Quality Act (CEQA, commonly pronounced "see kwa") are against urban infill housing, not new development in natural areas.[51]

As a result, California has the second-highest cost of living in the country, behind only Hawaii, with just a handful of lucky people benefiting from rent control.[52] Forty-three percent of California voters and 61 percent of those aged 18–34 said in 2019 that they couldn't afford to live in the state.[53] One-third of Californians say they have seriously considered moving out of the state entirely due to housing costs.[54] Few people are aware of how unfair rent control has become. "We have people making $500k+ in rent-controlled apartments all over town," tweeted Michelle Tandler. "In SF we have surgeons living in Atherton subletting out their med school apts. How is this equitable?"[55]

Newsom campaigned and was elected on a pledge to build 500,000 new units of housing every year from 2019 to 2025, but California's housing production *declined* in both of the years Newsom has been in office, 2019 and 2020. New housing construction in 2020 declined 10 percent with just 100,550 new building permits issued, one-fifth of what Newsom had promised.[56]

But the trend started long before Newsom. For over a century California added 300,000 new residents a year on average, expanding faster than any other state. California increased its population by half as much between 2000 and 2020 (17 percent) as it did between 1980 and 2000 (43 percent).[57] In 2019, the state gained just 90,846 residents, an increase of 0.2 percent.[58] In 2021, California lost a congressional seat due to its stagnation relative to other states.

Opposition to new housing has ideological roots. American progressives went from optimism in the 1950s about making middle-class living standards attainable for all Americans, and overcoming the legacy of racism, to deep pessimism just twenty years later. The pessimistic discourse on both the environment and on social progress has been the basis for much of the supposedly "progressive" opposition to new housing since the 1970s.

But NIMBYism also benefits homeowners. By restricting development, property owners reduce supply and drive up prices. Such a strategy is obviously inconsistent with liberal and progressive values since it hurts poor and working people the most. And so progressive San Franciscans have justified their NIMBYism by insisting that more housing actually hurts the poor, particularly poor people of color. They point to cases of badly done redevelopment, such as the bulldozing of San Francisco's historically African American neighborhood, the Fillmore, as proof.

O ver the last decade, demand for new housing in San Francisco and around the country has come from urban Millennial professionals who have formed a yes-in-my-backyard (YIMBY) movement to counter NIMBYs. In early 2018, state senator Scott Wiener from San Francisco introduced YIMBY-backed legislation that would have radically increased the number of apartments, condos, and duplexes near train and bus stations across California. The year before, the California legislature had passed Wiener's legislation to streamline residential housing approvals. But his new legislation was stronger. It would have changed zoning to allow apartments in half of all single-family neighborhoods in Los Angeles and nearly 100 percent of them in San Francisco.

Opponents of the legislation accused Wiener of proposing a takeover of something that had in the past been controlled locally. The Los Angeles City Council opposed the legislation unanimously.[59] Wiener responded that local control had failed to keep up with demand. "In education and healthcare," Wiener noted, "the state sets basic standards, and local control exists within those standards. Only in housing has the state abdicated its role."[60] Laura Foote, the executive director of YIMBY Action, a grassroots pro-housing group that supported the bill, agreed. "If we make the decisions at the neighborhood level, we're always going to have a collective action problem because there are too many incentives to say the next town over should build the housing."[61]

Wiener's boldness inspired left-of-center reporters and columnists. Over the next several months, they penned optimistic articles and columns for the *New York Times*, *Atlantic*, *Bloomberg Opinion*, and other national news media outlets. Newsom appeared to endorse Wiener's idea as he campaigned for governor in 2018 on a promise to create 3.5 million housing units, or 700,000 per year between 2019 and 2023. I, too, was swept up in the youthful, idealistic passion of the progressive pro-housing YIMBY and its demands for radical increases in housing.

But by spring 2019, Wiener's legislation was in trouble. Opponents said it would result in high-rise buildings in residential neighborhoods. Wiener responded by reducing the maximum height in "transit rich" areas to four or five stories. He also agreed to exempt from his bill areas near bus stops that had infrequent service outside of rush hour. None of it was enough. The committee killed Wiener's bill in a 6–4 vote. Wiener introduced an updated version later in 2019, which similarly failed. In response, the leadership of the legislature, where Democrats hold a super-majority, moved Wiener out of any leadership role on housing legislation. A group of seven legislators formed a moderate alternative to Wiener and the YIMBYs on one side and NIMBY legislators on the other. The goal was to build consensus around policy that could pass in 2020.

YIMBY leaders were optimistic in spring 2020, even after the coronavirus pandemic had begun, that they would pass legislation. "COVID has revealed the fragility of housing scarcity and has made it more urgent for us to not exacerbate it," a pro-housing leader who asked to remain anonymous told me. "Something inspired by [Wiener's legislation] SB50 will ram through."[62] But nothing of significance did.

Opposition to new housing is strong at state and local levels. "The average home value in my district is $1.7 million and I want it to stay that way," an influential Democratic state senator from Southern California reportedly told a pro-housing leader.[63] Said a homelessness advocate, "Gavin worries he can't do anything as governor because of opposition to building shelters by mayors. Nobody wants to build more housing. No one! How do you mandate local politicians to do housing? They don't want to or they'll be voted out of office."

Pro-housing leaders said Newsom could have withheld money from the counties that did not build more housing. "I think that it's no secret that Gavin's administration has not followed through on what would have been necessary to actually achieve the housing goals that he set forth when he was running for office," said Foote. "He didn't put a lot of pressure on the state legislature to pass some of the packages that needed, and they needed a governor to push and usher them through."[64]

A pro-housing leader in Sacramento who wished to stay anonymous agreed. "He has the inherent legal authority. He just lacks the courage to use it."[65]

At this point, the person started laughing.

"Why are you laughing?" I asked.

"Because there is no other way to say it than the rude way! He is being a coward about it. I would be the same if I were running for president. It takes a certain kind of leader to raise his middle finger. And I don't know if Gavin is the kind of leader to do the right thing when it's unpopular. He's more reactive and transactional. I don't know why he has that political strategy. I would just categorize it as, 'He doesn't because he's afraid to,' and it's not more complicated than that."[66]

The obstacle for YIMBYs and others who want to require that cities build more housing in existing neighborhoods is not lack of democracy but too much democracy. California's likely voters tend to be older, NIMBY homeowners. Californians over the age of 55 are one-third of the adult population but nearly half of voters. Young people aged 18–34 are one-third of adults but 22 percent of likely voters. Just one out of five likely voters has no college education. And two-thirds of likely voters are homeowners, while just one-third are renters.[67] "It's the worst possible opponent because it's Big Voter," said the pro-housing advocate, laughing. "Big Voter doesn't want you to succeed."[68]

Big Voter appears to be the biggest obstacle YIMBYs face in San Francisco. In November 2020, *SF Weekly* reported that San Francisco's progressive Board of Supervisors blocked a nominee to the city's transportation board simply because the person was a member of SF YIMBY. Wrote the *Weekly*, "YIMBY has become politically toxic among progressives."[69]

Even so, YIMBYs keep pursuing the right message for progressives. They promote more housing for greater livability and walkability. They emphasize solving climate change by reducing driving. And they point to remedying historic racism. "Maybe we can get enough people to believe that ending systemic racism is important," said Foote, "and therefore we have to reform our land use policies."[70]

Maybe. Or maybe California's progressives will keep voting NIMBY and assuage whatever guilt they feel by supporting more funding for the homeless, voting for candidates who promise to defund the police, and putting Black Lives Matter signs in their windows.

18

Responsibility First

In 1893, the historian Frederick Turner wrote a celebrated essay about the importance of the frontier to how Americans think about freedom. On the frontier, he noted, families and communities were mostly on their own, and thus in a different cultural, economic, and political environment than either New England or the South. Already the American Revolution had created a culture whereby "individual liberty was sometimes confused with absence of all effective government," noted Turner.[1] The experience of living on the western frontier "produces antipathy to control, and particularly to any direct control."[2]

No state embodies the frontier more than California. What happened during the 1960s in the counterculture's attempt to escape traditional obligations was an extension, not rejection, of the American frontier notion of freedom as the *absence* rather than *presence* of strong ties. To some extent, the frontier always romanticized the disaffiliated man, from the gold miner, to the entrepreneur, to the hobo. But there was always also a civic spirit, a dream of creating a better society together, and an appreciation of the norm of reciprocity, until the 1960s, when the progressive left sought to replace the principle of gratitude for charity with an attitude of entitlement.

It is thus not just in the name of compassion that Californians allow our most vulnerable fellow humans to live on the street. It is also in the name of liberty. San Francisco embodies an extreme version of the American Dream. Americans come from all over the country, as do immigrants from all over the world, to San Francisco, Los Angeles, and Seattle. These cities' liberal coastal nature and their distance from the established rules and norms of the East Coast establishment encouraged a bohemian, libertarian culture.

"I think it's the left combined with libertarianism around substances," said Keith Humphreys, "that is actually the mix that makes it really hard to manage these problems. The West is far more libertarian about lots of things. . . . Out west, it's more, 'Do whatever you want,' and, 'No one has a right to interfere with your view.' Sometimes that is terrific. We're the home of gay rights. But it doesn't work well for addiction. The pursuit of allegedly individual freedom ends up ultimately killing the person, and does enormous damage to everybody else. That's the basis of a lot of intervention [by friends and family of addicts]. But it's been politically nullified out in the [American] West. And that's why we don't have Portuguese outcomes."[3]

We commonly assume that left and right are opposites. Yet the libertarian right and the progressive left have been in a tacit alliance against greater government action on addiction and mental illness for at least fifty years. True, most of the right simply opposed stronger public action on mental illness out of discomfort with psychology and government spending on social services. But the power of libertarian ideas and institutions within the Republican coalition, along with broader confusion about psychiatry and drugs, meant that conservatives largely went along with progressive demands to shut down psychiatric hospitals, replace contingency management with Housing First, and underinvest in addiction treatment and recovery.

In 2012, the novelist Kurt Andersen made a similar observation. "What has happened politically, economically, culturally and socially since the sea change of the late '60s isn't contradictory or incongruous," he wrote. "It's all of a piece. For hippies and bohemians as for businesspeople and investors, extreme individualism has been triumphant. . . . 'Do your own thing' is not so different than 'every man for himself.' "[4]

Some people have told me that they thought San Francisco's Safe Sleeping Sites looked like a natural disaster. But with city-funded social workers providing services to the people in tents, it looked to me more like a medical experiment, albeit one that no board of ethics would ever permit. At the Sites the city isn't providing drug treatment; it's providing easy access to drugs. That includes, as we have seen, cash in the form of welfare payments with which to purchase drugs, and the equipment with which to inject them.

While San Francisco's approach to homelessness can be fairly described as pathological altruism, it would be unfair to call it Munchausen syndrome by proxy, which is when a parent deliberately makes their child sick so they can feel important. Many of the drug-addicted and mentally ill homeless are, in fact, sick, and most progressives have good intentions. But it is not unfair to point out that the city's approach of playing the Rescuer is resulting in worsening addiction and rising overdose deaths. Nor is it unfair to point out that we limit people's potential for freedom by labeling them Victims and "centering" their trauma, rather than viewing victimization as an opportunity for heroism. Nor is it unfair to point out, as I have attempted to do by describing the history, that San Francisco's political, business, and cultural leaders should all know better by now.

People suffering addiction and living on the street are ill. To mix them up in speech and policy with people who are merely poor is deceptive. Leading scholars have for thirty years denounced the conflation of the merely poor with disaffiliated addicts. Yet progressive advocates for the homeless continue to engage in the same sleight of hand by using the single term "homeless," tricking journalists, policy makers, and the public into mixing together groups of people who require different kinds of help. Progressives justify their discourse and agenda in the name of preventing dehumanization, but the effect has been the opposite. In defending the humanity of addicts, progressives ended up defending the inhumane conditions of street addiction.

The morality of victimology contains a version of all six values identified in Moral Foundations Theory. The problem is that those values are oriented around those defined as Victims in a particular context, to the exclusion of everyone else. But not even the most devoted homeless activists could do whatever drug-addicted homeless people demand of them. The demand that we give Victims special political authority is thus really a demand to give special political authority to those who claim to represent the supposed Victims, namely homelessness advocates.

The power of victimology lies in its moralizing discourse more than in any single set of laws. I was struck in my research that progressive civil society actors like Jennifer Friedenbach, Margot Kushel, and Sam Tsemberis have had a far greater impact on public policy, and the reality on the streets, than countless progressive politicians. It is notable that while Friedenbach, Kushel, and Tsemberis are the most influential individuals in shaping homeless policy in San Francisco and Los Angeles, they are also the least accountable. As the problem has worsened, their cultural and political power has grown, while voters understandably blame their local elected leaders for the crisis.

Progressive advocates and policy makers alike blame the drug war, mass incarceration, and drug prohibition for the addiction and overdose crisis, even though the crisis resulted from liberalized attitudes and drug laws, first toward pharmaceutical opioids, and then toward all drugs. This view is, on the one hand, a defensive and ideological reaction. But it is also an abdication of responsibility.

One of my motivations in writing this book was to understand how anarchism, or what is sometimes called left-libertarianism, gained so much power in progressive West Coast cities. I believe part of the answer lies in its lack of accountability, which is itself a kind of power. Anarchists can cheerlead disruptive and even violent actions and then evade responsibility when things go wrong. It is notable that America's most influential anarchist, Noam Chomsky, selects a few points in history—a ten-month period in Spain in 1936 when large regions of the country were governed autonomously and locally, and the early kibbutzim in Palestine before the creation of the state of Israel, when Jews, Muslims, and atheists all supposedly lived together in harmony—as models of anarchist rule.[5] Are those episodes really models for how to govern a large city, state, or nation today? Of course they aren't. But naming such episodes as the anarchist ideal allows Chomsky to reject responsibility for anarchist actions that go terribly wrong, such as in the occupied zones in Seattle and Minneapolis.

While we should hold our elected officials responsible, we must also ask hard questions of the intellectual architects of their policies, and of the citizens, donors, and voters who empower them. What kind of a civilization leaves its most vulnerable people to use deadly substances and die on the streets? What kind of city regulates ice cream stores more strictly than drug dealers who kill 713 of its citizens in a single year?[6] What kind of people moralize about their superior treatment of the poor, people of color, and addicts while enabling and subsidizing the conditions of their death?

O ver a decade ago, Jonathan Haidt warned that progressives needed to have a broader moral vision. They needed to value more things. Wrote Haidt, "self-control over self-expression, duty over rights, and loyalty to one's groups over concerns for out-group" are values necessary to the functioning of civilization. Such values, Haidt warned, "cannot be supported by the Care and Fairness foundations alone. You have to build on the Loyalty, Authority, and Sanctity foundations as well."[7]

My research for *San Fransicko* leads me to agree and build on Haidt's argument by adding that *how* we value matters as much as what we value. And so it is to reconstructing a new moral foundation, one capable of uniting moderate conservatives and progressives, that we can now turn.

Cities are sacred and thus there must be rules for behavior in them. It is simply not okay to allow people to sleep on sidewalks, in parks, and on the sides of highways. Nor is it okay for people to sit on the sidewalk and shout threats and profanity at people who walk by, nor for people to defecate in front of retail offices and stores. If restaurants and other businesses want to serve their customers at tables and chairs on sidewalks, they must apply for special permits. That was still the case even during the pandemic. People must not be exempted from this because we feel sorry for them and label them Victims.

When we allow for the chronic violation of laws and social norms, we erode the foundation of our cities and civilization. The city is sacred because it is, or can be, the place of highest human possibility, flourish, and freedom. The public's horror at open-air drug use and defecation stems from a justified disgust at the violation and contamination of shared, public, and common spaces. Homeless encampments damage the social fabric that makes cities possible.

The same goes for criminal justice. Abuses by the police undermine the public's trust in government, and thus loyalty to the city, state, and nation, which contributes to collective safety and public order. And high rates of homicide destroy the fabric of cities and communities. Coastal, progressive cities have shown us that we cannot effectively address past racial injustices without also addressing homicides in our cities, or we will worsen the wrongs we seek to rectify. All Americans, of all political ideologies, religions, social classes, and races, have an interest in focusing our attention, finally, on our nation's tragically high homicide rates.

Stigmatizing hard drug use and breaking up the open-air drug markets will not end drug dealing, but it will significantly reduce the violence associated with drugs by moving the drug trade indoors and thus dispersing it. Doing so may have the added benefit of increasing costs for dealers and users. The American people are capable of distinguishing between stigmatizing fentanyl use without stigmatizing the sick person who is using fentanyl. The person requires our compassion, but the behavior requires our condemnation.

We need a new, pro-human, pro-civilization, and pro-cities morality. Freedom is essential, but without order it can't exist in cities. If we are not safe, if our cities are not walkable, then we don't have a civilization. In some ways the new morality may seem like a return to an older, Enlightenment morality. But the morality we need would define Liberty more around affiliation than disaffiliation, and value the freedom that comes from taking responsibility more than the freedom to reject it.

Social norms are always individual and social. Most are never enforced, because nobody wants to feel the social embarrassment of being caught *not* picking up after their dog. One of the most important discoveries of sociologists in the late twentieth century, as they sought to understand rising crime rates, was that most people obey the law not because they are afraid of being caught violating it but because they believe in the law, and that it's being administered fairly.[8] The fact that a significant number of elected progressive Democrats, including district attorneys and supervisors in Los Angeles, Seattle, and San Francisco, have in recent years openly called for enforcing the law differently according to race and class, and have started doing so, is a disturbing threat both to public order and to the principle of equal justice under the law.

In 2018, Patrick Collison, the CEO and cofounder of Stripe, an Internet financial services firm, published an essay that described why he opposed Proposition C, the initiative written by Jennifer Friedenbach and championed by Salesforce's Marc Benioff. "Stripe is highly motivated to help solve homelessness," he wrote. "We're happy to pay higher taxes as part of doing so, a position we've made clear from the start. Stripe employees, and Stripe itself, have long worked to help housing-related causes and homeless service providers." But, he added, "[i]f homelessness was just a question of money, this issue would already be solved."

Collison had run the numbers. "While cities report inconsistently, San Francisco currently spends around $430 per city resident per year on services and programs for the homeless, compared to $260 in New York City and $110 in Los Angeles. Yet the problem in our city is worse." He called for "systemic changes" and "effective accountability."[9]

Progressives including Benioff criticized Collison sharply, but he found an unlikely ally in Riva Tez, a Britain-born, San Francisco–based tech entrepreneur who had been homeless as a girl. Tez's mother suffered schizophrenia, and they both squatted illegally and lived in a shelter. "[Living in a homeless shelter] really shaped me," said Riva. "I think that experience as a child made me much more sympathetic to those situations because I can see my mother in all of them."

But Tez does not share the views of progressive homelessness advocates. "I had a friend who went to work in an NGO," Tez said. "She is the most high-integrity person I know. After a year she had completely changed all her views. She said she never realized how much of an industry poverty was." The Proposition C campaign upset Tez. "They manipulated the narrative to be, 'Are you for or against the homeless?'" she said. "If you said you're against Prop C, people would say, 'You hate the homeless.' I'm like 'There are better things to do to help the homeless, because it doesn't seem like the problem in San Francisco is that the homeless [service providers] don't have enough money. It seems like we don't have enough accountability.'"[10]

Collison's decision could not have been easy. "[Patrick] put himself on the line because he was going against the homeless narrative," said Riva. "I mean, they had protests outside the Stripe offices. . . . There was bravery in that."[11] Said a writer for a San Francisco venture capital firm, Michael Solana, "There is a broader problem in our culture right now where people don't feel comfortable to speak. The city was a culture of new things. But then, politically, it became hostile to new things, from new housing to new technologies."[12]

Chris Rufo similarly pointed to the need to confront taboos. "The chief of psychiatry in a public hospital system in one of the largest California cities told me, 'I know for a fact, and all of my colleagues know, that what we actually need to deal with the problem in the biggest cities in California is long-term residential secure psychiatric care. But I can't say that publicly because I would be disemboweled by the activist left. My job would be in jeopardy. My reputation would be in jeopardy. My whole life would get turned upside down for even broaching the subject of expanding secure mental health facilities and compulsory mental health treatment.' And I said, 'So what's the solution?' and this person said, 'We muddle through.'"[13]

Stanford's Keith Humphreys described something similar. "The mayors of cities call me and they'll agree privately. 'Yeah. We can't just have a model where you use as much [hard drugs] as you want, wherever you want, and nothing bad ever happens to you.' And I say, 'Okay, here's some ways to change.' 'Nope.' 'Whoa, wait.' 'Nope, nope.' 'No pressure allowed.' 'No accountability allowed.'"[14]

W hen you dealt with the heroin epidemic in the eighties and nineties," I asked Rene Zegerius in Amsterdam, "were there activists who said that you should not do anything? That you should let people be addicts?"

"'Helping,' 'Helping,'" said Rene. "'We should help them.' Today we have policing forums. But that was not the case in the beginning of the epidemic. Then, we just had to help the poor bastards."

"Did the conservative parties say, 'No, you have to have law enforcement'?" I asked.

"The people and the politics are more to the right today than in the eighties," he said. "We had very large left-wing political parties then. Most of them formed the government. Now, Dilan's party, which is a little right of the middle, is the ruling party. But they were small in the eighties."[15]

Could a similar change occur on the progressive West Coast?

After I told Rufo that I had found openness among some progressives to greater mandatory treatment of the seriously mentally ill, he said, "I think there probably is [openness] among the center-left. But the problem, too, is that the real power holders in these conversations are the activist organizations. You have disability rights groups, the American Civil Liberties Union, and the umbrella of individual rights and rights protection groups for people who are mentally ill and people who are addicted. And they have manipulated the legal system into codifying their preferences and basically bully and bowl over any public officials that would cross their path for even a moderate compromise."[16]

Part of the reason I have focused on Amsterdam as a potential model is precisely because it is so liberal. It proves that cities with very progressive attitudes toward sex and drugs are not doomed to skyrocketing overdose deaths, open drug scenes, and homeless encampments. Gay and lesbian people were out in Amsterdam in the 1920s, forty years before they were in the Castro, Harvey Milk's neighborhood, in San Francisco. It was one of the first developed nations to decriminalize marijuana, and allow its relatively open use. Prostitution is legal and regulated.

And yet the Dutch have managed to maintain the safety and sanctity of the city and protect human dignity. Amsterdam is one of the few large cities in the world where one is relatively safe walking around in almost every neighborhood, even in the middle of the night. Its treatment of people suffering from mental illness and addiction is world-class. And it even allows for some experimentation with psychedelic drugs, which hold significant therapeutic potential.[17]

Conservative thinkers whom I interviewed all said they favored taxpayer support for housing the people who genuinely need it. "Good people who really care about mental health reform are generally supportive of the idea that seriously mentally ill people are disabled," said Stephen Eide. "If you're really schizophrenic, if you are mentally disabled, you probably will need the government to give you housing for the rest of your life. You'll need health care. You'll need an income source."[18]

Rising overdose deaths, the vacuum of leadership and vision, and the sheer disruption caused by the COVID-19 pandemic made some people wonder if the crisis had created a real opportunity for change on the West Coast. When I asked her what she thought was possible, given how many reform-minded tech workers had left San Francisco, Riva said, "It does feel like the end of an era, and makes me sad." At the same time, she said, "There's a lot of people trying to think like, how do we fix this?"[19]

In normal times, we pay our taxes and expect that, in return, police will prevent and investigate crimes, sidewalks and streets will be as clean and clear as possible, and our children can expect from their schools a decent education. When Bill Maher says, "I don't know what I'm getting for my super high taxes," he's saying something important: nobody knows what the exchange between rights and responsibilities is, as taxpayers and as citizens.[20] It is time to spell out what we should expect for our super high taxes.

California's state auditor and the Legislative Analyst's Office imply that homelessness can be solved through "coordination," but everybody knows that when you want to get something done you need a hierarchy, with a clear line of command and with leaders at the top who have both authority and accountability.

What California needs is a new, single, and powerful state agency. Let's call it Cal-Psych. It would be built as a separate institution from existing institutions, including state and county health departments and health providers. Cal-Psych would efficiently and humanely treat the seriously mentally ill and addicts, while providing housing to the homeless on a contingency-based system. Cal-Psych's CEO would be best-in-class and report directly to the governor. It is only in this way that the voters can hold the governor accountable for the crisis on the streets.

Cal-Psych would have significant buying power, be attractive to employees, and be able to move clients to where they need to be. It would be able to purchase psychiatric beds, board and care facilities, and treatment facilities from across the state. And it would be able to offer the mentally ill and those suffering substance use disorders drug and psychiatric treatment somewhere other than in an open-air drug scene.

Cal-Psych would start in one city, learn rapidly, and then grow, ultimately taking over from the counties. We must learn from the mistakes of the past. We shut down state mental hospitals before we had created the alternative. Cal-Psych would be scaled up over time, replacing various institutions that are currently doomed to failure. Legislation would be required to reallocate resources currently being wasted through the Mental Health Services Act. California must apply for the Medicaid waiver to expand psychiatric beds. Cal-Psych would attract an A-list workforce, including assertive social workers with a whatever-it-takes mandate.

Cal-Psych would do as much as legally, ethically, and practically possible to establish voluntary drug treatment and psychiatric care and would also work with the courts and law enforcement to enforce involuntary care through assisted outpatient treatment and conservatorship. The low-hanging fruit, according to Rene, is getting twenty-something-year-old opioid addicts off the street and into medically assisted treatment programs, since we have good substitutes for opioids in the form of Suboxone and methadone. The higher-hanging fruit is helping service-resistant people suffering from serious mental illness. All of Cal-Psych's involuntary treatment programs would work with California's criminal justice system to protect individual rights, expand alternatives to jail, and get people the care they need.

California is overdue for a turn toward pragmatism and moderation when it comes to these issues. Californians do not want to return to mass incarceration nor to *One Flew Over the Cuckoo's Nest*. At the same time, Californians want and deserve public order, which has broken down. Assisted outpatient treatment and conservatorship protect individual rights through the courts and allow non-jail and non-prison alternatives focused on psychiatric care. The ACLU has, in the past, done much good to protect rights, but they have taken an extreme position against conservatorship such that they are actively contributing to the current crisis.

Surveys find voters support a balanced, carrot-and-stick approach. Eighty-nine percent of voters support greater involuntary commitment of homeless individuals with severe mental illness and behavioral issues. While voters generally prefer local solutions, noted a pollster, "they are so frustrated with lack of action that Californians now put responsibility for solving the homelessness problem on state officials over local officials, by a 62 to 38 percent margin."[21]

And while some counties may resist Cal-Psych, many others recognize that they cannot solve the problem. They may be happy to let go of the responsibility of caring for the chronic homeless, so long as they are reassured that they will not lose funding or control over county programs for those with milder mental illness such as depression, which are best handled at the county level.

Assisted outpatient treatment, which treats the mentally ill outside of hospitals, would play a central role. Treatment in the community would be preferred over hospitals so no one is treated in a hospital if they don't have to be. However, sometimes severely mentally ill individuals need to be stabilized or cared for with treatments provided only by hospitals. We need to increase the number of mental health beds in hospitals, whether public or private, to the California Hospital Association's standard of 50 beds per 100,000 people. We should also expand conservatorship so loved ones can better care for their severely mentally ill kin.

Cal-Psych would also fight drug addiction through expanded drug treatment. The key time to offer drug treatment to a person suffering from addiction is when they are revived from the brink of death with Narcan. It is an existential moment par excellence: you have nearly died by smoking too much fentanyl and were saved by one of your fellow Americans. The Cal-Psych worker who revives you would be able to offer you drug treatment, available immediately, where you will have the opportunity to detox and get therapy. Cal-Psych would help lengthen court-ordered drug treatment and provide enough resources so that recovering addicts aren't forced to leave rehab right when their cravings peak. Sobering centers would also be provided to individuals still struggling with addiction.

Cal-Psych would get homeless people off the streets. For the one-third of the homeless who have severe mental illness, Cal-Psych compels treatment and supervised care. Cal-Psych would intervene at two different moments in the homeless addict's life, either when he is revived from overdose or after he is caught repeatedly committing nuisance crimes like public defecation, shoplifting, or public intoxication. In the latter case, drug treatment would be offered as an alternative to jail. In both instances, Cal-Psych would offer opportunities to learn to work and build a new life. Cal-Psych would help homeless drug addicts and mentally ill individuals stay healthy and housed by offering a variety of housing on a contingency basis.

Through Cal-Psych, California would dramatically increase the types of shelter and housing available to the homeless. Every homeless person should have access to shelter every night and must use it. Purchasing residential homes and converting the Project Roomkey hotels into abstinence-contingent hotels would be a key first step. The governor could issue state-of-emergency declarations to acquire shelters and housing.

Cal-Psych caseworkers would have a whatever-it-takes mandate to get people off the street. They would track their clients when they go into a hospital, jail, or shelter. Caseworkers would also know if their client relapsed or stopped taking medication. Greater court-ordered supervision would allow caseworkers to impose the order and structure missing from the chaotic lives of the mentally ill so they can get the psychiatric and therapeutic help they need to eventually live more independently.[22] Cal-Psych would have mobile units capable of performing on-the-spot psychiatric evaluations, enrollment in programs, and the replacement of medical identification cards, which homeless drug users tend to lose.

Cal-Psych would work with law enforcement to break up the open drug scenes in the Tenderloin, Skid Row, and the Blade, reimpose consequences for petty crimes through drug courts and mental illness courts, and redevelop run-down infrastructure, allowing for a larger, more diverse, and more functional community.

There are models of effective and humane responses to the mentally ill and street addicts in the United States. Arizona and Texas have police officers trained to handle mental health calls. They track down people who have violated court orders for treatment. They check in on people. They often have social workers with them. Crucially, their status allows them to handle people who might be in a violent, psychotic state, which social workers are usually not equipped to handle.[23]

Positive relationships between health-care providers and police are possible. And there are even the seeds of Cal-Psych in pragmatically minded health professionals in California. LA street doctor Susan Partovi spoke optimistically about the Los Angeles Police Department's head of mental evaluation. "He does not come off as a cop at all," she said. "Most compassionate guy I've ever met. Doesn't have that arrogance. Really cares about this population. He said, 'I want my police to know who's gravely disabled and a danger to self.'"

Susan and the officer created a checklist for police officers to use when interacting with homeless people in psychotic states. Together they are seeking to apply legal conservatorship to mentally ill homeless. "Let's see if they're willing to start taking medications on the streets."[24]

The money for Cal-Psych could come from three sources: California's failed Mental Health Services Act (Proposition 63), Medicaid, and, over time, the city and county funding currently being allocated to unaccountable nonprofit service providers. "Braid your money," said John Snook, "get your Prop 63 money, get your federal housing funds, your Housing First funding, everything together. [Cal-Psych] would have then the authority. That's where it breaks down in California. All of these random nonprofit service providers that are letting things fall through the cracks."

Opposition to Cal-Psych may come from some existing mental health-care providers, but what's going for the idea is the spectacular failure of the current system. "When there are quiet conversations, a lot of people are saying it doesn't make a ton of sense for every single county in the Bay Area to be doing something different," said Snook. "Somebody walks across an imaginary border and suddenly you don't have any ability to engage them in a program. I think a lot of people recognize that."[25]

Opposition may also come from some libertarians and conservatives, but Cal-Psych would not socialize a private market, and thus should not arouse their fears. The government already treats the mentally ill, but in prisons instead of hospitals and outpatient centers. Services for the severely mentally ill and drug-addicted are not a market for anyone except the very wealthy, who can afford private rehabilitation centers like the one that dispenses tough love in Malibu, which could continue to operate independently of Cal-Psych's mandate to treat the severely mentally ill homeless. Some may hesitate to support centralizing government mental health services, but doing so would enable efficiencies, cut government waste, and reverse the mass incarceration of the severely mentally ill, which are outcomes that should be persuasive to people with either libertarian or progressive leanings.

As such, Cal-Psych, and the creation of universal psychiatric care for the severely mentally ill homeless, could represent a moral, human, and technological frontier for California. After the closing of the formal frontier California pioneered frontiers of space exploration, medicine, information and communications technology, and alternative medicines including psychedelics, which show promise for many, from cancer patients to rape victims. Imagine the sense of pride Californians could feel for Cal-Psych. After vacationing in Italy, Dr. Thomas Insel said, "I jumped in a cab to go to the airport. The cabdriver was showing me all the sites when, at one point, he turned to me and said, 'We have the best mental health care in the world, here.' And I thought, 'That's pretty weird. I've never had a cabdriver in California say that to me.' But that was part of who they are. There's tremendous pride around that."[26]

Progressives say they want livable, walkable cities, but by allowing the continued operation of open-air drug scenes, they are making cities unlivable and unwalkable, as well as inhumane. No psychologist or psychiatrist in America believes meth and fentanyl are appropriate medicines for schizophrenia, bipolar disorder, or depression. And yet taxpayers in the San Francisco Bay Area, Seattle, and Los Angeles are, in effect, subsidizing their use and abuse by giving away free hotel rooms, cash, food, and much else.

Too often progressive idealism creates greater loyalty to a highly romanticized view, one that allowed progressives to justify defunding and shutting down core institutions, including psychiatric hospitals, police stations, and homeless shelters. "We have these very high ideals about making criminal justice problems public health problems," San Francisco supervisor Rafael Mandelman acknowledged. "We haven't begun to figure out how to organize and operationalize a public health structure that would allow public health to assume responsibility for that kind of transformation. We ripped down an ugly, problematic system that in some ways worked, and in a lot of ways didn't, and failed to replace it with anything adequate to managing the challenge. And now it feels like we're doing something similar with criminal justice."[27]

Like Mandelman, other elected officials are beginning to stand up to the more ideological advocates of harm reduction and Housing First, and advocating the expansion of temporary shelters. "It's estimated that it will take till 2035 or 2040 to build enough permanent housing," Sacramento mayor Darrell Steinberg said to Housing First advocate Margot Kushel at a televised event in 2019. "The only question I'm asking is, 'What do we do in the meantime?' "[28]

But many progressive advocates, more powerful than ever, had become more dogmatic. The founder of Drug Policy Alliance, Ethan Nadelmann, turned out to be a relative moderate in comparison to his successor. "They have really changed since he's left," said Humphreys. "I knew Ethan and a lot of the people there. There's been quite a turnover, and the viewpoint is much more towards the San Francisco model. There were more people there then who at least were a little more grounded in evidence than ideology than is the case now."[29]

The political establishment in California and progressive West Coast cities has plainly failed, but voters are still not being offered a genuine alternative to status quo policies. Cal-Psych offers voters an alternative between lawlessness and mass incarceration, and between chronic homelessness and chronic institutionalization. A new political vision, agenda, and leadership are needed to overcome the divisions and chaos. "The central conservative truth is that it is culture, not politics, that determines the success of a society," noted the late Democratic senator Daniel Patrick

Moynihan. "The central liberal truth is that politics can change a culture and save itself from itself."[30]

California residents, as noted above, appear ready for the state to take over where counties have failed. And when the context broadens from San Francisco to California, more seems possible. "I actually think there's hope for the state of California," said Michael Solana. "There are a lot of people who are cognizant of the state government's failures and want to see meaningful change."[31] Said Stephen Eide, "Revolutions in social policy do happen sometimes, and it's conceivable that something like that could happen with homelessness."[32]

19

Civilization's End

Next door to Amsterdam's red-light district, the Zeedijk neighborhood had a reputation for jazz and heroin, just like the Tenderloin in San Francisco. Jazz great Chet Baker, who played at the Black Hawk in the Tenderloin in the 1950s, played frequently in Zeedijk. A singer and trumpet player, Baker sat in on bebop sessions in 1950, when he was in the Presidio Army Band. Two years later he moved to Los Angeles to play with Charlie Parker and accompanied Gerry Mulligan in his famous piano-less quartet. But his addiction to heroin dragged him down. Baker's music suffered. Police arrested him repeatedly in both the United States and Europe. And he was nearly beaten to death in 1968.

Zeedijk's decline mirrored Baker's. By the 1980s it had become an open drug scene for heroin dealers and users. Neighborhood residents abandoned buildings and squatters took over. "There were a lot of houses that were abandoned and really falling apart," recalled a former resident. "Nobody wanted to invest in the area."[1]

It was the residents themselves who demanded that the neighborhood be cleaned up. In the spring of 1983, they came to a City Council meeting and threw at council members little bags of sugar mislabeled "Heroin," grabbing public attention. And so, in addition to breaking up Zeedijk's open drug scene, the city government also redeveloped it through a public-private venture.[2]

Amsterdam is home to some of the world's finest row houses, and is as fussy about architecture as San Francisco. The city redeveloped Zeedijk in a way that preserved and enhanced existing structures, including the original seawall. Today Zeedijk is viewed as a crown jewel of Amsterdam's revitalization.

In San Francisco, progressives have for fifty years suggested that redevelopment *must* result in evictions and the bulldozing of whole neighborhoods, but that's not what happened in Zeedijk. The city extended rental subsidies to tenants so they would not be driven out as rents rose. One-third of the housing stock is rent-controlled. "We could make a higher revenue on our portfolio, but we choose to keep diversity," the housing developer explained. "The money is reinvested in new properties and also more affordable housing in the area, unlike some landlords, where it is probably being invested in their holiday villa." The model was so popular that it is now being used in the neighboring red-light district.[3]

All redevelopment comes at a price. It can result in a change to the demographics of the neighborhood. Critics of Zeedijk's transformation complain of too many tourists, too few jazz clubs, and rising rents for those units that do not receive subsidies. "We have people who rent property with us who are also our main critics," said the public housing developer, who had a good attitude about it. "We believe that only when you are open to criticism, can you really make your neighborhood better."[4]

But the price of not redeveloping is much higher: the destruction of human dignity and civil society. Redevelopment makes housing more abundant and can reduce the concentration of poverty. It grows the tax base and generates revenue to improve schools and transportation. That's what happened in New York City after the closure of open-air drug markets in the Alphabet City area of the Lower East Side, and its subsequent redevelopment.[5]

Redevelopment is a chance to make the Tenderloin, the Blade, and

Skid Row walkable, livable, and beautiful. I was surprised to find little opposition to redevelopment, and even some enthusiasm. When I asked LA street doctor Susan Partovi, "Can we redevelop Skid Row?" she said, "Absolutely. Let's make it pretty."[6]

Given California's stagnation, we cannot allow our response to the untreated addiction and mental illness crisis to depend upon significantly expanding the overall housing stock. Human dignity, and the sanctity of our cities, must come before the political agendas of NIMBYs, YIMBYs, and everyone else in between. At the same time, the Tenderloin, Skid Row, and the Blade cannot be the only sites of new housing development. Attempting to make them that would be unfair and impractical. If California ever chooses to return to population growth, while reducing the impact of historic injustices, the state will need to build a lot more housing, from apartments and condos downtown to fourplexes and adjacent dwelling units in the suburbs.[7]

In exchange for more apartments downtown, Californians could agree to more suburbs on former farmlands. YIMBYs sometimes misdescribe how cities add housing. Cities around the world, from Tokyo to Atlanta, become more dense *and* grow outward at the same time. Some pro-density advocates have pointed to Tokyo as a city that grew its population without taking up more land, but Tokyo's area increased 54 percent from 1990 to 2010. Its rate of expansion doubled during this time and it became less dense overall.[8] Housing in suburbs is far cheaper to build than in the cities, which is how cities from Tokyo to Atlanta have been able to keep overall housing prices comparatively low.[9]

Many of us who move to the Bay Area, and pay dearly to remain, do so in part to enjoy California's spectacular natural environments. These public areas should remain off-limits to any kind of development. But allowing for suburbanization of California's ranches and farmlands would still allow for strong protections of California's scenic natural areas like Yosemite, the redwoods, and oak woodlands and green spaces near cities.

The obvious way to do so is by rescinding the regressive tax breaks California and other states give to uneconomic farms and ranches. Over the last several decades, a declining amount of California's land was converted from farming to housing.[10] In 2009, five times more of California's land was used for pasture (17 percent) and farming (8 percent) than for cities and suburbs.[11] People should be free to use their land for uneconomic purposes, but they should not be subsidized by taxpayers, particularly when the land would have far higher value as housing.

Some conservatives recognize the need for more housing. "I'm not one of those conservatives who rejects the idea that homelessness is a housing problem," said Stephen Eide. "Homelessness is a housing problem, at least in part. There's no way to understand how this developed and changed over the last fifty, sixty years without thinking about what happened to housing at that time. In particular, at the very lowest end of the housing market."[12]

But whether or not housing can be significantly expanded in California, we should redevelop neighborhoods that have been taken over by open-air drug scenes for strictly humanitarian, and public order, reasons. In this regard, Zeedijk serves as both inspiration and warning. When redevelopment finally arrived, it was too late to save Chet Baker. In 1973, police found his body under the second-story window of his hotel room, with cocaine and heroin in his room and his body. He was only fifty-eight.[13]

The crisis on the streets has led some progressives to recognize the need for building more temporary shelter. "We need to do the New York model and create a lot of housing," said Berkeley homeless service provider and advocate Boona Cheema. "Half the world lives in shanty-towns. Come on. That's the part that irritates me the most. How can you be anti-shelter unless you have affordable housing?"

"But the consensus seems to be pretty anti-shelter," I said.

"You've been talking to heavy-duty advocates," she said. "When you talk to service providers like me, we feel very differently because we've seen people fall out of Housing First because nobody showed up to check in on them and they were out of [psychiatric] meds and came back to the street."[14]

Chris Herring, who works closely with Jennifer Friedenbach, said his own thinking had evolved. "In 2000 when I started with the National Coalition on Homelessness, and in 2003 when I did my undergrad work, I became really critical of the shelter industrial complex and short-termism," he said. "But when you really start doing the ethnographic field research, going between the streets and the shelter, it's very hard to hold this sort of theoretical position that we need to just do Housing First and stop talking about shelter. In the last twenty years all I hear from city officials is 'Housing First' and 'We're not doing shelter because we need more housing.' But now we've got even more homeless on the street and more suffering."[15]

Susan Partovi agreed. "Interim housing is fine," she said. "As long as they're in interim housing, we can be working on their permanent housing. That can take a year or even more. They could die before that happens."[16]

Americans not suffering from serious mental illness should have a right to shelter, not to a studio apartment, much less one in one of the most expensive downtown real estate markets in the world. Shelters should be safe, clean, and humane. But they also must be low-cost, basic, and not so nice as to serve as an incentive to homelessness. And better housing should be earned, not given away unconditionally.

Would voters support such an agenda? In 2020 and 2021, I conducted two polls of California voters through Google Surveys, which surveyed a random and representative sample of the public, to find out. In both, I found strong support for the basic principles I have outlined here.

More than two-thirds of voters support enforcing laws against using hard drugs and defecating in public, and support using mandatory drug treatment and mental health care as alternatives to jail and prison. The 2020 survey was of 403 California voters. It found that 71 percent of respondents agreed with the statement, "People who defecate or use hard drugs in public should be arrested and evaluated for mental health and/ or drug treatment," and 42 percent strongly agreed, while just 11 percent disagreed, 4 percent strongly.

Most voters in 2021 still felt homelessness was the number one problem that required addressing. In January 2021, most respondents agreed that violent crime was increasing (52 percent) and that we need more housing, not less, to reduce rents and eviction (83 percent). Forty-three percent said mental illness and drug addiction were the main causes of homelessness, and 49 percent agreed with the statement, "We need to break up the open-air drug markets and offer mandatory drug treatment as an alternative to jail." Eighty-eight percent of Democrats and 29 percent of Republicans agreed.[17]

Other public opinion surveys find that California voters support a balanced approach. A 2019 poll found they "support a mix of compassionate and no-nonsense actions." A policy described as "involuntary commitment of homeless individuals who have severe mental/behavioral issues that may be a danger or harm to themselves or others in the community" had 89 percent support. Support for "more homeless shelters" stood at 86 percent. And 74 percent of voters said the state should recriminalize the serial thefts that Proposition 47 in 2014 decriminalized.[18]

Over the last two years we have seen a disturbing rise in politically motivated disorder, from the anarchist takeovers of autonomous zones in Seattle, Portland, and Minneapolis to the storming of the US Capitol by supporters of former president Donald Trump. In each case, elected officials not only failed to respond swiftly and decisively, they contributed to the undermining of law and order. In every case I felt an anxiety I had never felt before, which was the fear of losing my country. I began to genuinely worry that America could become like one of the undemocratic and unfree nations I have visited over the decades. Disorder and the loss of freedom go hand in hand. Political leaders who fail to maintain order are often replaced by leaders who sacrifice freedom.

I wish more Americans could experience life in a closed society to properly appreciate just how special and precious civilization and freedom are. Around the world I have met people whose loved ones were raped because the police had been kicked out of an area controlled by rebel factions. And I have interviewed journalists gripped with fear that the people at the table next to us were government spies who would take them to prison, or worse, simply for talking with me.

Many of the people who enjoy some of the highest levels of prosperity and freedom in human history are also the least grateful, and least loyal, to the civilization that made it possible. The progressive obsession with changing the names of schools and tearing down statues of people allegedly guilty of genocide in the past comes at a time when our greatest global rival is actually guilty of committing one in the present. In 2021, the US State Department declared China's treatment of its Uighur Muslim minority "genocide." Meanwhile, during the pandemic, China has behaved in increasingly menacing ways toward US allies in the Asia Pacific region, such as Australia, Japan, South Korea, Taiwan, and the Philippines, and continues to seek to steal from American entrepreneurs and high-tech firms.[19]

Today, America is so divided that some progressives are openly proposing that America split apart.[20] This suggestion raises a question similar to the one Victor Frankl demanded of his depressed clients: *Why doesn't America commit suicide? What should America live for?*

The traditional answer is freedom, but Americans are deeply divided over its meaning. Where progressives are concerned primarily with the freedom of victims, notes Jonathan Haidt, conservatives are concerned primarily with the freedom from constraints. In the United States "liberals are most concerned about the rights of certain vulnerable groups (e.g., racial minorities, children, animals)," he writes, "and they look to government to defend the weak against oppression by the strong. Conservatives, in contrast, hold more traditional ideas of liberty as the right to be left alone, and they often resent liberal programs that use government to infringe on their liberties in order to protect the groups that liberals care most about."[21]

In his famous essay, Frederick Turner argued that, to balance the American notion of freedom as self-reliance and rugged individualism, we needed to remind ourselves that the frontier was also a place of solidarity and reciprocity, and that we needed governmental and other shared institutions. Turner reminds us that much of the so-called freedom of the frontier was often not true freedom at all. The West was the meeting point between "savagery and civilization." Psychologist Viktor Frankl agreed. "Freedom is only part of the story and half of the truth," he wrote. "In fact, freedom is in danger of degenerating into mere arbitrariness unless it is lived in terms of responsibleness."[22]

The good news, noted Turner, is that the frontier is also characterized by the capacity for "perennial rebirth," and "beginning over again." Today that starts with valuing freedom as a state of affiliation, not disaffiliation, and of responsibility to, not freedom from, one another as fellow Americans. And we must return to a view of freedom that is universal, and not just for people designated Victims. We must affirm equal justice under, and enforcement of, the law.

In the same spirit, we should recommit to Martin Luther King's commandment to judge each other by the content of our character, not by the color of our skin. We are responsible for our behavior, not that of our group, nor that of our ancestors. The arc of the universe does indeed bend toward justice, as King claimed, and we thus dishonor the sacrifices of our forebears when we suggest things are as bad or worse today than before the 1964 Civil Rights Act. We must build upon our shared progress against inequality, not deny its existence.

By the spring of 2021, it appeared that a backlash against identity politics, and perhaps even victimology more broadly, was finally under way. Facing widespread criticism and a recall campaign, the San Francisco Unified School District's Board of Directors paused its school renaming initiative, ostensibly so it could focus on reopening the schools. Several well-known and respected scholars, journalists, and activists, including Columbia University's John McWhorter, former *New York Times* columnist Bari Weiss, Harvard's Steven Pinker, Coleman Hughes, and Chris Rufo, announced the creation of a new organization called Foundation Against Intolerance and Racism, to push back against racial essentialism and intolerance.[23] And in New York, New Jersey, and Virginia, Asian parents filed lawsuits to fight racial discrimination in high school admissions and defend meritocracy.[24]

No serious historian today would rank Harvey Milk's advocacy of requiring people to pick up after their dogs as a particularly important aspect of his legacy. Milk's legacy is normalizing gay, lesbian, bisexual, and transgender relationships by encouraging people to come out of the closet to their friends and families, and helping to kill a ballot initiative that would have fired gay teachers. But historians remind us that some things which appear trivial at first reveal themselves to be of greater importance over time.

Milk didn't get elected on a platform of gay rights. It was too narrow, even for San Francisco. He was elected to solve a problem of public disorder, of feces where they didn't belong. In the process of solving an issue trivialized as a mere nuisance, Milk went from being "the gay candidate" to the people's candidate. He transcended the politics of identity to arrive at a politics of community. Behavior matters, particularly in cities.

The dog poop law was, fundamentally, an effort to change behavior by changing social norms. Recall that when a reporter expressed skepticism that police would be able to enforce the law, Milk said the law would be enforced through "peer pressure." Said Milk, "when a San Franciscan is walking down the street and sees someone breaking the law you say 'Hey!'—with a smile—'You broke the law.' And after a while, when enough people do that, the message will be clear."[25]

When our manic character, born of the flight from oppression and the adventure of the Wild West frontier, is unbalanced by more sober virtues, lawlessness and disorder result. Great freedom depends on great responsibility. When conservatives say that freedom isn't free and that we should be grateful for our military families and veterans, it sounds to many progressives as it did to me once, as a justification for militarism, and in some cases it may be that. But it also speaks to the recognition of something much more profound and significant, which is that peace requires security, and that security requires responsibility.

The Statue of Liberty, noted Frankl, symbolizes something that is at once essential about the United States but also incomplete. The American frontier closed over a century ago, and the values of the West increasingly define the whole of the United States, as Turner predicted. But we are not living up to our role as leaders, or to our duty to one another as fellow humans and citizens. As such, it is time for us to grow up. That should start in California, the state that most embodies the American frontier spirit, and our love of freedom, and in San Francisco, the city that most embodies its ingenuity. And so it is here, perhaps in the bay that connects the city to America, that we should complete the American project and build what Frankl proposed: a Statue of Responsibility.[26]

Epilogue

In spring 2021, I watched a *Vice* documentary on YouTube about Mexican families living near the US border whose children had been abducted or killed by the drug cartel. At a press conference a group of them held up large photos of their children, something that is common in protests in Latin America. It made me wonder: would mothers of the San Francisco Bay Area do something similar to protest the drug dealers preying on their addicted children in the Tenderloin? I decided to ask two of the mothers I had interviewed, whose sons are addicted to fentanyl and homeless in the Bay Area.

"I would definitely consider doing that," said Kelly Stamphill, who said she had just seen her son, Morgan, a few days earlier. "I walked through those eleven drug dealers and a guy stopped me and said, 'You are dressed too well to be in the Tenderloin.' I showed him a picture of my son, and he knows him. They kept trying to sell me drugs. It took every bit of coolness and calmness to not become a crazy person and scream, 'Don't sell drugs to my son!' But they also had machetes, and I knew that wouldn't end well."

And so, after thinking more about it, Kelly, understandably, decided against it. "He's living in a tent city, a Safe Sleeping Site. He said, 'Mom, get out of the TL.' He was really worried about my safety but also was embarrassed that I'm showing these drug dealers a picture of him because he's there all the time. I don't want to put his life in jeopardy. A month ago, before I knew where he was, I wanted to start doing harm to the dealers, and bringing them down in justice. But now that I know where he's at, I'm scared for him."[1]

I also spoke with Jacqui Berlinn, whose son, Corey, compared San Francisco to Pleasure Island in *Pinocchio*. I asked her how he was doing.

"My anxiety level is very high right now," she said. "The last time I heard from him was mid-January. He usually contacts me once a month. He knows that I get anxious. I haven't heard if he's alive. I don't even know how I would find out if he's a victim of a crime on the streets. I can't find him in the hospital because he'd be under an alias. He's literally out there alone."

I asked, "Have you ever attended a protest?"

"No," she said, and then started to laugh, which made me laugh.

"Why are *you* laughing?" I asked.

"I work in law enforcement," said Jacqui. "I'm a legal process clerk for the Alameda County sheriff's office [across the bay from San Francisco]. Recent protests have affected my life. I work at the courthouse in Oakland, which was a target of graffiti, breaking windows, and trying to set fires. They boarded up the windows and I didn't have sunshine. They didn't know when they would go crazy. So when I think of protest I think of it in terms of violence. I don't believe in destroying property."

Then, before I had mentioned any specifics, Jacqui said, "I would be willing to hold up a huge picture of my son and walk around with it."

"What makes you say that?" I asked.

"I saw the tweet by T. [Tom] Wolf today," said Jacqui. "He said he counted eleven dealers in a picture he posted. I thought, 'Would I have the guts to stand across from them with a picture of my son on a sign, and tell them not to sell to my son?' I know they're very powerful. They have gangs. And I would put myself at risk. But I would. Absolutely."

"I was literally about to ask you if you would do that," I said

"I thought it was bold that Tom posted a picture of them," Jacqui said. "I was imagining if they saw him taking a picture of them. He's putting himself at risk. Being in law enforcement, I know what a risk it is to stand up against them. But why is it okay for eleven dealers to sell drugs to our children? Every single time they sell something, it's an opportunity for our children to die."[2]

As I listened to her, I reminded myself that protesting fentanyl dealers connected to international drug mafias might not be the safest thing in the world. As Kelly said, "they also had machetes."[3] On the other hand, if we are too intimidated to peacefully protest foreign drug dealers poisoning our children and fellow human beings in downtown San Francisco, degrading the fabric of civic life, then we are in some way participating in civilization's end.

I found myself thinking about the progressive and Christian concepts of witness. In the Bible, a witness is not only someone who sees something important, she is also somebody who takes responsibility by sharing what she sees. In the 1980s, a progressive activist research group called Witness for Peace documented human rights violations in Central America. It was that role, as Witness, not the role of Rescuer, I realized at that moment, which was the right role for me.

And so I told Jacqui that I would stand with her as her witness, even if it ended up just being the two of us, and promised to investigate how to do it in a safe way for everyone, including by speaking with the San Francisco Police Department beforehand. I told her we could take inspiration from the Mothers of the Plaza de Mayo in Buenos Aires in the late 1970s. Their quiet courage galvanized protests that ultimately resulted in the downfall of the government, and the advent of a new political era. Before ending our call, we both agreed to look for allies.

I reached out to Adam Mesnick, the Deli Board restaurateur who discovered that fentanyl addicts describe coming to San Francisco to die from overdose. I told him about our idea. "I'd love to help," he said, without hesitation. "How do people not hear when a parent writes on Twitter, 'My daughter or my son is on the streets of the Tenderloin, people are running around like it's a party, and my kid is going to die'?" Said Mesnick, alluding to San Francisco's 713 drug overdose deaths in 2020,

"I have no idea how many people died in San Francisco from COVID-19 last year, but I know it wasn't 700."[4] (It was 252.)[5]

What would a movement to save our cities, and states, look like? We might start with the people most impacted: the residents of the neighborhoods invaded by violent anarchists; the restaurant and store owners; the residents of the Tenderloin, Skid Row, and the Blade, and other neighborhoods degraded by open-air drug dealing; people who like parks; parents and families of homicide, overdose, poisoning, and addiction victims; all who believe cities are sacred and that sidewalks should be safe, clean, and clear for everyone, including children, the elderly, and the disabled.

It made sense to me that some of the leaders of such a movement might be mothers and that their power would emerge from overcoming their shame. Harvey Milk understood this power better than anyone else. He knew that social values and norms weren't fixed. They change. We change them. It wasn't shameful to not pick up one's dog's poop before Milk made it shameful. It was shameful to be gay before he made it unshameful. It was shameful to inject hard drugs on sidewalks, and should be so again.

Kelly emphasized that she supported the idea even if she couldn't join us on the streets. "It would draw attention," she said. "Maybe people will say, 'These people like Corey and Morgan have parents and friends.' "[6]

The mothers who fight for their children should not be ashamed. Kelly and Jacqui have nothing to be ashamed of. They have been fighting for their sons' lives for over a decade against a system that refuses to help them, ostensibly out of fairness and compassion to their sons. "I used to hide my story out of shame," said Jacqui. "But I realized a few years ago that that didn't help my son or myself. I have been speaking up ever since."[7] The people who most need to feel shame are those who failed to take responsibility for the situation and allowed it to worsen for decades: all of us.

Acknowledgments

In the summer of 2020, not long after deciding to write this book, I got in touch with the other board members and donors to my nonprofit research organization, Environmental Progress. I wanted to talk to them about why I felt the need to write it, and why I felt that research and policy development to address what is called homelessness was consistent with the organization's mission of nature and prosperity for all.

The environment and homelessness are not obviously connected. "Prosperity requires cities," I explained, "and our cities are being ruined." But that made my desire sound more rational than it probably was. The truth is that I couldn't explain very well why I felt the need to investigate the problem. What I do know is that while researching and writing *San Fransicko* was emotionally draining, it was also cathartic because it gave me a Franklian goal to pursue during COVID.

As such, I am grateful to the board, staff, and friends of Environmental Progress for making a deeper leap into the social and human dimensions of our environment than most environmental think tanks are willing to go. Frank Batten, Bill Budinger, John Crary, Paul Davis, Steve Kirsch, Ross Koningstein, Michael Pelizzari, Jim Swartz, Matt Winkler, and Kristin Zaitz have been loyal and loving supporters and friends. My colleagues Sid Bagga, Lea Booth, Gabrielle and Mark Nelson, and Emmet Penney contributed significantly to all aspects of this project, including research and collaboration on the development of Cal-Psych, and other aspects of our positive proposal. I am grateful to Claire Lehmann at *Quillette* for encouraging many of the ideas here, and hosting a wider conversation that informed my thinking, to Chris Helman at *Forbes* for allowing me to veer outside of my swim lane from time to time, and to Dr. Drew Pinsky for helping me think more deeply about an issue I had initially viewed through the lens of housing. I thank Eric Nelson at HarperCollins for helping me to conceptualize this project and entrusting me with it. And I am grateful to Helen Lee, Luke Thompson, Dalton Conley, Mark Sagoff, Scott Winship, and Kim Shellenberger for their thoughtful comments on early drafts.

Finally, I thank all who consented to share their views with me: Adam Mesnick, Andy Bales, Andy Mullan, Anne Harrington, Art Agnos, Beau Kilmer, Bill Zimmerman, Boona Cheema, Carl Hart, Carmen Best, Chris Block, Chris Herring, Chris Rufo, Christopher Jencks, Christopher Young, Cory Clark, Cristin Evans, Dalton Conley, Dan Abrahamson, Dan O'Flaherty, David Young, Dennis Culhane, Dilan Yeşilgöz, Drew Pinsky, Duncan Moore, Ethan Nadelmann, Eve Garrow, Jabari Jackson, Jacqui Berlinn, Jamie Crook, Jane Kim, Jeff Bellisario, Jen Loving, Jennifer Friedenbach, Keith Humphreys, Kelly Kruger, Kelly Stamphill, Ken Rosenberg, Kerry Jackson, Kristen Marshall, Laura Foote, Liz Breuilly, Louis Chicoine, Margot Kushel, Marsha Rosenbaum, Matt Haney, Michael Solana, Michelle Tandler, Monique Tula, Norman Yee, Paneez Kosarian, Patt Denning, Paul Boden, Paul Linde, Philip Mangano, Rafael Mandelman, Randolph Roth, Randy Shaw, Rene Zegerius, Richard Rosenfeld, Riva Tez, Robert Okin, Ron Book, Sam Tsemberis, Scott Winship, Stanton Peele, Stefan Kertesz, Stephen Eide, Steve Berg, Susan Mizner, Susan Partovi, Thomas Insel, Tom Wolf, Tracey Helton Mitchell, Victoria Beach, and Victoria Westbrook.

Notes

Epigraph

1. Charles Herbermann, ed., "St. Francis of Assisi," *Catholic Encyclopedia* (New York: Robert Appleton Company, 1913).

Introduction

1. "What's Driving California's Mass Exodus?" CNBC, January 23, 2021, YouTube video, 19:08, www.youtube.com.

2. Janelle Cammenga, "State and Local Sales Tax Rates, 2021," Tax Foundation, January 6, 2021, www.taxfoundation.org; Janelle Cammenga, "State Gasoline Tax Rates as of July 2020," Tax Foundation, July 29, 2020, www.taxfoundation.org.

3. Bill Maher, *Real Time with Bill Maher*, accessed through Joseph A. Wulfsohn, "Maher slams California's 'super high taxes,' cites Joe Rogan, Ben Shapiro as part of the state's 'exodus,'" Fox News, October 9, 2020, www.foxnews.com.

4. Christopher Jencks, *The Homeless* (Cambridge, MA: Harvard University Press, 1994); Richard W. White Jr., *Rude Awakenings: What the Homeless Crisis Tells Us* (Lanham, MD: Institute for Contemporary Studies Press, 1992); Alice S. Baum and Donald W. Burnes, *A Nation in Denial: The Truth About Homelessness* (Avalon, 1993).

1 "I Just Want to Clean Up the Mess"

1. Srdja Popovic and Matthew Miller, "Harvey Milk's First Crusade: Dog Poop," *Politico*, February 15, 2015, www.politico.com.

2. John M. Crewdson, "Harvey Milk, Led Coast Homosexual-Rights Fight," *New York Times*, November 28, 1978, www.nytimes.com.

3. SF History Center Archivist, "A Dog's Life: Scoop the Poop Act 1978," *What's on the 6th Floor?* (blog), May 1, 2010, www.sfhcbasc.blogspot.com.

4. Laura Perkins, "Milk Says Poop Scoop Ordinance Is a 'Step in the Right Direction,'" *SF Gate*, August 29, 2003, www.sfgate.com.

5. "Harvey Milk in Duboce Park on Pooper Scooper Law," aired August 29, 1978, on KQED, video, 2:31, https://diva.sfsu.edu.

6. Bigad Shaban, Robert Campos, and Anthony Rutanashoodech, "SF Mayor: 'There's More Feces . . . Than I've Ever Seen,'" NBC Bay Area, July 16, 2018, video, 3:33, www.nbcbayarea.com.

7. "311 Cases," database, DataSF, www.datasf.gov; cited in Bigad Shaban et al., "Survey of Downtown San Francisco Reveals Trash on Every Block, 303 Piles of Feces and 100 Drug Needles," NBC Bay Area, updated December 16, 2018, www.nbcbayarea.com.

8. Thomas Fuller, "Life on the Dirtiest Block in San Francisco," *New York Times*, October 8, 2018, www.nytimes.com.

9. "311 Cases," database, DataSF, www.datasf.gov.

10. Phil Matier and Andy Ross, "SF's Appalling Street Life Repels Residents—Now It's Driven Away a Convention," *San Francisco Chronicle*, July 2, 2018, www.sfchronicle.com.

11. Binyamin Appelbaum, "America's Cities Could House Everyone if They Chose To," *New York Times*, May 15, 2020, www.nytimes.com.

12. Nathan Heller, "A Window onto an American Nightmare," *New Yorker*, June 1, 2020, www.newyorker.com.

13. Kevin Corinth and David S. Lucas, "When Warm and Cold Don't Mix: The Implications of Climate for the Determinants of Homelessness," *Journal of Housing Economics* 41 (2018): 45–56.

14. "CoC Homeless Populations and Subpopulations Reports," HUD Exchange, accessed July 17, 2021, www.hudexchange.com.

15. Spencer Michels, "San Francisco's last working-class neighborhood gets left behind in boom times," *PBS NewsHour*, February 11, 2014, YouTube video, 7:34, www.youtube.com.

16. Audrey Cooper, "Year After Homeless Project Began, Struggle for Solutions Continues," *San Francisco Chronicle*, June 25, 2017, www.sfchronicle.com.

17. Joe Fitzgerald Rodriguez, "Proposition C Court Win Delivers Nearly $500 Million for San Francisco's Homeless. But How Will it Be Spent?" KQED, September 12, 2020, www.kqed.org.

18. Marc Benioff, "Marc Benioff Sees 'Crisis of Inequality' in San Francisco," interview by Emily Chang, *Bloomberg Politics*, October 31, 2018, YouTube video, 9:23, www.youtube.com.

19. Ibid.

20. Rosalie Chan, "Salesforce CEO Marc Benioff on His Twitter Beef with Jack Dorsey: You're Either 'for the Homeless' or 'You're for Yourself,' " *Business Insider*, October 15, 2018, www.businessinsider.com.

21. Laura Kurtzman, "UCSF Launches New Benioff Homelessness and Housing Initiative with $30M Gift," May 1, 2019, www.ucsf.edu.

22. Jill Cowan and Conor Dougherty, "What Would It Take to End Homelessness?" *New York Times*, January 13, 2020, updated February 20, 2020, www.nytimes.com.

23. Ibid.

24. Chris Glynn and Alexander Casey, "Homeless Rises Faster Where Rent Exceeds a Third of Income," Zillow, December 11, 2018, www.zillow.com.

25. Otis R. Taylor Jr., "Oakland Homeless Camps Point to Racial Bias," *San Francisco Chronicle*, July 1, 2017, www.sfchronicle.com.

26. Housing Instability Research Department, "San Francisco Homeless Count and Survey: Comprehensive Report, 2019," Applied Survey Research, 2019, www.nhipdata.org.

27. "CoC Homeless Populations and Subpopulations Reports."

28. Ibid.

29. Ibid.

30. Ibid.

31. Ibid.

32. Ibid. In 2020, San Francisco counted 1,908 unsheltered chronically homeless individuals, and 929 chronically homeless in emergency shelter.

33. Ibid.

34. Ibid.

35. Glynn and Casey, "Homeless Rises Faster Where Rent Exceeds a Third of Income."

36. "CoC Homeless Populations and Subpopulations Reports," HUD Exchange, accessed February 24, 2021, www.hudexchange.com; "Zillow Observed Rent Index (ZORI)," Zillow, accessed February 24, 2021, www.zillow.com.

37. "311 Cases," database, DataSF, www.datasf.gov.

38. Wilson Walker, "Junkies Take Over Corridors of San Francisco Civic Center BART Station," KPIX CBS SF Bay Area, April 25, 2018, YouTube video, 2:21, www.youtube.com.

39. Fuller, "Life on the Dirtiest Block in San Francisco."

40. Ibid.

41. Dominic Fracassa and Trisha Thadani, "SF Counts 4,000 Homeless, Addicted and Mentally Ill, but Timeline for Help Still Unclear," *San Francisco Chronicle*, December 31, 2019, www.sfchronicle.com.

42. Doug Smith and Benjamin Oreskes, "Are Many Homeless People in L.A. Mentally Ill? New Findings Back the Public's Perception," *Los Angeles Times*, October 7, 2019, www.latimes.com.

43. Angela Alioto et al., *The San Francisco Plan to Abolish Chronic Homelessness* (San Francisco Ten Year Planning Council, 2004), www.sfgov.org; W. Liu, McMillan Stabilization Pilot Project, unpublished report, 2004; Kelly M. Doran et al., "Substance Use and Homelessness Among Emergency Department Patients," *Drug and Alcohol Dependence* 188 (2018): 328–33, doi:10.1016/j.drugalcdep.2018.04.021; Alice S. Baum and Donald W. Burnes, *A Nation in Denial: The Truth About Homelessness* (Boulder, CO: Westview Press, 1993).

44. Stefan G. Kertesz et al., "Personal and Community Characteristics Associated with Unsheltered Status Among Veterans Who Have Experienced Homelessness," *American Journal of Preventive Medicine*, 2021.

45. Erica Sandberg, "Harm Reduction in San Francisco: The City by the Bay Has Embraced a New Religion: Drug Normalization," *City Journal*, February 14, 2019, www.city-journal.org; Joshua Sabatini, "SF's New Needle Cleanup Team to Get Van and Branded Jackets," *San Francisco Examiner*, May 25, 2018, www.sfexaminer.com.

46. City of San Francisco, *311 Cases*, (July 13, 2021), distributed by Data SF, www.datasf.org.

Notes

47. City of San Francisco, *311 Cases: Needle-Related Cases After January 1, 2017* (January 22, 2021), distributed by Data SF, www.datasf.org.

48. Fuller, "Life on the Dirtiest Block in San Francisco."

49. Cowan and Dougherty, "What Would It Take to End Homelessness?"

50. Utah Department of Workforce Services, "Utah's Chronic Homelessness Approaching 'Functional Zero' State Achieves Goal Ten Years in the Making," April 28, 2015, www.findinghousing.utah.gov; Kevin C. Corinth, "On Utah's 91 Percent Decrease in Chronic Homelessness," American Enterprise Institute, March 2016, www.aei.org; "Utah Reduced Chronic Homelessness by 91 Percent; Here's How," *NPR*, December 10, 2015, www.npr.org; Terrence McCoy, "The Surprisingly Simple Way Utah Solved Chronic Homelessness and Saved Millions," *Washington Post*, April 17, 2015, www.washingtonpost.com.

51. John M. Glionna, "Utah Is Winning the War on Chronic Homelessness with 'Housing First' Program," *Los Angeles Times*, May 24, 2015, www.latimes.com.

52. Jacob Rascon, "Utah's Strategy for the Homeless: Give Them Homes," NBC, May 3, 2015, www.nbcnews.com.

53. Sam Tsemberis et al., "Housing First, Consumer Choice, and Harm Reduction for Homeless Individuals with a Dual Diagnosis," *American Journal of Public Health* 94, no. 4 (2004): 651–56, doi:10.2105/AJPH.94.4.651.

54. Cowan and Dougherty, "What Would It Take to End Homelessness?"

55. Steve Berg, "Ten-Year Plans to End Homelessness," *2015 Advocates' Guide*, National Low Income Housing Coalition, accessed May 17, 2021, www.nlihc.org /sites/default/files/Sec7.08_Ten-Year-Plan_2015.pdf.

56. "Bay Area Homeless: Concern or Crisis Part 2," KTVU Fox 2 San Francisco, September 18, 2017, YouTube video, 52:07, www.youtube.com.

57. "CoC Housing Inventory Count Reports," HUD Exchange, accessed February 22, 2021, www.hudexchange.com.

58. Ibid.

59. "CoC Homeless Populations and Subpopulations Reports," HUD Exchange, accessed July 10, 2021, www.hudexchange.com.

60. Heather Knight, "Jennifer Friedenbach, Champion of S.F. Homeless," *SF Gate*, February 4, 2012.

61. Jennifer Friedenbach, interview by the author, January 13, 2021.

62. Randy Shaw, interview by the author, October 1, 2020.

63. Jamie Crook and Eve Garrow, interview by the author, February 28, 2020.

64. Christopher Jencks, *The Homeless* (Cambridge, MA: Harvard University Press, 1994), 97.

65. Ibid., 98.

66. Ben Austen, *High-Risers: Cabrini-Green and the Fate of American Public Housing* (New York: HarperCollins, 2018).

67. William Tucker, "The Source of America's Housing Problem: Look in Your Own Back Yard," *Cato Institute Policy Analysis* No. 127 (February 6, 1990), www.cato.org.

68. Ibid.

69. Boona Cheema, interview by the author, February 11, 2021.

70. Jencks, *The Homeless*, 41.

71. Art Agnos, *Beyond Shelter: A Homeless Plan for San Francisco*, August 1989; Department of Public Health, "Single Room Occupancy Hotels in San Francisco: A Health Impact Assessment," Spring 2016, https://www.pewtrusts.org/-/media/assets/external-sites/health-impact-project/sfdph-2016-sroh-report.pdf; Brian J. Sullivan & Jonathan Burke, *Single-Room Occupancy Housing in New York City: The Origins and Dimensions of a Crisis*, Winter 2013; Whet Moser "The Long, Slow Decline of Chicago's SROs," *Chicago Magazine*, June 14, 2013.

72. Kelly R. Knight et al., "Single Room Occupancy (SRO) Hotels as Mental Health Risk Environments Among Impoverished Women: The Intersection of Policy, Drug Use, Trauma, and Urban Space," *International Journal of Drug Policy* 25, no. 3 (May 2014): xx, doi:10.1016/j.drugpo.2013.10.011.

73. Thomas Wolf, interview with the author, October 23, 2020; Thomas Wolf, "San Francisco's $1 Billion Homeless Industry Is Fueled by Organized Crime and Compassion Politics," interview by John Sung Kim, October 2, 2020, YouTube video, 55:20, www.youtube.com.

74. Richard W. White Jr., *Rude Awakenings: What the Homeless Crisis Tells Us* (Institute for Contemporary Studies Press, 1992), 98; Baum and Burnes, *A Nation in Denial*.

75. Tracey Helton Mitchell, *The Big Fix: Hope After Heroin* (Berkeley, CA: Seal Press, 2016), 43.

76. Alexander Cockburn, "Feed a Vagrant, Go to Jail in San Francisco: The City by the Bay Is Almost Medieval in Its Treatment of the Homeless as Inhuman," *Los Angeles Times*, September 22, 1994, www.latimes.com.

77. Jane Meredith Adams, "Crackdown on Homeless Dividing San Francisco," *Chicago Tribune*, January 1, 1994.

78. Randy Shaw, "The Real Story of Care Not Cash," *Beyond Chron* (blog), May 5, 2009, www.beyondchron.org.

79. Teresa Gowan, *Hobos, Hustlers, and Backsliders: Homeless in San Francisco* (Minneapolis: University of Minnesota Press, 2010), 246.

80. John King, "Brown Baffled by Homeless Problem—Summit Canceled—Distrust on All Sides," *SF Gate*, September 17, 1996, www.sfgate.com.

81. Ibid.

82. "A start on ending homelessness," *San Francisco Chronicle*, December 12, 2004.

83. Gowan, *Hobos, Hustlers, and Backsliders*, 265.

84. Rone Tempest, "San Francisco Rethinks Cash Aid to Homeless," *Los Angeles Times*, August 26, 2002, www.latimes.com; Gowan, *Hobos, Hustlers, and Backsliders*, 265.

85. Gowan, *Hobos, Hustlers, and Backsliders*, 268.

86. Alioto et al., *The San Francisco Plan to Abolish Chronic Homelessness*.

87. Lee Romney, "S.F. Has a Plan for Homeless Problem," *Los Angeles Times*, July 1, 2004, www.latimes.com.

88. Kevin Fagan, "Mayor picks panel to tackle homelessness, Board council of 33 members has until July to craft new plan." *SF Gate*, March 12, 2004, www.sfgate.com.

2 Pleasure Island

1. Stephen Talbot, *To Have and Have Not*, KQED, 30:00, aired March 2, 1983.

2. Richard W. White, Jr., *Rude Awakenings: What the Homeless Crisis Tells Us* (Institute for Contemporary Studies Press, 1992).

Notes

3. Kerry Jackson et al., *No Way Home: The Crisis of Homelessness and How to Fix It with Intelligence and Humanity* (New York: Encounter Books, 2021), 67.

4. T. J. Johnston, "The Cost of Criminalizing Homelessness," *Street Sheet*, July 1, 2016, www.streetsheet.org.

5. Heather Knight, "Rogue Sit/Lie Ads Going Up—and Coming Down—from Muni Bus Stops," *SF Gate*, October 25, 2010, www.sfgate.com.

6. Heather Knight, "Sit/Lie Law Primarily Enforced in Haight," *SF Gate*, August 4, 2012, www.sfgate.com.

7. Teresa Gowan, *Hobos, Hustlers, and Backsliders: Homeless in San Francisco* (Minneapolis: University of Minnesota Press, 2010), 255.

8. Kevin Fagan, "The Situation on the Streets," *San Francisco Chronicle*, June 28, 2018, www.sfchronicle.com.

9. Daniel Duane, "The Tent Cities of San Francisco," *New York Times*, December 17, 2016, www.nytimes.com.

10. City of Phoenix, 2020–2021 Adopted Budget; City and County of San Francisco, Proposed Budget FY 2020–2021; The Council of the City of New York, Fiscal 2021 Budget; County of Los Angeles, 2020–2021 Adopted Budget; City of Chicago, 2021 Budget Overview.

11. Ibid.

12. Ibid.

13. US Census Bureau, 2018 Annual Survey of State and Local Government Finances. "Direct Cash Payments" includes the sum of "Welfare-Categorical Cash Assistance" and "Welfare-Cash Assistance" for respective cities.

14. "Left Behind: Homeless Crisis in San Francisco," Fox News, August 20, 2019, YouTube video, 9:46, www.youtube.com.

15. "The View from Outside," Tipping Point, April 2, 2019, www.tippingpoint.org; "San Francisco Homeless Count and Survey Comprehensive Report 2019," San Francisco Department of Homelessness and Supportive Housing, 2019, www.hsh .sfgov.org; "County Adult Assistance Programs," San Francisco Human Services Agency, accessed May 13, 2021, www.sfhsa.org.

16. Christopher Herring, "Cruel Streets: Criminalizing Homelessness in San Francisco," PhD diss. (University of California, Berkeley), 75.

17. "Robert and Elizabeth are homeless in San Francisco," interview by Mark Horvath, *Invisible People*, August 24, 2013, YouTube video, 2:03, www.youtube.com.

18. Gowan, *Hobos, Hustlers, and Backsliders*, 63.

19. Trisha Thadani, "A ticket out of Town," *San Francisco Chronicle*, July 29, 2019, www.sfchronicle.com.

20. Gowan, *Hobos, Hustlers, and Backsliders*, xv.

21. Ibid., xiii.

22. Rone Tempest, "San Francisco Rethinks Cash Aid to Homeless," *Los Angeles Times*, August 26, 2002, www.latimes.com.

23. Jacqui Berlinn, interview by the author, March 20, 2021.

24. Matt Haney, interview by the author, February 12, 2021.

25. Herring, "Cruel Streets," 73.

26. Paul Linde, "Ex-ER psychiatrist: More inpatient treatment needed in SF," interview by Heather Knight, *San Francisco Chronicle*, October 9, 2018, podcast audio, 24:21, www.sfchronicle.com.

27. Margot Kushel, "West Coast a Magnet for Homeless," *Conversation*, June 14, 2018, www.theconversation.com.

28. Jonathan Martin, "King County's Former Homeless 'Czar' on Homelessness: 'The Causes . . . Are Far More Complex Than I Even Knew,'" *Seattle Times*, February 21, 2018, www.seattletimes.com.

29. Nathan Heller, "A Window onto an American Nightmare," *New Yorker*, June 1, 2020, www.newyorker.com.

30. Phil Matier, "SF a Magnet for Homeless Seeking Free Hotel Rooms During Coronavirus Pandemic," *San Francisco Chronicle*, May 3, 2020, www.sfchronicle.com.

31. "Bay Area Homeless: Concern or Crisis Part 2," KTVU Fox 2 San Francisco, September 18, 2017, YouTube video, 52:07, www.youtube.com.

32. Joel John Roberts, *How to Increase Homelessness: Real Solutions to the Absurdity of Homelessness in America* (Bend, OR: Loyal Publishing, 2004), 57.

33. Thomas Wolf, interview by the author, March 12, 2020.

34. Heller, "A Window onto an American Nightmare."

Notes

35. Dennis Culhane, interview with the author, March 29, 2021.

36. Kale Williams and Evan Sernoffsky, "Homeless Encampment on SF's Division Street Cleared by City," *SF Gate*, March 2, 2016, www.sfgate.com.

37. Herring, "Cruel Streets."

38. "A Start on Ending Homelessness," *San Francisco Chronicle*, December 12, 2004.

39. Marisa Kendall, "These Homeless Oaklanders Refused to Be Moved. Now, They're Pioneers," *Mercury News*, March 11, 2021, www.mercurynews.com.

40. Kurtis Alexander, "Police Strive to Focus on Referrals, Not Arrests," *San Francisco Chronicle*, June 27, 2017, www.sfchronicle.com.

41. Andria Borba, "Neighbors Build Wooden Wall to Deter Homeless, Crime in SF's Ingleside," KPIX CBS SF Bay Area, October 14, 2019, YouTube video, 2:33, www.youtube.com.

42. Thomas Wolf, interview by the author, March 23, 2020.

43. Christopher Jencks, *The Homeless* (Cambridge, MA: Harvard University Press, 1994), 104.

44. Jennifer Friedenbach, interview by the author, January 13, 2021.

45. Paul Boden, *House Keys Not Handcuffs: Homeless Organizing, Art and Politics in San Francisco and Beyond* (San Francisco: Freedom Voices Publisher, 2014), 87.

46. Victoria Beach, interview with the author, January 7, 2021.

47. Heather Knight, "Tent Camp Cast a Cloud over Potrero Hill Street," *San Francisco Chronicle*, June 30, 2017, www.sfchronicle.com.

48. Thomas Wolf, interview by the author, February 12, 2021.

49. Mark Horvath (@hardlynormal), "I tweeted how @forbes pays writers bonuses for more pageviews," Twitter post, September 13, 2019, 10:44 am, https://twitter.com/hardlynormal.

50. Jane Kim, interview by the author, November 6, 2020.

51. "Hate, Violence, and Death on Main Street USA: A Report on Hate Crimes and Violence Against People Experiencing Homelessness 2008," National Coalition for the Homeless, August 2009, www.nationalhomeless.org; Annie Leomporra and Megan Hustings, "Vulnerable to Hate: A Survey of Bias Motivated Violence Against People Experiencing Homelessness in 2016–2017," National Coalition

for the Homeless, December 2018, www.nationalhomeless.org; Jeffrey M. Jones, "Worry About Hunger, Homelessness Up for Lower-Income in US," Gallup, March 30, 2017, www.news.gallup.com.

52. Thomas Wolf, interview by the author, August 27, 2020.

53. Willie Brown, *Basic Brown: My Life and Our Times* (New York: Simon & Schuster, 2008) 273, 274.

54. John King, "Brown Baffled by Homeless Problem—Summit Canceled—Distrust on All Sides," *SF Gate*, September 17, 1996, www.sfgate.com.

3 The Experiment Was a Success but the Patients Died

1. Bill Maher, *Real Time with Bill Maher*, episode 30, season 17, aired October 11, 2019, on HBO, video, 58:16, www.hbo.org.

2. Jennifer Friedenbach, "Defending San Francisco's 6,000 homeless," interview by Art Bruzzone, SFunscriptedTV, May 1, 2011, YouTube video, 14:01, www.youtube .com.

3. Jennifer Friedenbach, interview by the author, January 13, 2021.

4. Jennifer Friedenbach, "A 'Shelter for All' Policy Sounds Good, but It Takes Resources Away from Long Term Solutions," *San Francisco Examiner*, April 15, 2021, www.sfexaminer.com.

5. Jamie Almanza et al., "Destination Health: Solving Homelessness" (discussion panel, Thought Leadership series, Commonwealth Club, San Francisco, August 14, 2019), audio, 1:12:26, www.commonwealthclub.org.

6. Sam Tsemberis, interview by the author, January 6, 2021.

7. Kevin Fagan, "Trump's New Tough-Love Homelessness Czar Might Surprise Skeptics," *San Francisco Chronicle*, February 24, 2020, www.sfchronicle.com.

8. Christopher Herring, interview by the author, December 14, 2020.

9. Stefan G. Kertesz et al., "Personal and Community Characteristics Associated with Unsheltered Status Among Veterans Who Have Experienced Homelessness," *American Journal of Preventive Medicine*, 2021; Ann Elizabeth Montgomery et al., "Homelessness, Unsheltered Status, and Risk Factors for Mortality: Findings from the 100,000 Homes Campaign," *Public Health Reports* 13, no. 6 (2016): 765–772.

Notes

10. Jennifer Friedenbach, interview by the author, January 13, 2021.

11. "CoC Homeless Populations and Subpopulations Reports," HUD Exchange, accessed January 17, 2021, www.hudexchange.com.

12. Ibid.; "CoC Housing Inventory Count Reports," HUD Exchange, accessed February 22, 2021, www.hudexchange.com.

13. Ibid.

14. Herring, "Cruel Streets," 72.

15. Rafael Mandelman, interview by the author, December 18, 2020.

16. Angela Alioto et al., *The San Francisco Plan to Abolish Chronic Homelessness* (San Francisco Ten Year Planning Council, 2004), www.sfgov.org.

17. Ron Galperin, "Meeting the Moment: An Action Plan to Advance Prop. HHH," Accessed July 20, 2021, www.lacontroller.org.

18. Andy Bales, interview by the author, September 11, 2019.

19. Christopher Herring, interview by the author, December 14, 2020.

20. Gabriel Petek, *The 2019–20 Budget: Considerations for Governor's proposals to address homelessness*, Legislative Analyst's Office (LAO), 2019, lao.ca.gov; Gabriel Petek, *2020–21 Budget: The Governor's Homelessness Plan*, Legislative Analyst's Office (LAO), February 11, 2020, lao.ca.gov.

21. Phil Matier and Andy Ross, "SF Voters All in Favor of New Tax to Help Homeless—Until They See the Cost," *San Francisco Chronicle*, September 12, 2018, www.sfchronicle.com.

22. Andy Bosselman, "Proposition C: Is It the Right Move for Homelessness Now?" *SF Curbed*, October 25, 2018, www.sf.curbed.com.

23. Shirin Ghaffary, "Here's Why Tech Billionaires Are Fighting over San Francisco's Prop C Ballot Measure," *Vox*, October 27, 2018, www.vox.com.

24. Jennifer Friedenbach, interview by the author, January 13, 2021.

25. Trisha Thadani, "A Ticket out of Town," *San Francisco Chronicle*, July 29, 2019, www.sfchronicle.com.

26. "For SF homeless residents 'rapid rehousing' means leaving the city (Via SF Public Press)," Mission Local, March 6, 2018, www.missionlocal.org.

27. Trisha Thadani, "S.F. has an unprecedented $1.1 billion to spend on homelessness. The pressure is on to make a difference," *San Francisco Chronicle*, July 16, 2021.

28. Joe Fitzgerald Rodriguez, "Proposition C Court Win Delivers Nearly $500 Million for San Francisco's Homeless. But How Will It Be Spent?" KQED, September 12, 2020, www.kqed.org.

29. Marc Benioff, "On San Francisco's homeless problem," interview, Fox Business, October 31, 2018, YouTube video, 5:19, www.youtube.com.

30. Ibid.

31. Maria C. Raven, Matthew J. Niedzwiecki, and Margot Kushel, "A randomized trial of Permanent Supportive Housing for Chronically Homeless Persons with High Use of Publicly Funded Services," *Health Services Research* 55, no. S2 (2020): 797–806, doi:10.1111/1475–6773.13553.

32. Marisa Kendall, "'It Works.' Groundbreaking Data Proves Success of Santa Clara County Homeless Housing Program," *Mercury News*, September 17, 2020, www.mercurynews.com.

33. Ibid.; Raven, Niedzwiecki, and Kushel, "A Randomized Trial."

34. Jen Loving, interview by the author, October 12, 2020.

35. Louis Chicoine, interview by the author, October 5, 2020.

36. Sam Tsemberis, interview by the author, January 6, 2021.

37. Brendan O'Flaherty, "Homelessness Research: A Guide for Economists (and Friends)," *Journal of Housing Economics* 44(C)(2019): 21, doi:10.1016/j.jhe.2019.01.003.

38. Kade Minchey et al., "A Performance Audit of Utah's Homeless Services," Report to the Utah Legislature 2018–12, Office of the Legislative Auditor General, December 2018, www.le.utah.gov.

39. CoC Homeless Populations and Subpopulations Reports," HUD Exchange, accessed January 17, 2021, www.hudexchange.com.

40. Eric R. Kessell et al., "Public Health Care Utilization in a Cohort of Homeless Adult Applicants to a Supportive Housing Program," *Journal of Urban Health* 83, no. 5 (September 2006): 860–73, doi:10.1007/s11524-006-9083-0.

41. Carol Pearson et al., "Housing Stability Among Homeless Individuals with Serious Mental Illness Participating in Housing First Programs," *Journal of Community Psychology* 37, no. 3 (2009): 404–17, doi:10.1002/jcop.20303.

42. Jill S. Roncarati et al., "Housing Boston's Chronically Homeless Unsheltered Population: 14 Years Later," *Medical Care* 59, Suppl. 2 (2021): S170–S174, doi:10.1097/MLR.0000000000001409.

43. National Academies of Sciences, Engineering, and Medicine, *Permanent Supportive Housing: Evaluating the Evidence for Improving Health Outcomes Among People Experiencing Chronic Homelessness* (Washington, D.C.: The National Academies Press), 5.

44. Sam Tsemberis, interview by the author, January 6, 2021.

45. Kertesz et al., "Housing first for homeless persons with active addiction."

46. Rebecca A. Cherner et al., "Housing First for Adults with Problematic Substance Use," *Journal of Dual Diagnosis* 13, no. 1 (2017), doi:10.1080/15504263.2017.1319586.

47. Joseph E. Schumacher et al., "Meta-Analysis of Day Treatment and Contingency-Management Dismantling Research: Birmingham Homeless Cocaine Studies (1990–2006)," *Journal of Consulting and Clinical Psychology* 75, no. 5 (2007): 823–28, doi:10.1037/0022–006X.75.5.823.

48. Kertesz et al., "Housing First for Homeless Persons with Active Addiction."

49. Stefan G. Kertesz et al., "Long-Term Housing and Work Outcomes Among Treated Cocaine-Dependent Homeless Persons," *Journal of Behavioral and Health Services Research* 34, no. 1 (2007): 17–33, doi:10.1007/s11414–006–9041-3.

50. Roncarati et al., "Housing Boston's Chronically Homeless Unsheltered Population 14 years later," *Medical Care* 59 (April 2021): 170–174, doi:10.1097/MLR.0000000000001409.

51. Randy Shaw, interview by the author, October 1, 2020.

52. Louis Chicoine, interview by the author, October 5, 2020.

53. Steve Berg, interview by the author, February 19, 2021.

54. Dennis Culhane, interview by the author, March 29, 2021.

Notes

4 The War on the War on Drugs

1. World Prison Brief, "United States of America," Institute for Crime & Justice Policy Research, accessed December 12, 2020, www.prisonstudies.org/country/united-states-america.

2. John Pfaff, *Locked In: The True Causes of Mass Incarceration—and How to Achieve Real Reform* (New York: Basic Books, 2017), 2.

3. Ibid., 150.

4. Marc Mauer, *Race to Incarcerate* (New York: New Press, 2006), 33, cited in Michelle Alexander, *The New Jim Crow: Mass Incarceration in the Age of Colorblindness* (New York: New Press, 2010), 6.

5. Pfaff, *Locked In*, 42.

6. Alexander, *The New Jim Crow*, 101.

7. Bureau of Justice Statistics, Federal Justice Statistics Program, 2019 (preliminary); National Corrections Reporting Program, 2018; National Prisoner Statistics, 2019; and Survey of Prison Inmates, 2016.

8. E. Ann Carson, "Prisoners in 2019," Bureau of Justice Statistics, October 2020, www.bjs.gov.

9. "Sourcebook of Criminal Justice Statistics," Bureau of Justice Statistics, 1990; Paige M. Harrison, "Prisoners in 2010," Bureau of Justice Statistics, December 15, 2011, www.bjs.gov.

10. Eric L. Sevigny and Jonathan P. Caulkins, "Kingpins or Mules: An Analysis of Drug Offenders Incarcerated in Federal and State Prisons," *Criminology and Public Policy* 3 (2004): 401–34, cited in Pfaff, *Locked In*, 32–33.

11. Pfaff, *Locked In*, 22.

12. Ibid., 32.

13. Zhen Zeng and Todd Minton, "Jail Inmates in 2019," Bureau of Justice Statistics, March 2021, www.bjs.gov; Carson, "Prisoners in 2019."

14. Heather C. West and William J. Sabol, "Prisoners in 2007," *Bureau of Justice Statistics Bulletin*, December 2008, www.bjs.gov; Zeng and Minton, "Jail Inmates in 2019"; Carson, "Prisoners in 2019"; Allen J. Beck and Darrell K. Gilliard, "Prisoners in 1994," Bureau of Justice Statistics, August 1995, www.bjs.gov.

15. Sevigny and Caulkins, "Kingpins or Mules."

16. "Crime in the United States, 2019: Persons Arrested," FBI: Uniform Crime Reporting, accessed April 4, 2021, www.ucr.fbi.gov.

17. Pfaff, *Locked In*, 41; E. Ann Carson and Elizabeth Anderson, "Prisoners in 2015," Bureau of Justice Statistics, December 2016, www.bjs.gov.

18. Pfaff, *Locked In*, 42.

19. Ibid., 37.

20. Ibid., 40.

21. Ibid., 46–48.

22. Ibid., 28–29.

23. John McWhorter, *Losing the Race: Self-Sabotage in Black America* (New York: Free Press, 2000), 14.

24. Pfaff, *Locked In*, 29.

25. Ibid., 32–34.

26. Christopher Lowen Agee, *The Streets of San Francisco: Policing and the Creation of a Cosmopolitan Liberal Politics, 1950–1972* (Chicago: University of Chicago Press, 2014), 8.

27. Randolph Roth, "American Homicide Supplemental Volume (AHSV): American Homicides Twentieth Century (AHTC)," October 2009, https://cjrc.osu.edu/sites/cjrc.osu.edu/files/AHSV-American-Homicides-Twentieth-Century.pdf.

28. Yolanda Young, "Analysis: Black Leaders Supported Clinton's Crime Bill," NBC, April 8, 2016, www.nbcnews.com; Vanessa Williams, "1994 Crime Bill Haunts Clinton and Sanders as Criminal Justice Reform Rises to Top in Democratic Contest," *Washington Post*, February 12, 2016, www.washingtonpost.com.

29. McWhorter, *Losing the Race*, 14.

30. CDC, Wide-ranging online data for epidemiologic research (WONDER). National Center for Health Statistics; 2020. Deaths are classified using the International Classification of Diseases, 10th Revision. Drug-poisoning (overdose) deaths are identified using underlying cause-of-death codes X40–X44, X60–X64, X85, and Y10–Y14. www.wonder.cdc.gov; "Vital Statistics Rapid Release:

Provisional Drug Overdose Death Counts," Centers for Disease Control and Prevention, accessed July 13, 2021, www.cdc.gov.

31. "Expanded Homicide Data Table 2: Murder Victims," Crime in the United States: 2019, Criminal Justice Information Services Division, Federal Bureau of Investigation, accessed January 21, 2021, www.ucr.fbi.gov; "Motor Vehicle Safety Data," Bureau of Transportation Statistics, accessed February 9, 2021, www.bts.gov.

32. Wide-ranging online data for epidemiologic research (WONDER). National Center for Health Statistics; 2020. Deaths are classified using the International Classification of Diseases, 10th Revision. Drug-poisoning (overdose) deaths are identified using underlying cause-of-death codes X40–X44, X60–X64, X85, and Y10–Y14. www .wonder.cdc.gov; Luke N. Rodda, "Report on Accidental Overdose Death—January to December 2020," Office of the Chief Medical Examiner, San Francisco, January 14, 2021, www.sf.gov; "Overdose Deaths," King County, Updated December 1, 2020, Accessed July 13, 2021, www.kingcounty.gov; "2020 Annual Report," Maricopa County Office of the Medical Examiner, Accessed July 13, 2021, www.maricopa.gov; "Chicago Police Department, Chicago Department of Public Health Announce Expansion of Narcotics Arrest Diversion Program," Chicago Department of Public Health, July 8, 2021, www.chicago.gov.

33. Barbara A. Garcia et al., "San Francisco Safe Injection Services Task Force: Final Report, 2017," San Francisco Department of Public Health, September 2017, www .sfdph.org; Luke N. Rodda, "Report on Accidental Overdose Deaths," Office of the Chief Medical Examiner, San Francisco, April 16, 2021, www.sf.gov.

34. Rodda, "Report on Accidental Overdose Deaths."

35. Phil Matier, "San Francisco Where Drug Addicts Outnumber High School Students," *San Francisco Chronicle*, January 30, 2019, www.sfchronicle.com.

36. Phil Matier and Andy Ross, "Why San Francisco Is Stuck with a Deluge of Needles," *San Francisco Chronicle*, May 30, 2018, www.sfchronicle.com.

37. Tracey Helton Mitchell, *The Big Fix: Hope After Heroin* (Berkeley, CA: Seal Press, 2016), 44–45.

38. Ibid., 50.

39. Phil Matier, "On SF's Larch Street, as the Tents Move in, the Residents Move Out," *San Francisco Chronicle*, June 17, 2020, www.sfchronicle.com.

40. Thomas Wolf, interview by the author, March 23, 2020.

41. Thomas Wolf, interview by the author, October 29, 2020.

Notes

42. Matthew S. Ellis, Zachary A. Kasper, and Theodore J. Cicero, "Twin Epidemics: The Surging Rise of Methamphetamine Use in Chronic Opioid Users," *Drug and Alcohol Dependence* 193 (2018): 14–20, doi:10.1016/j.drugalcdep.2018.08.029.

43. Between 2015 and 2017 the percentage of individuals reporting heroin use in the past month who also reported using meth tripled from 9 to 30 percent. Justin C. Strickland, Jennifer R. Havens, and William W. Stoops, "A Nationally Representative Analysis of 'Twin Epidemics': Rising Rates of Methamphetamine Use Among Persons Who Use Opioids," *Drug and Alcohol Dependence* 204 (2019): 107592, doi:10.1016/j.drugalcdep.2019.107592. The percentage of people admitted into heroin treatment programs who also used meth rose 490 percent between 2008 and 2017, from 2 to 12 percent. Christopher M. Jones, Natasha Underwood, and Wilson M. Compton, "Increases in Methamphetamine Use Among Heroin Treatment Admissions in the United States, 2008–17," *Addiction* 115, no. 2 (2020): 347–53, doi:10.1111/add.14812.

44. Guy Johnson and Chris Chamberlain, "Homelessness and Substance Abuse: Which Comes First?" *Australian Social Work* 61, no. 4 (2008): 342–56, doi:10.1080/03124070802428191; Kelly M. Doran et al., "Substance Use and Homelessness Among Emergency Department Patients," *Drug and Alcohol Dependence* 188 (2018): 328–33, doi:10.1016/j.drugalcdep.2018.04.021.

45. Harper Sutherland, Mir M. Ali, and Emily Rosenoff, "Individuals Experiencing Homelessness Are Likely to Have Medical Conditions Associated with Severe Illness from COVID-19," ASPE Issue Brief, HHS Office of the Assistant Secretary for Planning and Evaluation, US Department of Health and Human Services, June 2020, www.aspe.hhs.gov; Robert W. Aldridge et al., "Morbidity and Mortality in Homeless Individuals, Prisoners, Sex Workers, and Individuals with Substance Use Disorders in High-Income Countries: A Systematic Review and Meta-Analysis," *Lancet* 391, no. 10117 (2018): 241–50, doi:10.1016/S0140-6736(17)31869-X.

46. Severin Campbell et al., "Performance Audit of the Department of Homelessness and Supportive Housing, Prepared for the Board of Supervisors of the City and County of San Francisco," Office of the San Francisco Budget and Legislative Analyst, August 6, 2020, www.sfbos.org.

47. Teresa Gowan, *Hobos, Hustlers, and Backsliders: Homeless in San Francisco* (Minneapolis: University of Minnesota Press, 2010), 161.

48. "Confessional Moments Like This Usually Occurred One-on-One," noted Gowan, "often inside my apartment, in fact." Gowan, *Hobos, Hustlers, and Backsliders*, xviii.

49. Ethan Nadelmann, interview by the author, December 30, 2019.

50. Ibid.

51. Ibid.

52. David Boyum and Peter Reuter, *An Analytic Assessment of US Drug Policy* (Washington, D.C.: AEI Press, 2005), cited in Mark Kleiman, *When Brute Force Fails: How to Have Less Crime and Less Punishment* (Princeton, NJ: Princeton University Press, 2010), 156.

53. Michael Botticelli et al., "National Drug Control Strategy, Data Supplement, 2015," Washington, D.C., White House, 2015, https://obamawhitehouse.archives.gov.

54. "Heroin prices in the United States, 2007–2017," United Nations Office on Drugs and Crime, accessed February 22, 2021, www.dataunodc.un.org.

55. "Meth Country—An Unstoppable Epidemic," *Vice*, October 28, 2019, YouTube video, 29:48, www.youtube.com.

56. Mark Kleiman, "Reducing the Prevalence of Cocaine and Heroin Dealing Among Adolescents," *Valparaiso University Law Review* 31, no. 2 (2011): 551–64, scholar.valpo.edu/vulr/vol31/iss2/17, cited in Kleiman, *When Brute Force Fails*, 155.

57. "Alcohol Facts and Statistics," National Institute on Alcohol Abuse and Alcoholism, accessed April 4, 2021, https://www.niaaa.nih.gov/publications/brochures-and-fact-sheets/alcohol-facts-and-statistics.

58. "Smoking & Tobacco Use," Centers for Disease Control and Prevention, last modified May 21, 2020, https://www.cdc.gov/tobacco/data_statistics/fact_sheets/fast_facts/index.htm.

59. "European Drug Report," European Monitoring Centre for Drugs and Drug Addiction, 2015, www.emcdda.europa.eu.

60. Naina Bajekal, "Want to Win the War on Drugs? Portugal Might Have the Answer," *Time*, August 1, 2018, www.time.com.

61. "Drug Decriminalisation in Portugal: Setting the Record Straight," Transform Drug Policy Foundation, November 14, 2018, www.transformdrugs.org.

62. Monique Tula, interview by the author, December 17, 2020.

63. "Proposition 36, California," Legislative Analyst's Office, passed November 2000, https://lao.ca.gov/ballot/2000/36_11_2000.html.

64. Nicholas Iovino, "San Francisco OKs Process to Open Safe-Injection Sites," *Courthouse News*, June 23, 2020, www.courthousenews.com.

65. Anna Staver, "Colorado Lawmakers Won't Vote on Safe Injection Sites in 2019. House Democratic Leader Blames Denver," *Denver Post*, February 19, 2019, www .denverpost.com; Elizabeth Hayes, "A Legal Site in Portland to Inject Heroin? Elected Officials, Advocates Explore the Idea," *Portland Business Journal*, March 15, 2018, www.bizjournals.com; Lee Harris, "Where Are the Safe Injection Facilities Cuomo Promised for New York?" *City*, March 30, 2021, www.thecity .nyc; Nina Feldman, "In Philadelphia, Judges Rule Against Opening 'Supervised' Site to Inject Opioids," NPR, January 14, 2021, www.npr.org.

66. "Alcohol Poisoning Deaths," Centers for Disease Control and Prevention, January 2015, www.cdc.gov.

67. Mark Kleiman, Jonathan Caulkins, and Angela Hawken, *Drugs and Drug Policy: What Everyone Needs to Know* (New York: Oxford University Press, 2011), 23.

68. Ibid.

69. Pfaff, *Locked In*, 45.

70. Kleiman, Caulkins, and Hawken, *Drugs and Drug Policy*, 22.

71. Keith Humphreys, interview by the author, March 16, 2021.

72. Pfaff, *Locked In*, 45.

73. Andy Bales, interview by the author, September 11, 2019.

74. Rosalie Liccardo Pacula et al., "Improving the Measurement of Drug-Related Crime," Office of National Drug Control Policy, White House, 2013, accessed April 4, 2021, www.obamawhitehouse.archives.gov, cited in Pfaff, *Locked In*, 44.

75. Jeffrey A. Miron and Jeffrey Zwiebel, "Alcohol Consumption During Prohibition" (NBER Working Papers No. 3675, Natural Bureau of Economic Research, Cambridge, MA, 1991).

76. Silvia S. Martins et al., "Changes in US Lifetime Heroin Use and Heroin Use Disorder: Prevalence from the 2001–2002 to 2012–2013 National Epidemiologic Survey on Alcohol and Related Conditions," *JAMA Psychiatry* 74, no. 5 (2017): 445–55, doi:10.1001/jamapsychiatry.2017.0113.

77. Gregory Midgette et al., *What America's Users Spend on Illegal Drugs, 2006–2016* (Santa Monica, CA: RAND Corporation, 2019), www.rand.org.

Notes

78. Beau Kilmer, interview by the author, February 19, 2021.

79. Gregory Midgette et al., *What America's Users Spend on Illegal Drugs, 2006–2016* (Santa Monica, CA: RAND Corporation, 2019), www.rand.org.

80. Silvia S. Martins et al., "Prescription Opioid Use Disorder and Heroin Use Among 12–34 year-olds in the United States from 2002 to 2014," *Addictive Behaviors* 65 (2017): 236–41, doi:10.1016/j.addbeh.2016.08.033.

81. SAMHSA, "2019 National Survey on Drug Use and Health: Detailed Tables," Substance Abuse and Mental Health Services Administration, August 2020, www.samhsa.gov.

82. Pfaff, *Locked In*, 25.

83. Ruixuan Jiang et al., "The Societal Cost of Heroin Use Disorder in the United States," *PLoS One* 12, no. 5 (2017): e0177323, doi:10.1371/journal.pone.0177323.

84. Kleiman, Caulkins, and Hawken, *Drugs and Drug Policy*, 107.

85. Victoria Westbrook, interview by the author, December 9, 2020.

86. Rachel Gonzales, Larissa Mooney, and Richard Rawson, "The Methamphetamine Problem in the United States," *Annual Review of Public Health* 31 (2010): 385–98, doi:10.1146/annurev.publhealth.012809.103600; SAMSHA, "Treatment Episode Data Set," National Admissions to Substance Abuse Treatment Services, August 03, 2017, www.samsha.gov.

87. SAMHSA, "2019 National Survey on Drug Use and Health: Detailed Tables."

88. Ibid.

89. Kelly Kruger, interview by the author, October 1, 2020.

90. Christopher Herring, interview by the author, December 14, 2020.

91. Trisha Thadani, "Can You Pay Someone to Stop Using Meth? Proposed California Legislation Would Boost Drug Treatment Option," *San Francisco Chronicle*, January 12, 2021, www.sfchronicle.com.

92. CDC, Wide-ranging online data for epidemiologic research (WONDER), National Center for Health Statistics, 2020, accessed May 18, 2021, www.cdc.gov.

93. Paul Linde, "Ex-ER psychiatrist: More inpatient treatment needed in SF," interview by Heather Knight, *San Francisco Chronicle*, October 9, 2018, podcast audio, 24:21, www.sfchronicle.com.

94. Kelly Kruger, interview by the author, October 1, 2020.

95. "The Crystal Meth Epidemic Plaguing Fresno," *Vice*, February 21, 2019, YouTube video, 18:57, www.youtube.com.

96. Based on overdose death rates out of the largest twenty-five metropolitan statistical areas (excluding the Inland Empire, MSA, which is outer Los Angeles), pulling from the most appropriate county for each. Source: CDC, Wide-ranging online data for epidemiologic research (WONDER). National Center for Health Statistics; 2020. Deaths are classified using the International Classification of Diseases, 10th Revision. Drug-poisoning (overdose) deaths are identified using underlying cause-of-death codes X40–X44, X60–X64, X85, and Y10–Y14. www.wonder.cdc.gov.

97. Rodda, "Report on Accidental Overdose Deaths."

98. CDC, Wide-ranging online data for epidemiologic research (WONDER), National Center for Health Statistics; 2020. Deaths are classified using the International Classification of Diseases, 10th Revision. Drug-poisoning (overdose) deaths are identified using underlying cause-of-death codes X40–X44, X60–X64, X85, and Y10–Y14. www.wonder.cdc.gov.

99. Wide-ranging online data for epidemiologic research (WONDER), National Center for Health Statistics, Center for Disease Control, accessed April 3, 2021, www.cdc.gov.

100. Keith Humphreys, interview by the author, March 16, 2021.

101. "Historical Data: The Birth of A.A. and Its Growth in the US/Canada," Alcoholics Anonymous, accessed December 24, 2020, www.aa.org.

102. Daniel J. Anderson, John P. McGovern, and Robert L. Dupont, "The Origins of the Minnesota Model of Addiction Treatment—A First Person Account," *Journal of Addictive Diseases* 18, no. 1 (1999): 107–14, doi:10.1300/J069v18n01_10.

103. "History of Drug Treatment," Desert Hope Treatment Center, August 21, 2020, www.deserthopetreatment.com.

104. Charles Perry, *The Haight-Ashbury* (New York: Random House, 1984), 125–26, cited in Henry Miller, *On the Fringe: The Dispossessed in America* (New York: Lexington Books, 1991), 95.

105. David Talbot, *Season of the Witch: Enchantment, Terror, and Deliverance in the City of Love* (New York: Free Press, 2012), 59.

106. Ibid.; Miller, *On the Fringe*, 104.

107. Talbot, *Season of the Witch*, 22.

108. James T. Wooten, "Carter Seeks to End Marijuana Penalty for Small Amounts," *New York Times*, August 3, 1977, www.nytimes.com; Marc Fisher and Richard Johnson, "A Brief History of Public Opinion on Marijuana Legalization," *Washington Post*, February 21, 2014, www.washingtonpost.com.

109. Fisher and Johnson, "A Brief History of Public Opinion on Marijuana Legalization."

110. Ethan Nadelmann, interview by the author, December 30, 2019.

111. Sam Quinones, *Dreamland: The True Tale of America's Opiate Epidemic* (New York: Bloomsbury Press, 2016), 94–95.

112. Elizabeth Devita, "Pain Killers," *New York*, February 7, 2000, www.nymag.com.

113. Ethan Nadelmann, interview by the author, December 30, 2019.

114. Quinones, *Dreamland*, 95.

115. Matthew Daubresse et al., "Ambulatory Diagnosis and Treatment of Nonmalignant Pain in the United States, 2000–2010," *Medical Care* 51, no. 10 (2013): 870–78, doi:10.1097/MLR.0b013e3182a95d86.

116. *The City of Nashua v. Purdue Pharma L.P. et. al*, Case 1:17 (District of New Hampshire 2017), 6, http://mediad.publicbroadcasting.net/p/nhpr/files/201712/11712000260.pdf.

117. Pradip K. Muhuri, Joseph C. Gfroerer, and M. Christine Davies, "CBHSQ Data Review, Associations of Nonmedical Pain Reliever Use and Initiation of Heroin Use in the United States," Substance Abuse and Mental Health Services Administration (SAMHSA), August 2013, www.samhsa.gov.

118. Stephen Lankenau et al., "Initiation into Prescription Opioid Misuse Amongst Young Injection Drug Users," *International Journal of Drug Policy* 23, no. 1 (2012): 37–44, doi:10.1016/j.drugpo.2011.05.014.

119. "Morbidity and Mortality Weekly Report," *Centers for Disease Control and Prevention* 63, no. 39 (October 3, 2014): 849–54, www.cdc.gov.

120. Ethan Nadelmann, interview by the author, December 23, 2020.

121. "Proposition 36, California"; "California Proposition 36, Probation and Treatment

for Drug-Related Offenses Initiative (2000)," Ballotpedia, accessed April 3, 2021, www.ballotpedia.org.

122. "UCLA issues new report on Prop. 36," press release, UCLA Health, October 14, 2008, www.uclahealth.org; Darren Urada et al., "Evaluation of Proposition 36: The Substance Abuse and Crime Prevention Act of 2000," UCLA, prepared for the Department of Alcohol and Drug Programs, California Health and Human Services Agency, 2008, www.uclaisap.org.

123. Elizabeth Evans et al., "Comparative Effectiveness of California's Proposition 36 and Drug Court Programs Before and After Propensity Score Matching," *Crime and Delinquency* 60, no. 6 (2010): 909–38, doi:10.1177/0011128710382342.

124. Andy Bales, interview by the author, September 11, 2019.

125. Kelly Kruger, interview by the author, October 1, 2020.

126. Andy Bales, interview by the author, September 11, 2019.

127. Thomas Wolf, interview by the author, May 22, 2020.

128. Mallory Moench, "'Out of Control': Organized Crime Drives S.F. Shoplifting, Closing 17 Walgreens in Five Years," *San Francisco Chronicle*, May 13, 2021, www.sfchronicle.com.

129. Phil Matier, "Rampant Shoplifting Leads to Another Walgreens Closing in S.F.," *San Francisco Chronicle*, updated October 19, 2020, www.sfchronicle.com.

130. Linde, "Ex-ER psychiatrist: More inpatient treatment needed in SF."

5 "We Can't End Overdoses Until We End Poverty and Racism"

1. Thomas Wolf, interview by the author, October 23, 2020.

2. "Meth Country—An Unstoppable Epidemic," *Vice*, October 28, 2019, YouTube video, 29:48, www.youtube.com.

3. Adam Mesnick, interview by the author, October 26, 2020.

4. Victoria Westbrook, interview by the author, December 9, 2020.

5. Adam Mesnick, interview by the author, October 26, 2020.

6. Christopher Herring, interview by the author, December 14, 2020.

7. Victoria Westbrook, interview by the author, December 9, 2020.

8. Vivian Ho, "San Francisco to Ban Tobacco Smoking in Apartments—but Not Cannabis," *Guardian*, December 3, 2020, www.theguardian.com.

9. "About Proposition 65," California Office of Environmental Health Hazard Assessment, accessed January 27, 2021, www.oehha.ca.gov.

10. "San Francisco supervisor: Drug overdose billboard sends wrong message," KTVU Fox News, March 6, 2020, www.fox5ny.com.

11. Kristen Marshall, interview by the author, September 24, 2020.

12. Paul Harkin, "Facts on Fentanyl," interview by GLIDE, August 2019, accessed February 20, 2021, www.glide.org.

13. San Francisco Human Services Agency, "RE: Public Records Request," email to the author, March 15, 2021.

14. Devon Link, "Fact Check: San Francisco Providing Drugs, Alcohol to Quarantining Homeless but Not on Taxpayers' Dime," *USA Today*, May 13, 2020, www.usatoday.com.

15. Thomas Wolf, interview by the author, September 23, 2020.

16. Kristen Marshall, interview by the author, September 24, 2020.

17. Paul Boden, interview by the author, December 10, 2020.

18. Bill Zimmerman, interview by the author, October 13, 2020.

19. Monique Tula, interview by the author, December 17, 2020.

20. Rafael Mandelman, interview by the author, December 18, 2020.

21. Victoria Westbrook, interview by the author, December 9, 2020.

22. Thomas Wolf, interview by the author, February 12, 2021.

23. Melanie Nagy and Alexandra Mae Jones, "B.C.'s overdose crisis killed 1,716 people last year, more than ever before: Coroner's Service," CTV News, February 11, 2021, www.ctvnews.ca.

24. Maia Szalavitz, "Dan Bigg Is a Harm-Reduction Pioneer and His Overdose Doesn't Change That," *Vice*, October 24, 2018, www.vice.com.

25. Trisha Thadani, "More Than One Person a Day Died in SF of an Overdose Last Year. This Year Is Expected to Be Worse," *San Francisco Chronicle*, August 31, 2020, www.sfchronicle.com.

26. "Mental Health Services Act: History and Orientation," County Behavioral Health Directors Association, California, accessed February 25, 2021, www.cibhs.org.

27. Neil Gong, "Between Tolerant Containment and Concerted Constraint: Managing Madness for the City and the Privileged Family," *American Sociological Review* 84, no. 4 (2019): 664–89, doi:10.1177/0003122419859533.

28. Ibid.

29. Ibid.

30. Ibid.

31. Rone Tempest, "San Francisco Rethinks Cash Aid to Homeless," *Los Angeles Times*, August 26, 2002, www.latimes.com.

32. Gong, "Between Tolerant Containment and Concerted Constraint."

33. Victoria Westbrook, interview by the author, December 9, 2020.

34. Tracey Helton Mitchell, *The Big Fix: Hope After Heroin* (Berkeley, CA: Seal Press, 2016), 55–56.

35. Ibid., 62.

36. Keith Humphreys, interview by the author, March 16, 2021.

37. A. Thomas McLellan and James R. McKay, *Bridging the Gap Between Practice and Research: Forging Partnerships with Community-Based Drug and Alcohol Treatment* (Washington, D.C.: National Academy Press, 1998), available at NCBI, accessed December 27, 2020, https://www.ncbi.nlm.nih.gov.

38. Denise C. Gottfredson and M. Lyn Exum, "The Baltimore City Drug Treatment Court: One-Year Results from a Randomized Study," *Journal of Research in Crime and Delinquency* 39, no. 3 (2002): 337–56, https://ccjs.umd.edu/sites/ccjs.umd .edu/files/pubs/bcdrug.pdf, cited in "Drug Courts as an Alternative to Incarceration," Stanford Network on Addiction Policy, accessed March 27, 2021, www .addictionpolicy.stanford.edu.

39. Ojmarrh Mitchell et al., "Assessing the effectiveness of drug courts on recidivism: A Meta-Analytic Review of Traditional and Non-Traditional Drug Courts," *Journal of Criminal Justice* 40, no. 1 (2012): 60–71, doi:10.1016/j.jcrimjus.2011.11.009.

40. "Drug Courts as an Alternative to Incarceration."

41. Harkin, "Facts on Fentanyl."

42. Victoria Westbrook, interview by the author, December 9, 2020.

43. Thomas Wolf, interview by the author, October 29, 2020.

44. Keith Humphreys, interview by the author, March 16, 2021.

6 Let's Go Dutch

1. Rene Zegerius, interview by the author, December 2020.

2. Helge Waal et al., "Open Drug Scenes: Responses of Five European Cities," *BMC Public Health* 14, no. 853 (2014), doi:10.1186/1471–2458–14–853.

3. Rene Zegerius, interview by the author, December 2020.

4. Amanda J. Abraham et al., "The Affordable Care Act Transformation of Substance Use Disorder Treatment," *American Journal of Public Health* 107, no. 1 (2017): 31–32, doi:10.2105/AJPH.2016.303558.

5. "Amsterdam Population 2020," World Population Review, accessed January 19, 2021, www.worldpopulationreview.com; "San Francisco County, CA Population 2020," World Population Review, accessed January 19, 2021, www.worldpopulationreview.com.

6. Matthew A. Winkler, "California Economy Soars Above the World," *Bloomberg*, April 24, 2019.

7. Daniel S. Nagin, "Deterrence in the Twenty-First Century," *Crime and Justice* 42, no. 1 (2013): 199–263, doi:10.1086/670398.

8. "CoC Homeless Populations and Subpopulations Reports," HUD Exchange, accessed January 17, 2021, www.hudexchange.com; Ron Book, interview by Lea Booth (research assistant to the author), March 29, 2021; "Miami Mayor Tomás Regalado May Have Mixed Up His Numbers," WLRN Miami South Florida, February 23, 2014, www.wlrn.org.

9. Ron Book, interview by Lea Booth (research assistant to the author), March 29, 2021.

10. Ibid.

11. Alex Haracopos and Mike Hough, "Drug Dealing in Open-Air Markets," *Problem Oriented Guides for Police* no. 31, Center for Problem-Oriented Policing, March 2010.

12. A. Thomas McLellan and James R. McKay, *Bridging the Gap Between Practice and Research: Forging Partnerships with Community-Based Drug and Alcohol Treatment* (Washington, D.C.: National Academy Press, 1998), available at NCBI, accessed December 27, 2020, https://www.ncbi.nlm.nih.gov.

13. Michael L. Dennis and Christy K. Scott, "Managing Addiction as a Chronic Condition," *Addiction Science and Clinical Practice* 4, no. 1 (2007): 45–55, doi:10.1151/ascp074145.

14. Victoria Westbrook, interview by the author, December 9, 2020.

15. Mark Kleiman, Jonathan Caulkins, and Angela Hawken, *Drugs and Drug Policy: What Everyone Needs to Know* (New York: Oxford University Press, 2011), 127.

16. Victoria Westbrook, interview by the author, December 9, 2020.

17. Keith Humphreys, interview by the author, March 16, 2021.

18. Kleiman, Caulkins, and Hawken, *Drugs and Drug Policy*, 96.

19. Kleiman, Caulkins, and Hawken, *Drugs and Drug Policy*, 126.

20. Dan Waldorf, "Natural Recovery from Addiction: Some Social-Psychological Processes of Untreated Recovery," *Journal of Drug Issues* 13, no. 2 (1983): 237–80, doi:10.1177/002204268301300205.

21. Kelly Stamphill, interview by the author, March 20, 2021.

22. Haracopos and Hough, "Drug Dealing in Open-Air Markets."

23. Monique Tula, interview by the author, December 17, 2020.

24. Jamie Crook, interview by the author, February 28, 2020.

25. Bill Zimmerman, interview by the author, October 13, 2020.

26. Rafael Mandelman, interview by the author, December 18, 2020.

27. Trisha Thadani, "More Than One Person a Day Died in SF of an Overdose Last Year. This Year Is Expected to Be Worse," *San Francisco Chronicle*, August 31, 2020, www.sfchronicle.com.

28. Matt Haney, interview by the author, February 12, 2021.

29. Keith Humphreys, interview by the author, March 16, 2021.

30. Rafael Mandelman, interview by the author, December 18, 2020.

31. Keith Humphreys, interview by the author, March 16, 2021.

32. Jacqui Berlinn, interview by the author, March 20, 2021.

33. Tracey Helton Mitchell, *The Big Fix: Hope After Heroin* (Berkeley, CA: Seal Press, 2016), 222.

34. Steve Berg, interview by the author, February 19, 2021.

35. Willie Brown and P. J. Corkey, *Basic Brown: My Life and Our Times* (New York: Simon & Schuster, 2008), 274–75.

36. Keith Humphreys, interview by the author, March 16, 2021.

37. Thomas Wolf (@MyTwolffamily), "I know 8 people that overdosed and died from illicit Fentanyl since 2018," Twitter post, March 1, 2021, 7:17 a.m., https://twitter .com/MyTwolffamily.

38. Adam Mesnick, interview by the author, October 26, 2020.

7 The Crisis of Untreated Mental Illness

1. Bill Zimmerman, interview by the author, October 13, 2020.

2. Susan Mizner, interview by the author, March 26, 2021.

3. Kelly Davis and Jeff McDonald, "In California, Jails Are Now the Mental Health Centers of Last Resort," *San Diego Union-Tribune*, September 20, 2019, www.san diegouniontribune.com.

4. "Bay Area Homelessness: A Regional View of a Regional Crisis," Bay Area Council Economic Institute, April 2019, www.bayareaeconomy.org.

5. *Deinstitutionalization, Mental Illness, and Medications*, hearing before the Committee on Finance, US Senate, 103rd Congress, 2nd session, May 10, 1994; H. Richard Lamb and Leona L. Bachrach, "Some Perspectives on Deinstitutionalization," *Psychiatric Services* 52, no. 8 (August 1, 2001): 1039–45; Ann Braden Johnson, *Out of Bedlam: The Truth About Deinstitutionalization* (New York: Basic Books, 1992), cited in Anne Harrington, *Mind Fixers: Psychiatry's Troubled Search for the Biology of Mental Illness* (New York: Norton, 2019), 116.

6. Andrew Scull, *Madness in Civilization: A Cultural History of Insanity, from the Bible to Freud, from the Madhouse to Modern Medicine* (Berkeley: University of California Press, 2019), 364.

7. Richard W. White Jr., *Rude Awakenings: What the Homeless Crisis Tells Us* (Institute for Contemporary Studies Press, 1992), 118.

8. Sarah Moore, "A brief history of mental health care in California," ABC10, updated April 17, 2018, www.abc10.com.

9. Peter H. Rossi, *Down and Out in America: The Origins of Homelessness* (Chicago: University of Chicago Press, 1989), 42.

10. Joni Lee Pow et al., "Deinstitutionalization of American Public Hospitals for the Mentally Ill Before and After the Introduction of Antipsychotic Medications," *Harvard Review of Psychiatry* 23, no. 3 (June 2015): 176–87, cited in Harrington, *Mind Fixers*, 111.

11. Richard D. Lyons, "How Release of Mental Patients Began," *New York Times*, October 30, 1984.

12. Ibid.

13. Kathleen Stone-Takai, "Mandating Treatment for the Mentally-Ill: Why So Difficult?" master's thesis (California State University, Sacramento, Spring 2009), www.antoniocasella.edu; Jim Shields, "Another Voice—Mental Health Myths," letter to the editor, *Ukiah Daily Journal*, June 9, 2013, www.ukiahdailyjournal.com.

14. "Social Security Cuts from Reagan Years Being Restored," *Chicago Tribune*, December 4, 1989, www.chicagotribune.com.

15. John F. Kennedy, "Message from the President of the United States Relative to Mental Illness and Mental Retardation," *American Journal of Psychiatry* 120, no. 8 (1964): 729–37; John F. Kennedy, "Remarks on Proposed Measures to Combat Mental Illness and Mental Retardation," February 5, 1963, accessed via the American Presidency Project on April 4, 2021, www.presidency.ucsb.edu, cited in Harrington, *Mind Fixers*, 112.

16. Kennedy, "Message from the President of the United States Relative to Mental Illness and Mental Retardation."

17. Andrew Scull, *Decarceration: Community Treatment and the Deviant: A Radical View* (Upper Saddle River, NJ: Prentice-Hall, 1977), 73; Thomas Szasz, *The Manufacture of Madness: A Comparative Study of the Inquisition and the Mental Health Movement* (Syracuse: Syracuse University Press, 1970); George S. Stevenson, "Needed: A Plan for the Mentally Ill," *New York Times*, July 27, 1947; Rael J. Isaac and Virginia C. Armat, *Madness in the Streets: How Psychiatry and the Law Abandoned the Mentally Ill* (Arlington County, VA: Treatment Advocacy Center, 1990), 69, cited

in Susannah Cahalan, *The Great Pretender: The Undercover Mission That Changed Our Understanding of Madness* (New York: Grand Central, 2019), 162.

18. Michelle Tandler, interview by the author, November 30, 2020.

19. ABC-KGO Channel 7 News, "San Francisco condo attack victim breaks down on stand during testimony," September 18, 2019; Phil Matier and Erin Allday, "Man Accused of Attacking Tenant Outside Her SF Embarcadero Condo Released from Jail," *San Francisco Chronicle*, August 15, 2019; Samuel Allegri, "Judge's Decision on Releasing Suspect That Allegedly Attacked Woman Condemned by Officials," NTD, August 16, 2019, www.ntd.com.

20. "Watermark Lobby Incident," uploaded by Jay Barmann, August 15, 2019, YouTube video, 9:58, www.youtube.com.

21. Evan Sernoffsky, "SF Embarcadero Attack: Victim Testifies Man Wanted to 'Kill the Front Desk Lady' to Save Her Life," *San Francisco Chronicle*, September 17, 2019, www.sfchronicle.com; "Watermark Lobby Incident."

22. "Watermark Lobby Incident."

23. "Mental Illness," National Institute of Mental Health, US Department of Health and Human Services, January 2021, www.nimh.nih.gov.

24. Kenneth Paul Rosenberg, *Bedlam: An Intimate Journey into America's Mental Health Crisis* (New York: Avery, 2019), xiii.

25. Marc de Hert et al., "Physical Illness in Patients with Severe Mental Disorders. I. Prevalence, Impact of Medications and Disparities in Health Care," *World Psychiatry* 10, no. 1 (2011): 52–77, doi:10.1002/j.2051–5545.2011.tb00014.x; John W. Newcomer and Charles Hennekens, "Severe Mental Illness and Risk of Cardiovascular Disease," *Journal of the American Medical Association* 298, no. 15 (October 2007); Amber Bahorik et. al., "Serious Mental Illness and Medical Comorbidities: Finds from an Integrated Health Care System," *Journal of Psychosomatic Research* 100 (September 2017): 35–45; "Common Comorbidities with Substance Use Disorders Research Report: Part 1: The Connection Between Substance Use Disorders and Mental Illness," National Institute on Drug Abuse, accessed May 14, 2021, www.drugabuse.gov.

26. "CoC Homeless Populations and Subpopulations Reports," HUD Exchange, accessed July 17, 2021, www.hudexchange.com. Figure includes homeless living with serious mental illness in all states and territories, Puerto Rico, and District of Columbia.

27. E. Fuller Torrey et al., "The Treatment of Persons with Mental Illness in Prisons and Jails: A State Survey," Treatment Advocacy Center, April 8, 2014, www.treat mentadvocacycenter.org, cited in Rosenberg, *Bedlam*, 69; Henry J. Steadman et al., "Prevalence of Serious Mental Illness Among Jail Inmates," *Psychiatric Services* 60, no. 6 (2009): 761–65, doi:10.1176/ps.2009.60.6.761, cited in "The Way Forward: Federal Action for a System That Works for All People Living with SMI and SED and Their Families and Caregivers," Interdepartmental Serious Mental Illness Coordinating Committee Report to Congress, December 13, 2017, www .samhsa.gov.

28. Tara Siler and Matthew Green, "New S.F. Pilot to Target Homeless Residents Most in Need of Mental Health, Addiction Services," KQED, September 4, 2019, www.kqed.org.

29. London Breed, "Mental Health Reform Press Event: Tipping Point and UCSF Benioff" (press conference, September 12, 2019), YouTube video, 24:01, www .youtube.com.

30. Virginia A. Hiday et al., "Criminal Victimization of Person with Severe Mental Illness," *Psychiatric Services* 50, no. 1 (January 1999): 62–68, cited in D. J. Jaffe, *Insane Consequences: How the Mental Health Industry Fails the Mentally Ill* (Buffalo, NY: Prometheus, 2017), 168.

31. "Premature death among people with severe mental disorders," World Health Organization, accessed May 18, 2021, www.who.int/mental_health/management /info_sheet.pdf.

32. Torrey et al., "The Treatment of Persons with Mental Illness in Prisons and Jails."

33. Paul Linde, "Ex-ER psychiatrist: More inpatient treatment needed in SF," interview by Heather Knight, *San Francisco Chronicle*, October 9, 2018, podcast audio, 24:21, www.sfchronicle.com.

34. "CoC Homeless Populations and Subpopulations Reports," HUD Exchange, accessed April 4, 2021, www.hudexchange.com.

35. Gale Holland, "Why L.A. County's Homelessness Crisis Has Been Decades in the Making," *Los Angeles Times*, June 5, 2019, www.latimes.com.

36. Linde, "Ex-ER psychiatrist: More inpatient treatment needed in SF."

37. Dale E. McNiel, Renee L. Binder, and Jo C. Robinson, "Incarceration Associated with Homelessness, Mental Disorder, and Co-occurring Substance Abuse," *Psychiatric Services* 56, no. 7 (2005): xx, doi:10.1176/appi.ps.56.7.840.

38. Linde, "Ex-ER psychiatrist: More inpatient treatment needed in SF."

39. Paneez Kosarian, interview by the author, February 3, 2021.

40. Bernard E. Harcourt, "An Institutionalization Effect: The Impact of Mental Hospitalization and Imprisonment on Homicide in the United States, 1934–2001," *Journal of Legal Studies* 40, no. 1 (January 2011), www.jstor.org/stable/10.1086/658 404, cited in Jaffe, *Insane Consequences*, 80.

41. "Serious Mental Illness (SMI) Prevalence in Jails and Prisons," Office of Research and Public Affairs, Treatment Advocacy Center, September 2016, www.treatment advocacycenter.org, cited in Rosenberg, *Bedlam*, 63.

42. Rosenberg, *Bedlam*, 64.

43. Susan Partovi, interview by the author, September 20, 2019.

44. "The Prevalence and Severity of Mental Illness Among California Prisoners on the Rise," advised by Michael Romano, Stanford Justice Advocacy Project, 2017, www.law.stanford.edu, cited in Jocelyn Wiener, "All too often, California's default mental institutions are now jails and prisons," *CalMatters*, February 4, 2019, updated September 17, 2020, www.calmatters.org.

45. Alisa Roth, *Insane: America's Criminal Treatment of Mental Illness* (New York: Basic Books, 2018), 52, 53, cited in Rosenberg, *Bedlam*, 63.

46. California Department of State Hospitals, 2018 Annual Report, www.dsh.ca.gov.

47. Dominic A. Sisti, Andrea G. Segal, and Ezekial J. Emanuel, "Improving Long-Term Psychiatric Care: Bring Back the Asylum," *Jama Network* 313, no. 3 (January 2015): 243–44, doi:10.1001/jama.2014.16088.

48. Robert Okin, "Silent Voices: A Psychiatrist's Quest to Understand Homelessness and Addiction," interview by Paul Linde, *Hippie Docs 2.0: Re-Humanizing Medicine*, September 30, 2020, podcast audio, 35:33, www.stitcher.com.

49. Jennifer Wadsworth, "Every San Jose Police Shooting in 2017 Has Involved Suspects with a History of Mental Illness," *San Jose Inside*, May 30, 2017, www.sanjoseinside.com, cited in "A Promising Start: Results from a California Survey Assessing the Use of Laura's Law," Treatment Advocacy Center, February 2019, www.treatmentadvocacycenter.org; Doris Fuller et. al, "Overlooked in the Undercounted: The Role of Mental Illness in Fatal Law Enforcement Encounters," Treatment Advocacy Center, December 15, 2021, www.treatmentadvocacycenter.org.

50. Vivian Ho, "S.F. Police Killing of Mentally Ill Man Exposes Reform Challenges," *San Francisco Chronicle*, February 1, 2016, www.sfchronicle.com.

51. Gary A. Harki, "Horrific Deaths, Brutal Treatment: Mental Illness in America's Jails," *Virginian-Pilot*, August 23, 2018, www.pilotonline.com, cited in "A Promising Start," 19–20.

52. Wilson Walker, "Victim Outraged After Man Who Attacked Her Outside San Francisco Home Released," KPIX5 CBS SF Bay Area, August 14, 2019, video, 2:43, www.sanfrancisco.cbslocal.com.

53. Ibid.

54. Dominic Fracassa and Jill Tucker, "Officials Condemn Judge's Decision to Release Suspect Accused of Attacking Woman," *San Francisco Chronicle*, August 15, 2019, www.sfchronicle.com.

55. Fracassa and Tucker, "Officials Condemn Judge's Decision to Release Suspect Accused of Attacking Woman"; Sara Stinson and Haaziq Madyun, "Judge Orders Homeless Man Who Attacked Woman in San Francisco to Wear Ankle Monitor," KRON4 News, August 16, 2019, www.kron4.com.

56. Dominic Fracassa and Emily Fancher, "After Outrage, Judge Orders Suspect in Attack of Woman Caught on Video to Wear Ankle Monitor," *San Francisco Chronicle*, August 16, 2019, www.sfchronicle.com.

57. Emily Turner, "San Francisco Condo Attack Suspect Austin Vincent Charged in Second Assault," KPIX5 CBS SF Bay Area, August 19, 2019, video, 1:32, www.sanfrancisco.cbslocal.com.

58. Heather Knight, "Another SF Attack Spotlights City's Mental Illness and Drug Addiction Crisis," *San Francisco Chronicle*, September 20, 2019, www.sfchronicle.com.

59. ABC7 News Bay Area, "Video Captures the moment a woman was attacked outside her home," August 14, 2019, YouTube video, 1:25, www.youtube.com.

60. Knight, "Another SF Attack Spotlights City's Mental Illness and Drug Addiction Crisis."

61. Paneez Kosarian, interview by the author, February 3, 2021.

62. Anne E. Parsons, *From Asylum to Prison: Deinstitutionalization and the Rise of Mass Incarceration After 1945* (Chapel Hill: University of North Carolina Press, 2018); Antonia Hylton, "Carceral Continuities: Tracing Black Bodies from the Asylum to the Penal State," unpublished undergraduate senior thesis, March 2015 (Harvard University), Harvard College Libraries, accession 2017.556, box 1, cited in Harrington, *Mind Fixers*, 118.

63. Okin, "Silent Voices."

64. Nathan Heller, "A Window onto an American Nightmare," *New Yorker*, June 1, 2020, www.newyorker.com.

65. "A Promising Start."

66. Marcia Gay Harden (mgh_8), Instagram post, January 22, 2021, www.instagram .com; Daniel Neira, "Cara Delevingne and Eva Longoria Team Up for Ground-breaking Film," *Hola!* January 26, 2021, www.us.hola.com.

67. Erin Allday, "The Streets' Sickest, Costliest: The Mentally Ill," *San Francisco Chronicle*, June 29, 2016, www.sfchronicle.com.

68. Kelly Kruger, interview by the author, October 1, 2020.

69. "California's Acute Psychiatric Bed Loss," California Hospital Association, February 26, 2019, accessed January 12, 2021, www.dir.ca.gov; "Psychiatric hospital beds per 100,000," World Health Organization, accessed May 12, 2021, https://gateway.euro.who.int.

70. "California's Acute Psychiatric Bed Loss"; Office of Statewide Health Planning and Development, "2020 Hospital Annual Utilization," CHHS Open Data, https://data.chhs.ca.gov/dataset/hospital-annual-utilization-report.

71. Linde, "Ex-ER Psychiatrist: More Inpatient Treatment Needed in SF"; Fred J. Martin Jr., "San Francisco Has Too Few Psychiatric Beds," *SF Gate*, June 28, 2013, www.sfgate.com.

72. "California's Acute Psychiatric Bed Loss"; California Health and Human Services, *2018 Calendar Year Hospital Utilization Pivot Table*, last updated January 7, 2020, www.data.chhs.ca.gov.

73. Kelly Kruger, interview by the author, October 1, 2020.

74. John Snook, interview by the author, October 21, 2020.

75. Stoddard Davenport, Stephen P. Melek, and Daniel J. Perlman, "Addiction and Mental Health vs. Physical Health: Analyzing Disparities in Network Use and Provider reimbursement rates," Milliman, December 2017, www.us.milliman.com, cited in "A Promising Start."

76. Jocelyn Wiener, "Overlooked Mental Health 'Catastrophe': Vanishing Board-and-Care-Homes Leave Residents with Few Options," *CalMatters*, April 15, 2019, www.calmatters.org.

77. Byrhonda Lyons, "Why California is struggling to provide adequate mental health," *PBS NewsHour*, August 8, 2019, video, 6:14, www.pbs.org.

78. Richard M. Scheffler and Neal Adams, "Millionaires and Mental Health: Proposition 63 in California," *Health Affairs* 24, no. 1(2005), doi:10.1377/hlthaff.w5.212.

79. Gavin Newsom, Mark A. Ghaly, and Will Lightbourne, "Mental Health Services Act Expenditure Report—Governor's Budget: Fiscal Year 2021–2022," California Department of Healthcare Services, February 2021, www.dhcs.ca.gov.

80. "California 2019 Mental Health National Outcome Measures (NOMS): SAMHSA Uniform Reporting System," Substance Abuse and Mental Health Administration, 2019, www.samhsa.gov.

81. Thomas Insel, interview by the author, March 22, 2021.

82. "Mental Health SF Legislation Approved Unanimously by Board of Supervisors" (press release), SF Mayor, December 10, 2019, www.sfmayor.gov.

83. Kristi Coale, "Why SF Added Homeless and Mental Health Services to the Prop A Parks Measure," *Frisc*, October 29, 2020, www.thefrisc.com; "San Francisco, California, Proposition A, Bond Issue (November 2020)," Ballotpedia, accessed May 14, 2021, www.ballotpedia.org.

84. John Snook, interview by the author, September 19, 2019.

8 Madness for Decivilization

1. Andrew Scull, *Madness in Civilization: A Cultural History of Insanity, from the Bible to Freud, from the Madhouse to Modern Medicine* (Berkeley: University of California Press, 2019), 36.

2. Ibid.

3. Augustine Thompson, O.P., *Francis of Assisi: A New Biography* (Ithaca and London: Cornell University Press, 2012), 14.

4. Ibid., 13–16. For more on medieval legal approaches to mental illness, see also Brandon T. Parlopiano, "Madmen and Lawyers: The Development and Practice of the Jurisprudence of Insanity in the Middle Ages," PhD diss. (Catholic University of America, Washington, D.C., 2013), www.cuislandora.wrlc.org/islandora/object/etd%3A349/datastream/PDF/view.

Notes

5.   Emil Kraepelin, "Concerning the Influence of Acute Diseases on the Causation of Mental Illness," unpublished PhD diss. (Institute of Psychiatry, London), cited in E. Fuller Torrey, *Out of the Shadows: Confronting America's Mental Illness Crisis* (Hoboken, NJ: John Wiley & Sons, 1997), 167.

6.   Scull, *Madness in Civilization*, 27.

7.   Donald Lupton, *London and the Countrey Carbonadoed and Quartred into Severall Characters* (London: Nicholas Oakes, 1632), 75, cited in Scull, *Madness in Civilization*, 85.

8.   César de Saussure, *A Foreign View of England in the Reigns of George I and George II: The Letters of Monsieur César de Saussure to His Family*, trans. and ed. Madame Van Muyden (Miami, FL: HardPress Publishing, 2012), cited in Kenneth Paul Rosenberg, *Bedlam: An Intimate Journey into America's Mental Health Crisis* (New York: Avery, 2019), 4–5.

9.   Alexander Cruden, *The London-Citizen Exceedingly Injured: Or, a British Inquisition Display'd . . . Addressed to the Legislature, as Plainly Shewing the Absolute Necessity of Regulating Private Madhouses* (London: Cooper & Dodd, 1739); Daniel Defoe, *Augusta Triumphans: Or, the Way to Make London the Most Flourishing City in the Universe* (London: J. Roberts, 1728), cited in Scull, *Madness in Civilization*, 139.

10. Defoe, *Augusta Triumphans*, cited in Scull, *Madness in Civilization*, 139.

11. J.-E. D. Esquirol, *Des Établissments des aliénés en France et des moyens d'améliorer le sort de ces infortunés* (Paris: Huzard, 1819), cited in Scull, *Madness in Civilization*, 190.

12. Susannah Cahalan, *The Great Pretender: The Undercover Mission That Changed Our Understanding of Madness* (New York: Grand Central, 2019), 16–17.

13. Frederick H. Wine, *Report on the Defective, Dependent and Delinquent Classes of the Population of the United States* (Washington, D.C.: US Government Printing Office, 1888), cited in E. Fuller Torrey, *Out of the Shadows: Confronting America's Mental Illness Crisis* (New York: John Wiley & Sons, 1997), 28.

14. Katie Dowd, "Historic Asylums and Sanitariums of Northern California," *SF Gate*, June 16, 2016, www.sfgate.com.

15. Ibid.

16. Neal L. Starr, "Stockton State Hospital: A Century and a Quarter of Service," *San Joaquin Historian* 8, no. 3 (1976).

17. Sarah Moore, "A brief history of mental health care in California," ABC10, updated April 17, 2018, www.abc10.com.

18. Cahalan, *The Great Pretender*, 13.

19. Ibid., 13.

20. Frank Leon Wright, "Out of sight, out of mind: A graphic picture of present-day institutional care of the mentally ill in America, based on more than two thousand eye-witness reports" (National Mental Health Foundation, 1947), available at Disability History Museum, www.disabilitymuseum.org, cited in E. Fuller Torrey, *American Psychosis: How the Federal Government Destroyed the Mental Illness Treatment System* (New York: Oxford University Press, 2013), 23.

21. Albert Q. Maisel, "Most U.S. Mental Hospitals Are a Shame and a Disgrace," *Life*, May 6 1946, available at PBS *American Experience*, accessed December 26, 2020, www.pbs.org.

22. Ellen Herman, *The Romance of American Psychology: Political Culture in the Age of Experts* (Berkeley: University of California Press, 1995), cited in D. J. Jaffe, *Insane Consequences: How the Mental Health Industry Fails the Mentally Ill* (Buffalo, NY: Prometheus, 2017), 184.

23. Torrey, *American Psychosis*, 64, 69.

24. Matthew Dumont, *The Absurd Healer: Perspectives of a Community Psychiatrist* (New York: Science House, 1968), cited in Torrey, *American Psychosis*, 67.

25. Liz Szabo, "Cost of Not Caring: Stigma Set in Stone," *USA Today*, June 25, 2014, www.usatoday.com.

26. Torrey, *American Psychosis*, 79.

27. Jaffe, *Insane Consequences*, 238.

28. Scull, *Madness in Civilization*, 365.

29. E. Fuller Torrey, *Nowhere to Go: The Tragic Odyssey of the Homeless Mentally Ill* (New York: Harper & Row, 1988), 55–57; Alex Sarayan, *The Turning Point: How Men of Conscience Brought About Major Change in the Care of America's Mentally Ill* (Washington, D.C.: American Psychiatric Publishing, 1994), cited in Torrey, *American Psychosis*, 23.

30. Torrey, *American Psychosis*, 48.

31. Ibid., 95.

32. *Community Mental Health Centers Amendments of 1969, Hearings on S. 2523, Before the Subcomm. on Health, Comm. on Labor and Public Welfare*, 91st Cong. 98 (statement of Horace G. Whittington), cited in Torrey, *American Psychosis*, 91.

33. James Miller, *The Passion of Michel Foucault* (New York: Simon & Schuster, 1993), 14.

34. Ibid., 113.

35. Anne Harrington, *Mind Fixers: Psychiatry's Troubled Search for the Biology of Mental Illness* (New York: Norton, 2019), 122–24.

36. Bruce J. Ennis and Thomas R. Litwick, "Psychiatry and the Presumption of Expertise: Flipping Coins in the Courtroom," *California Law Review* 62, no. 3 (1974); cited in Cahalan, *The Great Pretender*, 124.

37. "The Discharged Chronic Mental Patient," *Medical World News*, April 12, 1974, cited in Torrey, *American Psychosis*, 150.

38. David Rosenhan, "On Being Sane in Insane Places," *Science* 179, no. 4070 (1973): 250–58, doi:10.1126/science.179.4070.250.

39. Cahalan, *The Great Pretender*, 35.

40. Allen Frances, *Saving Normal: An Insider's Revolt Against Out-of-Control Psychiatric Diagnosis, DSM-5, Big Pharma, and the Medicalization of Ordinary Life* (New York: William Morrow, 2013), 62, cited in Cahalan, *The Great Pretender*.

41. Cahalan, *The Great Pretender*, 160.

42. Jeffrey Lieberman, "Imagine There Was No Stigma to Mental Illness" (lecture, TEDx, Charlottesville, January 11, 2016), YouTube video, 22:07, www.youtube.com.

43. Elinore F. McCance-Katz, "The Federal Government Ignores the Treatment Needs of Americans with Serious Mental Illness," *Psychiatric Times*, April 21, 2016, www.psychiatrictimes.com, cited in Jaffe, *Insane Consequences*, 99–100.

9 Medication First

1. Laura's Law, AB 1421, September 28th, 2002, leginfo.ca.gov; "A Promising Start: Results from a California Survey Assessing the Use of Laura's Law," Treatment Advocacy Center, February 2019, www.treatmentadvocacycenter.org.

2. Ibid.

3. J. D. Jaffe, *Insane Consequences: How the Mental Health Industry Fails the Mentally Ill* (Buffalo, NY: Prometheus, 2017), 92.

4. Raisa Small, "Response to SB 1045 and Possible Expansion of Conservatorship," *Berkeley Daily Planet*, October 15, 2018.

5. Robert Garrova, "Why LA County wants to expand involuntary psych holds for some homeless," 89.3 KPCC, November 1, 2017, www.scpr.org.

6. Jaffe, *Insane Consequences*, 159.

7. Petro Nava et al., "Promises Still to Keep: A Decade of the Mental Health Services Act," Little Hoover Commission, Report 225, January 2015, www.lhc.ca.gov.

8. Sammy Caiola and Emily Zentner, "As An Overhaul Of California's Mental Health Spending Gets Shelved, One Mother Pushes For Reform," CapRadio, July 2, 2020, www.capradio.org; Hannah Dreier, "California Mental-Health Spending Often Bypasses the Mentally Ill," *Los Angeles Daily News*, July 28, 2012, www.dailynews.com, cited in Jaffe, *Insane Consequences*, 159.

9. Heather Knight, "Why Are More Mentally Ill People Wandering SF Streets? Report Gives Answers," *San Francisco Chronicle*, July 30, 2019, www.sfchronicle.com.

10. Ibid.

11. Nuala Sawyer Bishari, "After Months of Contentious Arguments, S.F. Passes Mental Health Conservatorship Bill," *SF Weekly*, June 5, 2019, www.sfweekly.com.

12. Thomas Fuller, "Life on the Dirtiest Block in San Francisco," *New York Times*, October 8, 2018, www.nytimes.com.

13. Bishari, "After Months of Contentious Arguments, S.F. Passes Mental Health Conservatorship Bill."

14. Ibid.

15. Rafael Mandelman, interview by the author, December 18, 2020.

16. John Fergus Edwards, "The Outdated Institution for Mental Diseases Exclusion: A Call to Re-examine and Repeal the Medicaid IMD Exclusion," Mental Health Policy Org., May 1997, accessed January 21, 2021, www.mentalillnesspolicy.org, cited in Jaffe, *Insane Consequences*, 186.

Notes

17. John Snook, interview by the author, October 21, 2020.

18. Ibid.

19. Allen Frances, "Fixing the Mental Health System: Snake Pits, Dungeons, and Back Alleys," *Psychiatric Times* 31, no. 12 (2014), www.psychiatrictimes.com.

20. Caiola and Zentner, "As an Overhaul of California's Mental Health Spending Gets Shelved, One Mother Pushes for Reform."

21. Susan Partovi, interview by the author, September 20, 2019.

22. Neil Gong, "'That Proves You Mad, Because You Know It Not': Impaired Insight and the Dilemma of Governing Psychiatric Patients as Legal Subjects," *Theory and Society* 46 (2017): 201–28, doi:10.1007/s11186–017–9288–0.

23. Willie L. Brown Jr., *Basic Brown: My Life and Our Times* (New York: Simon & Schuster, 2011), 272–73.

24. Susan Partovi, interview by the author, September 20, 2019.

25. Lissa Dutra et al., "A Meta-Analytic Review of Psychosocial Interventions for Substance Use Disorders," *American Journal of Psychiatry* 165, no. 2 (2008): 179–87, doi:10.1176/appi.ajp.2007.06111851; Nancy M. Petry et al., "Effect of Prize-Based Incentives on Outcomes in Stimulant Abusers in Outpatient Psychosocial Treatment Programs: A National Drug Abuse Treatment Clinical Trials Network Study," *Archives of General Psychiatry* 62, no. 10 (2005): 1148–56, doi:10.1001/archpsyc.62.10.1148; Stephen T. Higgins et al., *Contingency Management in Substance Abuse Treatment* (Guilford Press, 2007).

26. John M. Roll et al., "Investigating the Use of Contingency Management in the Treatment of Cocaine Abuse Among Individuals with Schizophrenia: A Feasibility Study," *Psychiatry Research* 125, no. 1 (2004): 61–64, doi:10.1016/j.psychres.2003.10.003; Richard K. Ries et al., "Outcomes of Managing Disability Benefits Among Patients with Substance Dependence and Serious Mental Illness," *Psychiatric Services* 55, no. 4 (2004): 445–47, doi:10.1176/appi.ps.55.4.445.

27. Danielle R. Davis et al., "A Review of the Literature on Contingency Management in the Treatment of Substance Use Disorders, 2009–2014," *Preventative Medicine* 92 (2016), doi:10.1016/j.ypmed.2016.08.008.

28. Stacey C. Sigmon and Maxine L. Stitzer, "Use of a Low-Cost Incentive Intervention to Improve Counseling Attendance Among Methadone-Maintained Patients,"

Journal of Substance Abuse Treatment 29, no. 4 (2005): 253–58, doi:10.1016/j.jsat.2005.08.004.

29. Alan Bellack et al., "A Randomized Clinical Trial of a New Behavioral Treatment for Drug Abuse in People with Serious and Persistent Mental Illness," *Archives of General Psychiatry* 63, no. 4 (2006): 426–32, doi:10.1001/archpsyc.63.4.426.

30. Michael G. McDonell et al., "Randomized Controlled Trial of Contingency Management for Stimulant Use in Community Mental Health Patients with Serious Mental Illness," *American Journal of Psychiatry* 170, no. 1 (2012), doi:10.1176/appi.ajp.2012.11121831; Davis et al., "A Review of the Literature on Contingency Management in the Treatment of Substance Use Disorders, 2009–2014."

31. Nancy M. Petry et al., "Contingency Management Treatment for Substance Use Disorders: How Far Has It Come, and Where Does It Need to Go?" *Psychology of Addictive Behaviors* 31, no. 8 (2017), doi:10.1037/adv0000287.

32. Marianne Promberger and Theresa M. Marteau, "When Do Financial Incentives Reduce Intrinsic Motivation? Comparing Behaviors Studied in Psychological and Economic Literatures," *Health Psychology* 32, no. 9 (2013): 950–57, doi:10.1037/hea0000036; Petry et al., "Contingency Management Treatment for Substance Use Disorders."

33. Rene Zegerius, interview by the author, December 2020.

34. Jamie Crook and Eve Garrow, interview by the author, February 28, 2020.

35. Susan Mizner, interview by the author, March 26, 2021.

36. John Snook, interview by the author, October 21, 2020.

37. Robert Okin, "Silent Voices: A Psychiatrist's Quest to Understand Homelessness and Addiction," interview by Paul Linde, *Hippie Docs 2.0: Re-Humanizing Medicine*, September 30, 2020, podcast audio, 35:33, www.stitcher.com.

38. Thomas Insel, interview by the author, March 22, 2021.

39. Boona Cheema, interview by the author, February 11, 2021.

40. Louis Chicoine, interview by the author, October 5, 2020.

41. Thomas Insel, interview by the author, March 22, 2021.

42. Susan Partovi, interview by the author, September 20, 2019.

10 Not Everyone's a Victim

1. Jabari Jackson, interview by the author, October 27, 2020.

2. Housing Instability Research Department, "San Francisco Homeless Count and Survey: Comprehensive Report, 2019," Applied Survey Research, 2019, 16, www.nhipdata.org.

3. Jennifer Friedenbach, interview by Michael Morrissey, August 8, 2017, YouTube video, 17:18, www.youtube.com.

4. Jen Loving, interview by the author, October 12, 2020.

5. Victoria Westbrook, interview by the author, December 9, 2020.

6. Adam Mesnick, interview by the author, October 26, 2020.

7. Paul Boden, "On the Homeless Industry and the Criminalization of Homelessness," interview by Mark Horvath, *Invisible People*, June 12, 2019, YouTube video, 39:29, www.youtube.com.

8. Kristen Marshall, interview by the author, September 24, 2020.

9. Andrew Woo, "Imbalance in Housing Aid: Mortgage Interest Deduction vs. Section 8," Apartment List, October 11, 2017, www.apartmentlist.com; Ezra Levin and David Meni, "The Biggest Beneficiaries of Housing Subsidies? The Wealthy," Talk Poverty, June 30, 2016, www.talkpoverty.org.

10. H. Luke Shaefer and Kathryn Edin, "Extreme Poverty in the United States, 1996–2011," *National Poverty Center Policy Brief* 28, February 2012, www.npc.umich.edu.

11. Jennifer Friedenbach, interview by Michael Morrissey, August 8, 2017, YouTube video, 17:18, www.youtube.com.

12. "No Safe Place: The Criminalization of Homelessness in US Cities," National Law Center on Homelessness and Poverty, July 16, 2014, www.homelessnesslaw.org.

13. Justin Keller, "Open letter to SF Mayor Ed Lee and Greg Suhr (police chief)," *Justin Keller* (blog), February 15, 2016, www.justink.svbtle.com.

14. Julie Carrie Wong, "San Francisco Tech Worker: 'I Don't Want to See Homeless Riff-Raff,'" *Guardian*, February 17, 2016, www.theguardian.com.

15. Richard Rothstein, *Color of Law: A Forgotten History of How Our Government Segregated America* (New York: Liveright, 2017).

16. Bruce Mitchell and Juan Franco, "HOLC 'Redlining' Maps: The Persistent Structure of Segregation and Economic Inequality," National Community Reinvestment Coalition, March 20, 2018, www.ncrc.org/holc.

17. Michael B. Gerrar, "The Victims of NIMBY," *Fordham Urban Law Journal* 21, no. 3 (1994): 495–522; Robert D. Bullard, *Dumping in Dixie: Race, Class, and Environmental Quality* (Boulder, CO: Westview Press, 2008); Jessica Trounstine, "The Geography of Inequality: How Land Use Regulation Produces Segregation," *American Political Science Review* 114, no. 2 (2020): 443–55, doi:10.1017/S0003055419000844.

18. Luke N. Rodda, "Report on Accidental Overdose Deaths," Office of the Chief Medical Examiner, San Francisco, February 17, 2021, www.sf.gov.

19. "Final Report on County Jail #4 Closure," Safety and Justice Challenge Subcommittee of the San Francisco Sentencing Commission, San Francisco Sentencing Commission, September 30, 2020, www.sfdistrictattorney.org.

20. Kristen Marshall, interview by the author, September 24, 2020.

21. David Finkelhor and Lisa Jones, "Have Sexual Abuse and Physical Abuse Declined Since the 1990s?" Crimes Against Children Research Center, November 2012, accessed January 15, 2021, www.unh.edu; Steve Olson and Clare Stroud, *Child Maltreatment Research, Policy, and Practice for the Next Decade: Workshop Summary* (Washington, D.C.: National Academies Press, 2012), www.ncbi.nlm.nih.gov.

22. David Finkelhor et al., "Corporal Punishment: Current Rates from a National Survey," *Journal of Child and Family Studies* 28, no. 7 (2019): 1991–97, doi:10.1007/s10826–019–01426–4.

23. Isabel V. Sawhill and Edward Rodrigue, "An Agenda for Reducing Poverty and Improving Opportunity," Brookings Institution, November 18, 2015, www.brookings.edu.

24. All figures in 2019 dollars. Hispanic per capita income data is available starting in 1973. US Census Bureau, *Historical Income Tables: People*, Table P-1. Total CPS Population and Per Capita Income, accessed April 1, 2021, www.census.gov.

25. Elaine L. Chao and Kathleen P. Utgoff, "100 Years of US Consumer Spending: Data for the Nation, New York City, and Boston," US Bureau of Labor Statistics Report 991, US Department of Labor, May 2006, accessed April 1, 2021, www.bls

.gov; "Consumer Expenditures—2019," news release, Bureau of Labor Statistics, September 9, 2020, www.bls.gov.

26. Ajay Chaudry et al, "Poverty in the United States: 50 Year Trends and Safety Net Impacts," US Department of Health and Human Services, March 2016, www .aspe.hhs.gov.

27. Austin Frakt and Toni Monkovic, "A 'Rare Case Where Racial Biases' Protected African-Americans," *New York Times*, November 25, 2019, www.nytimes.com.

28. Sally Satel, "The Truth About Painkillers," *National Affairs* 47, Spring 2021, www.nationalaffairs.com.

29. US Department of Transportation, National Highway Traffic Safety Administration, National Center for Statistics and Analysis, personal communication, October 16, 2018, November 6, 2019, and January 6, 2021, cited in "Motor Vehicle Safety Data," Bureau of Transportation Statistics, accessed April 1, 2021, www.bts.gov.

30. "Historical Background and Development of Social Security," Social Security Administration, accessed March 12, 2021, www.ssa.gov; "Annual Statistical Report on the Social Security Disability Insurance Program, 2010," Social Security Administration, August 2011, www.ssa.gov.

31. Margot Crandall-Hollick and Gene Falk, "The Earned Income Tax Credit (EITC): How It Works and Who Receives It," Congressional Research Service, updated August 7, 2020, www.crsreports.congress.gov.

32. Heather Long, Alyssa Fowers, and Andrew Van Dam, "Biden Stimulus Showers Money on Americans, Sharply Cutting Poverty and Favoring Individuals over Businesses," *Washington Post*, March 6, 2021, www.washingtonpost.com; Jacob Pramuk, "Biden Covid relief plan gives bigger boost to lower-income Americans than Trump tax cuts, study says," CNBC, March 9, 2021, www.cnbc.com; Maria Morava and Scottie Andrew, "Here's how unhoused people can get the $1,400 stimulus check—and how others can help," CNN, March 18, 2021, www.cnn.com.

33. Richard Fry and D'Vera Cohn, "Women, Men and the New Economics of Marriage," Pew Research Center's Social & Demographic Trends Project, January 19, 2010, www.pewresearch.org.

34. "Historical Income Tables, Families, Table F-22. Married-Couple Families with Wives' Earnings Greater than Husbands' Earnings," United States Census Bureau, accessed July 21, 2021, www.census.gov.

Notes

35. Sheree Gibb, David M. Fergusson, and L. John Horwood, "Gender Differences in Education Achievement to Age 25," *Australian Journal of Education* 52, no. 1 (2008), doi:10.1177/000494410805200105; Renato Gil Gomes Carvalho, "Gender Differences in Academic Achievement: The Mediating Role of Personality," *Personality and Individual Differences* 94 (2016): 54–58, doi:10.1016/j.paid.2016.01.011; Androulla Vassiliou et al., *Gender Differences in Educational Outcomes: Study on the Measures Taken and the Current Situation in Europe* (Brussels: Eurydice, 2009), doi:10.2797/3598.

36. Randolph Roth, *American Homicide* (Cambridge, MA: Harvard University Press, 2009), 470.

37. Justin McCarthy, "Gallup First Polled On Gay Issues in '77. What Has Changed?" Gallup, June 6, 2019, www.news.gallup.com; Justin McCarthy, "Record-High 70% in U.S. Support Same-Sex Marriage," Gallup, June 8, 2021, www.news.gallup.com.

38. *Edwards v. California*, 314 US 177 (1941), cited in Kerry Jackson et al., *No Way Home: The Crisis of Homelessness and How to Fix It with Intelligence and Humanity* (New York: Encounter Books, 2021), 23–24.

39. *Papachristou v. City of Jacksonville*, 405 US, cited in Jackson et al., *No Way Home*, 25.

40. *Loper v. New York City Police Dep't*, 999 F. 2d 699, 704 (2d Cir. 1993), cited in Jackson et al., *No Way Home*, 75.

41. *Jones v. City of Los Angeles*, 444 F. 3d 1118 (9th Cir. 2006), *vacated by* 505 F. 3d 1006 (9th Cir. 2007), cited in Jackson et al., *No Way Home*, 62.

42. *L.A. All. For Human Rights*, No. 20-cv-02291-DOC-KES, Doc. 108, at 2, 4 (injunction and order dated May 15, 2020); *L.A. All. For Human Rights v. City of Los Angeles*, No. 20-cv-02291-DOC-KES, 2020 WL 2615741, at 5 (C.D. Cal. May 22, 2020), *vacated as a result of stipulation*, cited in Jackson et al., *No Way Home*, 93.

43. Aidin Vaziri, "San Francisco Expands Who Can Get a Vaccine, Beyond California Eligibility Rules," *San Francisco Chronicle*, March 15 2021, www.sfchronicle.com.

44. Abigail Stewart-Kahn, "San Francisco's Homelessness Response System, Budget Overview and System Gaps," Department of Homelessness and Supportive Housing, November 2020, www.sfcontroller.org; Adam Brinklow, "SF had a renaissance in homeless aid this decade—and it barely mattered," *SF Curbed*, December 19, 2019, www.sf.curbed.com. In 2018 San Francisco spent about 2.5 percent

of its budget on homelessness, whereas New York City spent 1.9 and Chicago spent 0.4. London Breed et al., "Mayor's 2019–2020 & 2020–2021 Proposed Budget," Mayor's Office of Public Policy and Finance, City and County of San Francisco, California, accessed March 12, 2021, www.sfmayor.org; Bill de Blasio et al., "Preliminary Budget, Fiscal Year 2019, Expense Revenue Contract," Office of Management and Budget, City of New York, accessed March 12, 2021, www.nyc .gov; Rahm Emanuel et al., "2019 Budget Overview," City of Chicago, accessed March 12, 2021, www.chicago.gov.

45. Jabari Jackson, interview by the author, October 27, 2020.

46. Thomas Wolf, interview by the author, November 19, 2020.

47. Teresa Gowan, *Hobos, Hustlers, and Backsliders: Homeless in San Francisco* (Minneapolis: University of Minnesota Press, 2010), 72.

48. Ibid., 93.

49. Ibid., xvi.

50. Ibid., 25.

51. Ibid., 18.

52. "Homeless man talks openly about being addicted to heroin. We have an opioid crisis in America," interview by Mark Horvath, *Invisible People*, June 19, 2011, YouTube video, 6:14, www.youtube.com.

53. Timothy Busby, "Opinion: With a New Nuts-to-Bolts Drop-in Center, Dorothy Day House Is Truly Helping the Homeless," Berkeleyside, November 4, 2019, www.berkeleyside.com.

54. Christopher Jencks, *The Homeless* (Cambridge, MA: Harvard University Press, 1994), 104.

55. Duncan Moore, interview by the author, March 8, 2021.

56. Boden, "On the Homeless Industry and the Criminalization of Homelessness."

57. Dennis Culhane, interview by the author, March 29, 2021.

58. Gowan, *Hobos, Hustlers, and Backsliders*, 46.

59. Stephen Talbot, *To Have and Have Not*, KQED, 30:00, aired March 2, 1983.

60. Bureau of Labor Statistics, "Unemployment Rate, 1929–2020," accessed April 2, 2021, www.bls.gov; Jencks, *The Homeless*, v.

61. Mary Ellen Hombs and Mitch Snyder, *Homelessness in America: A Forced March to Nowhere* (Washington, D.C.: Community on Creative Non-Violence, 1982), cited in Jencks, *The Homeless*, 1.

62. Cynthia J. Bogard, *Seasons Such as These: How Homelessness Took Shape in America* (New York: Walter de Gruyter, 2003), cited in Gowan, *Hobos, Hustlers, and Backsliders*, 47.

63. William Tucker, "The Source of America's Housing Problem: Look in Your Own Back Yard," *Cato Institute Policy Analysis* no. 127 (February 6, 1990), www.cato.org.

64. Charles Solomon, "Cartoonists to Help Homeless," *Los Angeles Times*, October 24, 1988, www.latimes.com.

65. Gowan, *Hobos, Hustlers, and Backsliders*, 49.

66. Ibid.

67. Courtland Milloy, "Mitch Snyder Found No Shelter from Pain," *Washington Post*, July 8, 1990, www.washingtonpost.com.

68. Phil Matier, "What's the Answer to Quality-of-Life Crimes in SF: DA Candidates Give Answers," *San Francisco Chronicle*, October 27, 2019, www.sfchronicle.com.

69. Gabe Stutman, "Chesa Boudin, San Francisco's D.A. Elect, Talks Homelessness, Jewishness and Taking on the Establishment," *Jewish News of Northern California*, December 26, 2019, www.jweekly.com.

70. Chesa Boudin, interview by Alicia Garza (Inforum series, Commonwealth Club, San Francisco, February 13, 2020), YouTube video, 1:07:54, www.youtube.com.

71. Phil Matier, "Shopping in SF's Tenderloin Is Wide Open—for Illegal Drugs, That Is," *San Francisco Chronicle*, September 13, 2020, www.sfchronicle.com.

72. Heather Knight, "The War on Drugs Destroyed People. But S.F.'s Passive Approach to the Drug Crisis Is Costing Lives, Too," *San Francisco Chronicle*, November 14, 2020, www.sfchronicle.com.

73. Mallory Moench, "S.F. Can't Ban People Charged with Dealing Drugs from Tenderloin, Court Rules," *San Francisco Chronicle*, May 14, 2021, www.sfchronicle.com.

74. Editorial Board, "Reject Seattle's Absurd Misdemeanor Proposal," *Seattle Times*, October 29, 2020, www.seattletimes.com.

75. Haddon Klingberg Jr., *When Life Calls Out to Us: The Love and Lifework of Viktor and Elly Frankl* (New York: Doubleday, 2001), 155.

76. Holcomb Noble, "Dr. Viktor E. Frankl of Vienna, Psychiatrist of the Search for Meaning, Dies at 92," *New York Times*, September 4, 1997, www.nytimes.com.

77. Viktor Frankl, *Recollections: An Autobiography* (New York: Basic Books, 2008), 114.

11 The Heroism of Recovery

1. Jean-Paul Sartre, *Existentialism and Humanism*, trans. Philip Mairet (London: Methuen, 1966), 34.

2. Roy F. Baumeister, E. J. Masicampo, and C. Nathan DeWall, "Prosocial Benefits of Feeling Free: Disbelief in Free Will Increases Aggression and Reduces Helpfulness," *Personality and Social Psychology Bulletin* 35, no. 2 (2009): 260–68, doi:10.1177/0146167208327217; Xian Zhao et al., "The Effect of Belief in Free Will on Prejudice," *PLoS One* 9, no. 3 (2014): e91572, doi:10.1371/journal.pone.0091572.

3. Davide Rigoni, Gilles Pourtois, and Marcel Brass, "'Why Should I Care?' Challenging Free Will Attenuates Neural Reaction to Errors," *Social Cognitive and Affective Neuroscience* 10, no. 2 (2014), doi:10.1093/scan/nsu068; Tyler F. Stillman and Roy F. Baumeister, "Guilty, Free, and Wise: Determinism and Psychopathy Diminish Learning from Negative Emotions," *Journal of Experimental Social Psychology* 46, no. 6 (2010): 951–60, doi:10.1016/j.jesp.2010.05.012.

4. Cory Clark, interview by the author, January 1, 2021.

5. Jabari Jackson, interview by the author, October 27, 2020.

6. Eric Berne, *Games People Play* (New York: Grove Press, 1964), 74–75. Berne notes that this dynamic is not limited to substance abuse but can play out with many other self-destructive behaviors.

7. Cory Clark, interview by the author, January 1, 2021.

8. Barbara A. Oakley, "Concepts and Implications of Altruism Bias and Pathological Altruism," in *In the Light of Evolution: Volume VII: The Human Mental Machinery*, Camilo J. Cela-Conde, Raúl Gutiérrez Lombardo, John C. Avise, and Francisco J. Ayala, eds. (Washington, D.C.: National Academies Press, 2014), 169–90, doi:10.17226/18573, cited in Kerry Jackson and Wayne Winegarden, "San Francisco's Homeless Crisis: How Policy Reforms and Private Charities

Can Move More People to Self-Sufficiency," Pacific Research Institute, June 2019, www.pacificresearch.org.

9. Shelby Steele, *The Content of Our Character: A New Vision of Race in America* (New York: St. Martin's Press, 1990), 14.

10. John McWhorter, *Losing the Race: Self-Sabotage in Black America* (New York: Simon & Schuster, 2001), xi.

11. Viktor Frankl, *Recollections: An Autobiography* (New York: Basic Books, 2008), 103.

12. Margot Kushel, interview by the author, March 1, 2020.

13. David Talbot, *Season of the Witch: Enchantment, Terror, and Deliverance in the City of Love* (New York: Free Press, 2012), 326–27.

14. Ron Eyerman, "Harvey Milk and the Trauma of Assassination," *Cultural Sociology* 6, no. 4 (2012): 399–421, doi:10.1177/1749975512445429.

15. Talbot, *Season of the Witch*, 329.

16. Ibid., 330.

17. Kurt Gray and Daniel M. Wegner, "Moral Typecasting: Divergent Perceptions of Moral Agents and Moral Patients," *Journal of Personality and Social Psychology* 96, no. 3 (2009): 505–20, doi:10.1037/a0013748.

18. Kurt Gray and Daniel M. Wegner, "To Escape Blame, Don't Be a Hero—Be a Victim," *Journal of Experimental Social Psychology* 47, no. 2 (2011): 516–19, doi:10.1016/j.jesp.2010.12.012.

19. Gray and Wegner, "Moral Typecasting: Divergent Perceptions of Moral Agents and Moral Patients."

20. Ekin Ok et al., "Virtuous Victimhood as Indicators of Dark Triad Personalities," *Journal of Personality and Social Psychology: Personality Processes and Individual Differences* (2020), doi:10.1037/pspp0000329.

21. Masi Noor et al., "When Suffering Begets Suffering: The Psychology of Competitive Victimhood Between Adversarial Groups in Violent Conflicts," *Personality and Social Psychology Review* 16, no. 4 (2012): 351–74, doi:10.1177/1088868312440048.

22. Daniel Luc Sullivan, "Competitive Victimhood as a Response to Accusations of Ingroup Harm Doing" (master's thesis, University of Kansas, June 2010),

www.kuscholarworks.ku.edu; Riana M. Brown and Maureen A. Craig, "Intergroup Inequality Heightens Reports of Discrimination Along Alternative Identity Dimensions," *Personality and Social Psychology Bulletin* (2019): 1–16, doi:10.1177/0146167219880186; Noor et al., "When Suffering Begets Suffering"; Isaac F. Young and Daniel Sullivan, "Competitive Victimhood: A Review of the Theoretical and Empirical Literature," *Current Opinion in Psychology* 11 (October 2016): 30–34, doi:10.1016/j.copsyc.2016.04.004; Francis Fukuyama, *Identity: The Demand for Dignity and the Politics of Resentment* (New York: Farrar, Straus & Giroux, 2018).

23. Ok et. al., "Virtuous Victimhood as Indicators of Dark Triad Personalities."

24. Dudley Clendinen and Adam Nagourney, *Out for Good: The Struggle to Build a Gay Rights Movement in America* (New York: Simon & Schuster, 2013), 296–311.

25. Talbot, *Season of the Witch*, 312.

26. Ibid., 311.

27. Ibid., 148.

28. Ibid., 313.

29. Ibid., 313.

30. "California Proposition 6, the Briggs Initiative (1978)," Ballotpedia, accessed March 9, 2021, www.ballotpedia.org.

31. Teresa Gowan, *Hobos, Hustlers, and Backsliders: Homeless in San Francisco* (Minneapolis: University of Minnesota Press, 2010), 129.

32. Ibid., 144.

33. Cary McClelland, *Silicon City: San Francisco in the Long Shadow of the Valley* (New York: Norton, 2018), 142.

34. Victoria Westbrook, interview by the author, December 9, 2020.

35. Keith Humphreys, interview by the author, March 16, 2021.

36. Kristen Marshall, interview by the author, September 24, 2020.

37. Jennifer Breheny Wallace, "Why Children Need Chores," *Wall Street Journal*, March 13, 2015, www.wsj.com; Sandra L. Hofferth and John F. Sandberg, "How American Children Spend Their Time," *Journal of Marriage and Family* 63, no. 2

(2001): 295–308, doi:10.1111/j.1741-3737.2001.00295.x; Wendy Klein, Anthony Graesch, and Carolina Izquierdo, "Children and Chores: A Mixed-Method Study of Children's Household Work in Los Angeles Families," *Anthropology of Work Review* 30, no. 3 (2009): 98–109, doi:10.1111/j.1548-1417.2009.01030.x.

38. Robert D. Putnam, *Our Kids: The American Dream in Crisis* (New York: Simon & Schuster, 2015), 117, cited in Greg Lukianoff and Jonathan Haidt, *The Coddling of the American Mind: How Good Intentions and Bad Ideas Are Setting Up a Generation for Failure* (London: Penguin, 2018), 174.

39. Jean-Jacques Rousseau, *Émile: or On Education*, trans. Allan Bloom (New York: Basic Books, 1979).

40. The term "salvation *by* the child" was initially coined by writer Malcolm Cowley in a 1951 description of the values of the bohemians of Greenwich Village in the 1920s. Sociologist Bennett Berger in 1967 reused the term to describe hippies, arguing that many of their core values were inherited from the 1920s bohemians. Malcolm Cowley, *Exile's Return* (United Kingdom: Penguin Books, 1994), 60; Bennet M. Berger, "Hippie Morality—More Old Than New," *Society* 5, no. 2 (1967): 12–27, doi:10.1007/bf02804803, cited in Henry Miller, *On the Fringe: The Dispossessed in America* (New York: Lexington Books, 1991), 85.

41. Miller, *On the Fringe*, 107.

42. Talbot, *Season of the Witch*, 114–15.

43. Christopher Lasch, "The Family as a Haven in a Heartless World," *Salmagundi* 35 (1976): 45, www.jstor.org/stable/40546941; Christopher Lasch, *The Culture of Narcissism: American Life in an Age of Diminishing Expectations* (New York: Norton, 1979).

44. Elinor Ochs and Tamar Kremer-Sadlik, *Fast-Forward Family: Home, Work, and Relationships in Middle-Class America* (Berkeley and Los Angeles: University of California Press, 2013), cited in Natalie Angier, "The Changing American Family," *New York Times*, November 25, 2013.

45. Hae In Lee et al., "Understanding When Parental Praise Leads to Optimal Child Outcomes: Role of Perceived Praise Accuracy," *Social Psychology and Personality Science* 8, no. 6 (2016): 679–88, doi:10.1177/1948550616683020.

46. Carl G. Jung, "The Psychology of the Child Archetype," in *Archetypes and the Collective Unconscious*, vol. 9, part 1, *The Collected Works of C. G. Jung*, trans. Gerhard Adler and R. F. C. Hull (Princeton, NJ: Princeton University Press, 1969),

151–81; Marie-Louise von Franz, *The Problem of the Puer Aeternus* (Toronto: Inner City Books, 2000).

47. Peter Gray, "The Decline of Play and the Rise of Psychopathology in Children and Adolescents," *Psychology Today*, January 2011, www.psychologytoday.com, cited in Lukianoff and Haidt, *The Coddling of the American Mind*, 176.

48. Jean M. Twenge, *iGen: Why Today's Super-Connected Kids Are Growing Up Less Rebellious, More Tolerant, Less Happy—and Completely Unprepared for Adulthood—and What That Means for the Rest of Us* (New York: Atria Books, 2017), 152.

49. McClelland, *Silicon City*, 105.

50. Sam Quinones, *Dreamland: The True Tale of America's Opiate Epidemic* (New York: Bloomsbury Press, 2016), 96.

51. Ethan Nadelmann, interview by the author, December 30, 2019.

52. *The City of Nashua v. Purdue Pharma L.P. et. al*, Case 1:17 (District of New Hampshire 2017), http://mediad.publicbroadcasting.net/p/nhpr/files/201712/11712000260.pdf.

53. Sally Satel, "The Truth About Painkillers," *National Affairs* 47, Spring 2021, www.nationalaffairs.com.

54. Victoria Westbrook, interview by the author, December 9, 2020.

55. Wendy Kaminer, *I'm Dysfunctional, You're Dysfunctional* (New York: Random House, 1993), 151.

56. Victoria Westbrook, interview by the author, December 9, 2020.

57. Gowan, *Hobos, Hustlers, and Backsliders*, 170.

58. Victoria Westbrook, interview by the author, December 9, 2020.

59. Jabari Jackson, interview by the author, October 27, 2020.

60. Victoria Westbrook, interview by the author, December 9, 2020.

61. Jabari Jackson, interview by the author, October 27, 2020.

62. Victoria Westbrook, interview by the author, December 9, 2020.

63. Paneez Kosarian, interview by the author, February 3, 2021.

64. Jabari Jackson, interview by the author, October 27, 2020.

65. Gowan, *Hobos, Hustlers, and Backsliders*, xix.

66. Jabari Jackson, interview by the author, October 27, 2020.

67. Rene Zegerius, interview by the author, December 2020.

68. Jabari Jackson, interview by the author, October 27, 2020.

69. Victoria Westbrook, interview by the author, December 9, 2020.

70. Keith Humphreys, interview by the author, March 16, 2021.

12 Homicide and Legitimacy

1. Victoria Beach, interview by the author, January 7, 2021.

2. Audra D. S. Burch and John Eligon, "Bystander Videos of George Floyd and Others Are Policing the Police," *New York Times*, updated May 29, 2020, www.ny times.com.

3. "George Floyd: What happened in the final moments of his life," BBC, July 16, 2020, www.bbc.com.

4. Rebecca Tan et al., "Protesters Paint 'Defund the Police' Right Next to D.C.'s 'Black Lives Matter' Mural," *Washington Post*, June 7, 2020, www.washingtonpost .com.

5. Chase DeFeliciantonio, "George Floyd Protest Briefly Shuts Down Golden Gate Bridge in San Francisco," *San Francisco Chronicle*, June 6, 2020, www.sfchronicle .com; Matthias Gaffni, Matt Kawahara, Tatiana Sanchez, "Protesters Block Bay Bridge After Peaceful Day Filled with Marches," *San Francisco Chronicle*, June 15, 2020, www.sfchronicle.com.

6. Rusty Simmons, "Black Lives Matter Protests Continue Around Bay Area for Fourth Weekend," *San Francisco Chronicle*, updated June 22, 2020, www.sfchronicle .com

7. Alexi Jones and Wendy Sawyer, "Not just 'a few bad apples': US police kill civilians at much higher rates than other countries," Prison Policy Initiative, June 5, 2020, www.prisonpolicy.org.

8. "Fatal Force," *Washington Post*, updated July 19, 2021, www.washingtonpost.com.

9. Nancy Krieger et al., "Trends in US Deaths Due to Legal Intervention Among

Black and White Men, Age 15–34 Years, by County Income Level: 1960–2010," *Harvard Public Health Review* 3 (2015), www.harvardpublichealthreview.org.

10. Cody T. Ross, "A Multi-Level Bayesian Analysis of Racial Bias in Police Shootings at the County-Level in the United States, 2011–2014," *PloS One* 10, no. 11 (2015), doi:10.1371/journal.pone.0141854.

11. Sarah DeGue, Katherine A. Fowler, and Cynthia Calkins, "Deaths Due to Use of Lethal Force by Law Enforcement: Findings from the National Violent Death Reporting System, 17 US States, 2009–2012," *American Journal of Preventative Medicine* 51, no. 5 (2016): S173-S187, doi:10.1016/j.amepre.2016.08.027.

12. Roland G. Fryer Jr., "An Empirical Analysis of Racial Differences in Police Use of Force" (NBER Working Paper Series No. 22399, National Bureau of Economic Research, Cambridge, MA, July 2016, revised January 2018), doi:10.3386/w22399.

13. Roland G. Fryer Jr., "What the Data Say About Police," *Wall Street Journal*, June 22, 2020, www.wsj.com.

14. Ibid.

15. Christopher Ingraham, "You Really Can Get Pulled Over for Driving While Black, Federal Statistics Show," *Washington Post*, September 9, 2014, www.washingtonpost.com; Rob Voigt et al., "Language from Police Body Camera Footage Shows Racial Disparities in Officer Respect," *PNAS* 114, no. 25 (2017): 6521–26, doi:10.1073/pnas.1702413114; Ben Poston and Cindy Chang, "LAPD Searches Blacks and Latinos More. But They're Less Likely to Have Contraband Than Whites," *Los Angeles Times*, October 8, 2019, www.latimes.com.

16. Emma Pierson et al., "A Large-Scale Analysis of Racial Disparities in Police Stops Across the United States," *Nature Human Behaviour* 4(2020): 736–45, doi:10.1038/s41562–020–0858–1.

17. Drew DeSilver, Michael Lipka, and Dalia Fahmy, "10 things we know about race and policing in the US," Pew Research, June 3, 2020, www.pewresearch.org.

18. Samuel R. Gross, Maurice Possley, and Klara Stephens, "Race and Wrongful Convictions in the United States," National Registry of Exonerations, Newkirk Center for Science and Society, March 7, 2017, http://www.law.umich.edu/special/exoneration/Documents/Race_and_Wrongful_Convictions.pdf; William H. Pryor et al., "Mandatory Minimum Penalties for Firearms Offenses in the Federal Criminal Justice System," United States Sentencing Commission, March 2018,

www.ussc.gov; "A Living Death: Life Without Parole for Nonviolent Offenses," ACLU, November 2013, www.laaclu.org.

19. Emily Owens, Erin M. Kerrison, and Bernardo Santos Da Silveira, "Examining Racial Disparities in Criminal Case Outcomes Among Indigent Defendants in San Francisco," Quattrone Center for the Fair Administration of Justice, University of Pennsylvania Law School, May 2017, https://www.law.upenn.edu/live/files/6793-examining-racial-disparities-may-2017-full; Mike Dorning, "Plea Bargains Favor Whites in Death Penalty Cases, Study Says," *Washington Post*, July 26, 2000, www.washingtonpost.com; Jonah B. Gelbach and Shawn D. Bushway, "Testing for Racial Discrimination in Bail Setting Using Nonparametric Estimation of a Parametric Model," *SSRN*, August 20, 2011, doi:10.2139/ssrn.1990324.

20. Jane Coaston, "Jaywalking While Black," *New York Times*, July 3, 2017, www.nytimes.com; Jesse Jannetta et al., "Examining Racial and Ethnic Disparities in Probation Revocation: Summary Findings and Implications from a Multisite Study," Urban Institute, April 2014, www.urban.org.

21. Thomas K. Hargrove et al., "Victim Characteristics 1976–2019," Murder Accountability Project, accessed February 15, 2021, www.murderdata.org; Thomas K. Hargrove, "Black Homicide Victims Accounted for All of America's Declining Clearance Rate," Murder Accountability Project, February 18, 2019, www.murderdata.org.

22. Alicia Bannon, "State Supreme Court Diversity," Brennan Center, July 23, 2019, www.brennancenter.org; Maya Sen, "Is Justice Really Blind? Race and Reversal in US Courts," *Journal of Legal Studies* 44, no. S1 (2015), doi:10.1086/682691; "Justice for All?" Reflective Democracy Campaign, July 2015, www.wholeads.us; Debra Cassens Weiss, "Lawyer Population 15% Higher Than 10 Years Ago, New ABA Data Shows," *ABA Journal*, May 3, 2018, www.abajournal.com.

23. Bruce Western and Becky Pettit, "Incarceration & Social Inequality," *Daedalus* 139, no. 3 (2010): 8–19, doi:10.1162/DAED_a_00019.

24. "Sworn Statements, Expert Analysis of Prince George's Police Department Exposes No Discipline for White Officers' Racial Slurs, but Retaliation for Black and Brown Officers Who Speak Out," ACLU Maryland, June 18, 2020, www.aclu-md.org; Alice Speri, "The FBI Has Quietly Investigated White Supremacist Infiltration of Law Enforcement," *Intercept*, January 31, 2017, www.theintercept.com; Kenneth Bolton Jr. and Joe R. Feagin, *Black in Blue: African-American Police Officers and Racism* (New York: Routledge, 2004).

25. Reade Levinson and Lisa Girion, "Key to Reforming US Policing Rests with State Legislatures," *Reuters*, November 17, 2020, www.reuters.com.

26. Christopher Ingraham, "Police Unions and Police Misconduct: What the Research Says About the Connection," *Washington Post*, June 10, 2020, www.washington post.com; Lindsey de Stefan, "'No Man Is Above the Law and No Man Is Below It': How Qualified Immunity Reform Could Create Accountability and Curb Widespread Police Misconduct," *Seton Hall Law Review* 47, issue 2, no. 5 (2017), https://scholarship.shu.edu/shlr/vol47/iss2/5; Jerome Skolnick, "Corruption and the Blue Code of Silence," *Police Practice and Research* 3, no. 1 (2002): 7–19, doi:10.1080/15614260290011309.

27. Kim Barker, Michael H. Keller, and Steve Eder, "How Cities Lost Control of Police Discipline," *New York Times*, December 22, 2020, updated January 6, 2021, www .nytimes.com.

28. Kimbriell Kelly, Wesley Lowery, and Steven Rich, "Fired/Rehired: Police Chiefs Are Often Forced to Put Officers Fired for Misconduct Back on the Streets," *Washington Post*, August 3, 2017, www.washingtonpost.com.

29. Barker, Keller, and Eder, "How Cities Lost Control of Police Discipline."

30. "Fatal Force"; Fryer Jr., "An Empirical Analysis of Racial Differences in Police Use of Force."

31. Fryer Jr., "What the Data Say About Police."

32. Roland G. Fryer Jr., "Reconciling Results On Racial Differences In Police Shootings" (NBER Working Paper Series No. 24238, National Bureau of Economic Research, Cambridge, MA, January 2018).

33. Fryer Jr., "What the Data Say About Police."

34. Phillip Atiba Goff et al., *The Science of Justice: Race, Arrests and Police Use of Force* (Los Angeles: Center for Policing Equity, July 2016), www.policingequity.org.

35. Krieger et al., "Trends in US Deaths Due to Legal Intervention Among Black and White Men."

36. D. Brian Burghart et al., "Fatal Encounters Google Sheet" (database), *Fatal Encounters* (blog), accessed February 15, 2021, www.fatalencounters.org; Fryer Jr., "An Empirical Analysis of Racial Differences in Police Use of Force."

37. Fryer Jr., "What the Data Say About Police."

38. Ross, "A Multi-Level Bayesian Analysis of Racial Bias in Police Shootings at the County-Level in the United States, 2011–2014."

39. Brandon Vaidyanathan, "Systemic Racial Bias in the Criminal Justice System Is Not a Myth," *Public Discourse*, June 29, 2020, www.thepublicdiscourse.com.

40. Chesa Boudin, interview by Alicia Garza (Inforum series, Commonwealth Club, San Francisco, February 13, 2020), YouTube video, 1:07:54, www.youtube.com.

41. Ibid.

42. "California Proposition 21, Treatment of Juvenile Offenders (2000)," Ballotpedia, accessed January 20, 2021, www.ballotpedia.org.

43. Krieger et al., "Trends in US Deaths Due to Legal Intervention Among Black and White Men."

44. The 1970s data is from Ellen G. Cohn and Lawrence W. Sherman, "Citizens Killed by Big City Police, 1970–84," Crime Control Institute, October 1986. Data for recent years is from D. Brian Burghart et al., "Fatal Encounters Google Sheet" (database), Fatal Encounters (blog), accessed July 13, 2021, www.fatalencounters.org. It is important to note that statistics from the 1970s, which rely upon official police department reports, are likely a lower-bound estimate of police killings, especially compared to the Fatal Encounters database, which includes both officially reported police killings and unreported police killings found in media reports.

45. Ibid.

46. David Leonhardt, "Where Police Reform Has Worked," *New York Times*, updated June 11, 2020, www.nytimes.com.

47. Evan Sernoffsky, "San Francisco Police Tout Use-of-Force Drop—No Shootings for Nearly a Year," *San Francisco Chronicle*, May 1, 2019, www.sfchronicle.com.

48. Justin M. Feldman, "Roland Fryer Is Wrong: There Is Racial Bias in Shootings by Police," *Justin M. Feldman, ScD* (blog), July 12, 2016, www.scholar.harvard.edu/jfeldman/blog; Melody S. Sadler et al., "The World Is Not Black and White: Racial Bias in the Decision to Shoot in a Multiethnic Context," *Journal of Social Issues* 63, no. 2 (2012): 286–313, doi:10.1111/j.1540–4560.2012.01749.x; David Jacobs, "The Determinants of Deadly Force: A Structural Analysis of Police Violence," *American Journal of Sociology* 103, no. 4 (1998): 837–62, doi:10.1086/231291; Ross,

"A Multi-Level Bayesian Analysis of Racial Bias in Police Shootings at the County-Level in the United States, 2011–2014."

49. Franklin E. Zimring, "Should We Defund the Police?" interview, *Real Talk Philosophy*, June 10, 2020, YouTube video, 20:12, www.youtube.com.

50. Fryer Jr., "What the Data Say About Police."

51. Victoria Beach, interview by the author, January 7, 2021.

52. Hayat Norimine, "Community Advocates Outraged Over Process, Urge Mayor to Consider Best for Police Chief," *Seattle Met*, May 30, 2018, www.seattlemet .com.

53. Carmen Best, interview by the author, January 18, 2021.

54. Victoria Beach, interview by the author, January 7, 2021.

55. Carmen Best, interview by the author, January 18, 2021.

56. Jenny Durkan, "Seattle mayor fires back after Trump threatens to intervene," interview by Chris Cuomo, CNN, June 11, 2020, YouTube video, 10:26, www.you tube.com.

57. Tammy Mutasa, "Black community leader confronts Capitol Hill protesters for destruction in neighborhood," KOMO News, October 27, 2020, www.komonews .com.

58. Carmen Best, interview by the author, January 18, 2021.

59. Lisa Baumann, "'Enough': 1 killed in shooting in Seattle's protest zone," AP News, June 29, 2020, www.apnews.com.

60. "Homicides," California Department of Justice, accessed July 13, 2021, https:// openjustice.doj.ca.gov/data.

61. Incarceration data from Bureau of Justice Statistics, accessed May 14, 2021, www .bjs.gov; "Jail Profile Survey," Board of State and Community Corrections, updated June 15, 2021, www.bscc.ca.gov.

62. "Victims of intentional homicide, 1990–2018," United Nations Office on Drugs and Crime, accessed July 20, 2021, www.dataunodc.un.org.

63. Roger Lane, *Violent Death in the City: Suicide, Accident, and Murder in Nineteenth-Century Philadelphia* (Cambridge, MA: Harvard University Press, 1979), 112–13.

64. "Homicide in the United States, 1950–1964," *National Center for Health Statistics* 20, no. 6 (October 1967), www.cdc.gov.

65. National Center for Health Statistics, Compressed Mortality File: Years 1968–1978 with ICD-8 Codes, 1979–1988 with ICD-9 Codes and 1999–2010 with ICD-10 Codes.

66. "Crime in the U.S.," FBI: Uniform Crime Reporting, accessed July 20, 2021, www.ucr.fbi.gov.

67. Niall McCarthy, "Major U.S. Cities Saw Unprecedented Murder Spike In 2020 [Infographic]," Forbes, January 12, 2021, www.forbes.com; "Monthly Neighborhood Offense Statistics," Strategic Services Division, Portland Police Bureau, updated June 8, 2021, www.portlandoregon.gov; "The Homicide Report," Los Angeles Times, accessed July 20, 2021, www.homicide.latimes.com; Uniform Crime Reporting, Federal Bureau of Investigation, accessed July 20, 2021, www.fbi.gov; "Violent Crime Survey - National Totals," Major Chiefs Association, February 21, 2021, www.majorcitieschiefs.com; Lori Lightfoot and David O. Brown, "2019 Annual Report," Chicago Police Department, accessed July 20, 2021, www.home.chicagopolice.org; Jonathan Levy, "Crime - 2020," updated July 20, 2021, City of Chicago, www.data.cityofchicago.org; "Supplementary Homicide Report," New York Police Department, accessed July 20, 2021, www1.nyc.gov.

68. Jon Hilsenrath, "Homicide Spike Hits Most Large US Cities," *Wall Street Journal*, August 2, 2020, www.wsj.com.

69. Monica Davey and Mitch Smith, "Murder Rates Rising Sharply in Many US Cities," *New York Times*, August 31, 2015, www.nytimes.com.

13 When the Law's Against the Laws

1. Richard Rosenfeld, interview by the author, January 23, 2021; see also Uniform Crime Reporting Program Data Series, Federal Bureau of Investigation, ICPSR, accessed July 21, 2021, www.icpsr.umich.edu/web/ICPSR/series/57?q=1960.

2. John Pfaff, *Locked In: The True Causes of Mass Incarceration—and How to Achieve Real Reform* (New York: Basic Books, 2017), 3–4.

3. "Crime in the U.S.," FBI: Uniform Crime Reporting, accessed May 13, 2021, www.ucr.fbi.gov/crime-in-the-u.s.

Notes

4. Jill Leovy, *Ghettoside: A True Story of Murder in America* (New York: Random House, 2015).

5. Pfaff, *Locked In*, 26, 34.

6. Richard Rhodes, *Why They Kill* (New York: Random House, 1999).

7. Randolph Roth, *American Homicide* (Cambridge, MA: Harvard University Press, 2009), xiv.

8. Ibid., xi–xii.

9. Ibid., xi-xii.

10. Ibid., 17.

11. Randolph Roth, "Yes We Can: Working Together Toward a History of Homicide That Is Empirically, Mathematically, and Theoretically Sound," *Crime, History and Societies* 15, no. 2 (2011): 131–45, doi:10.4000/chs.1296.

12. Roth, *American Homicide*, 17.

13. Steven Pinker, *Better Angels of Our Nature* (New York: Penguin, 2011).

14. Eric Cummins, *The Rise and Fall of California's Radical Prison Movement* (Palo Alto, CA: Stanford University Press, 1994), 8–9.

15. Ibid., photo insert.

16. Ibid., 26, 28.

17. Michel Foucault, *Discipline and Punish: The Birth of the Prison*, trans. Alan Sheridan (New York: Vintage Books, 1977), cited in James Miller, *The Passion of Michel Foucault* (New York: Simon & Schuster, 1993), 224.

18. Foucault, *Discipline and Punish*, 18, 188.

19. Miller, *The Passion of Michel Foucault*, 230.

20. Foucault, *Discipline and Punish*.

21. William J. Chambliss and Robert B. Seidman, *Law, Order and Power* (Boston: Addison-Wesley, 1971).

22. Steve Tombs and Dave Whyte, *Unmasking the Crimes of the Powerful: Scrutinizing States and Corporations* (New York: Peter Lang, 2003).

Notes

23. William J. Chambliss and Milton Mankoff, *Whose Law? What Order? A Conflict Approach to Criminology* (New York: Wiley, 1976).

24. Cummins, *The Rise and Fall of California's Radical Prison Movement*, viii.

25. Dan Berger, *Captive Nation: Black Prison Organizing in the Civil Rights Era* (Chapel Hill: University of North Carolina Press, 2014), 10.

26. Miller, *The Passion of Michel Foucault*, 200, 231.

27. Malcolm X, "Message to the Grassroots" (speech, Detroit, MI, December 10, 1963), available at Black Past, accessed May 14, 2021, www.blackpast.org.

28. Malcolm X, "The Harlem Hate-Gang Scare" (speech, Militant Labor Forum Hall, New York, May 29, 1964), in *Malcolm X Speaks*, ed. George Breitman (New York: Grove Press, 1965), 64–71.

29. Cummins, *The Rise and Fall of California's Radical Prison Movement*, 221.

30. Lucinda Franks, "The Seeds of Terror," *New York Times*, November 22, 1981, www.nytimes.com.

31. George Jackson, *Blood in My Eye* (Baltimore, MD: Black Classic Press, 1990), 18, 19.

32. Cummins, *The Rise and Fall of California's Radical Prison Movement*, 167.

33. Ibid., 228; Simeon Wade, *Foucault in California: A True Story—Wherein the Great French Philosopher Drops Acid in the Valley of Death* (Berkeley, CA: Heyday, 2019), 34.

34. Foucault, *Discipline and Punish*, cited in Miller, *The Passion of Michel Foucault*, 224.

35. Miller, *The Passion of Michel Foucault*, 200, 231.

36. Ibid., 206.

37. Michel Foucault and Noam Chomsky, "Human Nature: Justice Versus Power," in *Reflexive Water: The Basic Concerns of Mankind*, A. J. Ayer and Fons Elders, eds. (London: Souvenir Press, 1974), 168, cited in Miller, *The Passion of Michel Foucault*, 203.

38. André Glucksmann, interview by James Miller, March 26, 1990, cited in Miller, *The Passion of Michel Foucault*, 204.

39. Cummins, *The Rise and Fall of California's Radical Prison Movement*, 147–49, 157, 190.

40. Ibid., 247.

41. Matthew Green, "How One Law Helped Pack California's Prisons," KQED, January 23, 2012, www.kqed.org.

42. Ibid.

43. Franklin E. Zimring and Gordon Hawkins, "The Growth of Imprisonment in California," *British Journal of Criminology* 83 (1994).

44. This figure includes Propositions 1 and 2 in 1982, Props 16 and 17 in 1984, Props 52 and 54 in 1986, and Props 80 and 86 in 1988. The electoral results and bond values can all be found through Ballotpedia at www.ballotpedia.org.

45. "California Proposition 4, Rules Governing Bail (June 1982)," Ballotpedia, accessed February 17, 2021, www.ballotpedia.org; BAIL, California Proposition 4 (1982), California Secretary of State, State Archives, accessed from the UC Hastings Scholarship Repository, https://repository.uchastings.edu/ca_ballots.

46. "California Proposition 8, Victims' Bill of Rights (June 1982)," Ballotpedia, accessed February 17, 2021, www.ballotpedia.org; Voter Information Guide for 1982, Primary, California Secretary of State, State Archives, accessed through the UC Hastings Scholarship Repository, https://repository.uchastings.edu/ca_ballots.

47. Zimring and Hawkins, "The Growth of Imprisonment in California," 83–96.

48. "California Proposition 114, Reclassification of Peace Officers Covered by the Death Penalty Act," Ballotpedia, accessed January 20, 2021, www.ballotpedia .org; Deborah Glynn, "Proposition 115: The Crime Victims Justice Reform Act," *McGeorge Law Review* 22, no. 3 (1991): 1010–37; "California Proposition 120, Prison Construction Bonds (1990)," Ballotpedia, accessed January 20, 2021, www .ballotpedia.org.

49. Evan Sernoffsky, "Kidnap Victim, First Scoffed at by Police, May Be Cross-Examined by Her Alleged Rapist," *San Francisco Chronicle*, September 19, 2018, www.sf chronicle.com; "California Proposition 115, the 'Crime Victims Justice Reform Act,'" Ballotpedia, accessed January 20, 2021, www.ballotpedia.org; Bob Baker, "Proposition 139 Would End State Ban on Hiring Out Inmates: Ballot: Initiative Sponsored by Deukmejian Would Let Businesses Set Up Shops on Prison Grounds," *Los Angeles Times*, October 22, 1990, www.latimes.com; "California Proposition 139, Prison Inmate Labor Initiative (1990)," Ballotpedia, accessed January 20, 2021, www.ballotpedia.org.

50. "Murder Punishment," UC Hastings Scholarship Repository, California Ballot Proposition and Initiatives, 1994, www.repository.uchastings.edu; "California Proposition 179, Punishment for Murders Committed with Firearms," Ballotpedia, accessed January 20, 2021, www.ballotpedia.org; Legislative Analyst's Office, *A Primer: Three Strikes—The Impact After More Than a Decade*, Brian Brown and Greg Jolivette, October 2005, www.lao.ca.gov; "California Proposition 184, Three Strikes Sentencing Initiative (1994)," Ballotpedia, accessed January 20, 2021, www.ballotpedia.org; "Bail Exception. Felony Sexual Assault," UC Hastings Scholarship Repository, California Ballot Proposition and Initiatives, 1994, www.repository.uchastings.edu; "California Proposition 189, No Bail for Felony Sexual Assault Charges (1994)," Ballotpedia, accessed January 20, 2021, www.ballotpedia.org.

51. "California Proposition 21, Treatment of Juvenile Offenders (2000)," Ballotpedia, accessed January 20, 2021, www.ballotpedia.org.

52. "Proposition 36 Victory," Drug Policy Alliance, accessed January 20, 2021, www.drugpolicy.org; "California Proposition 36, Probation and Treatment for Drug-Related Offenses (2000)," Ballotpedia, accessed January 20, 2021, www.ballotpedia.org.

14 "Legalize Crime"

1. Christopher Young, "A Cop Debunks Four Core Myths of the #DefundPolice Movement," *New York Post*, December 27, 2020, www.nypost.com.

2. Christopher Young, interview with the author, March 1, 2021.

3. Evan Sernoffsky, "SF Supervisor Leads Anti-Police-Union 'F-the POA' Chant at DA Election Party," *San Francisco Chronicle*, November 6, 2019, www.sfchronicle.com.

4. Rachel Swan, "Oakland City Council Approves Budget with $14.6 Million Cut to Police Department," *San Francisco Chronicle*, June 24, 2020, www.sfchronicle.com.

5. Rachel Swan, "Collision in Oakland: Move to Defund Police Meets Homicide Spike," *San Francisco Chronicle*, November 1, 2020, www.sfchronicle.com.

6. Christopher Young, interview by the author, March 1, 2021. The article Young referenced is Colin Kaepernick, "The Demand for Abolition," Level, Medium, October 6, 2020, https://level.medium.com/the-demand-for-abolition-979c759ff6f.

Notes

7. David Gutman and Sydney Brownstone, "'Everybody Down!': What Happened at the Shooting That Killed a Teenager and Led to CHOP's Shutdown," *Seattle Times*, July 8, 2020, www.seattletimes.com.

8. Lee Brown, "Portland's Red House 'Autonomous Zone' Dismantled After Mayor Apologizes," *New York Post*, December 14, 2020, www.nypost.com; Lee Brown, "Portland Cops Authorized to Clear Protesters' Armed Occupation of House," *New York Post*, December 9, 2020, www.nypost.com; Shane Dixon Kavanaugh, "Activists Work to Block Journalists from Full, Accurate Coverage of Occupation Outside 'Red House' in N. Portland," *Oregonian*, December 11, 2020, www.oregon live.com.

9. Andrea Blackstone, "Black-Owned Businesses Struggle at George Floyd Square, Plead for Financial Help," *Black Enterprise*, April 23, 2021, www.blackenterprise .com.

10. "NewsNation Goes Inside Minneapolis 'Autonomous Zone' Called George Floyd Square," *NewsNation Now*, March 17, 2021, YouTube video, 8:19, www.you tube.com.

11. "Man shot and killed near George Floyd Square in Minneapolis," AP News, March 7, 2021, www.apnews.com; "NewsNation goes inside Minneapolis 'autonomous zone' called George Floyd Square"; Danielle Wallace, "FBI to monitor Minneapolis 'autonomous zone' in George Floyd Square amid Derek Chauvin trial," Fox News, March 18, 2021, video, 4:44, www.foxnews.com; Jared Goyette, "Amid Complaints of Violence, Minneapolis Moves to Reopen Intersection Where George Floyd Was Killed," *Washington Post*, March 18, 2021, www.washington post.com.

12. Lizzie Johnson, Trisha Thadani, and Kevin Fagan, "Tensions High in SF, Oakland in George Floyd Protests; Looting Spreads to Walnut Creek," *San Francisco Chronicle*, June 2, 2020, www.sfchronicle.com.

13. Kelly Kruger, interview by the author, October 1, 2020.

14. Aaron Mesh, "Federal Police Buy 1,000 Pairs of Sunglasses to Protect Officers from Protesters' Lasers," *Willamette Week*, July 25, 2020, www.wweek.com.

15. Joaquin Palomino, "Windows Smashed, Courthouse Lobby Set ablaze Following Huge Saturday Night Rally in Oakland," *San Francisco Chronicle*, July 26, 2020, www.sfchronicle.com; Roland Li, Steve Rubenstein, and Greg Griffin, "Officer Injured, 6 Arrests Made in Oakland Saturday Night as More Clashes Erupt Between Protesters, Police," *San Francisco Chronicle*, August 30, 2020,

www.sfchronicle.com; Kelly Kruger, interview by the author, October 1, 2020; Lauren Hernández et al., "'Together Our Voices Are Stronger': Hundreds March Through Bay Area Cities," *San Francisco Chronicle*, June 2, 2020, www.sfchronicle .com.

16. Elisha Fieldstadt, "Man sentenced for using Molotov cocktails to burn police cars during Seattle protest," NBC News, March 30, 2021, www.nbcnews.com; Young, "A cop debunks four core myths of the #DefundPolice movement."

17. Daniel Beekman and Jim Brunner, "Seattle Mayor Jenny Durkan Won't Run for Reelection," *Seattle Times*, December 7, 2020, updated December 9, 2020, www .seattletimes.com.

18. "California Proposition 36, Changes in the 'Three Strikes' Law (2012)," Ballot-pedia, accessed January 20, 2021, www.ballotpedia.org.

19. "Proposition 47: The Safe Neighborhoods and Schools Act," California Courts, accessed January 20, 2021, www.courts.ca.gov; "California Proposition 47, Reduced Penalties for Some Crimes Initiative (2014)," Ballotpedia, accessed January 20, 2021, www.ballotpedia.org.

20. "California Proposition 57, Parole for Non-Violent Criminals and Juvenile Court Trial Requirements (2016)," Ballotpedia, accessed January 21, 2021, www.ballot pedia.com; "Proposition 57, The Public Safety and Rehabilitation Act of 2016," California Department of Corrections and Rehabilitation, accessed January 20, 2021, www.cdcr.ca.gov.

21. "Crime in the U.S.," FBI: Uniform Crime Reporting, accessed January 8, 2021, www.ucr.fbi.gov/crime-in-the-u.s.

22. Magnus Lofstrom et al., "California's Future: Criminal Justice," Public Policy Institute of California, January 2020, www.ppic.org.

23. Katie Canales, "San Francisco Car Break-ins Are So Common That the City's District Attorney Is Proposing Reimbursing Residents Whose Windows Are Smashed," *Business Insider*, February 13, 2020, www.businessinsider.com.

24. "Destination Health: Solving Homelessness" (discussion panel, Thought Leadership series, Commonwealth Club, San Francisco, August 14, 2019), audio, 1:12:26, www.commonwealthclub.org.

25. "The San Francisco County Jails," San Francisco Sheriff, San Francisco Department of Public Health, April 8, 2016, www.sfdph.org/dph/files/jrp/WG -MeetingCombined.pdf.

Notes

26. Chesa Boudin, interview by Alicia Garza (Inforum series, Commonwealth Club, San Francisco, February 13, 2020), YouTube video, 1:07:54, www.youtube.com.

27. Kate Wolffe, "'Recycled Approach': Some SF Leaders, Activists Bristle at Plan to Ban Dealers from Tenderloin," KQED, September 25, 2020, www.kqed.org.

28. Michael Solana, interview by the author, January 8, 2021.

29. Lauren Hernández, "Chesa Boudin Offers Theories on Why Burglaries Are on Upswing in Bernal Heights," *San Francisco Chronicle*, February 11, 2021, www.sfchronicle.com.

30. Thomas Wolf, interview by the author, May 22, 2020.

31. Ben Dugan, "San Francisco Board of Supervisors Public Safety & Neighborhood Services Committee Meeting" (presentation, Zoom, May 13, 2021), www.sfgov.legistar.com; Mallory Moench, "'Out of Control': Organized Crime Drives S.F. Shoplifting, Closing 17 Walgreens in Five Years," *San Francisco Chronicle*, May 13, 2021, www.sfchronicle.com.

32. "Major San Francisco Bay Area Retail Theft Ring Busted; Five Suspects Arrested; $8 Million in Stolen Merchandise Recovered," CBS Local, October 6, 2020, www.sanfrancisco.cbslocal.com.

33. Megan Cassidy, "Suspect in Fatal S.F. Crash Faced Another, Separate DUI Charge Weeks Earlier," *San Francisco Chronicle*, February 6, 2021, www.sfchronicle.com.

34. Dion Lim, "Exclusive: Wife of man killed in SF crash tells heartbreaking story of California dream turned nightmare," ABC 7 News, February 6, 2021, www.abc7news.com.

35. "Police Discover Body Burning Amid Debris Pile on San Francisco Side Street," KPIX5 CBS SF Bay Area, October 25, 2020, www.sanfrancisco.cbslocal.com.

36. Adam Mesnick, interview by the author, October 26, 2020.

37. Victoria Westbrook, interview by the author, April 1, 2021.

38. Victoria Beach, interview by the author, January 7, 2021.

39. Beth Odonnell (@BethOdo_SF), "Spotted in Diamond Heights. In case anyone is confused about why SF is crazy," Twitter post, February 4, 2021, 7:01 p.m., https://twitter.com/BethOdo_SF.

40. Christine Byers, "Crime Up After Ferguson and More Police Needed, Top St.

Louis Area Chiefs Say," *St. Louis Post-Dispatch*, November 15, 2014, www.stltoday .com.

41. Richard Rosenfeld, "Documenting and Explaining the 2015 Homicide Rise: Research Directions" (Washington, D.C.: US Department of Justice, June 2016), 2, www.ncjrs.gov.

42. Ibid., 19.

43. Justin Nix and Justin T. Pickett, "Third-Person Perceptions, Hostile Media Effects, and Policing: Developing a Theoretical Framework for Assessing the Ferguson Effect," *Journal of Criminal Justice* 51 (2017): 24–33, doi:10.1016/j.jcrimjus .2017.05.016.

44. Fryer Jr., "What the Data Say About Police."; Tanaya Devi and Roland G. Fryer Jr., "Policing the Police: The Impact of "Pattern-or-Practice" Investigations on Crime" NBER, June 2020 www.ssrn.com.

45. Kamala Harris (@VP), "America has confused having safe communities with having more cops on the street. It's time to change that," Twitter post, June 9, 2020, 5:35 p.m., https://twitter.com/VP.

46. Steven Mello, "More COPS, Less Crime," *Journal of Public Economics* 172 (2019): 174–200, doi:10.1016/j.jpubeco.2018.12.003.

47. Aaron Chalfin and Justin McCrary, "Are US Cities Underpoliced? Theory and Evidence," *Review of Economics and Statistics* 100, no. 1 (2018): 167–86, doi:10.1162 /REST_a_00694.

48. Ibid.

49. Sarit Weisburd, "Police Presence, Rapid Response Rates, and Crime Prevention," *Review of Economics and Statistics*, December 16, 2019, doi:10.1162/rest _a_00889.

50. Charles Fain Lehman, "The 'Great Crime Decline' Is Stalled Out," *Washington Free Beacon*, September 15, 2020, www.freebeacon.com.

51. Richard Rosenfeld, interview by the author, January 23, 2021.

52. Randolph Roth, "Criminologists and Historians of Crime: A Partnership Well Worth Pursuing," *Crime, History & Society* 21, no. 2 (2017): 387–99, doi:10.4000/chs.2064.

53. Carmen Best, interview by the author, January 18, 2021.

54. "Crime in the U.S.," FBI: Uniform Crime Reporting, accessed July 20, 2021, www.ucr.fbi.gov/crime-in-the-u.s; "Violent Crime Survey - National Totals," Major Chiefs Association, February 21, 2021, www.majorcitieschiefs.com; "Supplementary Homicide Report," New York Police Department, accessed July 20, 2021, www1.nyc.gov.

55. Franklin E. Zimring, *The City That Became Safe: New York's Lessons for Urban Crime and Its Control* (New York: Oxford University Press, 2013), 166.

56. Ibid., 209.

57. Mark H. Moore, "Sizing Up Compstat: An Important Administrative Innovation in Policing," *Criminology and Public Policy* 2: 469–94, cited in Mark Kleiman, *When Brute Force Fails: How to Have Less Crime and Less Punishment* (Princeton, NJ: Princeton University Press, 2009), 106.

58. Heather Mac Donald, "It's the Cops, Stupid!" *New Republic*, February 1, 2012, www.newrepublic.com.

59. Ibid.

60. Zimring, *The City That Became Safe*, 91, 99.

61. Kleiman, *When Brute Force Fails*, 47.

62. Ibid.

63. Daniel S. Nagin, "Deterrence in the Twenty-First Century," *Crime and Justice* 42, no. 1 (2013): 199–263, doi:10.1086/670398.

64. Ibid.

65. Angela Hawken and Mark Kleiman, "Managing Drug Involved Probationers with Swift and Certain Sanctions: Evaluating Hawaii's HOPE," National Institute of Justice, December 2009, www.nij.ojp.gov; Keith Humphreys and Beau Kilmer, "Still HOPEful: Reconsidering a 'Failed' Replication of a Swift, Certain, and Fair Approach to Reducing Substance Use Among Individuals Under Criminal Justice Supervision," *Addiction*, May 7, 2020, doi:10.1111/add.15049; Sam Kornell, "Probation That Works," *Slate*, June 5, 2013, www.slate.com.

66. Kornell, "Probation That Works."

67. Ibid.

68. Humphreys and Kilmer, "Still HOPEful."

Notes

69. Victoria Westbrook, interview by the author, December 9, 2020.

70. Carmen Best, interview by the author, January 18, 2021.

71. Gary Horcher, "'I refuse to work for this socialist City Council': Resigning SPD cops cite low morale, safety and city leaders as reasons for leaving," KIRO7 News, October 20, 2020, www.kiro7.com.

72. "Police/Chief Retirements in 50 Largest Cities," unpublished data from an analysis of local newspapers, Environmental Progress, 2021.

73. Zusha Elinson, "Cities Are Losing Police Chiefs and Struggling to Hire New Ones," *Wall Street Journal*, October 8, 2020, www.wsj.com; "New Haven Police Chief to Retire This Spring," NBC Connecticut, January 5, 2021, www.nbc connecticut.com.

74. "Annual Survey of Public Employment & Payroll (ASPEP)," US Census, accessed April 2, 2021, www.census.gov; "Police Employee Data," FBI: Uniform Crime Reporting, accessed July 20, 2021, www.ucr.f bi.gov/crime-in-the-u.s.

75. "Report on the Police Department Staffing Study: San Francisco, California," Matrix Consulting Group, March 6, 2019, https://assets.documentcloud.org /documents/6807617/SFPD-Staffing-Study.pdf.

76. Phil Matier, "SF Police Appear to Be Doing Their Own Defunding as Cops Leave in Record Numbers," *San Francisco Chronicle*, August 16, 2020, www.sfchronicle .com.

77. Alex Nester, "Mayor de Blasio: NYC Is Safer with Fewer People in Jail," *Washington Free Beacon*, July 17, 2020, www.freebeacon.com.

78. Rocco Parascandola, "'Blue Flight' Retirements Thinning NYPD Ranks to Levels Not Seen in Nearly a Decade," *New York Daily News*, October 8, 2020, www .nydailynews.com.

79. Matier, "SF Police Appear to Be Doing Their Own Defunding as Cops Leave in Record Numbers."

80. Samantha M. Riedy, Drew Dawson, and Bryan Vila, "US Police Rosters: Fatigue and Public Complaints," *Sleep* 42, no. 3 (2019), doi:10.1093/sleep/zsy231.

81. Swan, "Collision in Oakland."

82. Franklin E. Zimring, *When Police Kill* (Cambridge, MA: Harvard University Press, 2017), 231.

83. Roth, "Criminologists and Historians of Crime."

84. Tarah Hodgkinson, Tullio Caputo, and Michael L. McIntyre, "Beyond Crime Rates and Community Surveys: A New Approach to Police Accountability and Performance Measurement," *Crime Science* 8, no. 13 (2019), doi:10.1186/s40163–019–0108-x.

85. Joshua Chanin and Salvador Espinosa, "Examining the Determinants of Police Department Transparency: The View of Police Executives," *Criminal Justice Policy Review* 27, no. 5 (2016): 498–519, doi:10.1177/0887403415596039.

86. Lawrence W. Sherman, "Preventing Avoidable Deaths in Police Encounters with Citizens: Immediate Priorities," *Annals of the American Academy of Political and Social Science* 687, no. 1 (2020): 16–226, doi:10.1177/0002716220904048.

87. Robert McCartney, "Police Critic Says Officers Need More Money and Less Stress, Along with Greater Accountability," *Washington Post*, June 22, 2020, www.washingtonpost.com.

88. Richard Rosenfeld, interview by the author, January 23, 2021.

89. Victoria Beach, interview by the author, January 7, 2021.

90. Allison Williams, "Minding the Ever-Wider Gap Between the Community and the Police," *Seattle Met*, August 4, 2020, www.seattlemet.com.

91. Tammy Mutasa, "Black community leader confronts Capitol Hill protesters for destruction in neighborhood," KOMO News, October 27, 2020, www.komonews.com.

15   It's Not About the Money

1. Joel John Roberts, "Is there a homeless industrial complex that perpetuates homelessness," *Save Marinwood-Lucas Valley* (blog), August 5, 2013, www.savemarinwood.org.

2. Joel John Roberts, *How to Increase Homelessness: Real Solutions to the Absurdity of Homelessness in America* (Bend, OR: Loyal), 19.

3. Bill Maher, *Real Time with Bill Maher*, episode 30, season 17, aired October 11, 2019, on HBO, video, 58:16, www.hbo.org.

4. Elaine M. Howle, "Homelessness in California: The State's Uncoordinated Approach to Addressing Homelessness Has Hampered the Effectiveness of Its Efforts," California State Auditor, February 2021, www.auditor.ca.gov.

Notes

5. Marissa Kendall, "California Bill Would Raise Corporate Taxes to Fight Home-lessness," *San Jose Mercury News*, January 13, 2021; "FY2021-22 and FY2022-23 HSH Proposed Budget," San Francisco Department of Homelessness and Sup-portive Housing, June 2021, https://hsh.sfgov.org/wp-content/uploads/2021/05 /HSH-FY21-23-Budget-Briefing-Deck_FINAL.pdf.

6. Kristen Marshall, interview by the author, September 24, 2020.

7. Internal Revenue Service, Form 990: Return of Organization Exempt from In-come Tax: Coalition on Homelessness, 2018, retrieved from Guidestar, March 25, 2021, www.guidestar.org.

8. Internal Revenue Service, *Form 990: Return of Organization Exempt from Income Tax: The Nature Conservancy*, 2018, retrieved from Guidestar, March 25, 2021, www.guidestar.org; Internal Revenue Service, *Form 990: Return of Organization Exempt from Income Tax: National Rifle Association*, 2018, retrieved from Guide-star, March 25, 2021, www.guidestar.org.

9. Jonathan Haidt, *The Righteous Mind: Why Good People Are Divided by Politics and Religion* (New York: Vintage Books, 2012), 212. See also Ravi Iyer et al., "Understanding Libertarian Morality: The Psychological Dispositions of Self-Identified Libertarians," *PLoS One* 7, no. 8 (2012): e42366, doi:10.1371/journal .pone.0042366.

10. Jesse Graham et al., "Moral Foundations Theory: The Pragmatic Validity of Moral Pluralism," Advances in Experimental Social Psychology 47 (2013): 55–130, doi:10.1016/b978-0-12-407236-7.00002-4; Jesse Graham et al., "Mapping the moral domain," Journal of Personality and Social Psychology 101, no. 2 (2011): 366 -385, doi:10.1037/a0021847.

11. Haidt, *The Righteous Mind*, 214.

12. Jennifer Friedenbach, interview by the author, January 13, 2021.

13. Kristen Marshall, interview by the author, September 24, 2020.

14. Karl Marx, "A Contribution to the Critique of Hegel's Philosophy of Right. In-troduction," *Early Writings* (New York: Penguin Classics, 1992), 256.

15. Teresa Gowan, *Hobos, Hustlers, and Backsliders: Homeless in San Francisco* (Minne-apolis: University of Minnesota Press, 2010), 40.

16. John Schwarzmantel, *The Routledge Guidebook to Gramsci's Prison Notebooks* (New York: Routledge, 2015), 75.

Notes

17. James Heartfield, "The New Social Movements Against the Old Left," *Damage Magazine*, June 24, 2020, www.damagemag.com.

18. Louis Menand, "The Making of the New Left," *New Yorker*, March 15, 2021, www.newyorker.com.

19. Heartfield, "The New Social Movements Against the Old Left."

20. Stewart J. H. McCann, "Big Five personality differences and political, social, and economic conservatism: An American State-Level Analysis," in *Geographical Psychology: Exploring the Interaction of Environment and Behavior*, ed. P. J. Rentfrow (Washington, D.C.: American Psychological Association, 2014), 139–60; David M. Amodio et al., "Neurocognitive Correlates of Liberalism and Conservatism," *Nature Neuroscience* 10 (2007): 1246–47, www.nature.com; Stewart J. H. McCann, "State Resident Neuroticism Accounts for Life Satisfaction Differences Between Conservative and Liberal States of the USA," *Psychological Reports* 121, no. 2 (2017): 204–28, doi:10.1177/0033294117725072.

21. Emilio Gentile, "Fascism as Political Religion," *Journal of Contemporary History* 25, no. 2/3 (May–June 1990), 229–51.

22. Karl Marx and Friedrich Engels, *The Communist Manifesto*, 1848.

23. Eric Cummins, *The Rise and Fall of California's Radical Prison Movement* (Palo Alto, CA: Stanford University Press, 1994), 126.

24. Fay Stender, quoted in Eve Pell and Members of the Prison Law Project, eds., *Maximum Security: Letters from California's Prisons* (New York: E. P. Dutton, 1972), cited in Cummins, *The Rise and Fall of California's Radical Prison Movement*, 127.

25. Gregory Armstrong, *The Dragon Has Come* (New York: Harper & Row, 1974), 183, cited in Cummins, *The Rise and Fall of California's Radical Prison Movement*, 176.

26. John Irwin, interview by Eric Cummins, 1988, cited in Cummins, *The Rise and Fall of California's Radical Prison Movement*, 169.

27. Jonathan Haidt, *The Righteous Mind: Why Good People Are Divided by Politics and Religion* (New York: Vintage, 2012), 217, 283, 317, 365.

28. Paschal Robinson, "St. Francis of Assisi," *Old Catholic Encyclopedia*, vol. 6 (New York: Robert Appleton, 1913).

29. Ibid.

30. Stefan Pfattheicher and Johannes Keller, "The Watching Eyes Phenomenon: The Role of a Sense of Being Seen and Public Self-Awareness," *European Journal of Social Psychology* 45, no. 5 (2015): 560–66, doi:10.1002/ejsp.2122; Ryo Oda, Yuta Kato, and Kai Hiraishi, "The Watching-Eye Effect on Prosocial Lying," *Evolutionary Psychology* 13, no. 3 (2015): 147470491559495, doi:10.1177/1474704915594959; Daniel Nettle, Kenneth Nott, and Melissa Bateson, "'Cycle Thieves, We Are Watching You': Impact of a Simple Signage Intervention against Bicycle Theft," *PLoS One* 7, no. 12 (2012): e51738, doi:10.1371/journal.pone.0051738; Melissa Bateson et al., "Do Images of 'Watching Eyes' Induce Behaviour That Is More Pro-Social or More Normative? A Field Experiment on Littering," *PLoS One* 8, no. 12 (2013): e82055, doi:10.1371/journal.pone.0082055; Keith Dear, Kevin Dutton, and Elaine Fox, "Do 'Watching Eyes' Influence Antisocial Behavior? A Systematic Review & Meta-Analysis," *Evolution and Human Behavior* 40, no. 3 (2019): 269–80, doi:10.1016/j.evolhumbehav.2019.01.006.

16 Love Bombing

1. Tim Reiterman and John Jacobs, *Raven: The Untold Story of Rev. Jim Jones and His People* (New York: Penguin Books, 2008); *Jonestown: The Life and Death of People's Temple*, produced and directed by Stanley Nelson, written by Marcia Smith and Noland Walker (2006; Firelight Media, aired April 9, 2007 on *American Experience*, PBS).

2. Richard Barrett Ulman and D. Wilfred Abse, "The Group Psychology of Mass Madness: Jonestown," *Political Psychology* 4, no. 4 (1983): 637–61.

3. David Talbot, *Season of the Witch: Enchantment, Terror, and Deliverance in the City of Love* (New York: Free Press, 2012), 278.

4. David Chidester, *Salvation and Suicide: An Interpretation of Jim Jones, the People's Temple, and Jonestown* (Bloomington: Indiana University Press, 2003), 71; E. Black, "The Reincarnations of God: George Baker Jr. and Jim Jones as Fathers Divine," *Alternative Considerations of Jonestown and Peoples Temple* (blog), San Diego State University, July 25, 2013, updated May 20, 2020, www.jonestown .sdsu.edu.

5. Talbot, *Season of the Witch*, 297.

6. Ibid., 279.

7. Ibid., 280.

8. Ibid., 261.

9. Ibid.

10. Ibid.

11. Ibid., 280.

12. Ibid.

13. Ibid., 272.

14. Estella Habal, *San Francisco's International Hotel: Mobilizing the Filipino American Community in the Anti-Eviction Movement* (Philadelphia: Temple University Press, 2007), xvii.

15. Reiterman and Jacobs, *Raven*; Ashley Harrell, "The International Hotel," *New York Times*, April 30, 2011, www.nytimes.com. After Four Seas demolished the hotel in 1979, they were unable to make the site profitable. After years of failed proposals, a new owner sold the land to the Catholic Church in 1994, and the city raised $8.7 million for affordable senior housing on the site. In 2005, the new International Hotel Manilatown Center finally opened, with residency determined by a lottery. For more on the history of the International Hotel after Jones's involvement stopped, see Habal, *San Francisco's International Hotel*, xvii–xviv.

16. Jeff Guinn, *The Road to Jonestown: Jim Jones and People's Temple* (New York: Simon & Schuster, 2017), 336.

17. Talbot, *Season of the Witch*, 284, 288–89.

18. James Richardson, *Willie Brown: A Biography* (Berkeley: University of California Press, 1996), 251.

19. Ibid.

20. Reiterman and Jacobs, *Raven*, 267.

21. Marshall Kilduff and Phil Tracy, "Inside Peoples Temple," *New West*, August 1, 1977, available at *Alternative Considerations of Jonestown and Peoples Temple* (blog), San Diego State University, accessed April 1, 2021, www.jonestown.sdsu.edu; Jack Doyle, "Murdoch's NY Deals, 1976–1977," Pop History Dig, September 25, 2010, updated January 23, 2020, www.pophistorydig.com.

22. Marshall Kilduff, "Dark Days: How an Important Story on Jim Jones Went Untold," *San Francisco Chronicle*, November 17, 2018, www.sfchronicle.com.

Notes

23. Talbot, *Season of the Witch*, 272.

24. Richardson, *Willie Brown*, 251.

25. Talbot, *Season of the Witch*, 295.

26. Ibid.

27. Ibid.

28. Ibid., 278.

29. "Death Tape," Q042 Transcript, Federal Bureau of Investigation, RYMUR 89–4286–2303, 11–42; RYMUR 89–4286–2375, 2–33; RYMUR 89–4286–2431, 3–35, *Alternative Considerations of Jonestown and Peoples Temple* (blog), San Diego State University, updated March 12, 2019, www.jonestown.sdsu.edu.

30. Ibid.

31. Richardson, *Willie Brown*, 252.

32. Talbot, *Season of the Witch*, 307.

33. Ibid., 333.

34. Guinn, *The Road to Jonestown*, 216.

35. Verena Daniel, "A look Behind the Curtain of Cult Psychology," *State News*, October 29, 2020, www.statenews.com.

36. Richard Barrett Ulman and D. Wilfred Abse, "The Group Psychology of Mass Madness: Jonestown," *Political Psychology* 4, no. 4 (1983): 637–61, doi:10.2307/3791059.

37. Eileen Barker, "Religious Movements: Cult and Anticult Since Jonestown," *Annual Review of Sociology* 12 (1986): 329–46.

38. Philip G. Zimbardo and Cynthia F. Hartley, "Cults Go to High School: A Theoretical and Empirical Analysis of the Initial Stage in the Recruitment Process," *Cultic Studies Journal* 2 (1985): 91–147, www.purl.stanford.edu/vv317cb6196.

39. Kevin Corinth and David S. Lucas, "When Warm and Cold Don't Mix: The Implications of Climate for the Determinants of Homelessness," *Journal of Housing Economics* 41 (September 2018): 45–56, doi:10.1016/j.jhe.2018.01.001.

40. Jeffrey M. Jones, "U.S. Church Membership Falls Below Majority for First Time," Gallup, March 29, 2021, www.news.gallup.com.

41. James Miller, *The Passion of Michel Foucault* (New York: Simon & Schuster, 1993), 309.

42. Ibid., 312.

43. *The Times of Harvey Milk*, directed by Rob Epstein, written by Judith Coburn and Carter Wilson (1984; TC Films International).

44. Talbot, *Season of the Witch*, 339–41.

45. Ibid.

46. Ibid., 344.

47. Ibid., 345.

48. Ibid., 395.

49. Ibid.

50. Nicholas Goldberg, "Column: Should the San Francisco School Board 'Cancel' Sen. Dianne Feinstein?" *Los Angeles Times*, December 9, 2020, www.latimes; "Dixie Flag Won't Rise Again, Feinstein Decides," *San Francisco Examiner*, April 18, 1984, accessed through Newspapers.com, March 21, 2021, www.newspapers .com. In March 2021, a local law firm brought a lawsuit against the School Board, alleging that the process was slapdash and misleading to the public. Greg Keraghosian, "SF School Board Pauses Renaming 44 Schools, Promises to Consult Historians in Future," *SF Gate*, February 21, 2021, www.sfgate.com; Jill Tucker, "SFUSD Faces Lawsuit over Controversial Renaming of 44 Schools," *San Francisco Chronicle*, March 19, 2021, www.sfchronicle.com.

51. Simeon Wade, *Foucault in California: A True Story—Wherein the Great French Philosopher Drops Acid in the Valley of Death* (Berkeley, CA: Heyday, 2019), 105.

52. Ibid., 69.

53. Bradley Campbell and Jason Manning, *The Rise of Victimhood Culture: Microaggressions, Safe Spaces and the New Culture Wars* (Cham, Switzerland: Palgrave Macmillan, 2018), 22.

54. Jim Logan, "For Shame," *Current*, University of California, Santa Barbara, February 22, 2016, www.newsucsb.edu.

55. Wade, *Foucault in California*, 72.

56. "SF School Board Votes to Change Admissions Process for Lowell High School," NBC Bay Area, February 10, 2021, www.nbcbayarea.com.

57. HereSay Media (@HereSayMedia), Twitter post, February 6, 2021, 2:03 a.m., www.twitter.com/HereSayMedia.

58. Eliza Shapiro, "Lawsuit Challenging N.Y.C. School Segregation Targets Gifted Programs," *New York Times*, March 9, 2021, updated April 5, 2021, www.nytimes .com; Asra Q. Nomani, "Op-Ed: The War on Merit in American Schools," *Center Square*, March 25, 2021, www.thecentersquare.com.

59. Emma Talley, "Lowell High School's Racial Demographics to Change Next Year, After Merit-Based Admissions Dropped," *San Francisco Chronicle*, March 25, 2021.

60. "English Language Arts/Literacy and Mathematics, Smarter Balanced Summative Assessments, District: San Francisco Unified," California Assessment of Student Performance and Progress, accessed July 20, 2021, www.caaspp-elpac.cde.ca.gov.

61. London Breed, "Statement from Mayor London Breed on School Renaming," Office of the Mayor, January 27, 2021, www.sfmayor.org.

62. Joe Eskenazi, "The strange and terrible saga of Alison Collins and her ill-fated Tweets," Mission Local, March 23, 2021, www.missionlocal.org.

63. Jill Tucker, "Mayor Breed Calls for S.F. School Board Member to Resign over Racist Tweets Directed at Asian Americans," *San Francisco Chronicle*, March 21, 2021, www.sfchronicle.com.

64. Ibid.

65. Thomas Wolf, interview by the author, March 26, 2021.

17 "It's a Leadership Problem"

1. Gavin Newsom, "State of the State Address" (speech, Sacramento, CA, February 19, 2020), accessed through *CalMatters*, www.calmatters.org.

2. "CoC Homeless Populations and Subpopulations Reports," HUD Exchange, accessed May 12, 2021, www.hudexchange.com.

3. "New USC Poll Reveals Likely California Voters' Sentiments on Homelessness Ahead of March 3 Primary Election," USC Price School of Public Policy, February 13, 2020, www.priceschool.usc.edu.

4. "The People's Voice: Voters Serious About Addressing Pandemic Consequences," CalChamber 2021 Business Issues and Legislative Guide, accessed February 6, 2021, www.calchamber.com/businessissues.

Notes

5. Newsom, "State of the State Address."

6. Erin Baldassari, "California Gov. Newsom Lays Out Framework to Address Homelessness," *Morning Edition*, NPR, aired February 21, 2020, 5:07 a.m., audio, 3:23, www.npr.org.

7. Kenneth Paul Rosenberg, *Bedlam: An Intimate Journey into America's Mental Health Crisis* (New York: Avery, 2019), 64.

8. Newsom, "State of the State Address."

9. Gabriel Petek, *2020–21 Budget: The Governor's Homelessness Plan*, Legislative Analyst's Office (LAO), February 11, 2020, 2–3, lao.ca.gov.

10. Kelly Stamphill, interview by the author, March 20, 2021.

11. Bobby Allyn, "California Governor Pushes $1.4 Billion Plan to Tackle Homelessness," NPR, January 8, 2020, www.npr.org.

12. Victoria Westbrook, interview by the author, April 1, 2021.

13. Mallory Moench, "S.F. Has to Find Housing for 1,700 Homeless People Now Living in Hotels Within Six Months. How?" *San Francisco Chronicle*, March 30, 2021, www.sfchronicle.com.

14. Trisha Thadani, "S.F. Pays $61,000 a Year for One Tent in a Site to Shelter the Homeless. Why?" *San Francisco Chronicle*, March 11, 2021, www.sfchronicle.com.

15. Jennifer Friedenbach, "A 'Shelter for All' Policy Sounds Good, but It Takes Resources Away from Long Term Solutions," *San Francisco Examiner*, April 15, 2021, www.sfexaminer.com.

16. Mallory Moench, "S.F. Debates Controversial Homeless Proposal to Make City Provide Shelter to All," *San Francisco Chronicle*, April 21, 2021.

17. Keith Humphreys, interview by the author, March 16, 2021.

18. Philip F. Mangano, interview by the author, December 31, 2020.

19. Housing Instability Research Department, "San Francisco Homeless Count and Survey: Comprehensive Report, 2019," Applied Survey Research, 2019, www.nhipdata.org.

20. Joel John Roberts, *How to Increase Homelessness: Real Solutions to the Absurdity of Homelessness in America* (Bend, OR: Loyal, 2004), 57.

21. Rafael Mandelman, interview by the author, December 18, 2020.

22. John Snook, interview by the author, October 21, 2020.

23. Dennis Culhane, interview by the author, March 29, 2021.

24. Thomas Insel, interview by the author, March 22, 2021.

25. Petek, *2020–21*, 24.

26. Victoria Westbrook, interview by the author, April 1, 2021.

27. Thomas Insel, interview by the author, March 22, 2021.

28. Ibid.

29. Jeff Bellisario, interview by the author, February 5, 2021.

30. "California Roars Back: Governor Newsom Announces Historic $12 Billion Package to Confront the Homelessness Crisis" (press release), Office of Governor Gavin Newsom, May 11, 2021, www.gov.ca.gov/2021/05/11/california-roars -back-governor-newsom-announces-historic-12-billion-package-to-confront-the -homelessness-crisis.

31. John Snook, interview by the author, October 21, 2020.

32. Richard Frank, Keith Humphreys, and Harold Pollack, "Policy Responses to the Addiction Crisis," *Journal of Health Politics and Policy Law,* January 22, 2021, doi:10.1215/03616878–8970796.

33. "Early Model-based Provisional Estimates of Drug Overdose, Suicide, and Transportation-related Deaths," National Center for Health Statistics, Centers for Disease Control and Prevention, accessed April 2, 2021, www.cdc.gov; Brian Mann, "Drug Overdose Deaths Spiked to 88,000 During the Pandemic, White House Says," NPR, April 1, 2021, www.npr.org.

34. Elisabeth Egan, "Hunter Biden's Memoir: 7 Takeaways from 'Beautiful Things,'" *New York Times*, March 30, 2021.

35. Arlette Saenz, Jake Tapper, and Betsy Klein, "White House staffers asked to resign or work remotely after revealing past marijuana use," CNN, March 19, 2021, www.cnn.com; Michael Medved, "Obama's Cocaine Confessional Won't 'Blow' His Chances," ABC News, January 5, 2007, www.abcnews.go.com; Devan Cole, "Harris says she has smoked pot and supports marijuana legalization," CNN, February 11, 2019, www.cnn.com.

36. Keith Humphreys, email to the author, May 13, 2021.

37. Scott Shafer, "When and Why Did the Bay Area Become So Liberal?" KQED, August 20, 2020, www.kqed.org.

38. William H. Mullins, "The Persistence of Progressivism: James Ellis and the Forward Thrust Campaign, 1968–1970," *Pacific Northwest Quarterly* 105, no. 2 (2014): 55–72, www.jstor.org/stable/24631886.

39. "Elections 1950–1959," JoinCalifornia, accessed February 25, 2021, www.join california.com; Hunter G. Goodman and Barbara Baker, eds., "State of Washington: Members of the Legislature, 1889–2014," Legislative Information Center, State of Washington, June 2014, www.leg.wa.gov.

40. Michael Dardia et al., *Military Base Closures: The Impact on California Communities* (Santa Monica, CA: RAND Corporation, 1996), available at RAND Corporation, www.rand.org; Dan Walters, "The Decline and Fall of California's Republican Party," *Orange County Register*, December 2, 2019, www.ocregister.com.

41. E. J. Dionne, "Washington Talk; Greening of Democrats: An 80's Mix of Idealism and Shrewd Politics," *New York Times*, June 14, 1989, www.nytimes.com.

42. Christopher Rufo, interview by the author, February 15, 2021.

43. Wayne Winegarden, interview by the author, February 3, 2021.

44. Stephen Eide, interview by the author, December 10, 2020.

45. Ethan Nadelmann, interview by the author, December 30, 2019.

46. Neil Gong, "Between Tolerant Containment and Concerted Constraint: Managing Madness for the City and the Privileged Family," *American Sociological Review* 84, no. 4 (2019): 664–89, doi:10.1177/0003122419859533.

47. Elaine M. Howle, "Homelessness in California: The State's Uncoordinated Approach to Addressing Homelessness Has Hampered the Effectiveness of Its Efforts," California State Auditor, February 2021, www.auditor.ca.gov; Trisha Thadani, "S.F. has an unprecedented $1.1 billion to spend on homelessness. The pressure is on to make a difference," *San Francisco Chronicle*, July 16, 2021.

48. William Tucker, "The Source of America's Housing Problem: Look in Your Own Back Yard," *Cato Institute Policy Analysis* 127 (February 6, 1990), www.cato.org.

49. Ibid.

Notes

50. Bernard J. Frieden, *The Environmental Protection Hustle* (Cambridge, MA: MIT Press, 1979), 178.

51. Jennifer Hernandez, "California's Environmental Quality Act Lawsuits and California's Housing Crisis," *Hastings Environmental Law Journal* 24, no. 1 (2018): 21–71, www.hklaw.com.

52. "Cost of Living Index by State 2021," World Population Review, accessed March 21, 2021, www.worldpopulationreview.com.

53. Douglas Schwartz, "California Dems Excited About Biden and Harris, Quinnipiac University Poll Finds; 43% of Voters Say They Can't Afford to Live Here," Quinnipiac University, February 6, 2019, www.poll.qu.edu.

54. David Byler, "Why California's Population Boom Has Stalled," *Washington Post*, March 31, 2021, www.washingtonpost.com; Mark Baldassare et al., "Californians and Their Government," Public Policy Institute of California, March 2021, www.ppic.org.

55. Michelle Tandler (@michelletandler), "I believe it is the anti-capitalistics solutions to housing that are the reason we have so little housing," Twitter post, March 16, 2021, 7:24 p.m., https://twitter.com/michelletandler.

56. Data from Construction Information Research Board report on California. Cited by Liam Dillon (@dillonliam), Twitter post, May 5, 2021, 11:23 a.m., https://twitter.com/dillonliam.

57. "Historical Population Change Data (1910–2010)," Census Bureau, accessed April 3, 2021.

58. Byler, "Why California's population boom has stalled"; "E-2. California County Population Estimates and Components of Change by Year–July 1, 2010–2020," California Department of Finance, December 2020, www.dof.ca.gov.

59. David Zahniser and Liam Dillon, "L.A. City Council Opposes State Bill That Would Lift Local Zoning Rules," *Los Angeles Times*, April 16, 2019, www.latimes.com.

60. Michael Hiltzik, "Column: California's Housing Crisis Reaches from the Homeless to the Middle Class—but It's Still Almost Impossible to Fix," *Los Angeles Times*, March 29, 2018, www.latimes.com.

61. Laura Foote, interview by the author, January 15, 2021.

62. YIMBY leader (name withheld), interview by the author, April 1, 2020.

63. Ibid.

64. Laura Foote, interview by the author, January 15, 2021.

65. YIMBY leader (name withheld), interview by the author, April 1, 2020.

66. Ibid.

67. "California's Likely Voters," Public Policy Institute of California, accessed January 21, 2021, www.ppic.org.

68. YIMBY leader (name withheld), interview by the author, April 1, 2020.

69. Benjamin Schneider, "Unpacking SF's Moderate/Progressive Divide," *SF Weekly*, November 11, 2020, updated November 13, 2020, www.sfweekly.com.

70. Laura Foote, interview by the author, January 15, 2021.

18 Responsibility First

1. Frederick J. Turner, "The Significance of the Frontier in American History," *Annual Report of the American Historical Association*, 1893: 197–227, available at American Historical Association, accessed January 19, 2021, www.historians.org.

2. Ibid.

3. Keith Humphreys, interview by the author, March 16, 2021.

4. Kurt Andersen, "The Downside of Liberty," *New York Times*, July 3, 2021, www.nytimes.com.

5. See Noam Chomsky, "On the Spanish Revolution," interview by Jorell A. Meléndez Badillo, 2009, available at libcom.org, November 7, 2013, www.libcom.org/library/interview-noam-chomsky-spanish-revolution-jorell-mel%C3%A9ndez-badillo-2009; Noam Chomsky, "A portrait of Chomsky as a young Zionist, interview by Gabriel Matthew Schivone," *New Voices*, November 7, 2011, available at Chomsky.info, accessed May 17, 2021, www.chomsky.info/20111107.

6. Heather Knight, "Bid to Open Ice Cream Store Turns into Bitter Saga," *San Francisco Chronicle*, October 2, 2020, www.sfchronicle.com.

7. Jonathan Haidt, "What Makes People Vote Republican?" Edge, September 8,

2008, www.edge.org, cited in Jonathan Haidt, *The Righteous Mind: Why Good People Are Divided by Politics and Religion* (New York: Vintage Books, 2012), 193–94.

8. See Randolph Roth, *American Homicide* (Cambridge, MA: Harvard University Press, 2009); Tom R. Tyler, *Why People Obey the Law* (Princeton, NJ: Princeton University Press, 2006).

9. Patrick Collison, "Proposition C" (press release), October 19, 2018, Stripe Newsroom, www.stripe.com.

10. Riva Tez, interview by the author, November 30, 2020.

11. Ibid.

12. Michael Solana, interview by the author, January 8, 2021.

13. Christopher Rufo, interview by the author, February 15, 2021.

14. Keith Humphreys, interview by the author, March 16, 2021.

15. Rene Zegerius, interview by the author, December 2020.

16. Christopher Rufo, interview by the author, February 15, 2021.

17. See Michael Pollan, *How to Change Your Mind* (Penguin, 2018).

18. Stephen Eide, interview by the author, December 10, 2020.

19. Riva Tez, interview by the author, November 30, 2020.

20. Bill Maher, *Real Time with Bill Maher*, accessed through Joseph A. Wulfsohn, "Maher slams California's 'super high taxes,' cites Joe Rogan, Ben Shapiro as part of the state's 'exodus,'" Fox News, October 9, 2020, www.foxnews.com.

21. "The People's Voice 2019: CalChamber's 5th Annual Survey of California Voter Attitudes," California Chamber of Commerce, 2019, accessed April 3, 2021, www.advocacy.calchamber.com.

22. John Snook, interview by the author, October 21, 2020.

23. Ibid.

24. Susan Partovi, interview by the author, September 20, 2019.

25. John Snook, interview by the author, October 21, 2020.

26. Thomas Insel, interview by the author, March 22, 2021.

27. Rafael Mandelman, interview by the author, December 18, 2020.

28. "Destination Health: Solving Homelessness" (discussion panel, Thought Leadership series, Commonwealth Club, San Francisco, August 14, 2019), audio, 1:12:26, www.commonwealthclub.org.

29. Keith Humphreys, interview by the author, March 16, 2021.

30. Quoted in Joe Klein, "Daniel Patrick Moynihan Was Often Right," *New York Times*, May 15, 2021.

31. Michael Solana, interview by the author, January 8, 2021.

32. Stephen Eide, interview by the author, December 10, 2020.

19 Civilization's End

1. Deborah Nicholls-Lee, "How a Dutch Housing Agency Rescued an Amsterdam Street from the Drug Trade," *Bloomberg*, November 12, 2018, www.bloomberg.com.

2. Ibid.

3. Ibid.

4. Ibid.

5. Mark Kleiman, *When Brute Force Fails: How to Have Less Crime and Less Punishment* (Princeton, NJ: Princeton University Press, 2009), 45; Andrew Jacobs, "A New Spell for Alphabet City; Gentrification Led to the Unrest at Tompkins Square 10 Years Ago. Did the Protesters Win That Battle but Lose the War?" *New York Times*, August 9, 1998, www.nytimes.com.

6. Susan Partovi, interview by the author, January 10, 2021.

7. "Black-White Homeownership Gap: A Closer Look Across MSAs," Urban Institute, June 2019, www.urban.org.

8. "Tokyo," Atlas of Urban Expansion, accessed April 3, 2021, www.atlasofurbanexpansion.org, cited in Michael Shellenberger, "Dear Fellow YIMBYs: Yes, Urban Density Is Wonderful. But We Also Need More Suburbs," *Forbes*, April 13, 2018, www.forbes.com.

9. Shellenberger, "Dear Fellow YIMBYs."

10. "Conservation Easement," California Council of Land Trusts, accessed April 3,

2021, www.calandtrusts.org; "Conservation Easements," Chicago Metropolitan Agency for Planning, accessed April 3, 2021, www.cmap.illinois.gov; Michael Shellenberger, "California in Danger: Why the Dream Is Dying and How We Can Save It," Environmental Progress, February 14, 2018, www.environmental progress.org.

11. "The Measure of California Agriculture," University of California Agricultural Issues Center, August 2009, accessed April 3, 2021, www.aic.ucdavis.edu.

12. Stephen Eide, interview by the author, December 10, 2020.

13. Tom Schnabel, "How Chet Baker Really Died," KCRW.com, January 17, 2012; Jon Pareles, "Chet Baker, Jazz Trumpeteer, Dies from a Fall at 59," *New York Times*, May 14, 1988; James Gavin, *Deep in a Dream: The Long Night of Chet Baker* (Chicago: Chicago Review Press, 2011); Phil Johnson, "Chet Baker: My Druggy Valentine," *Independent*, November 19, 2013.

14. Boona Cheema, interview by the author, February 11, 2021.

15. Christopher Herring, interviews by the author, December 14, 2020, and February 17, 2021.

16. Susan Partovi, interview by the author, January 10, 2021.

17. Michael Shellenberger, "California Homelessness Survey 2021," Google Surveys. Full results can be found at https://surveys.google.com/reporting/survey ?utm_source=google&utm_medium=email&utm_campaign=survey_bought &hl=en&survey=cc4zcmorsl2ao5bcjm4izpgv2m.

18. "The People's Voice 2019: CalChamber's 5th Annual Survey of California Voter Attitudes," California Chamber of Commerce, 2019, accessed April 3, 2021, www .advocacy.calchamber.com.

19. "U.S. Subpoenas Chinese Communications Firms in Probe of National Security Risks," *Reuters*, March 17, 2021, www.reuters.com; Edward Wong and Chris Buckley, "U.S. Says China's Repression of Uighurs Is 'Genocide,'" *New York Times*, January 19, 2021, www.nytimes.com.

20. David French, *Divided We Fall: America's Secession Threat and How to Restore Our Nation* (New York: St. Martin's Press, 2020), 27.

21. Jonathan Haidt, *The Righteous Mind: Why Good People Are Divided by Politics and Religion* (New York: Vintage Books, 2012), 212.

22. Viktor E. Frankl, *Man's Search for Meaning* (Boston: Beacon Press, 2006), 132.

23. Bari Weiss (@bariweiss), "Join me, Coleman Hughes, Daryl Davis, John McWhorter, Glenn Loury, Melissa Chen, Megyn Kelly, Stephen Pinker and so many more," Twitter post, March 4, 2021, 11:30 a.m., https://twitter.com/bariweiss.

24. Asra Q. Nomani, "The War on Merit," *Real Clear Education*, March 24, 2021, www.realcleareducation.com.

25. "Harvey Milk in Duboce Park on Pooper Scooper Law," aired August 29, 1978, on KQED, video, 2:31, www.diva.sfsu.edu.

26. Frankl, *Man's Search for Meaning*, 132.

Epilogue

1. Kelly Stamphill, interview by the author, March 20, 2021.

2. Jacqui Berlinn, interview by the author, March 20, 2021.

3. Kelly Stamphill, interview by the author, March 20, 2021.

4. Adam Mesnick, interview by the author, March 19, 2021.

5. "COVID-19 Cases and Deaths," DataSF, accessed March 28, 2021, www.data.sf gov.org.

6. Kelly Stamphill, interview by the author, March 20, 2021.

7. Jacqui Berlinn, interview by the author, March 20, 2021.

Index

Index

Index

Index

Index

on payments to volunteers, 19
World Health Organization,
  89–90

Yesilgöz, Dilan, 73, 266
Young, Christopher, 189–190

Zegerius, Rene, 73–75, 78, 114,
  116, 155–156, 159–160,
  265–266, 268
Zimmerman, Bill, 64–65, 80–81,
  85
Zimring, Frank, 171–172,
  199–200

About the Author

MICHAEL SHELLENBERGER is the nationally bestselling author of *Apocalypse Never*, a *Time* magazine "Hero of the Environment," the winner of the 2008 Green Book Award from the Stevens Institute of Technology's Center for Science Writings, and an invited expert reviewer of the Assessment Report for the Intergovernmental Panel on Climate Change (IPCC). He has written on energy and the environment for the *New York Times*, the *Washington Post*, the *Wall Street Journal*, *Nature Energy*, and other publications for two decades. He is the founder and president of Environmental Progress, an independent, nonpartisan research organization based in Berkeley, California.